Thunderstruck

Jamie Sheffield
2016

"Thunderstruck"
© Jamie Sheffield, 2016

Published by SmartPig through CreateSpace and Amazon.com KDP.
This is a work of fiction. Names, characters, places and incidents are
either products of the author's imagination or are used fictitiously.
While the descriptions are based on real locations in the Adirondack
Park, any resemblance to actual events or persons, living or dead, is
entirely coincidental.

ISBN-13: 978-1518792922
ISBN-10: 1518792928

This book is dedicated to my wife Gail, she nurtures my words, my body, and my soul (*if such a thing exists, and I have one*) …

and to Tyler, and all the Tylers.

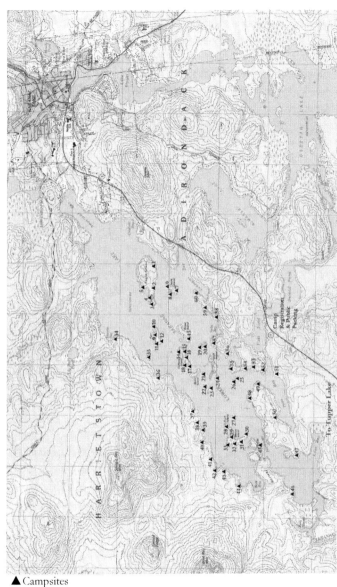

▲ Campsites

Portion of USGS 7.5-minute image map for Saranac Lake, New York
U.S. Department of the Interior U. S. Geological Survey

Lower Saranac, under cover of night

As the glow from another spectacular Adirondack sunset faded unnoticed in the sky behind him, the killer crept across the water in his boat. To his way of thinking, the Richards' family were already dead, they just didn't know it yet.

Vanilla had spent the afternoon and evening hours visiting dozens of campsites, selling bundles of wood and bags of ice and taking people's garbage. The fact that he made decent money while cruising the sixty campsites on the big lake was nearly beside the point; he was able to pinpoint his targets. Residents and tourists alike were used to seeing his boat on the water at all hours during the season. To them, everyone, he faded into the background, became invisible.

He helped things along by timing his kills for just after sunset, painting his boat a dark and neutral splotchy grey, and buying the quietest engine he could find for the barge. The running and safety lights were on a dimmer switch, and he'd dialed them down to the barest glow by the time he cut the engine and nosed into some reeds about thirty yards from the sign for the Richardses' campsite.

Vanilla stepped carefully down into the lake, feeling for the sandy bottom through the cold water, listening for voices, looking for lights. He could hear low voices and the crackling of a fire in the family's campsite, but nothing else. They, and now he, were distant and visually shielded from other campsites... one of the reasons he'd picked them. Vanilla tied his barge to a sturdy-enough tree and crept carefully into the woods, feeling with his foot for the path he'd seen there this afternoon.

Crouching on the path, just able to see by the light left in the sky and that thrown by the Richardses' campfire, Vanilla's heartbeat raced. The woman struggled up from the low camp-chair Vanilla had seen when he helped them carry wood and ice up to the campsite this afternoon, and walked over to check on the girl in their tent.

Beast woke, and stretched and flexed and readied himself. He smelled the campsite coffee, the husband's cigar, felt the vibrations come through the ground. Power flooded in Beast's veins, rushing strength to every muscle and sharpening his senses. He felt a stick flex under his left foot and stopped putting weight on it before it snapped. As he bent over to pick it up and thread it into his belt, he smiled. Once he had closed to within ten yards, he rustled off the path and into the adjacent bushes as quietly as possible, feeling around inside for Vanilla, bringing him back to the front for a final check.

Vanilla had always been the thinker, the planner. Beast was the doer. Vanilla looked around the camp and listened and eventually gave a slow and satisfied nod to them both. Beast huffed three times in quick succession, as he had once heard a bear do outside of Vanilla's tent, just loud enough to likely be heard.

"What was that?" the woman asked. "Keith, I know I heard something that time."

"Nothing, Ange," the man replied. "Just a squirrel or some shit. Don't freak yourself out."

Beast's fingers stroked the stick, flexing and caressing it for half a minute until it snapped loudly in two. The sound had an immediate effect on Angela and Keith

Richards. The woman jerked as if slapped and looked toward the tent while the man swung his head around to look into the woods, nearly at Beast. The part of his mind that still hosted Vanilla knew Keith's night vision was shot from staring into the campfire. Regardless, it felt as though he had looked straight at Beast who had put the two halves of the stick down on the ground, reached into his shirt pocket for the Schrade folding knife and opened the large blade. Beast ran his finger along the shaving-sharp edge and waited.

As the man stood and spoke to the woman, the blood began to pound in Beast's ears—crowding out thoughts and fears and plans—crowding out Vanilla. The man walked to the edge of the campsite clearing while the woman, consciously or not, put herself between Beast and the tent where her daughter slept. When the wind shifted, Beast had a moment's concern that the man would catch his scent, but he was city-soft and stupid and had smoked a cigar recently enough to kill his nose anyway. The man passed within a foot of Beast, unaware of the foot that shot out to trip him. He fell perfectly, as Beast and Vanilla had imagined, along the path and into the dark, away from the camp and the woman.

"Ow," Keith Richards said. "Crap! I'm all right, Ange, I just …"

Beast opened his neck.

It happened while the man was on all fours, shaking off the fall. Beast stood partway, moving between the man's legs, yanking the top of Keith's head up by the hair, and making a smooth, deep cut across his neck. As planned, his victim didn't have time for surprise, or a scream, only a wet and noisy exhalation along with some thrashing in the bushes while he bled out. Beast crouched back into the bushes to wait.

A broad and savage grin broke Beast's face open. The woman had no idea what had happened, just that something was wrong. Beast watched with hungry pleasure as surprise turned to worry and fear and then terror when her man didn't say anything further. She froze, trapped by the newness and unfamiliarity and unexpectedness of the developments in the last minute of her family vacation. Beast raised the knife to his lips and let his tongue dart out to taste the first blood of the night while savoring the anticipation of the next kill, and most especially the one after that, the girl. A few seconds later, the woman chose her move and nearly ruined Beast's plans.

"Edith," she called over her shoulder into the tent. "Daddy's hurt, and I need the headlamp and first-aid kit. Didja hear me, baby?"

Beast had started moving before the woman finished and by the time she turned fully back around, he was only a few yards from her with the knife arcing toward its soft target under her chin. She had time for half of a high-pitched scream before Beast's knife, which he thought of like a claw, dismantled the fragile nexus of her speech and respiratory and circulatory machinery. Beast was covered in and temporarily blinded by the initial spray of the woman's blood, which probably was the only thing that saved the child's life.

Edith Richards heard her mother's call and partial scream and what sounded like a bear or lion grunting and growling and savaging her mother, and without thinking, the child reached up above her head to the zipper for the tent's back door. She unzipped it partway and crawled out into the darkness created by the tent eclipsing the firelight. Edith turned, in time to see her mother falling in the dirt and her attacker wiping his face and eyes. The fire was behind him, so she only saw silhouettes, her mother spinning and falling gracelessly, and the Beast, a split second before he started moving toward her.

On instinct, she ran in the opposite direction, tearing her tender, bare feet open on rocks and sticks while fleeing through the bushes … her hands blindly held in front until she splashed down and into the water, twisting an ankle and tripping on the rocks. Even though the Beast yowled when he heard the splash, and leaped after her, he was unlucky enough to land on a downed tree at the water's edge and fell away from the child.

Edith heard the splash, which sounded near, and screamed long and loud, before taking in a deep breath and diving into the black water and away from the island; she stayed underwater until her lungs burned, stroking and kicking as hard as she could, coming up about fifty feet from the island in the middle of the dark lake. Although scared of whatever had violated her campsite a minute before, she also imagined the hungry and angry denizens of the lake homing in on her toes and fingers in the dark, warm, and still, night-water.

The Beast saw the girl's head break the surface too far away for pursuit, howled his rage at the night, then slunk back onto land to clean up while desperately calling for Vanilla.

Vanilla stopped and bent double to catch his breath and listen. The child kept screaming, but her panicked, breathless state had initially reduced the reach of her cries, now getting louder by the second. He slapped his head, both in frustration and to clear his mind from the hunt. Getting the girl, Edith Richards, was out of the question; getting clear of the area was the only possible course of action.

He couldn't clean the campsite as he normally did,

but he took a minute to pick up and toss items that could possibly lead people in his direction into the fire. That done, before leaving camp, Vanilla quickly squatted by Angela Richards' corpse, dabbing up and tasting a sweet and salty fingerful of blood for Beast. He moved back to the barge, as fast as seemed prudent, where he untied and pushed it out into deeper water and climbed aboard.

Within three minutes of the stick snapping in the darkness outside the Richardses' camp, Vanilla was quietly motoring toward home while cursing the Beast's poor luck, but still exultant in the powerful rush he got during the hunting trips.

A Sphagnum Swamp near Butternut Point,
Upper Saranac Lake, NY
Thursday, 7/9 2015, 9:47 a.m.

We'd been circling each other for nearly a minute on the trampoline surface of the sphagnum when my foot caught on a blueberry bush. His foot shot out and up and knocked me back onto the wet and giving ground. After a second, my attacker reached a hand out to help me back to my feet.

"You see, Tyler," John said. "It's mostly about waiting for the other guy to make a mistake, not making one of your own, and being ready to take advantage of that split second opening when it comes."

"The extensive training in Special Forces probably helps too," I said as he reached down to pull me up.

John and I have known each other for years. We originally met during one of my very earliest cases/investigations/adventures and formed an alliance, if not a friendship. (*I don't exactly do friendship, or at least not very well or broadly.*) Over the years, we have helped each other in minor ways from time to time. He had recently offered to help me develop my physical strength and speed and to give me some basic instruction in unarmed combat (*which he called variously, "scuffling" or "street-fighting" or "The Ancient and Noble Art of Fook Yu"*). He had suggested his dojo in Lake Placid would be a good place to practice, and I countered with this place that I'd discovered in my wanderings of the woods near Upper Saranac Lake.

The access to our swamp is a snowplow turnaround roughly halfway between Moss Rock Road and Beaverwood Road. Once we'd parked there, he'd cursed and bug-slapped and groaned while ducking limbs and climbing over monstrous downed trees as we made our way East-South-East toward the lake. A hair over a kilometer of straight line travel (*we had never traveled in a straight line for more than ten seconds at a time during our walk*) from my Element, the old-growth forest opened up to a sphagnum bog the size of a few football fields. Walking across it gave me the same feeling this time as it had the first time I'd found it … the ground gave too much. If you stood in the same place too long, it settled and you would be standing in water up to your ankles, lending itself to feeling the ancient pond under the sphagnum floor/ ceiling/cover.

I had once spilled out of my Hornbeck canoe at a portage not far from our current location and slid under the sphagnum at the carry. When I swam upward, my hands pushed against a yielding but stubborn, foot-thick, mat of sphagnum. Upon opening my eyes, the density of moss and crud suspended in the water made it impossible to see; panic and claustrophobia threatened to close in and render me useless/stupid/dead, but the rational thinkers in the back of my skull ordered me to search the records for a memory of turning around in the water. Failing that, to feel my way back along the sphagnum for a few feet until my hand found warm air and the feeling of sunshine on my slimy finger.

The memory of being under the swamp is still as fresh today as it was when I crawled from the muck on the day it happened at the portage from Fish Creek across to Follensby Clear Pond; I could feel the water, deep and dark and (*somehow*) hungry below me, beneath the mat of sphagnum, and I considered telling John the story.

"I don't know how to watch you, your feet and hands, and the ground where I'm placing my feet, and also make a plan," I said, circling him again, and thinking about landing my first punch or kick. "Keeping all of those things active in my head at the same time makes it difficult to do more than stay on my feet. How do you know when to hit/strike/kick/punch?"

"It's tough at first," John said. "That's why you practice, even the simple stuff, ten thousand times so your body and brain can take care of most of it without your having to think about it. Beyond that, watch his middle, his belt, for signs of what he's planning on doing next, and wait for him to make a mistake. Never force a move unless time is pressing on you. Even then, know that you'll likely fuck up and die. If you feel confident, though, and have the time, you can alter the flow or movement parameters like I'm doing right now."

I hadn't noticed prior to his mention of it, but he had been crowding me on my left and forcing a retreat that I hadn't been aware of until the tamarack sapling was at my back. I stole a microsecond to make sure of my footing … it was then he cuffed the side of my head with an open hand, and sent me falling into/onto the sapling. A branch broke on my way down/into the tree; I smelled citrusy sap and felt the sharp end open my scalp (*behind my right ear, and partway down to my neck*) in the same instant. By the time I was on the ground, I could see from John's face (*and felt from the splash/drip/flow on my neck*) that our training session was over.

John used the kit in my backpack to clean and

bandage my wound. He tipped my chin back (*although I understand and appreciate his reason/motivation, and am as comfortable with John as nearly any of the people in my life, I didn't/don't/wouldn't like the intimacy of this kind of touch*) to check my injury. He sensed my flinch/stiffness and cut his examination short with a gruff comment about me probably not bleeding out then he drank the rest of his thermos of coffee while I wandered around for a few minutes taking pictures and marking GPS locations of/in the sphagnum field with my iPhone. When he finished his coffee, he shrugged his way into an ancient green canvas pack, threadbare and full of holes, to return his and then led the way back through the thick woods. Although I never saw him consult a map or compass, we came out right next to the Element (*something I have trouble doing in this stretch of woods even with my well-developed internal mapping systems*). More bugs seemed awake on our way out of the woods than on our way in, and after I had finished slapping a final few and feeling for seepage on my bandage, we got into the SUV and drove off.

SmartPig Offices, Saranac Lake, NY
Thursday, 7/9 2015, 10:23 a.m.

John didn't comment when I headed out and away from
home on Route 30, past what used to be The Wawbeek
Resort, and turned onto Panther Mountain Road for a
needless/pointless shortcut (*since I'd taken the long way home,
and the smaller road takes longer anyway*).

He understands my drive to explore and map and
maintain/increase familiarity with my world ... even if he
thinks of it in terms of situational awareness, where I
simply need to (*without knowing exactly why*). The maps in
my head are constantly being added to and refined, in my
driving and walking and paddling tours of the
Adirondacks, by virtue of the cartographers in the back of
my skull pasting together an ongoing collage of
walked/driven/paddled distances, sightlines of the lakes
and islands and points and peaks. (*Now I was able to see
Corey and Birch islands off to our left on the lake as I stole my eyes
from the road for a moment to lock in another image/location.*)

The rest of the drive back to Saranac Lake was
standard, without any significant deviation in the sights I
was used to seeing (*because I always try to add a new reference
point or two on any drive, to improve/reinforce the maps*); I did
notice, however, more law enforcement and rescue
vehicles than usual at the state boat launch for Lower
Saranac Lake, between First and Second ponds and

wondered if someone had been injured jumping from one of the cliffs on Bluff Island. (*It happens from time to time, injury, not jumping. The jumping happens continuously … something that makes no sense at all to me … jumping off of a perfectly stable island for no reason.*)

I interrupted the silence when I saw John reach for the radio (*and then retract his arm*) on the console for the fourth time, "Have you given any thought to the playlist I mentioned a few weeks ago?" I asked.

Dot had set me up with a couple of playlists on my iPhone, to supplement audiobooks, during my trip to the southwest last winter. What had begun as a kindly diversion on her part evolved into a research project on my part. I have noted that music has played an important role in mood and personality, areas in which I am untrained/unfamiliar/uncomfortable. I'd asked the important people in my life to produce a playlist of ten to fifteen songs that they felt was representative of themselves, or a mood, or facet of their lives. I'd gotten some interesting (*and unexpected*) results and was interested in pushing the last few holdouts in my inner circle to hand in their homework.

"I don't have one of those phones, Tyler," John said, "and I don't know how to cram myself into ten tracks of music."

"It doesn't need to be on a phone. It can just be a list … on paper, or whatever. It doesn't need to be representative of your whole life either … take it from a chunk that makes sense to you. Maybe from Sunday morning reading, or late night coffee drinking and pipe smoking with Nick, or something from your life before you moved up to the Adirondacks, and Helgafel."

He nodded, and looked up at the ceiling. "I can do that. I'll get something to you some time."

"Sounds good," I said, thankfully not broadcasting my frustration with the incredible vagueness of his assurance.

I pulled into the parking lot behind the SmartPig offices, where John and I had met early that morning, and maneuvered over to the beat-up farm truck he had driven. Before the Element came to a stop, he was sitting up and craning his neck around to take in all corners of the lot, nearby roofs, and the bridge that was the sole way out of the lot.

"Shit," he said flatly. "This might be for me. You should let me out here, and pull ahead a bit. Can I leave something in your car, Tyler?"

"What might be for you?" I said, looking around, "And what do you have that you need to leave/hide in my car? That being said/asked, yes, you can leave it, whatever it is, with me."

He pointed to Frank Gibson, an SLPD member, and another man getting out of an unmarked car I didn't recognize (*which meant I hadn't seen it, because I would have remembered*), and then to a pair of men dressed significantly too *city* for the Adirondacks walking in such a way as to partly block the bridge.

"The suit with Gibson, and the two minions on the bridge," he said, "mean something serious. As to the other, I have a handgun in my pack, which I'm going to wrap in your fleece and put under the back seat."

Without another word, he shuffled my fleece back behind us and under the seat and climbed out of the car and walked toward Frank and the other guy, who I was now close enough to recognize (*even after 12.25 years*).

I quickly pulled into a spot (*not one of the three I prefer in this lot, but expedient*), and honked, which surprised everyone and stopped John from walking into something he didn't need to walk into. Jumping out of the car, I jogged over to catch up with, then pass, John.

"I'm pretty sure they're here for me. Leave the fleece for now. I'll call you later," I whispered as I passed.

When closing in on Frank and the other man, I waved to grab their attention in a non-threatening manner while John hopefully beat a discrete/discreet retreat. (*I wondered if some buried nervousness or nerves had promoted that unfortunate string of rhyming words, and then dismissed the thought/worry as I got within quiet speaking range of the two men.*)

"Agent Brimley," I said, "are you here looking for a murderer?"

He and Frank appeared shocked, and Brimley's hand reached partway across his body, toward, but not for, the gun in a shoulder holster. In my peripheral vision, I watched the two men on the bridge start toward us, and slide hands onto, but not draw, guns on their hips, spreading out each from the other as they closed on us, on me.

"Whoa, let's everybody relax a few notches," Frank spoke up with a mix of his friendly and commanding voices. "I bet dollars to donuts that Tyler's talking about the last time you were here, Brimley, looking at him for the bomb thing."

They hadn't known it was a *bomb thing* when they came searching for me barely more than 12 years ago. I had figured that out for them ... that and a great deal more, including the cryptogram and the identity of the would-be assassin. Although, in any just/fair world, I should have come out of the episode looking like a hero, smelling like a rose, there had been a definite lack of rosy smell and heroic aspect to me in their eyes when all was said and done. My unusual approach and lateral thinking had made Brimley uncomfortable and suspicious (*and apparently still did)*. Frank Gibson had grown to know, and even occasionally work with, me over the years since then. (*The fact that his wife was one of the people I was closest with in the Adirondacks, further helped, and sometimes complicated, matters.*)

"Tell me about the wound on your neck and the blood on your shirt?" Brimley asked, not acknowledging Frank. "Whose is it?"

"The wound, the neck, and the blood are all mine," I began, perhaps too literally, while watching Frank wince a bit. "I got the cut working out in the woods about forty-five minutes ago. John bandaged it."

I pointed an elbow behind me showing where John's truck was bouncing over the bridge, maybe seven miles an hour too fast for the potholed state of the road/bridge. Frank muttered something about Grasshopper snatching the goddamned pebble from someone's hand.

"Where were you last night from roughly seven to nine?" Brimley said, consulting a notebook (*perhaps a bit of theater, since it wasn't a lot to memorize*), "And would you be willing to submit a DNA sample, for exclusion purposes, of course?"

Frank started to speak, but I held up a hand. "I've got this, Officer Gibson, don't worry. I'm aware of my rights, possibly more so than Agent Brimley, but I'd prefer to get out from under this, whatever this is, as soon as possible. This time, it's easy ... especially if you've got DNA for a comparison."

I carefully peeled the bandage off. The bleeding had stopped, but it held a decent amount of blood, and sap, and a few tamarack needles. Agent Brimley waved at one of the minions (*both seemed to have relaxed based on the less-threatening course the exchange had taken in the last 30 seconds*), who produced a big Ziploc-y evidence bag from a pocket inside his jacket with a flourish better suited to a magic show than a potential crime scene, and held it open for me to drop in my sample.

"Last night I was enjoying dinner with Dot and Lisa and the pastor from their church," I said, speaking mainly to Frank (*who I assumed would provide their bonafides to Brimley*). "I arrived a few minutes before six, and didn't leave until nine forty."

Brimley glanced at Frank, who nodded ever so slightly, but positively/affirmatively that I wondered if he practiced the move or had taken an in-service training on it at some point in his law enforcement career. The agent scrunched his face in what I took to be annoyed disappointment (*I study facial expressions, lacking much of the emotional programming to make many of my own*), and his posture eased as he leaned back against a car.

"Well, dammit," he said, mostly to himself. "That probably would have been too easy. Now we'll, or at least I'll, have to settle down here in the boonies until we can figure out this mess."

"What mess?" I asked, again facing Frank because I assumed he would be the one, if any, to give me an answer.

"A family camping out on Lower Saranac was attacked last night," he began, "parents killed, daughter survived."

I didn't gasp or make a dramatic face, but after waiting for a pair of long seconds, I glanced at Brimley so Frank could, hopefully, make the logical jump without my having to ask ... he did.

"Brimley's here because he's some kind of regional information processing supervisory agent," he said. "Means he spends his days looking at paper for patterns in crime. He thinks there may have been a number of disappearances in recent years, all involving summer people from out of state, campers, all involving the Tri-Lakes."

Brimley coughed/cleared his throat at this moment, bringing Frank to a brief halt until the FBI agent had finished.

"He thinks there may be a serial killer operating in the region," Frank continued, ignoring the shushing facial and hand gestures which Brimley made. (*I was able to pick them up, so he must have been telegraphing them, which led me to believe that Frank was choosing to overshare with me on purpose, for reasons I didn't/couldn't guess or understand.*) "He was hoping it might be you, so he could be back in his office in Albany by lunchtime, preparing his *Aw shucks* look for the uber-suits."

I wasn't interested in Brimley's office politics, his reasons for thinking and/or wanting me to be a serial killer (*which, by the strictest of definitions, I am*), Frank messing with him or *them*, or the people who got killed the previous night. (*People get killed all the time, and it seldom concerns/interests me*) … I was, however, interested in the idea of a serial killer in the Adirondacks, and wanted to participate, for a variety of reasons.

"I want in," I said, to all of them, even the minions. "I can help with this investigation."

Faces clouded and got interested in me again, and I held up a pause-hand. "You'll say *no* right now, and that's cool … I've got other stuff to do in the short term. If you find the guy in the next few hours, I wouldn't have been interested in the case anyway. If your investigation doesn't go anywhere, I'd be happy to help. I have a good eye and brain for details and research and think differently enough that I can help when and if you get stuck."

My face shaped into what experience told me was a knowing look, and I gave both Frank and Brimley a dose of it, ignoring the minions.

Before they could answer, I turned and headed up to SmartPig to change into a new shirt (*my current one was significantly bloody*), do some deep thinking and Coke drinking and a bit of refresher research on a couple of things that had occurred to me in the last 137 seconds.

I had a feeling Frank and/or Brimley would be back in touch with me before long.

I grabbed a fresh shirt from the top of a pile on my couch
as I walked in the door to SmartPig, my workspace, living
space, and bat-cave … it would be my sanctum
sanctorum if what I did was the least bit spiritual. (*It's not,
so it's not.*)

When I first moved to the Adirondacks, I initially
rented both an apartment and an office, but I shortly
found out that I spent all of my time in the office, so I
got rid of the apartment. I'd done the owner of the
building/office a significant (*he felt*) favor, and in return he
had been disposed to look the other way with regard to
my habitation of a workspace. It works comfortably for
me now, which is the guiding principle of my life and
lifestyle, at present.

I drank a pair of super-cooled Cokes from a special
fridge I'd ordered from a scientific supply company a
number of years ago to keep my Cokes chilled to just
below 30 degrees Fahrenheit (*beyond that, they begin to slush.
But at this temperature, they're my single greatest pleasure*) while
opening a panopticon of tabs on my laptop browser to
check email and what social media I participate in and
various websites and blogs and e-zines and databases and
forums and listservs. I ran through the most
recent/important materials and messages in the time it

took me to work through another pair of Cokes. My mind went, unbidden, to Hope.

I could still smell her in the single big room *("probably the couch cushions" an unwelcome voice whispered from the back of my head)*, and I breathed her scent in, deeply, picturing her face at every stage and important milestone of our relationship. It had been 267 days since she'd left me … 256 mornings that I'd reached for her first thing in the morning … and talked to her before remembering that she was gone. I was completely and utterly without Hope *(and aware, every time I thought about it, that I could recognize it as a double-entendre but not see the utility or humor in the pun, albeit certain my old speech therapist would likely be proud of me).*

My dog, Hope, an ancient and sickly and ill-tempered beagle-mix from the local shelter *(Tri-Lakes Animal Shelter, TLAS)* had died, out West in Navajo Country, last year during a lengthy trip we took to avoid the coldest part of the year in one of the coldest places in the Lower-48. *(In her later years, the cold had bothered her more and more, and I wanted to spare her the discomfort during what would be her last winter.)* I missed, and mourned, her in the only way I knew, by a painful and throbbing awareness of the absence of an accustomed part of my life. One day she was with me driving through the bright and red and dry country in northern Arizona, the next day I was driving alone through the same country … talking to the space she had occupied on my passenger seat, grabbing her leash when I stopped near other people and dogs *(Hope had a nasty disposition, and would start a fight with a grizzly bear or Mother Teresa, or Mother Teresa riding a grizzly bear, without blinking an eye or caring a whit that she would lose, which she inevitably did, even when fighting baby duckies)*, and sliding a filled water bowl into the shade created by the opened tailgate.

My iPhone rang. I recognized the ringtone, so I shunted the call to voicemail ... I'd deal with it later. I simply couldn't deal with a call from Mickey right now ... since too much was going on in my head, the dual pulls of thinking about the possibility of a serial killer and my inability to produce any new or productive research into the problems/issues/concerns about Mickey for weeks. The frustration of this duality made me nearly shake, and I didn't want to be in this frame of mind when I spoke to him, of all people.

I leaned forward off the couch, listening to both knees crack like sticks, and grabbed my in-town go-pack, shoving a zippered folio of library gear into the open mouth from a pile on the big round table I used for reading and writing and eating and fly-tying and painting and sewing/cementing clothes and outdoor gear together. (*Almost everyone who calls the Adirondacks home ends up wearing more than one hat. I find myself trying out lots of things in the pursuit of a living and staying busy and keeping entertained.*) While turning a full circle before leaving, I stopped just short of telling Hope I'd be back soon, and stomped down the stairs, headed to the library, in search of something not only to hold my eye and interest, but something to change the direction of my luck, and life.

"I've seen most of these before," I nearly shouted, minutes later, in a back room at the library. "Last week, I'm pretty sure. And the ones that are new are referential of the older ones. I need the ones I highlighted last time I was here ... electronic format would be better, so I don't have to translate from German and French, but I'll take whatever I can get ... of the new ones."

Jill, the newest Library Media Specialist to join the staff of the Saranac Lake Public Library (SLPL), leaned back and away from me when I delivered this missive (*missile?*), and it occurred to me that my tone and volume and even the words I was using were inappropriate. Even so, I was disturbed on a number of levels (*and for a number of reasons*) and having some trouble modulating my output. Over the years, lots of people have noted, sometimes benefited (*and/or suffered*) from the fact, that my brain processes and orders data differently than many/most other people on the planet … faster, more efficiently, and able to make connections that others might/would miss. In this instance (*and in fact, for the last few weeks*), I'd been trying to apply my talents to a problem (*or challenge, or opportunity, as one of my mentors/teachers used to suggest*) with very little success. A significant part of my problem was the difficulty in gaining access to current research suggesting new and effective treatments of cerebral aneurysms. But, to be fair/honest/realistic, an even bigger part of the problem was my lack of objectivity and calm/patience/rationality in my approach to the research/challenge/opportunity. Mickey, the most important person in my world, bar none, had nearly died on May 6th, although he assured me it was far less serious than I inferred from our discussions, and my snooping while he was in the hospital for the second worst week of my life. (*The worst week of my life had begun on a Tuesday morning in September of 2001 when my parents went to work at their jobs in the Twin Towers before a pair of airplanes flew into both buildings, and they, along with 2604 other people, never made it home*).

Since May 6th, I'd been reading everything I could get my eyes and hands and ears on having to do with the treatment of cerebral aneurysms, specifically with reducing symptoms and improving both long- and short-term outcomes for people so afflicted. I had read thousands of journal articles, dozens of books, and spoken directly or through email/Skype/FaceTime with leading experts (*and crackpots and quacks and people on the fringes of the medical world*) looking for some way to save the life and mind of Mickey Schwarz. He was getting the best treatment in the best hospital from the best doctors; it likely wouldn't be enough to make much difference ... chances were good he'd be dead or living with significantly diminished cognitive facilities within a year.

His was the sole mind I had experienced on this planet, in this life, that truly understood and appreciated and challenged and possibly equaled mine, and it was literally maddening (*nothing figurative about it*) to think that I might lose it/him for want of some obscure article I simply couldn't get in front of my eyes/brain.

"Tyler, I—" Jill began.

"Jill, I'm sorry," I interrupted, "about the way I talked to you just now, for the last few weeks really, I have been unconscionable/unacceptable. You've all been patient with me, too patient. I'll take what we've got here, and go. Please accept my apologies and tell everyone else they'll get a break from me. Also, lunches are on me for the next little while ... pizza and Chinese, from the good place."

"Oh, Tyler, you don't have to ... it's all right," she said, but not convincingly (*even to me*), not as though she meant it.

I scooped up the tall pile of printouts and journals and books, and stomped off and out and away, with angry, useless, meaningless tears pouring down my cheeks ... back to SmartPig to read and sift and think and take notes and reach out to too-busy researchers for an hour or so before my swim date later in the afternoon.

Best Western Mountain Lake Inn, Saranac Lake, NY
Thursday, 7/9/2015, 3:37 p.m.

As I mounted the steps up to SmartPig, my iPhone rang again; again with the ringtone I'd heard, and ignored, before … this time, I answered.

"Hi, Mickey, what's the weather like in the Big Apple?" I asked.

Mickey is a weather addict. Despite living in the most controlled environment I've ever experienced (*his apartment and office, even his car, have fine controls for adjusting the temperature and humidity and air circulation, along with ambient noises and smells*), he is in love with tracking weather and weather outbreaks all over the planet. My moving up to Saranac Lake was a godsend for him (*because he gets to call me a dozen or so times every year to let me know how cold it is, and that I'm living in the coldest spot in the continental United States*).

"Hey, kiddo," he began, "it might hit ninety today, but the humidity is the real villain of the story. There may be showers this afternoon. Looks like it got down into the forties in your neck of the woods last night. That's windows open weather unless you were camping."

Mickey knows I sleep outside roughly half of the nights in any given year, hammock camping on state land in the woods around Saranac Lake. (*Other times, in rough weather, or when I'm feeling lazy, I sleep on the couch in SmartPig.*)

He thinks it's bizarre, but he loves me, and assumes, rightly, that I know what I'm doing. He's the only person on Earth, besides Dot, who knows exactly what I do, what I've done, as the Adirondacks' only consulting detective … it makes him nervous/scared/queasy to think or talk about some of the worst things I've done in the commission of my avocation, but there's also some level of pride.

Last summer, during the early stages of a particularly nasty piece of work, he made a fantastic, logical case for my using the unique confluence/configuration of skills and abilities that I was endowed with to help people. Having made/tested the argument, he stood by his words, and was/is my biggest supporter.

"It was cool down by the water," I said, "and the lakes are warm enough that they develop a fog layer in the early hours every morning. I went for a swim and then a paddle as the sun was coming up this morning (*at 5:21 a.m., I could feel both of us think, across the distance of our phone call*), it was quite nice."

"How are Anne and the girls?" I continued. "Are you still thinking of coming up here at the end of the summer?

"They're fine," he said. "Anne's excited to come up and see you (a *lie, but a permissible one, given the parameters and duration of our relationship*). Mindy is deep into her MFA program and is already making noises about begging off, and Becky is excited to take a trip with her new boyfriend … Greg, no, Tom, no …"

"How are you feeling?" I asked, without thinking, before I could pull the words back. I actually winced a bit, imagining his hurt face at the other end of the cell phone call. He'd always had nearly perfect recall and access to the stunning amount and diversity of information in his head, and not only would this embarrass him, but my calling attention to it would embarrass him further.

They say that doctors make the worst patients … that wasn't at all the case with Mickey. He was an excellent patient, both at the hospital during the crisis and in his frequent/regular checkups in the weeks since. That being said, though, he didn't like that the aneurysm had left him with the feeling/perception of weakness, of letting us down, of being slightly less than … and being reminded of it made it all worse.

I'd slipped up because Mickey lived and thrived, most of all in his mind. My biggest worry when he was struck by the defective blood vessel, in that otherwise miraculous skull, had been that he would lose himself, the part of himself he most valued, his razor-sharp mind. His intellect, most specifically his ability to hold crap-tons (*Dot assures me this is a valid unit of measure*) of information and turn it this way and that, in relation to other information, and reach conclusions nobody else was capable of … those were the waters he and I swim/swam in, alone perhaps, at least unparalleled on this planet.

He has a berry aneurysm of almost 18mm across (*17.9mm exactly, the diameter of a dime, which has, foolishly/stupidly, stopped me carrying those coins, and places it/his comfortably in the large aneurysm class*). In the early days of May, it swelled enough to press on something in that priceless, perfect, brain of his, and his vision experienced a rapid loss of focus. He fell down a number of times one morning as he puttered around the kitchen fixing and drinking the first of many cups of coffee for the day. I wanted to dig into his Circle of Willis myself and correct/excise/fortify the faulty vessel and bring him back into line with my, and his, image of himself. The more I looked into it and the oceans of information about it, the more I have come to the same conclusion he came to in the days immediately after the vomiting and crippling headaches and medical imaging and first tentative diagnoses and treatments began.

"I feel trapped in this stupid aging, dying body, kiddo," he said. "I spend all day feeling around in my skull and all over my body for symptoms that I'm getting better or about to die. A headache scares the shit out of me. I'm wearing slippers and loafers because I read an article about some guy who blew his aneurysm tying a shoelace."

He stopped and breathed for nine seconds, respiration rattling in my ear while sweat popped out everywhere I had pores.

"I'm taking it day by day, kiddo," he said, voice steady and strong ... and Mickey-esque, back at the wheel again. "Today, I'm here, and tomorrow Anne and I are heading in to talk with Dr. Patil about the center's ongoing debate with itself about coiling versus clipping. Are you conversant with this stuff, Ty?"

He'd asked me this before, numerous times, and I was glad for my generally flat affect on the phone to mask the fear inspired by answering it again, "Yes, Mickey, I've read up on it. Based on my understanding of the research and your circumstances, your aneurysm is sized and located so your neuro team is rightly split on which approach is indicated in your case. Coiling seems to have a lower mortality rate, but a higher recurrence of bleeding than does clipping. Using a vessel from elsewhere in your head or body was not a viable treatment approach, I gather."

"These guys are the tops in the world, Ty," he said, a quaver sliding around the edge of his voice/tone, "and in these meetings, it seems as if we've arrived at a coin-toss when it comes to picking a solution to the time bomb in my noggin. Anne is drinking so much, and so early some days, that I'm worrying about her as much as me."

"I've read—extensively—on the subject, and in the research both old and new," I said, not wanting to climb into the mess that was Anne, Mickey's wife, and her drinking, "and if it was me, and my team of doctors was really split, I'd go with the clipping … take the higher initial risk in exchange for a lower chance of recurrence."

What I wasn't saying … what both of us thought but wouldn't say … was that I'd rather be dead than diminished to an ever-increasing amount, by repeated bleeds in my head. I live in my head, as does Mickey. Losing that essential me-ness *(or him-ness)* was very nearly as hard to imagine as simply dying.

"I think you and I are on the same page," he said. "Anne is seduced by the better mortality numbers up front with coiling. I'm not sure what we'll have to talk about tomorrow because it's all been said … I miss you, kiddo," he said, continuing after a brief pause. "I know you hate coming to the city, but I'd love to see you before the surgery."

He stopped there, waiting for me, probably not wanting to say the stupid things people say in movies at this point in these discussions.

"I'll head down in a few days," I blurted, unaware that I'd been going to say it. "There's nothing up here that can't wait *(even though I wasn't positive of this, thinking about Brimley and the idea of a serial killer in the Adirondacks but could see no reason to flavor my stew with this poop, as Dot liked to say)*."

I could hear him smile at the phone by the way his next words came out, "That's great, Ty! That's really great. I hope you'll stay with us this time."

Mickey and Anne had recently moved to an apartment near Columbus Circle, and the last time I'd gone down to NYC, I'd chosen to set up my hammock in Central Park and had gotten a ticket from a member of the NYPD, who apparently had no serious crimes/criminals to pursue/prosecute.

"I'd love to," I said, lying.

"I'll tell Anne. She'll be so excited," he said, also lying. "Now, though, I'm going to lie down and take a little nap (*something he'd never done in all the years I'd known him*). They've been changing my meds a lot lately, and either that or the brain-bomb makes me sleepy." (*He only referred to it by that name with me, knowing his gallows humor wouldn't break me, possibly incorrectly, but I'd never tell him, or let on.*)

"Take care of yourself, Mickey," I said. "I'll send an email when I know more about my trip down (*even though I would always speak with Mickey on the phone, I vastly prefer communicating via email, with everyone/anyone*)."

"I love you, boy," he said, his traditional (*comforting*) closing.

"Love you too," I said, my traditional closing, which I had always felt was an acceptable lie, but which recent events/shift/thinking had me at least considering it might be true (*after a fashion, to the extent that I could love people*).

I heard the phone connection terminate and felt my heart rate start to drop. Sweat began to dry on all surfaces (*and in all crevices*), and the feeling of helplessness/hopelessness I'd been feeling since May 6th slowly receded to a manageable level again.

While changing into my bathing suit, I grabbed a different stuff-sack to drop into my in-town pack, chugged a Coke from the Coke fridge quickly enough to effectively simulate an aneurysm (*at which thought I felt guilty enough to skip the trick I knew to ameliorate cold-headaches*), and headed back down to the parking lot in back of my building to drive the Element over to the Best Western to keep my swim date with Xander.

I met Xander Kovac last August after his sister was brutally murdered, apparently (*to everyone but me*) at Xander's hands. He was innocent, and in the course of a messy (*in every negative sense of the word*) investigation, Xander was cleared and out of danger from the real killer. I now had a standing date to meet him for an hour or so of swimming at the Best Western Mountain Lake Inn on Wednesdays and Saturdays. I am a creature of habit/pattern/repetition/ritual, and so is Xander, which is no real surprise since we are both people living somewhere along the autistic spectrum.

Although I often feel lost and alone and overwhelmed and out of place in the sea of humanity in which I find myself (*even in tiny Saranac Lake, which counts its residents in thousands, as opposed to New York City, the place of my birth, which numbers in the millions*), Xander has more of a difficult time relating to/with people than I do. Whatever input-processing and communication and social issues I have are much less significant than his. We've both found ways to make our worlds work for us, with the help of those who love and aid us getting around and through, in a world we often have trouble dealing with. I mostly face the world on my own, whereas Xander has the constant help of one of his parents or an aide.

I didn't know which I would see today when I walked through the hotel lobby as if I owned the place (*which I have found is a key to getting into hotels, among other places*) but had heard Xander had a new aide who was working out tremendously well. Apparently, the new one was with Xander this afternoon because there was a significantly tattooed young man I didn't recognize (*that's saying something in Saranac Lake where I know most people, and their cars, and their addresses ... and their phone numbers)* swimming laps in proximity to Xander, who was floating face down with mask and snorkel as he likes to do. I waved to the presumed aide, said hello to a non-responsive Xander *(who nevertheless must have registered my arrival, as his starfished body mysteriously rotated so his head was facing toward me as I stripped out of all of my non-bathing suit clothing)*, and slid into the pool to join them.

"Hope, to sit, and then shake," Xander said from around his snorkel.

Xander had liked giving my dog, Hope, treats; Hope had liked receiving treats. The two of them had built a relationship on the basis of this exchange/interaction, and Xander was having some difficulty internalizing Hope's death *(in much the same way he had had difficulty dealing with his sister Danica's ...and possibly in much the same way I was not able to effectively deal with the possibility of Mickey's)*.

"Xander Kovac," I began. It seemed to work best with him when starting a discussion. "Hope was a good girl *(not really, but who did it hurt to polish the past a bit)*, but she died last winter. We did the same *trick* with the big black dog, Puck, at the shelter with Dot last week, do you remember?"

"Yes," he said before reacquiring the snorkel with his gums and dunking his head back down into the water.

"He talks about Hope a lot," the aide said, "and you. You must be Mr. Cunningham. I'm Mark Devlin, nice to meet you."

"Nobody on Earth," I said, "except for Xander and disgruntled law enforcement types, refers to me as Mr. Cunningham. Please, call me Tyler, Mark. It's nice to meet you."

He didn't seem put off, or confused by my not

offering to shake hands, so he must have heard something about me, beyond what Xander had said.

"It's awesome that you make time in your week to come and swim with the big guy," he said, pointing with an elbow to Xander, who was taller than both of us, and probably weighed the same as the two of us put together. "I love working with him, hanging with him, but it's sure not for everyone."

"After last summer, I feel as though we get along and understand each other and have even more in common than before."

It felt like obvious, low-hanging fruit, but he missed or ignored it. "I'm going through a therapeutic rec program at Paul Smith's College. Working with him is an awesome experience and pretty good money. I heard a little about what went down last year. That's some crazy shit."

"Xander," I said, (*hopefully*) redirecting/deflecting/distracting Mark from this line of talk where/while Xander could listen to us, "I've got some diving rings, would you like to do some hunting?"

"Yuph," he replied, which I took to mean *yes*, so I climbed out of the pool and fetched the rings from the stuff-sack.

I chucked the rings into the corners and deep spots all over the pool, and Xander started working his way around, diving and sometimes getting two or three rings with a single breath.

"Dude," Mark said, "I'm sorry, I didn't think. It was insensitive to you and Xander. Mea Culpa, no offense meant."

"No worries," I said. "I don't take offense, or have a problem talking about what happened (*especially the scrubbed version that everyone but Dot and Mickey got*), but the *big guy* was pretty broken/malfunctioning about what happened to (*I lowered my voice to say her name*) Danica."

"What I meant was what you did for him, for the whole family, was awesome," he said. "You totally saved his life. Iskra (*Xander's mother*) said that if you hadn't gotten involved, he would have ended up in some institution, probably forever. I can't fuckin' imagine that because he's so into the outdoors."

"I think it's likely the police would have figured out what happened without me, given time," I said. "His ... theirs was an interesting problem, and that's what grabbed me at first ... it wasn't until later, once I got to know him, that I knew I had to do whatever I could." (*This wasn't entirely true, but the truth sounded colder and didn't translate well to more traditionally programmed humans, as Mark seemed to be.*)

"Before I started at PSC, I served for sixteen months in Afghanistan. I found my way up here thanks to a buddy who's in the state troopers," Mark said. "He told me a bit about the inside of the house that day and what happened back in the canoe area (*the Saint Regis Canoe Area, a motorless wilderness across which Xander and I had been chased by a man intent on killing us*)."

Xander chose that moment to bring me the rings and look back over his shoulder at the pool, his message clear ... I chucked the rings again, distributing them perfectly throughout the pool.

"It was terrifying," I agreed. "But/and I don't much want to talk about it with him right here ... he hears everything, you know ... everything."

"I'm an ass," Mark said. "That's not what I was driving at, Tyler. I don't need details, and I know how much he takes in. I just wanted to say I know a bit about what you must have gone through. I think you're brave, maybe a hero. Getting to know Xander, hearing him talk about Hope and you these weeks since they hired me, I'm grateful for what you did. He can't say it, so I am. If I can do something for you someday, just ask. I'd be happy. It'd make me happy."

"Thanks, Mark," I said, probably as awkwardly as I felt at that moment … I struggle with emotions and emotional moments, and this interaction was replete with both.

We swam and dove and snacked and juice-boxed and talked about dogs and paddling and hiking and snowshoeing and camping … all of which was much more comfortable for me than what we had been speaking about previously. Every once in a while, during a normal conversation lag, I would catch Mark looking at me speculatively; eventually, when Xander wandered off into the locker room to use the bathroom, I asked why.

"Well," he said after a moment's pause, "I've heard the story from his parents, and from my friend Devin in the troopers, and from people talking when they hear that I'm working with him, but I've also heard him say some things that don't exactly fit. Things about what happened back in the woods, between the carries."

I felt a chill and actually checked my arms for goosebumps (*stupid, involuntary response*). Xander had seen, and been a part of, things that happened in those woods that didn't make it into any of the official reports/stories. I had counted on a combination of people wanting the simple/easy story and Xander's difficulties with expressive communication to prevent those details and events from getting out in the open.

"I think I need to get going," I said. "It was nice to meet you, Mark. Please say goodbye to Xander for me."

"Please don't," he said. "Remember, you asked. I

wasn't going to say anything. Won't say anything, about what he said, or what I think he said about what happened while he and Hope were watching 'Alias,' which I love too, by the way, back at Fish Pond."

Xander re-entered the pool area, and started making his way back toward us, so Mark leaned his head closer to mine, "That kind of situation never works out as neatly as civilians (*said with an emphasis which I took to mean people who don't know*) want them to. I believe you did what you needed to do in order to come out of the woods intact with Xander, oh yeah, and Hope. Whatever it was, you did a good job back there, and what I said earlier still stands. I'm happy to never talk about any of this again."

I nodded noncommittally (*something I excel at*), got up, said my goodbyes to Xander, waved to Mark, and wandered out into the bright, hot afternoon, head swimming a bit, and more than ready for a pile of nearly frozen Cokes, some Netflix, and as many donuts as I could eat before I fell asleep ... a great summer afternoon.

On my way to the door, I snuck a look at my watch and noted the time was 3:37 p.m. ... smiling, I turned around and called out the time to Xander.

Mark gave me a *so what?* look, and I said, "Give it, give him, a minute."

Xander glanced up at the ceiling while he lumbered down the steps into the pool ... I worried for a minute that he might trip and fall (*which was not the point of the exercise*), then gave his barking version of a laugh, made solid eye contact with me for a second and launched himself back into the water to float again.

Mark literally scratched his head for a few seconds, and then said, "Okay, Tyler, give. What the fuck was that? What does the current time mean? Did something funny happen at 3:37 to you two? I can go days without seeing that much animation from him, he almost never looks me in the eye, and I've never heard him laugh before."

"Nothing like that," I said. "337 is a prime … a prime number."

Mark shook his head, repeating the *so what?* look.

"Xander has some skills in mathematics," I said. "One of those skills is recognizing primes (*something we have in common, actually*). Because 337 is a prime number … beyond that it's a permutable prime, meaning that any way you arrange those numbers, 373 or 733, it's still a prime." (*It occurred to me that it was even possible that he knew it was star number … the 8th one.*)

"Okay," he said. "So how did you know that? Or did you make a plan to leave at 3:37?"

"Like I said," I answered after a moment, "Xander and I have a lot of things in common … math being one of those things."

Netflix and Cokes and all the donuts I could stack on a plate … it was a plan so perfect that I should have known it wouldn't work out the way I envisioned (*that's sort of a thing with me and plans*) … Frank and Brimley were waiting for me on the small landing at the top of the stairs outside of SmartPig.

Lower Saranac Lake, NY
Thursday, 7/9/ 2015, 7:23 p.m.

"For a guy with NVMS, you can be a hard man to find,"
Agent Tyson Brimley said as I clomped up the stairs to
SmartPig, savoring the slapping noise of my flip-flops and
the feel/smell of chlorinated water drying in my hair.

"That's cop talk for *No Visible Means of Support*,
Tyler," Frank said.

"I know what it means, Officer Gibson," I answered.
Addressing him more formally than I might when over to
his house for dinner seemed the best approach until I was
sure of my position, and his, with Brimley. "But I have
lots of jobs, Agent Brimley, and I'm a little bit rich on top
of that. All of that aside, I cannot see what that has to do
with your presumed serial killer."

"What he's trying to do with the talk about your lack
of a nine-to-five," said Frank, "and with whatever's in the
folder one of the Phils (*Frank later explained that both of the
FBI windbreakers I had met earlier were named Phil*) gave him
on our way up here is establish dominance … lay the
groundwork for a subordinate relationship."

"What the hell, Gibson?" Brimley said in an
exasperated tone. "Whose side are you on? His?"

Frank straightened slightly, and leaned in/over/
toward Brimley, before growling down at him, "I'm on
the side of that mother and father who were left in a

bloody mess all over an island inside my jurisdiction. I'm on the side of the twelve-year-old girl who saw her parents killed and hid from their killer by treading water in a dark lake until I could coax her into the rescue boat and hold her shivering body while she screamed for her mommy." He took a deep breath, and continued, "If you think messing around with Tyler will help the investigation, then by all means continue. My feeling is that dick-measuring won't get anything accomplished, and I'd rather just get Tyler out to the crime scene and make use of that brain of his before we lose daylight."

Agent Brimley reddened, and I watched … I love watching emotions, even ones I don't fully understand, play out on people's faces. He seemed to run the various options in his head, and I saw different things flit across his face for seconds, until he nodded, and turned to speak to me. "We've been at it since late last night, and as Officer Gibson pointed out, we're losing daylight."

"There is probably a touch less than four hours of usable light left today," I said. "I assume you've got lights out there, but what I've read on the subject (*which was, predictably, extensive*) would suggest that the spectral quality and non-diffused directionality of scene lights tend to have a negative impact on crime scene surveys, especially when compared to regular daylight."

"It has been suggested," he said, giving a nod in Frank's direction, "and based on our history, I would agree, that another set of eyes, and more specifically your eyes, would be beneficial in working the crime scene."

I waited, and he looked as though it pained him slightly to ask. "Mr. Cunningham, would you be willing to help us with our investigation?"

When I nodded, he got out a sheaf of papers for me … I signed everything. I sampled blocks of text while flipping through the fifty-some pages, and it appeared to be a mix of nondisclosure, non-interference, per diems and expense formulas, and possibly some nonsense sheets just to see if someone was reading and/or paying attention to what they were signing. I autographed and initialed and dated and had witnessed. Six minutes later, I grabbed my light duty outdoor pack, with a first-aid kit stuff-sack and some Cokes and beef jerky and peanut butter M&Ms jammed inside to facilitate as many hours of on-site investigation as the FBI and SLPD would allow me.

Although my understanding was that everyone who was going to die had been dead for nearly 20 hours, Frank punched the lights and sirens on his cruiser and rocketed through a nearly empty downtown (*it was too late for lunch and too early for dinner in town … the summer people were either taking a nap or still on the water/trail on this gorgeous day*) with us following. I sat next to Brimley in his multiply-antennaed, but determinedly generic-looking government sedan. The silence would have been awkward for most people (*probably was for him*), but I'm not most people … I'm happy/comfortable with silence, for days if/when possible. I waited until we got to the spot on Route 3 where we passed Lonesome Bay and watched out the window at the lake (*which looked like the lake on any other day, which seemed wrong, somehow*) before asking the question I'd been sitting on for hours. "What makes you think this killing is part of a pattern," I asked, "and not a run-of-the-mill homicide for money or sex or jealousy or because the person at the next campsite got drunk/high/crazy and found themselves with a knife and nothing better to do?"

Brimley eased his foot off the gas, enough that we slowed on the uphill after crossing Lonesome Bay, and he looked at his GPS.

"We're a little less than two road miles from the turnoff for the boat launch," I said. "At your present rate of speed, it will take you a few seconds under two minutes until the turn … I need to know why you made a connection that suggests a serial killer to you when other people didn't reach that same conclusion."

I noticed his fingers tighten slightly on the steering wheel, as he slowed down a bit more.

"Don't defend your theory, or the foundation upon which it was built, to me," I said. "That can come later if you feel it's important. For now, I just want to know what data came across your desk that moved your thoughts in that direction. I sift mountains of data myself and know what it's like to see patterns nobody else does/can/will. If you can tell me everything that led you to respond so quickly to this pair of murders in the next eighty-seven seconds, I promise both that I'll be more useful/ effective/efficient at the crime scene, and that I won't make fun of your flights of fancy if they turn out to be in error … I'm actually impressed that the 'suit' (*Frank's word, but Brimley would know what I meant*) I met twelve and a quarter years ago would be interested in, and willing to, color outside the lines to that extent."

He must have pulled his right foot back another micrometer, (*I looked at the GPS to verify my guesstimate*) and then he spoke without looking in my direction, "I started at the data-hub in Albany almost ten years ago. I manage a staff and extensive computing resources that process information from all over the country with reference to New York State and potential interstate criminal activity, and the various other crimes the FBI takes an interest in."

I nodded to encourage him to continue, and hopefully speed up, stifling the urge to interject with the FBI's mission and charter for the sake of maximizing efficiency.

"I admit that I kept an eye on the Adirondacks," he said, "and more particularly on you, in the years since our first encounter. Your name is green-boxed (*a term I was unfamiliar with, but could infer the meaning of*), and has come across my desk a number of times in the intervening decade, most notably in the last few years. More subtle, but noticed, perhaps, as a byproduct of my lingering interest in you, by my staff and the algorithms we've set up, was a handful of disappearances of people from out of state. All of them had little to nothing in common except neighbors and coworkers who, when interviewed, indicated that prior to their disappearance they had all been heading to the Adirondacks for a vacation. I only know one *gimp* in this area, and it's you, so I paid attention over the years."

"I appreciate the way you think," I said, "even though I was targeted by what I assume was an inappropriate use of government people and computing. It seems a bit thin though (*thinking again that my speech therapist would be pleased with my use of figurative language*) to get you and those guys in windbreakers you had with you earlier, to come up here for whatever happened out at that campsite on Lower Saranac."

"The FBI and I have significant resources, and it's simple enough, and entirely appropriate, to set the data-skimmer for whatever I want," he said. "In this case, one of my ongoing searches included the key terms: multiple murder, Adirondack, no arrest, no person of interest, not drug related (*which thankfully would have excluded one of the big opportunities for Brimley to have come across me and my extra-legal activities*). These searches generate no shortage of results, but we have lots of people, and smartish computers to look at them and separate the possible wheat from the certain chaff. The latest popped up around one o'clock this morning and was interesting and likely enough to make it past the algorithms and my night shift guy, and he took some initiative and woke me up. I was up here and on scene by five o'clock. You know the rest."

He finished his statement at the same moment he flicked the turn signal down with his pinky, slowed and pulled into the state boat launch area at the bridge between First Pond and Second Pond.

On a normal day, the concrete ramp leading into the water is constantly occupied by a mix of cars/trucks/vans/boats/barges/canoes/kayaks. Today was clearly not a normal day. It looked as though the local PD, state troopers, and FBI had taken over and diverted ninety percent of the regular boaters/traffic elsewhere (*probably Ampersand Bay and Crescent Bay, I guessed*). Not much seemed to be going on at the moment, but a barge was being loaded with lights and generators and gear and scuba divers with headlamps. An ambulance idled by the edge of the ramp with its lights slowly blinking a coded message of *no hurry*. A number of marked and unmarked cars, and their occupants/drivers, lounged around the ramp area in that busy/impatient/indolent way that only LEOs can manage to pull off.

We were waved out of our intended route straight to the water by a nearly frantic SLPD drone who clearly couldn't deal with the crowd of local and state and federal police all wanting to be at the center of things, all at the same time. A number of cruisers and unmarkeds and special response vans and ambulances and the SLFD's water rescue trucks and trailers were all blocking the straight line from Route 3. We had to detour around and through the big parking lot, likely filled because of people camping on Lower Saranac (*as day trippers would have had to launch, today at least, from Marcy Bridge or Ampersand Bay)*. In the seventy-three seconds it took us to wend our way in and around the hundred or so parked cars, I noted that a bit less than two-thirds of the plates/cars/people were from out of state. This got me thinking, but I was forced to file my thoughts due to Frank waving his arms and yelling out his window at the cars poking along in front of him. Brimley got on the radio with him and spoke in low tones for only a few seconds before Frank turned on the flashers and started talking through the PA system on his cop-bar, telling all of the cars between us and the water to make a hole "right fucking now" (*an uncharacteristic use of profanity while in uniform, which confused me somewhat*).

With Frank's cruiser in the lead, and us on his bumper, we nosed our way through the mess, all the way up to the front. A Boston Whaler apparently for us, was tied up at the dock on the right, which was normally reserved for canoe and kayaks waiting to launch/unlaunch. We walked over, under stares of people who had been, until seconds ago, furiously busy (*or seeming to be*). Frank settled behind the wheel of the boat without asking, and nodded his chin at me and then the two ropes securing us to the dock; I undid the slip-hitches and kicked us away from the dock while Frank started the boat and backed us out into the river.

He motored the Whaler up and around and into Lower Saranac significantly faster than the posted 5-MPH (*but they always do, even when they aren't on their way to a crime scene*). Coming out of the narrows, we were faced with the tall cliffs of Bluff Island. As always, people were jumping and climbing and watching other people jumping and climbing. There was something both comforting and somewhat off-putting about activities in the Adirondacks progressing as per normal when I was on my way to what

I assumed was the site of a gruesome murder (*murders, I corrected myself*). Without slowing down, Frank threaded the needle/Whaler between Bluff Island and the boats and the smaller facing islands called simply the Little Twins by everyone. (*Hope and I had stopped at the shallow and rocky shelf between them a number of times for shallow swimming and splashing and snacking while exploring Lower Saranac Lake in the previous few summers.*) As he pushed the Whaler's throttle to the stops and leaned into the acceleration, I watched Agent Brimley stagger and grab wildly at a railing, and saw Frank smile for a moment before scrubbing it from his face with a tiny shake of his head. I called up my personal/internal map of Lower Saranac, asking the cartographers living in the back of my skull to overlay the basic map with campgrounds and private residences.

Lower Saranac Lake has sixty campsites, sixty-two if you include those down by First Pond and Second Pond, near the boat launch … I didn't (*both because they're not in the lake proper, and because they'd make horrible places to commit murders and hope to get away with it*). I'd spent a few nights in various campsites there with people I knew who invited me out for a night or two while they stayed on the lake. But, in general, I preferred to find my own, wilder (*and free*) campsites elsewhere in the six-million-acre park where I live. The campsites felt too close/closed-in to me after the deep woods spots and bandit camping I had grown used to in my explorations of the park in the last thirteen and a half years. I tried to imagine a killer or killers thinking they could get in, kill a couple of people, and make their way out without getting caught.

I leaned over to speak into Agent Brimley's ear (*the wind and noise of the boat's engine made the proximity necessary, if not welcome*). "You imagined that I did this, whatever this is? It's like murdering someone in the middle of Times

Square."

He turned part way toward me, not letting go of the railing he had previously grabbed, and spoke out of the side of his mouth, "Are you kidding, Cunningham? We're on the dark side of the moon compared to some killings I've investigated."

His response tickled something in a dusty corner of my brain, and I took a mental picture of his words so I could revisit them later to prime the pump on whatever was going on (*or wanted to start going on*) back there ... I forced myself to refocus while Frank was slowing down and arcing in the direction of a campsite that struck me as profoundly interesting.

The encampment on Hocum Point Island, campsite #35, looked, even from a distance, to have been thoroughly trampled. The camping season had been going on long enough that there had likely been dozens of families and individuals staying there. Whatever had happened last night brought a legion of local and state and federal investigators ... each group likely with their own forensics teams and photographers and detectives. I recognized one of the SLPD officers holding station 25 yards off the island, taking pictures of every boat that passed, near or far, and handing Frank a clipboard to sign as we approached.

"Please list everyone on your boat," he said. "Anyone who'll be setting foot on the island needs to sign for themselves, along with agency affiliation, reason for visit, and they have to sign out again on their way out." He sounded nervous, and as though reading off a card.

Frank scribbled for a few seconds and then handed the clipboard to Agent Brimley, who apparently signed for me before giving the clipboard back to Frank, who returned it back across the gap between the boats, along with a can of Coke and a Snickers bar. "Long day, is that correct, Bryce? You were one of the first on the scene, right, came in last night after I got the girl to the hospital?"

"Yeah, Jesus though, what a fuckin' mess," he said. "I'm glad I pulled clipboard and camera duty on this one. The woman's blood sprayed all the way up to the underside of some maple leaves ... ten, twelve feet up. Skinny Tom hadda leave. He couldn't stop barfin'."

"Skinny Tom's vomit aside," Agent Brimley asked, "are you confident of the integrity of the scene?"

"What? Yeah, sure, I been here all day, and they've been careful logging people and evidence in and out on the island the whole time."

Frank looked back at me and rode over the possibility of more exchange between the two of them by speaking loudly to me, pointing, "The girl went into the water off the southwest tip of the island. We think the unsub or unsubs accessed the island from the northeast nubbin, so we've been makin' everyone walk in on the rocks that almost make up an isthmus at the northwest end of the island."

"Nice word, Frank," I said. "Isthmus."

"I know, right," he said, cracking a toothy grin. "That tear-off calendar you gave me for my birthday is really starting to pay off."

He started to motor slowly, pointing out details as we went. "I pulled Edith, the girl, out of the water about here. No shoes o' course, she'd been in bed when it started. She heard her mother scream and went out the back door of the tent, saw the guy put her mom down and ran into the water. She cut up her feet pretty bad and broke a coupla toes and fingers getting from the tent to the water. Edith said the guy followed her in, but she

46

dove and swam straight out. He didn't follow, and once he turned back for land, she started hollerin' like bloody murder, which I guess it was. Believe it or not, you can get fair cell service out here, and we musta had a half dozen calls to the station in the first few minutes of her screamin'. I was up at a friend's boathouse smoking a cigar after supper when I got the call. We took my buddy's boat cuz it was quicker 'n waiting for the rescue boat, and she was still screaming when I got on-scene, mebbe twenty minutes after the first call came in."

Frank maneuvered the Whaler up and around some big glacial erratics stranded by the last ice age, and slowly ran the boat up and into/onto some smaller rocks making up the correctly identified/aforementioned isthmus. "By the time I got out here, it was dark enough I needed a handheld spotlight to find the girl. A little white face in all that black water. I shined the light on my face, on myself, and my badge, talking her into letting me help her into the boat. She was exhausted, and just hung there while I pulled her up into the Whaler and wrapped her in my fleece and a dirty towel layin' on the bottom of the boat. Once she was on board and told me what she thought happened, I left her with Ted and splashed in and waded ashore with my light and piece and found the parents, and called it in and made tracks for the hospital with the girl. I was admittedly distracted, but failed to see other people or boats on my way here or back to the dock."

I looked at Frank and Agent Brimley, and down at my feet. "Do I have to wear those little blue paper booties or something?"

"Only if we're gonna be on TV, Tyler," Frank said. "But I bet you got some gloves in that bag of yours, and those might be useful if you find something. Don't step on, or near any little yellow flags you see. If there's an

47

area looped in string or tape, don't step inside it. If you see something that might be evidence that everyone else missed, whistle for me, but don't touch it if you can help yourself."

I stepped out of the boat and onto the rocks leading to shore and out to the island. Picking my way carefully toward the busy-cop-noise and occasional flashing of cameras, I tried to will the sun back up higher in the sky, wanting to hold back the night/dark. I pushed through the low scrub at the edge of the island, my feet naturally finding a narrow path leading clockwise around to the greatest concentration of noise and activity on the northeast side of the roughly circular island (*about 170 feet in diameter, if you were wondering, or for those who hunger for details*). A mix of crime scene geeks was working the shoreline for clues. It seemed an uphill slog for all of them because halfway through the summer this island had been pawed over and crashed into and peed/pooped/littered/bled on by dozens, if not hundreds of people from all over the country/world.

"Is there a blood trail coming back from the campsite to this side of the island?" I asked whoever would answer me ... I assumed someone would. "That would be a good sign that the killer, or killers, came back this way after killing the ... what were the names of the deceased?"

"Angela and Keith Richards," Frank offered, from somewhere behind me, "but not *that* Keith Richards."

There were a couple of snorts from the crime scene techs working around me, so I assumed Frank had said something funny, but not necessarily pertinent. He came up and touched my shoulder lightly before handing me a short stack of printed photographs taken last night and today of various aspects of the scene and the Richardses ... as found, when turned over. The snapshots included close-ups of their wounds and hands and injuries they'd sustained in the seconds leading up to their deaths that would never have time to bruise or bleed or swell (*much less heal*).

"We've found human blood samples from two distinct blood groups but haven't yet matched it to either of the decedents," said an Alpha-geek (*I don't say this in a pejorative sense. They stand out if you know what to look for … and I do*) working half in and half out of the water. "We're hoping for a sample from a third donor, or for one of the two to be the killer's, but it seems a lot to hope for given the state of the bodies at the scene."

I spent the next few seconds looking around the spot where the killer most likely came ashore to kill the Richards family. It soon became apparent that the techs were competent, and would certainly find anything there was to find. If the killer could be caught using their methods, they would do it. I turned on my heel and walked through the scrub (*the trail was too littered with little flags and markers and tape and string to be passable*) heading to the southern end of the island … toward the (*it's hard to write this in a way that doesn't sound dramatic, so I won't bother*) kill zone.

I was expecting the blood to look red, and for there to be more of it. (*My understanding is that a typical adult has between five and six liters of blood inside them.*) This killer had violently exsanguinated both Angela and Keith Richards … it didn't appear as though there were three gallons of blood spread/sprayed around the campsite. What little there was, was dark brown to black in color and was already blending in with the pine and hemlock needles littering the ground around Campsite #35. A solid rain would erase the Richardses' blood from the ground/trees/leaves/rocks as if they had never been there. Already, if not for their abandoned/orphaned camping gear and the detritus of the scene techs, one could almost dismiss the clutter as the result of messy tenants having stayed at the campsite the night before. (*I'd been to campsites after high school/college parties that looked worse.*)

Mr. Richards had been taken about 35 feet from the campfire pit (*which makes a convenient center point of the campsite from which to measure distances. So that's what I decided to do*). The pictures indicated he'd died face down, spilling his blood into a puddle the size and shape of the china server my mother used two or three times a year for turkeys and hams … when we had company. His clean/intact hands showed he hadn't scratched up either his killer or the ground beneath him, suggesting that he went relatively quickly (*if not gently*) into that good night. I was certain that Quincy or Kay Scarpetta could have ascertained the strength and height and handedness and weapon preference of his assailant from the wound pictures. But I couldn't seem to (*although I tried and made a note of things I needed to research further in the future*), except to say that this person (*or people, although I leaned toward person, based on a lifetime of reading*) had killed Keith with a single, strong/deep cut. (*It was the same with Angela, but more on that in a paragraph or two.*) I noticed bootprints in the blood next to his body, not huge, not tiny … just man boot-sized to my eye. The geeks would be able to work all of that out. (*Brimley and Frank had me at the scene for other, higher, purposes.*) I spent another minute studying the dark serving dish-sized stain on the ground, flipping back and forth between pictures of Keith Richards from different angles before moving in closer to the campfire (*which I thought of as point 0,0, the origin of the crime scene … if you know, you know, if you don't, luckily it doesn't matter much*).

Everything about the death of Angela Richards was faster, more violent, more powerful … it made her husband's death seem almost peaceful by comparison (*although, you know, not if you thought about it much*). The killer's boot strides lengthened and deepened in his approach to her, which I took to mean he sped up on his way toward her; the killer must have been moving fast and swinging his weapon hard, as her head was nearly severed from her body. One extremely detailed photograph showed a significant notch in the vertebra the knife/machete had finally run into after cutting through the rest of her neck. Angela Richards' blood had sprayed far and wide. Based on their relative presumed positions, the knife had been swinging/arcing up and to the left when it made devastating contact with that bridge between body and mind, mouth and stomach, and the home of the voice she'd used in her last seconds to warn, and save, her daughter. A notation on the back of one picture mentioned tiny droplets of blood on a maple sapling at the edge of the campsite where contact between killer and killee must have occurred, suggesting a void in the spray from Angela's neck wound had likely been occupied by the killer. Said perpetrator must have gotten covered in a significant amount of blood (*enough that they presumably couldn't stop for gas or McDonald's or check into a hotel without it being noted/noticed*). It looked from the mess of tiny footprints and extensive fountaining of blood in all directions, that Angela Richards had spun at least one full circle before collapsing in front of the tent where all three had planned on sleeping during their stay in the Adirondacks.

Moving forward, past the campfire pit, to the tent, I took a brief glance inside. An inventory in my pile of pictures and papers showed a list of what I assumed a

51

of this approach...

small family would likely have with them for a multi-day vacation in what they saw as wilderness. I committed the list to memory and walked around to the back of the tent. The girl, Edith, had only unzipped the vertical zipper, which given years of use, would have resulted in zipper failure in the back door (*from the stress of this common practice of people, especially kids, unzipping one, but not both zippers in tents with doors like this one had*). That useless detail stuck in my head awhile, and I turned to look at the crime scene laid out before me, imagining the terror/helplessness/ hopelessness/worry of her parents as their lives literally drained away, unable to do anything to help their daughter (*or see her grow up and do whatever she would do with them out of the picture*). My mouth filled with spit and I felt dizzy and hot and swayed some, reaching out to steady myself on a stubbly balsam tree not far from the tent. I tore the hand out of my glove, grabbed another from my pack, shook my head to clear away thoughts of my parents, and walked to the water's edge.

I spotted a reddish/brownish/whitish speck caught in a crack in a rock partly covered by a low-hanging branch and whistled and raised my hand, catching Frank's attention before I pointed. A ballet of tired/grumpy/ resentful/embarrassed crime scene weenies swooped in with cameras and flags and bags and tweezers and swabs and vials, blocking us from view of the rock and whatever I'd seen for a minute while the recovered/recorded it.

"Blood, tissue, and most of a toenail," announced the Alpha-geek I'd heard from (*as opposed to spoken with*) earlier. "Likely it's from Edith Richards. She apparently sustained injuries along these lines fleeing the tent while headed to the water, and I can't imagine our guy taking off his shoes just to leave us some evidence."

I stepped into the lake, surprised as I always was, at

how warm the lakes got during the summer months. Walking out the length of a tree near where she, the girl, must have gone into the water, I waded deeper until something nagged me into turning around. When I did, I saw it … a shiny dent in the weather-greyed tree.

Again, I whistled and pointed. "I'm not sure that's anything. It might have been there for a week or a month, but I don't think so. I believe your bad guy fell across the tree when he started to follow the girl into the water, and something, maybe a belt-buckle, maybe his knife, maybe a button/zipper, came between his weight and the tree. If I fell here, and if he's about as tall as me, I would have touched the tree … here-ish. As long as you're already running a big tab at the forensics lab, you might as well swab the hell out of this tree wherever his hands might have touched it … there could be skin cells or blood."

I bent low, then squatted in the water, on both sides of the tree, looking for what I didn't know; I guess I was hoping that something might have fallen out of one of his pockets … a wallet or library card maybe. (*I gave a short and sharp huffing laugh at my inappropriate fantasy/dream/hope, then felt awkward and tried to cover it all with a cough.*)

Running back the tape of the time in my mind since we'd arrived at the island/campsite/crime-scene, poking and prodding and running it forward and backward to see if I'd missed obvious things I should look for … I couldn't see/think of any.

"I need to see and talk with the girl now," I said, "before too much time passes, or anyone starts to help her getting over, or comfortable with, the pain of what happened last night. I need it, need her, raw and red and dripping and crying and broken. Frank, can we go?"

"We just got here, Tyler," Frank said, (*which wasn't at all true*). "It'll be another hour at least before Brimley and

I finish checking in with people and making sure they've got the scene, and new evidence, wrapped."

"Okay," I said. "Then give me one of your steno pads and a pen, and I'll go back to the boat to write down some thoughts/questions/theories. As soon as you can, we should get to the hospital or wherever you're holding her."

"We're not holding her," Agent Brimley spoke over Frank's shoulder at me. "We got a pair of statements last night, and again this morning. She's being treated at the hospital, and waiting for family to come and pick her up. Edith is not a witness, she's a victim. If we grant you an opportunity to talk with her, you will do well to remember that: victim, not witness."

"Puh-tay-toe, puh-tah-toe," I said. "I'll be in the boat."

I grabbed the pad and pen Frank held out for me as I walked by, and made my way back to the Whaler, looking forward to the snacks and drinks in my pack and hoping the Cokes would still be cold. (*I'd wrapped them in a towel on my way out, so I had high hopes.*)

Adirondack Medical Center, Saranac Lake, NY
Thursday, 7/9/ 2015, 9:18 p.m.

The Cokes were cold enough to drink and enjoy but not
at optimal temperatures. Although the M&Ms had melted
internally, they were saved (*as so often happens*) by the candy
shell. The jerky was perfect, as it always seemed to be. I
was happy to be alone with my thoughts about what had
happened on Hocum Point Island the previous night.
Somewhere roughly five miles east-north-east of me, a
young girl was likely much less happy to be alone, in a
hospital room, moving restlessly on starchy bedding,
aware at some level of her parents' ruined bodies in the
morgue two floors below her. I projected my map in that
direction and tried to picture her alone and sad and scared
and life-ruined in a hospital bed in a strange place with no
parents to check on her. I couldn't change her past or
present, but I might just have a shot at altering/
improving the trajectory of her future … I resolved to do
just that, regardless of any resistance I might encounter.

I rode to the hospital in the front of Frank's cruiser,
no lights, with Agent Brimley trailing us. Neither of them
were enthused about my plan/desire/need to speak with
Edith Richards, for all sorts of reasons which they had
detailed, at length, on the ride back to the boat launch; I
factored large numbers in my head and ignored them
until they finished, nodding at randomly timed intervals

and occasionally saying "yup" when they paused.

Once we were in his cruiser and Frank could aim for AMC on autopilot, he speed-dialed his wife, Meg, and spoke with her about my wish to interview the girl, as if I weren't in the car with him/them. (*Despite his insistence that he doesn't understand me at all, Frank seems to get me more than most people in the world.*) After an initial data dump, Frank mostly listened, occasionally angling his head to look at me slyly/not-slyly from two feet away. I assume she was reminding him that I too had lost both of my parents in a single, violent event at a young age and that the girl and I might, in fact, have some deeper things in common ... I was comfortable using his, or their, pity/compassion/ understanding in this situation; it was wasted otherwise, but might finally come to some use tonight. When I asked about talking with Edith, Frank said that an aunt would arrive from Pennsylvania late that night or the next, and until then, she'd be staying at AMC for observation and care and protection. He said he'd talked Agent Brimley into letting me speak to her in pursuit of getting a feasible angle/crack/approach in working the case. (*He nearly said "our case," which might, in other circumstances be cause for celebration, but I was happy just to get a shot at the girl ... I wanted to work on this, on her, for a number of reasons, six.*)

I followed Frank and Agent Brimley into the hospital and down the halls. (*I hate every single thing about hospitals, except their stated function, and tend to shut down most of my sensory/cognitive array the moment I enter one, to avoid discomfort.*) A state trooper stood, leaning against the wall outside of her door, reminding me of something John had said recently about the police force being more a detritivore than guardian/keeper of the peace as we would like (*and they would like us*) to believe. It was clear when we walked into her room that Edith Richards was physically fine, and essentially being warehoused in the short term. Both feet were bandaged, and her right-hand index finger had one of those metal splints on it, but she seemed otherwise mobile and alert and fully functional. She had no trouble with the remote for the wall-mounted TV and had made the best of horrific food options, based on the remains of her dinner tray.

Lying down in the bed, Edith Richards was longer than I had anticipated and skinny ... elbows and knees sticking out a bit under the slightly grey hospital sheets. She had bright blue eyes, huge and noticeable on her ashen face, and slightly sunken into their sockets. I smelled disinfectant and tape and Betadine and, underneath it, Johnson's Baby Shampoo from her long and still-braided blonde hair. (*This scent evoked a memory of my own mother washing my hair with the no-tears shampoo years ago, and made me sad/angry/determined before we'd even spoken.*)

She smiled reflexively at Frank, who was first through the door. (*I would probably do the same thing if I was the kind of person who smiled, but I'm not.*) While Frank was mumbling/fumbling his way through an awkward greeting/regrets segment, Agent Brimley moved out from behind him, and her entire aspect/carriage/demeanor changed ... she stiffened, the smile fled for parts unknown, and what color she had in the parts of her I could see, drained as though some dam had broken. (*It occurred to me that Agent Brimley might have been lacking in bedside manner with young Edith in an earlier interview/talk about what had happened.*) I stepped in beside Brimley, and she didn't even register my presence ... I was just another old person up in her grill on the worst day of her life. I could tell by looking at her, and from the memory of my own version of the day she was living, that she hadn't slept since her mother's scream the previous evening ... she'd be tired and vulnerable, and I could use that to get more of what I needed if I could get Frank and Brimley (*and their delicate sensibilitie*s) out of the room for a few minutes.

After an awkward few seconds while she struggled with muting some reality show, she shut the TV off entirely and looked up at all of us, but mostly Frank, and said with a tiny voice, "Hello."

"Hi, Edith," Frank said. "You remember Agent Brimley (*she nodded, but didn't look his wa*y)? This is my friend, (*possibly an exaggeration or misnomer, but certainly acceptable in these circumstances*) Tyler Cunningham. He runs a business called SmartPig ... get it, Cunning-ham, Smart Pig?"

She smiled awkwardly in my direction, and then felt guilty about smiling and her eyes got shiny, "Why's he here?"

"Besides being my friend and a nice guy (*again, possibly a stretch*)," Frank began, "Tyler's maybe the smartest person I know. He likes puzzles and mysteries and codes and stuff and sees and knows and thinks things other people don't. We, Agent Brimley and I, asked him to help us figure out what happened last night."

It was as if the curtain fell on her attention and participation at that point. Her hands clenched and wrestled on the stiff white sheets over her hidden lap; her eyes dropped to watch the hands, got still shinier, and big drops started metronomically pulsing out of one and then the other eye in turn. Her breathing sped up and got less regular than it had been when we'd first entered the room, and the skin on her chest and neck and face started blotching with red and white spots.

"You don't have to talk with Tyler, or any of us, if you don't want to, honey," Agent Brimley said. "Your Aunt Peggy will be here in the morning to take you home (*at which word, Edith started sobbing quietly, still looking down at her hands*), but any help you can give us could help prevent other people getting hurt like your mommy and daddy."

I lack lots of the basic social/emotional software that every person comes pre-installed with, and after only 51 words, I wanted to throw a bedpan at Agent Brimley … preferably full.

"Edith," I said, wondering what I would follow up with, "do you like solving puzzles? (*She had tilted her head when Frank mentioned my interests/skills a minute ago, and nodded now, without raising her eyes … yet.*)

I picked the pillaged food tray off her bed table, and drew a circle with a Sharpie from my pocket, marking it with the six words I'd just said and corresponding dots along the rim of the circle. "Agent Brimley spoke fifty-one words a minute ago. I used six words when I spoke eight seconds ago. These two numbers are related. Fifty-one is the sixth Motzkin number, which means you can make fifty-one lines that don't cross between these six points. I'll bet you this twenty dollar bill that you can't make fifty-one non-intersecting lines using these six points and the straws from your dinner before I get back with all the Jell-O I can find in the cafeteria and an … orange soda. I'll give you this hundred dollar bill (*glad that I had brought my wallet along for this trip … money gets the attention of twelve-year-olds, even nerdy and bereaved ones*) if you can make more than fifty-one. Sound fair (*she nodded, eyes locked on the Franklin*)?"

Both Frank and Agent Brimley looked as though they were about to object to, or say, something … which I didn't want at this juncture. "When I come back with the Jell-O and soda, and to check your math, would it be okay if we talked for a minute (*the tiniest nod imaginable*). I'll tell you a story I guarantee you'll like." (*Another quick bob, and her head leaned in to look at my drawing of the circle, the straws, and the bills decorating her bed table … I had her, even though I was lying about the story.*)

"Great, I'll see you in five minutes and thirty-two seconds, Edith," I said, grabbing the tray and using it to shunt Frank and Agent Brimley back out the door. "Thanks for agreeing to play with me. These guys are boring … nice, but boring."

Out in the hall, as soon as the door swished shut, Frank and Brimley both spoke at once, I interrupted before they could get rolling … gain traction. "She was shutting down, and I need to talk to her. I got her back … I think. Which of you two has the necessary juice to hustle up six or eight little tubs of Jell-O, flavors unimportant? I also need an orange soda (*people are always impressed when you identify them as liking orange soda, it makes them feel special, even though 92 percent of the world likes orange soda, and doesn't know that other people also do*) and a Coke … just bottles or cans, no hospital cups."

They were good sports about it, once they realized they really had no choice in the matter. They'd invited me to the party, and since I hadn't announced my plans to beat or consume the child, they had no real reason to object to my scheming/manipulation. While Frank went off after the Jell-O and pointed me to the soda machine, Brimley stalked off, saying he wanted to check on preliminary postmortems on the parents. I went to the bathroom to offload some used Cokes and splash my face (*apologies for crossing the TMI-line, but if I got lucky and Edith started talking, I didn't want to have to leave to un-gum tired eyes or find a bathroom*).

Frank came back with a tray full of little cups of Jell-O about the same time I found and had gotten what I needed from the soda machine.

"Don't fuck this up, Tyler," he said. "She seems okay, but her world ended a bit last night, and she hasn't fully figured it out yet. If you make things tougher for her, even in the service of investigating this case, I'll stab you in your eye. The left one, I think."

"Got it," I said. "Make the kid cry, and I get to wear my eyepatch all year, not just on Halloween."

"That was almost a fucking joke, Tyler," Frank said, impressed (*I have a sense of humor, but it's not in line with the majority of humanity, which is almost exactly like not having one*). "Did it hurt?

"I stole it from Dot ... it seemed to fit at the moment," I said. "No, it didn't hurt, but I had a moment of doubt, nearly worry, when I launched it, so thanks for affirming that it worked/landed."

He shook his head, snorted (*which made me wonder if I'd been funny again*), handed me the tray, and left, saying over his shoulder that he'd be at the nurses' station when I was done.

I tapped on the door to Edith's room, heard a noise from inside that I took to be assent/invitation, and pushed in, past the trooper.

"Hey, kiddo," I said. "How'd you do?" (*Mickey has always, always, called me kiddo and I've always liked it.*)

She held up a few sheets of paper, "I had to use paper to keep my solutions straight. I found fifty-three."

She slid the twenty and the hundred across the table with a pair of fingertips, and then stopped, looking up at me. I grabbed the papers out of her outstretched hand, and quickly scanned the messily drawn circles ... I smiled down at her and retrieved my hundred, leaving the twenty.

"You only found fifty," I said. "Solutions twenty-two, thirty-seven, and fifty-three are repeats, so you still owe me one, but you were quick, so I think we're good … fair?"

I slid the tray of Jell-O and the orange soda across to her, covering the math/geometry geekery, hopefully signaling effectively enough that we could move on. (*She seemed pretty bright. Twelve-year-olds are by the term's original definition, morons, so I didn't want to go too fast for her.*)

While I opened one of my Cokes and drank, I looked around the room, generally waiting and trying to give her a bit of space/time.

"You were going to tell me a story," she said, after what must have seemed to her a long and quiet minute and forty-three seconds. "Is it about a brave little girl who helps the cops after her parents are … get …?"

Her breathing and skin color and eyes fell apart again (*she looked as if she'd been hit by lightning or a frying pan*), but I didn't react (*which is thankfully, remarkably easy for me*). Instead, I let her breathe and drip and sniffle through it while we each sipped some soda, and I slyly grabbed the Jell-O cup closest to me and slurped a few cubes over the rim (*lacking a spoon or the desire for one*).

"Nope, it's about a young man," I said, "older and bigger and tougher and weirder than you … it's debatable whether or not he loved his parents, or even could love them. Nevertheless, one bright and sunny Tuesday at the end of the summer, but not quite into fall yet, a group of angry men hijacked a bunch of airplanes and flew them into buildings all over the east coast, including, by horrible coincidence, the buildings his parents worked in. The young man didn't know how or when, or even for sure if, his parents died, but they never came home that day or any other day. All of a sudden, he was entirely alone in an unfair and demonstrably mean-spirited world. Have you heard this one?"

Edith Richards was still slowly leaking tears, but her breathing was normalizing, and her color was better. "Your parents were killed in 9/11?"

It occurred to me that she'd been born after that bright, sunny morning turned smoky and confusing and dark and full of flying bits of things … I had wandered the streets for hours, looking at thousands of shell-shocked faces for the ones I wanted/needed, all of their eyes wet and red in the middle of uniformly dusty white faces and hair and bodies. It was an historical event to Edith, through no fault of her own, like Pearl Harbor or the Civil War or the Big Bang … something that had once happened and changed everything for some other people. It was likely too big, too far away, for her to really grasp, or relate to.

"We, my mom and dad and I, had plans to go out for Chinese food at this great dumpling place for dinner (*Noodles on 28th, which had recently relocated to 29th Street, but kept the old name, which bothered me more than it did anyone else on the planet*)," I said. "When they didn't come home, I ordered in, to wait for them. When the dumplings got cold and gross, I threw them out and ordered another batch … again and again for days."

My world had been based on order, and their disappearance/loss/death erased that order, or the illusion of order I'd pasted over the world. I had to flee the newly terrifying city and start over again; Edith was probably in a similar place. When I didn't say anything else, she filled the quiet with her own story (*something I've found works more often than you'd think*).

"I was lying in the tent in my sleeping bag," she began. "My lips felt sticky from the s'mores, and I was thinking about getting up to get a drink and rinse off the marshmallow, but I liked being there, warm in the

63

slippery bag, listening to Mom and Keith talking quietly by the fire. It was a little like nights at home, but different. Then the noises and voices changed, and Mommy sounded scared and asked me to bring her first-aid stuff for Keith. He fell down, I guess."

She reached for a container of cherry Jell-O (*red, anyway, who knows what flavor Jell-O is, and does it really matter?*), seemed to think better of it and grabbed a container filled with yellow cubes (*a safe bet it was lemon*) before continuing. "I don't want to talk about what went on after that."

She picked up the pen and started doodling, gripping Frank's pen hard enough that each knuckle was highlighted in white … a rough drawing that even upside down I could translate/interpret. She drew a square topped by a triangle, seemingly without thinking about it … home. She didn't have a home anymore, not like she had 24 hours ago. My understanding from articles I'd read (*if I talked to myself more, lots, maybe most, of my sentences would begin this way*), was that after pictures of themselves, this form of home image was incredibly common among both very young children, and those who have family snatched from them by some flavor of disaster … the earliest pictures I remembered drawing, and those I scribbled on the takeout menu from the dumpling place that Tuesday night were nautilus/Fibonacci shells, spiraling and growing and looping endlessly and perfectly outwards, from nothing to everything (*the exact opposite of me*).

"Keith's not your dad?" I asked, using the present tense to see/test, not as a device of cruelty (*I don't do cruel, by and large*). "I'm just asking because you referred to them as Mom and Keith."

"My dad had a heart attack a few years ago," she said

quietly, looking at her hands, knotting and unknotting them on the thin sheets in front of her, like restless kittens. "Keith moved in a little over a year later; he makes, made, I guess, Mom happy and was nice to me. Camping was his idea, and it was fun ... until."

She started crying, silent gasping sobs and huge tears rolling down her cheeks; I was almost certain I'd blown it and would get nothing more.

"Edith, I'm okay with you not talking about what happened," I said, lying ... I was hoping to trick this little girl into giving me something to get my mental/research hooks into. "My friend, Frank, Officer Gibson, is the one who pulled you out of the water. That must have been weird, night swimming for that long. I sometimes go out into the middle of one of the lakes or ponds around here to float and think ... I always imagine that I can feel the fish/turtles/leeches in the water around me."

She shivered (*leeches, I thought, it's the leeches*), but I'd gotten her thinking about something besides the person who'd bled her parents dry, so I counted it a victory.

"It wasn't so bad," she said. "The water's warmer than I thought."

I was thinking about marine iguanas and Charles Darwin and Edith Richards when she said this. Darwin famously (*at least in my mind*) spent an afternoon hurling marine iguanas into the ocean; they kept swimming straight back to shore, crawling ashore at his feet only to be chucked into the sea again. They kept returning despite the annoyance because they'd long been programmed to fear the dangers of the sea, sharks mostly, but also seals and sea lions (*ears/earholes, to answer your inevitable question*), and to a lesser degree whales. The iguana faced no predators/threats on land (*except for annoying young biologists*), so they swam as quickly as possible back to

65

land, despite young Charles and his tireless pitching arm.
Edith was an example of the same response to stimuli,
only reversed … there might be minor annoyances or
things she feared in the dark waters of the lake, but
nothing so serious as the man she'd seen kill her mother
and (*I assumed from her language*) stepfather. She would have
stayed out in the lake until she sank.

I noisily slurped a cube of the red Jell-O into my
mouth and squished it between my teeth, like my father
and I used to do. (*It drove my mother crazy, but that was
apparently part of the fun, for my father anyway … I just got
accustomed to it, which is 90 percent of the story of my life.*) Once
I'd thoroughly flossed with the gelatin, I swallowed it,
tipping my head back as we always used to do. When I
leaned forward again, I saw the hint of a smile in Edith's
eyes, if not on her mouth. She pulled a cube of
yellow/lemon into her mouth, and inexpertly swished it
around.

"What did you and that putz, Agent Brimley, talk
about?" I asked, trying my hand at impugning him to get
her on my side (*not something I am particularly gifted at/in, but
she's only 12, so I figured that I might have a chance*).

"He doesn't like you much, does he?" she asked. "He
kept asking the big man if they really needed your help.
They were out in the hall and thought I couldn't hear
them (*which made me wonder for a second what she'd heard earlier
when I was talking with Frank and Brimley outside her room*).

"No, he doesn't like me much," I said. "But maybe
because I once helped him figure out something on an
important case. He thinks I'm weird."

This last was non-specific enough that Edith could
attach her own meaning to it … which I hoped she
would. (*Meg, Frank's wife, a counselor in the local school system
often tells me that most kids in middle and high school think they're*

weird, or think/fear that other kids perceive them to be so.) My bet was Edith wasn't in the confident/well-adjusted five percent and could relate. I was enjoying *hacking* this conversation, and girl, and situation, for my own purposes. (*Thankfully, she was tired and susceptible to my, admittedly, clumsy psyops.*)

"People think I'm weird too," she said (*ka-ching!*). "How'd ja help him, that man, the putz (*she rolled the word around in her mouth a bit, getting a feel for it, like Jell-O)?*"

"I think, and see things, a little differently than other people, especially Agent Brimley of the FBI," I said with the tonal flourish of Hannibal Lecter in 'Silence of the Lambs' (*which was almost certainly inappropriate, but also, thankfully, sailed over Edith's head, a wasted reference*). "I figured out a code and picked the bad guy out of a crowd using my particular skills (*which sounds way better than saying that I read through cubic yards of paperwork and eliminated possible suspects until only one viable candidate remained*)."

"And it worked?" she asked. "You did it? Solved the mystery, saved the day, caught the bad guy?"

"I was able to figure out what he was going to do," I said, "and from there, I found out who he was, and then I let the cops and suits, Officer Gibson and Agent Brimley and their minions, get the bad guy."

"Is that what you wanna do here, with me?" she asked. "But how can you do that? He already …"

I let her marinate in that for a second before responding. "Agent Brimley would tell you, did tell me, that we may be able to help prevent what happened to you and your mom and Keith (*I hoped that my referring to him as she had would further place me inside her trust circle, and not seem too familiar and/or creep her out*) happening to other people. He thinks all of this has happened before and will happen again (*I had an intense Battlestar Galactica and Jimi*

Hendrix moment and wondered why, infinitesimally, before going on … I trust the mind-minions in the back rooms, and try to leave them alone while things are cooking). He may be right."

"What do you think, Mr. Cunningham?" Edith asked, tiny face looking up at me in earnest … if I had a heart in the way most people mean when they talk about it (*and not just a muscle the size and weight of a can of Coke in my chest that moved blood/oxygen/nutrients/waste around my body*), I might have paused, or stopped, or considered (*but maybe not. We'll never know*).

"If you're comfortable with it, Edith, I'd prefer you call me Tyler," I said. "After taking a trip out there (*she seemed ready to tense up and/or shut down, so I didn't get any more specific*) and talking with him, I tend to think he's probably right."

She appeared uncomfortable, and I grafted thoughts from my version of her day onto her, today. "I bet you feel angry and sad and guilty and not too interested in *the greater good*, in helping people you've never met … when your parents are gone." (*I was walking a tightrope at this point in my manipulation, and not well, but it could work.*)

She nodded, to herself, eyes looking past me, thinking/remembering/wishing. "I left. I ran and hid while that …"

"Yup, you did," I said, which was obviously not what she expected/wanted to hear, "and it's exactly what your mom and Keith would have wanted … did want … you to do. They wanted you to live. That's probably all they wanted, all they thought about, in their last seconds … and if they knew you did, they'd be deliriously happy."

"This sounds weird even while I'm saying it, Tyler," she said, "but I don't care. Don't care about doing the right thing, helping to protect the next people, don't care about the next family he'll get."

"I understand, Edith," I said, thinking of Dawkins's book, *The Selfish Gene*. "How about if I give you another reason, a better reason, than Officers Gibson or Brimley could?" (*I had her, I could see it in the way her head/chin tilted up and toward me, mouth open showing canine teeth in what some might mistake for a grin.*)

"What if I could give you revenge?" I asked simply, quietly. "If you give me access to everything inside your head that you can remember, even stuff you don't remember, I'll help. I'll make sure the guy who hurt your mom and Keith ends up in a small concrete box for the rest of his life."

"I want him dead," she whispered, looking around the room as if there might suddenly be witnesses to her shocking/horrible/reasonable wish. "He shouldn't get to watch TV and eat mac and cheese if they can't. I want him dead. Can you give me that?"

The fact that she was bargaining meant I'd won, but my limited experience/study with these things indicated that I shouldn't give in too much, too fast. "I don't know, Edith, there would be lots of moving parts, lots of people involved, in the sort of operation/investigation that Agent Brimley, and even Officer Gibson will be running." (*I let the final words dribble out, hopefully implying there was more to my thoughts along this line ... there wasn't, but I was hopeful she could supply her own.*)

"But if you had to ..." Now she was trying to talk me into helping her. "If you really needed to, you could do it, right?"

"I think so, I guess it's what I wanted for my parents," I said. (*I didn't ... revenge is a dish best eaten by muttonheads, an expensive luxury item that costs a lot and benefits very little, in the final analysis, but it always seems an easy button to push with people.*)

Finding this guy was important for a number of reasons, none of them revenge-based. I have always found pattern killers fascinating. I didn't want Brimley and his ilk up here any longer than was absolutely necessary. I didn't like the idea of people in my life getting hacked up by somebody. I also knew Frank would tell Meg about the possibility of a pattern killer in the Adirondacks, and also about Edith and her family, and she would be sad about it (*which I didn't want because Meg's better company when she's happy*). I can acknowledge these reasons, acknowledge that they are perhaps not the ordinary response to this specific set of stimuli, not noble reasons, and still accept them as my way of interacting with the world … I consider this progress/growth in my ongoing evolution.

"If you promise to try and make sure that at the end of all this (*whatever she imagined 'this' to be*), that you'll do your best for him to be dead." (*She wanted it, but couldn't ask me specifically to kill him, which I thought was probably a good thing, a positive indicator, for her.*)

"I will," I said. "I promise. And while I'm not, in general, a big fan of secrets between twelve-year-old girls and grown-up men, you have to promise not to talk about our deal with Brimley or Gibson or anyone … including your BFFs or your aunt when she gets here tomorrow, deal?"

"Deal," she said, and in a sweetly dim show of faith, she reached across the bed table strewn with now-empty Jell-O cups, and stuck out a gently trembling/bobbing hand for me to shake … I did (*despite my aversion to the practice*).

"Now tell me everything you heard and saw from the moment you described a few minutes ago, when you were considering getting up to get a drink and wash off errant marshmallow residue," I said.

"I told them, him, everything a couple of times last night and again this morning," she said. "And I told you everything I can remember earlier."

"Was it dark in the tent?" I asked. "Could you smell the fire? Do you remember when the sound of your mom and Keith talking changed? Did you hear another person speak?"

I'd be happy with an answer to any of those … anything to get the ball rolling.

"The wall of the tent was green, and I saw light from the fire coming through it," she said, "flickering. The only things I could smell were Keith's wet socks and that nasty seam sealer we'd used to waterproof the bottom of the tent."

She looked up at the ceiling for a few seconds, trying to pull something useful out of the mess that last night was, had become … I hoped she wouldn't try so hard that she would make things up. (*Your brain can do that, even without you wanting to, if you're eager/desperate enough.*)

"I just heard their voices," she said. "Nobody else was talking. He didn't make a sound until I was out of the tent. He grunted when he swung his arm at Mom, and then growled like a bear when he saw me. Wait! I did hear a loud noise, like a clap or a stick breaking, a little bit before Mom called out to me about Keith falling down. I figured that he tripped walking away from the fire to go pee, Keith, not the guy."

Edith stopped talking for a moment and looked up and out the window, at the darkness outside, perhaps remembering the previous night.

"The zipper for one door of the tent was by my head, and it was easier than crawling all the way down to the other door, so I went out that door, and heard something.

71

I turned in time to see his arm swinging and my mom falling down. I couldn't see Keith at all. As soon as the man saw me, he came toward me, and I didn't even think about what came next. Then, I knew I was in the water, a long ways from the island, and my feet hurt like crazy. A little while later, I saw this light coming toward me, and the big guy, Officer Gibson, pulled me over the side into the boat."

"Do you remember anything else from this period of time?" I asked. "Could you hear or see anything from back on the island?" (*I assume she focused on it since that's where the thing she was most scared of was at that moment, so she had probably kept her sensory array aimed in that direction.*)

"I was yellin' the whole time." Her cheeks flushed a bit when saying this. "My throat's still sore from screaming for so long. I didn't hear anything until Officer Gibson leaned down to talk to me. I could see his shadow, the guy's, moving in and around the camp for a while, in the light of the campfire. I don't know what he was doing."

"That's great, Edith," I said, uncertain if it was. (*I'd have to let the guys in the back of my skull toss everything I had learned in the last few hours, and would learn in the coming days, around and see if it made any sense to them once they'd sorted it all into usable/useful piles.*) "I think that should be …"

"Wait!" she nearly shouted, "I just remembered something. I'm not sure if it'll be useful to you or them, but it just popped into my head while I was thinking about floating in the lake before the boat came to pick me up."

I was able to avoid grabbing her and telling her to get to it, but just. Thank goodness for reduced emotional responses.

"A few minutes before Officer Gibson came to pull

me out of the lake, I saw something," she said. "I was in the water (*obviously, I thought*), but whatever it was blocked the light from some building or something at the other end of the lake." (*I wanted to ask her if she could vague that up for me a bit, but again, managed to resist, and compose my face into what the feel of the muscles told me would look patient and helpful.*)

"If I drew a map, or picture, of the island and the lake, do you think you could show me about where you were, and where the thing, and light, you saw were?"

Edith nodded, and I grabbed a sheet of paper from the clipboard at the foot of her bed. (*She wasn't sick … what did they need all of that paper for?*) I drew a reasonably accurate map of their campsite, the island they'd been camping on, along with the general shape of nearby islands and shoreline at that end of Lower Saranac Lake. I was torn between my desire for accuracy and the feeling that Frank and Agent Brimley would come through the door soon and disrupt the spell/mood/microclimate Edith and I had established, so I aimed for some degree of balance between detail and speed. I turned the map around and started to explain it when she jammed her finger down and began talking. "That's where I went into the lake. I swam out to about there," she said, with some confidence. "Whatever it was, I guess maybe a boat or something, came out here and blocked out lights down here. (*She was indicating with the index finger of her other hand that his boat had swung out from the north end of the island heading south and then east and then north and blocked out what I assumed were boathouse lights along the northeastern end of the lake.*) It seemed to stay still (*which I took to mean kept up a reasonably steady heading moving away from her*) for a few minutes, and then I saw the lights from Officer Gibson's boat, and I lost track of the other thing."

I pictured one of the big platform barges that infest

the bigger lakes during the summer, sneaking up on, and then away from the island. Drawing a few hasty conclusions, I threw them, and some half-formed thoughts into the back of my skull for the mind-minions to chew over while I finished with Edith.

"That's great, Edith," I said. "Thanks a lot."

I heard Frank and Brimley clomping down the hall in our direction, and wanted to wrap things up.

"Remember our deal, Mr. ... Tyler," Edith said.

"I will," I answered, giving her an often practiced *earnest* look. "You too. Let me talk to them, okay? You should tell them you're tired and need to get some rest, which you probably are, and probably do. It'll be easier for me to keep our deal if you let me share with them in my way. Does that make sense?"

"A little," she said.

"That's enough, as long as you trust me," I said, unsure of any reason she should actually trust me, but certain she could provide one if she wanted/needed to badly enough.

"Why?" she asked. It was a simple question ... imprecise (*I would like to lobby, or start a letter writing campaign, for the word to be changed to 'unprecise' ... is all I'm saying*) and open-ended, but I knew what was on her mind.

"I don't know why, Edith," I said, "and anybody who says they do is trying to sell something." (*Mickey said that particular phrase to me 2,371 times before I turned 18, and I don't fully understand/ believe it, but it sticks with me, obviously.*) "I'm not sure why this man hurt your mom and Keith ... not sure why it wasn't the people at one of the remote sites on Eagle Island instead (*I actually did have some ideas about that, but nothing that would benefit Edith at this moment*), or what made him do it in the first place. Humans are the most bizarre creatures on this bizarre planet, and that's including anglerfish and legless lizards and platypodes. The reason why may or may not have much to do with me finding/catching this guy. Last year, I worked a case where this outwardly normal person murdered a couple of people (*and would have happily murdered a few more, myself included*) for money. Imagine that … for money."

She nodded, but I caught the fairytale hope still lingering in her eyes.

"Assuming I can work with the suits and cruisers, Agent Brimley and all of the Officer Gibsons, and drill down to the *who*, you have to be ready to accept that there may not be a *why* … that's a level of closure I can't promise you. Nobody can, especially not them (*pointing out the door to the hall, where we could hear Brimley and Gibson discussing coming in*)."

I gave her one my SmartPig cards and told her to get in touch with me once she got her phone back, or if she had any questions for me, not the cops.

"A guy I know (*John, in a late night conversation with Barry, over brandy-laced coffee, Cokes, and imaginary tumblers of Wild Turkey*) once said that the cops aren't alpha wolves protecting the pack from predation, as we like to imagine. They're crows, or raccoons, picking through roadkill or garbage on the side of the road. They serve a purpose, to be sure, just not the one they're selling."

I noticed some partial understanding glow to life in her eyes as the door opened and admitted two of my favorite detritivores. It's a lesson that is only learned at the pointy end of a tragedy, and the world always feels/looks different after learning it. My point, and John's, and even Barry's, isn't/wasn't that policing isn't a societal necessity, but that people should have a clear understanding of the difference between what's on the box, and what's in the box. (*Look at me, comfortably using figurative language like a boss!*)

I held a finger alongside my nose, the same way I'd seen Mickey do several times when enjoying a shared secret, and she did the same thing and gave me a small smile as my favorite cop and least-favorite suit walked into the room. Edith was a bit abrupt in telling them that she was tired and just wanted to go to sleep, but Frank and Agent Brimley were nothing if not sensitive to the needs of this young *victim, not witness*, and we quickly left. When we walked out into the cool evening, I told them I had lots to think about, but would love to meet them in the morning for breakfast at Dunkin' Donuts, once I had sorted through all of my impressions of the day.

It was mostly true, but I had a pretty good idea of what I was going to say to them already … I just wanted time to work out the plan and actions that I'd be running inside their various plans and actions. I cast my eyes out over the Adirondack Medical Center parking lot, at the few cars and trucks cruising by on Route 86, and at the somewhat cloverleaf-shaped Lake Colby … thinking about Edith and Angela and Keith Richards (*now determined to research the other one, which this was not, had not been*) … the setting, the methodology, the post-game, and most of all … the killer.

Adirondack Medical Center (AMC), under cover of night

Vanilla slowed down as much as seemed prudent when he passed the front of the hospital. He had rolled the passenger side window down, and looking out that way at the rows of windows, he briefly traded places with Beast, momentarily relinquishing control.

Beast inhaled huge lungsful of the cooling night air, willing himself to catch the scent of the girl, the survivor, his meat, that bitch. He could not. While pushing his senses out toward the fluorescent green squares of light, he reached out for the one who got away, the only one he'd missed. He caught a flicker of connection from a room where a light was just turning off as he passed, also from the trio of men walking to the parking lot from the main entrance. Beast rolled up the window, pushed his foot down on the gas pedal, and headed back into the darkness, driving toward Paul Smiths and Malone, but first, Donnelly's Corners.

The ice cream stand was closed, of course, but Vanilla pulled in, shut off the car, and got a Mountain Dew from the soda machine glowing by the quiet shack. He tramped back to his car, leaned against the hood, opened the bottle, and drank it while facing the mountains on the far side of the Bloomingdale Bog.

Beast wanted to storm the hospital, find the girl, open her up, and paint the white room red. Vanilla was scared and excited, but mostly scared. The game had taken a leap forward and sideways, one he was not ready for. Odd, because he was the one who was always ready. Vanilla had been playing the game for sixteen summers, and the rule he and Beast had discovered when they began years ago was that it always got harder. The game had to get more complex, more challenging, each time they played.

The first time was beautiful, perfect, sublime. Vanilla had planned everything, every contingency, and Beast had executed the plan, and Fred Tidwell, to perfection. Tidwell's blood was a holy sacrament, tasted like life, brought both the Beast and Vanilla back from the brink of despair, from giving up and giving in to the grey life. The second game they'd played, Vanilla had planned a repeat of the first; the victory was hollow, and the blood of his victim tasted like ash in the Beast's mouth.

Vanilla cursed and thought, while Beast howled madly in the cage of his mind, cursed and thought and thought and cursed and drank. In the depths of a nearly bottomless drunk, Vanilla had a moment of clarity, a vision. The game, the kill, had to vary every time, slightly new and different, slightly more complex. It had to have more challenge for Vanilla, place more demands on the Beast, to stretch them both each and every time they played.

Vanilla had immediately found another victim, a new playing field, and a new challenge. Tidwell, the first, had been old and weak and too friendly. The third time, Vanilla and Beast went after a woman, a solo camper, young and strong and not so trusting as Tidwell had been. This game took more planning, more work, had many more contingencies to take into account. Vanilla was challenged and exhausted and frustrated and exultant. The Beast had to defuse and confuse and lull her long enough to get inside his effective range, and even then she had nearly gotten clear of him, nearly. He had drunk deep of her that night, and she tasted like the sun shining on his face as a boy, and warm naps in the cold winter, and a full belly when hunger was written on other faces.

From that point on, they worked together to improve the game in some way every time they played. Over the years they had added better opponents, and then more opponents; this had been their only game played against three. In the first years, Vanilla had limited himself to, and been satisfied with, one game each summer season; more recently they'd play multiple games each summer. In 2014, they'd played four times. They were perfect and deadly artists. They were special.

Initially, Vanilla had found Beast at the end of the road, in a year when his work and home and family all came down like a line of dominoes, both chaotic and predictable when seen from a distance. The last straw felt like a mile of rough road behind him. Vanilla had the barrel of his father's shotgun in his mouth, tasting Hoppe's #9 and thinking about the noise and mess he'd be leaving behind when the Beast spoke to him for the first time.

"Why kill yourself when you could kill someone who's not you?"

The logic was simple and irrefutable. They had stayed up all night, shotgun put away in the hall closet, after a cleaning, and worked out the basics by morning. Beast wanted something spectacular and showy, with splatter and a car chase, ending in a glorious gunfight and death.

"You were ready to die, why not like this?" Beast asked.

Vanilla had argued that if they liked killing, they could keep doing it. Not getting caught could be a part of the fun. They'd agreed, liked the way it went with Tidwell, and the years and games and bodies piled up and rolled by while they kept score in blood, and laughed at the world that couldn't see them playing their murderous sport. The game was about more than killing, more than not getting caught, even more than the thrill. It was about the power they stole from their victims and the addiction to that control and blood and thrill that Vanilla and Beast shared and reveled in.

They had taken a couple in June. Campsite #13, on Green Island, was surrounded by other campsites to a degree that required finesse and swift brutality, appealing to them both. The New Jersey couple's blood had been nectar on the blade. The risk and daring and power flooded through them and Vanilla and Beast were excited to try a threesome for the first time for their July 2015 game, less than a month later.

The game at campsite #35 had gone perfectly until the instant it didn't. In the hours following the girl's unexpected dive into the lake, and subsequent shrieking, Vanilla had been going over his plan in minute detail. Beast had been raging, wanting to drink the child. Vanilla worried about the police and being exposed and sought for the first time. Beast exulted in the new shape and challenge of the game, insisting it would be better now, that this was the direction they had always been heading.

Vanilla had to agree that he felt alive in a way he hadn't, and hadn't even noted or missed, since the first few kills; he recalled the taste of the Richardses' blood even now, electric and spicy and deeply satisfying. When Beast had insisted they go and collect the girl, Vanilla hadn't pushed back with more than a few desultory entreaties to planning and caution; they were both eager and determined and ready to finish, and win, the game.

While Beast looked up at the stars and listened to the night sounds, Vanilla drained the bottle of Dew and worked out a plan. In his previous life, Vanilla had helped once when a convict fled a work crew in the Saranac Lakes Wild Forest, via the tip of the southern end of Upper Saranac Lake. When the flatlander finally stumbled out of the woods to give himself up, he was in rough enough shape to need a trip to the hospital before going back to FCI Raybrook. A suite of rooms in the AMC was designed for security and containment, and Vanilla assumed that was where the girl would be. Beast wanted this to be the end, a grand storming of the halls, knives in hand, taking everyone in their path and winning in a glorious flood of death and blood and magic. Vanilla had talked him out of it, suggesting they could count coup by ghosting in, killing the girl, sneaking out again, and living to fight and kill another day.

Beast and Vanilla drove back to the hospital, parked out beyond the lights of the main building, behind the day-use offices adjoining AMC. Once they had parked in darkness and waited a full minute to see if anyone or anything was moving nearby them, they approached the ER while staying deep in shadows, unseen. The emergency room area was Thursday-night quiet, but with enough people that Vanilla stayed outside to let bolder, braver, Beast take over once they reached the building, confident the Beast could manage any needed improvisations once things started moving.

The girl's room, complete with a trooper holding up the wall outside the door, was less than a minute from the darkened supply station where Beast lit a fire. He filled a metal garbage can with plastic and paper containers of bandages and crumpled paper towels, then ignited it with his grandfather's Zippo, surprised at how quickly the flames flared. He walked away as fast as possible from the burgeoning flames and rolling smoke, hoping to get clear before someone pulled an alarm; he did.

Beast was sitting in the far stall of a bathroom twenty feet from the girl's room when the siren sounded in the hallway, and a flashing light started strobing in the bathroom. Within seconds, announcements began and the sounds of panicked people in the hall changed the hospital from a place of routine to one of chaos. Beast didn't know how the different zones of the hospital would react to a fire, but he assumed there would be some degree of upset. That would give him an improved chance of getting into, and out of, the girl's room.

He counted off forty-five seconds, and then exited the bathroom, turning immediately toward the girl's room, and nearly running into the state trooper. The sentry stood up from his leaning position against the wall, and fully blocked the doorway, and much of the hall, with his bulk and height and hat. Beast saw himself opening the oaf's throat, stepping over the body, closing out the girl and the game with one quick slice, and walking back out into the starry night; then he heard a voice from the other side of the door, just inside the girl's room.

"Everything okay?" said the voice, deep and male and implying a large person.

"Yeah," the trooper said, "just a fire drill or something."

He shifted his focus to the Beast, looking him up and down for a second before speaking. "Sir, you'll need to proceed to the nearest fire exit, and leave the building. Go back down at the end of this hallway and turn to your left."

Beast stopped and stood for a moment, considering the trooper, one hand in his windbreaker pocket, running a thumb along the naked blade of his smaller knife, with enough pressure to part a few layers of skin, but no more. Then, he thanked the guard and turned and left the building, Vanilla's voice whispering a steady stream of calming promises into his ear.

SmartPig Offices, Saranac Lake, NY
Friday, 7/10/ 2015, 12:29 a.m.

I called ahead to the Good Chinese Place for a big order
of spicy fat and protein on a bed of sticky carbohydrates.
Some of the things that made them the good place were
that they were: open until ten every night, happy to make
custom food to order, close to SmartPig, happy to
welcome my dog Hope into their place of business (*despite
it being against the law, and the fact that she was decidedly
unpleasant/unfriendly to everyone on the planet except me and two
or three others, depending on the weather and her mood*).

The food was waiting for me when I entered. I
walked in, paid, and left, under the watchful and grumpy
eyes of a trio of the drunk/tired/patchouli-scented
trustafarians that Saranac Lake seems to attract in droves.
When I first arrived, nearly thirteen years ago, I had been
able to lose myself among their numbers; that was no
longer the case. (*I could no longer pass as a shiftless college
student and was now faced with the more challenging task of passing
as a shiftless thirty-something.*)

I climbed the stairs to SmartPig, locked and barred
the door (*since although I hadn't said so to Frank or Brimley, I
was reasonably certain a long-term pattern killer had been operating
in Saranac Lake, and I was planning on placing myself between
him and the things he wanted*). I unpacked the food, took out
the first three ice-cold Canadian Cokes of the evening

(*I've said it before, but in case you're new here, or suffered some memory loss since the last time, the real sugar in Canadian Cokes makes it taste better, especially when chilled to just this side of the slush-point*), and took out an array of pens/paper/Post-its to organize my impressions and thoughts about what I'd seen that day on Lower Saranac Lake, and, later, talked about with Edith Richards.

I was quickly and easily able to build a solid argument for the killings being a long-term serial killer, as opposed to either a random or a motivated single event. The pattern Brimley had noted, along with the scene I'd visited, and the fact that it appeared to have been successfully done multiple times in a row with clean getaways … spoke to a reasonably organized and intelligent killer. (*Frank was fond of pointing out that most homicide investigations involve finding a drunk boyfriend on the floor next to a dead body, blood/DNA with evidence over everything, weapon in hand.*)

While already formulating some ideas about how to find him/them (*I suspected just 'him' but was open to other possibilities*), in the next few hours I even generated a few more. The real trick was in building a plan, or rather a series of nested plans for finding him that would satisfy each of my nominal masters: Agent Brimley and the FBI, Frank and the state and local police, Edith Richards and the ghosts of her parents (*if I could have Barry, my own personal ghost, who's to say there couldn't be other ghosts in this large and varied world, of which I've only seen a tiny portion*), and my own interests/conscience and/or sense of justice.

I wanted to take each layer into account in my planning and have all parts of the overall machinations work with, and within, each other. It took a while, but by the time I'd worked through the half-dozen containers of Chinese food and apps, along with eight cans of Coke cold enough to give me hypothermia from the inside, I felt as though I had a good foundation from which to continue my work in the morning. I was also able to acknowledge my desire to find him first because of the challenge and insult presented by Brimley and his minions.

Barry mumbled incoherently, and incorporeally (*since I hadn't yet seen him today, although I'd heard his voice a number of times, sometimes in my head, and other times from specific places around the rooms I'd been in*) about something, and I turned to the place the sound seemed to be coming from. "What, Barry, What? I'm tired and want to catch a few hours of sleep before the FBI buys me breakfast in the morning."

My ghostly companion became instantly present, sitting at the far end of the couch that takes up a fair amount of the floor space in the world headquarters of SmartPig. "It's a great plan that'll never fuggin' work, monkey-nuts."

"Why not?" I asked.

"Two big reasons," Barry said. "First, it's got too many moving parts. Too many things can, and probably will, go wrong. Second, as always, you entirely fail to plan for people doing something other than what you'd do in the same situation."

"So, do you have ideas for patching my plans up, or should I scrap it all and start over?"

"I got a coupla ideas," he said. "Mainly, you gotta work on making it as simple as you can, and not counting on people to do the rational thing as you see it."

We hammered at my plans, Barry poking holes, me trying to patch them, neither of us discussing the bizarre nature of our relationship, or the reason for the recurrence of my on again, off again hallucination. (*I believe Barry to be an unusual manifestation of PTSD, and as such, it makes sense that he would come back into my life when unusual stress and violence return as well ... that or I'm slipping deeper into insanity, but that doesn't leave me much to work with, so I ignore that option.)* We re-finished shortly after midnight, and I lay down on the couch at 12:29, which I took as a good sign. *(When things start going wonky and/or sideways in my life, I look to numbers for stability and sometimes even omens, and 1229 is not only a prime number, but it's the number of prime numbers between 0 and 10,000, which I took as a great sign ... beyond that, it can also be multiplied by the third prime to give me the last four digits of the phone number for The Good Chinese Place.)*

"Stop it, and just go to sleep already," Barry said out of the darkness. "You're making me hungry again."

"If I have to be haunted," I said, "why did it have to be you? Why couldn't it be Hope?"

"Dunno," he said. "Maybe it's a soul versus no soul deal. That or God hates you." He snickered and then I heard him clomp to the comfy chair by the back window.

The metaphysical conundrums presented by my version of Jacob Marley kept me from sleep for an extra seventeen seconds.

Dunkin' Donuts, Saranac Lake, NY
Friday, 7/10/2015, 5:58 a.m.

I woke up at 4:43, sent a group text message to Frank and Agent Brimley telling them to meet me at DD when they opened at 5 a.m. The next step in the plan I'd mostly generated last night (*I'd left some ends loose wiggling, certain that the tireless minions in the back of my head would keep working on things while I slept … they had*) involved sending emails asking John and Dot and Xander's new aid Mark to play a role in the plan within the plan, if willing; I had Dot and John's email addresses already, and it didn't take much digging to find Mark's through the PSC website.

Texts are more intrusive and immediate than emails, which is what I'd been going for when I'd sent the ones to Frank and Brimley. I got answering *boops* within a few minutes with grudging confirmations for 5:30. (*I suspected they'd colluded upon receiving, and before answering, my texts.*) I was happy with the others responding to their emails whenever they got around to it, so long as it was sometime that morning.

Lacking the facilities for a shower or bath in SmartPig (*I sometimes go to the sports complex at NCCC if I really feel the need for a more thorough cleansing, but mostly just get by, sometimes a little stinky/sticky*), I did a lean-over splash and rinse at the sink, brushed my teeth, and grabbed the relevant notes before heading downstairs and out the back door to the parking lot and my Element, managing this time to not grab for Hope's leash or whistle her to the door for a walk.

I pulled into my usual early morning parking spot at a few minutes after five and debated waiting for Frank and Agent Brimley so they could buy my donuts/breakfast. Hunger and lack of self-control won out (*as they nearly always do with me*) and while ordering a perfect dozen (*my current formula is four each of glazed, chocolate glazed, and regular jellies*), I consoled myself with thoughts of per-diem and expenses the FBI might actually be giving me this time.

As nearly always happens (*despite the fact that I dine at DD 5-7 times each week*) the person behind the counter was quite insistent on suggesting coffee to go with my donuts. I don't enjoy the taste and experience of hot beverages, in general, and especially detest coffee, so I demurred once again, pulling my own Canadian Coke out of my backpack to show them that I did, in fact, have something to wash my donuts down with … they didn't seem relieved/assuaged, but I was able to conclude the transaction and grab one of the big tables to wait for Frank and Brimley.

They arrived five donuts and two Cokes later. Brimley, seeing my dozen box started to sit, but Frank assured him that they were all mine and that he wanted the biggest coffee, along with a couple of donuts, since the FBI was buying. In just slightly longer than it should have taken with four kids behind the counter filling a simple order for two coffees and four donuts, Frank and Brimley joined me at the table. Brimley looked fresh and pressed, as though he'd already had coffee and caught some bad guys this morning; Frank, on the other hand, appeared as if he'd been rolled around the floor of a dirty basement for a while by an angry mob. He was rumpled and wrinkled and his hair was pointing in odd directions, and he had significant eye-boogers along with too much of the white stuff that accumulates in the corners of your mouth sometimes. Agent Brimley gestured for me to begin, but I let Frank inhale a donut and drink down half of the giant mug of coffee before I spoke. I had notes on paper in front of me but didn't need them ... with only a few points to make, I knew them and could see them floating in a bulleted list in my mind.

"Before you start your, 'I suppose you're all wondering why I've called you here' thing, Tyler," Frank said, "let me first tell you that a small fire was started at AMC last night shortly after we left, and although we want to assume it's connected with the killings, and with Edith, there's no direct evidence linking the two. She was never at risk, so far as we can tell."

"Wait a second," I said. "Tell me about the fire, how and where it started, how it ties to the investigation, and most importantly, what's being done to ensure Edith's safety?"

"It appears to have started in a supply closet," Brimley began, rolling over Frank who appeared ready to answer me. "Clinic administrators think it was possibly an employee sneaking in a smoke break. A state trooper was stationed at the Richards girl's door, and one of my guys happened to be inside the room, taking a final statement from her at the time the fire broke out. We locked her down, and she was never in any danger from either the fire or the possibility of the person who killed her parents trying to get at her."

"Assuming it was him (*which seemed more likely than a coincidental fire in what has been, during my tenure in Saranac Lake, a fire-free hospital*)," I said, "what's being done to make sure he doesn't try again?"

"One of my guys took her out early this morning, under escort from Brimley's people," Frank said. "They met the aunt in Watertown and are driving them both the rest of the way to the aunt's house in Pennsylvania. We reached out to the state police in PA, and they're going to attach a rotating team to Edith for the foreseeable future, thanks to a nudge from the FBI (*he said with a nod in Brimley's direction*)."

I ran my brain over what they both had said, felt relieved, and took a deep breath to replace an oxygen deprivation I hadn't been aware of a minute before.

"Now you can begin," Frank said.

"The killing of Angela and Keith Richards, at campsite number thirty-five on Lower Saranac Lake in the early evening of July 8th, is interesting for a number of reasons," I said. "I tend to agree with Agent Brimley's assessment that it was the work of a pattern killer. This tentative conclusion (*a contradiction in terms, but I stand by the word choice*) hinges on two related sets of information and impressions (*both of them winced a bit at the word impressions, but what can you do?*) and a nested series of questions I asked in approaching the available information."

I looked across the table, and saw that Brimley was taking notes on a tall/thin steno pad, and Frank was looking at the bottom of his now-empty coffee cup ... he held up a finger and hurried back up to the counter for a refill.

"Well?" said Brimley.

"I don't want to do it twice," I replied, "and Frank will want to hear my reasoning."

"Damn skippy," Frank said upon rejoining us at the table with a steaming quart-sized cup of black coffee, the smell of which almost put me off my donuts ... almost.

"First," I said, "was it a random murder? This would

be the *escaped madman from a local asylum* or wandering violent hobo who are often scapegoated in some brands of English mysteries. The answer is *no*, for a couple of reasons. We didn't catch the blood-soaked killer waiting for a bus or ordering a dozen donuts. The Richardses were killed efficiently, and although messy, the scene and their bodies were not indicative of a frenzy."

Picking up another jelly, I noted, with some concern that I was on the downslope of my box, and entirely out of jellies (*after finishing the one in my hand/mouth*). Frank can, on occasion, be a sensitive soul, and somehow he noted/interpreted my pause, and traded a jelly on his plate for one of the chocolate glazed left in my box.

"The next thing to think about is whether or not Keith and Angela brought the trouble with them," I said. "I tend to think not, but that's the kind of thing the Bureau is perfect at researching."

"Why not," Brimley asked. "I agree, but we're paying for your brain, so I'd like to hear how you got there."

"It's too tricky," I said. "It would be far easier for someone with a grudge against Angela or Keith Richards to kill one or both of them at home. That being said, it's still worth checking out Edith's Aunt, full financials on everyone, running backgrounds on friends and family and business partners back in their hometown, and checking local credit card receipts and hotels for any crossover. Their being killed with a knife also argues, to me at least, in favor of a pattern killer. A gun would be easier and less messy than the knife, or whatever sharp instrument, he used. Also, something that came up yesterday when we were going out to the island stuck with me. Agent Brimley talked about the remote location of the killing, but the truth is that, like lots of the Adirondacks, it's more crowded than you think. Escape routes are limited and controlled by a few key chokepoints. If the killer came up from Pennsylvania with the Richards family, he likely would have run afoul of these ... been seen at one of the two boat launches controlling Lower Saranac or some such. Also, he would have needed access to a boat to get to and from the site."

I skipped over Frank's gift-jelly, in favor of one of my remaining chocolate glazed.

Saving the last jelly for my summation (*and a possible distraction, if needed*), I continued, "The most likely option, and most difficult to work (*I didn't actually think so because I was fairly confident I could catch the guy with a couple of long nights of paper surfing, but I needed Brimley, and to a lesser degree, Frank, to be in the search for the long haul*) is that there's a pattern killer in the Tri-Lakes. I'll need access to some of Agent Brimley's resources to confirm it, but I believe not only is there a pattern killer, but he's been operating in the area for years ... for long enough to become proficient, and possibly bored, with what he's doing."

"No chance, Tyler," Frank said. "All respect, but there's no chance of something like that going on in Saranac Lake for years without the PD, or me, or you, noticing."

"The FBI estimates between thirty and fifty serial killers are operating in the U.S. at any given time," I said, pointing to Brimley, who nodded. "And unless they're the disorganized type, or devolving, they can remain hidden for years, or forever, in their home community. The knife and his use of it, speak to me as evidence that you're, we're (*this was a bit of theater, which apparently they were willing to let me get away with*), dealing with a serial killer. It's personal and nasty and he's good at using it ... spectacular, really."

"Glad you're so happy about it, Tyler," Frank said.

"He killed two people in a relatively very short time and did it with two strokes of the knife," I said. "No hesitation cuts. Neither Keith nor Angela had time or sufficient warning to react enough to generate defensive wounds ... their killer is fantastic with his knife. Sorry if my saying so upsets you, but it means he's done it before ... lots of times. Also, the fact that he got hosed down with Angela's blood on site and still made it home, shows that he's done some planning and trial runs ... a guy like this won't count on luck. It can be assumed, if you'll allow my previous suppositions (*suddenly, Barry was sitting at the next table, behind Agent Brimley, and said, loudly, although, of course, only I could hear him, 'I'll allow you your previous suppositories, dickweed!' I found it odd that he seemed to have trouble accepting my arguments, given that he existed solely in my head, but I've never been in charge of my PTSD*), he's got to have a way to get in and out of the area ... and doesn't seem to balk at the prospect of leaving the scene covered in blood."

I paused, slurping some Coke and demolishing the new/final jelly, hoping against hope that Brimley or Frank would jump in and push this discussion to the next step so I wouldn't have to. Even though I had more (*and more specific*) reasons in support of my theory, I wanted to save, or at most imply, them, if possible. Frank bailed me out, as he often does, unwittingly (*I assume*), also as he often does.

"Nothing revolutionary there, Brain," he said. "So, where does that leave us? Where does it leave you?"

"The various law enforcement agencies allied against your, our, unknown subject need to split their efforts among a couple of things. Some of them are probably a waste of time, but they're the kinds of things you need to waste time on in this sort of investigation." (*I was speaking from vast experience with police/FBI procedural novels I'd read in the last 25 years.*) "Get people at both boat launches, asking everyone getting onto and off the water if they heard or saw anything on the night in question," I said, in my list tone. "Send people to campsites one through sixty to ask the same thing, and get a few agents on the phone to follow up with anyone who's already left for home. (*I tried to force my flattest affect here, as this was at the edge of what I wanted to focus my efforts, and innermost layer of my investigation, on*). Check boat rentals in the days and weeks leading up to the killings. Run credit cards against lists of friends and family and business connections of the Richards family, along with anyone with a criminal record ... most specifically a record of violence against humans/animals."

I swept the table clear of the accumulated sugar and crumbs, taking note as I did so of the way my napkin left streamers of crumbs and sugar particles like a river or rake does with sediment/leaves of different sizes and densities.

"I assume the FBI," I said, looking back up at Agent Brimley, "will activate/alert, or has already activated/alerted, the Behavioral Analysis Unit for a profile and further recommendations?"

Brimley gave a long answer, dense with FBI-speak, and Frank slipped away to get another refill on his coffee while I pretended to listen. When Brimley tipped his head down toward something he'd pulled out of a manila folder, I snuck a careful wink at Barry ... he and I had spoken before about the similarities and likely usefulness of FBI profiling.

"Do those things actually ever help in catching these bugs," Frank asked. "They seem awfully generic."

"After the FBI catches this pattern killer," I said, chucking Brimley a small bone (*because I was planning on being the one to catch this killer*), "he'll turn out to be a white male, between thirty and fifty, with a history of head injury and animal abuse and bed-wetting and starting fires and sexual abuse in his childhood. He'll have grown up a loner, who is able to form functional, if shallow, relationships with the people around him. He's capable of being quite charming and reasonably intelligent, but will have been fired from, and/or quit lots of jobs throughout his adult life."

"Sounds like a lotta guys I know," Frank said. "Except for some of the more private, background stuff, which can be tough to find out up front. Sounds a bit like you, Tyler. Brimley, maybe you were right, huh?"

I assumed he was joking, but Brimley looked up from his scribbling to goggle at me for a few seconds before getting back to scratching down things he already knew.

"I've never knowingly injured an animal in my life, except insofar as I'm not a vegetarian. I'm lucky, and perhaps unusual, not to have ever been the victim of sexual abuse (*or even sexual contact, but that's another issue, one Frank was likely not interested in*). I'm not charming, am largely unable to form functional relationships, am well outside the normal/accepted IQ range for pattern killers, and have never been fired from a job."

Frank raised his eyebrows at the gaps in my defense.

I continued, "I wet the bed until the age of fourteen, and was quite uncoordinated as a child, resulting in lots of minor head injuries. I have always liked fires, which is probably one of the big reasons I enjoy camping."

Frank and Brimley looked embarrassed, a look I often get when I talk about myself (*which is one of the reasons I don't do it much*).

"All of that will be interesting when we catch the killer, but not particularly helpful until such time," I said.

"Yeah," said Agent Brimley, "but it could help, and it'll keep the bug-hunters in Behavioral busy. Speaking of which, since your recommendations all sound like stuff for Frank and I to do, what are you going to do to keep yourself occupied?"

"I'm glad you asked." And I was, and also that he'd not picked up on the gaps I'd left in my conclusions (*but more on that later*).

"I'll need the help of one of your tech guys, and for you to apply some of your influence to get some big piles of data for me to sift through (*a widely, and correctly, acknowledged strength of mine*)," I said.

"As long as my guy can work with you (*and spy on me and look over my shoulder and get in my way the whole time, I added parenthetically, as you can see, since this is all in parentheses*)," he said. "That shouldn't be a problem. Give me an idea of what you need, and I can figure out who to pair you with, and how to apply the needed pressure."

"I think you may get lucky with the avenues of inquiry I've already suggested," I said. Frank's head went up a degree at this, as he has heard my lecture (*catalog #47, if you're interested*) on the stupidity of counting/believing in luck. "But I'm interested in delving more deeply into his selection of the site, his getaway, his base of operations, and the mechanisms he must have had in place for disposal of bodies/evidence (*all said quickly and lightly and in an order designed to distract them from the first of my tasks, which I deemed the most useful/important and likely to bear fruit*). The first item will require significant computer resources and influence. The others will likely be a matter of map work and county rolls and exploring on foot and in a canoe. I'll drop it in an email to you, along with my expenses to date, and estimated incidentals in the coming days, and weeks if needed." (*I anticipated*

closure on this investigation in less than a week, not least because I needed to vacate the Adirondacks and head down to The City to spend time with Mickey, but didn't want to imply I wouldn't be giving the impossible 110 percent Brimley would expect from me.)
"But for now, I've got to head out to another important meeting at the other end of town."

Frank smiled. Brimley sputtered. I grabbed my mostly empty box of donuts and left. It only occurred to me after I was pulling out onto Route 86, heading back to town, that Dot might want (*would want, who was I kidding*) donuts … so I pulled a U-turn, and drove into the drive-thru lane for another dozen (*hoping for some reason that Frank and Brimley wouldn't see me*), including a mix of the Manager's Specials, the carnival rides of frostings and fillings and sprinkles that Dot loves more than anything on Earth except for her wife Lisa, the dogs and cats at the Tri-Lakes Animal Shelter (TLAS), and, sometimes, me.

Tri-Lakes Animal Shelter (TLAS), Saranac Lake, NY
Friday, 7/10/2015, 8:03 a.m.

I sped through the still mostly empty early morning quiet
in Saranac Lake, glad the monstrous hotel development
plan for the lakefront near Mountain Mist, (*Ice Cream and
More!*) seemed to have sunk without a ripple after months
of contentious debate among locals. Fog was climbing
out of Lake Flower and onto the shore down by the band
shell in the park near the big intersection at the town hall
and abandoned gas station and pizza place (*with a too-
boring-for-words phone number, factorable into a small pile of single-
digit numbers*). I went up the hill, out of town, and past the
elementary/middle school, the athletic fields, and then
the high school on my ride in the direction of the boat
launch I'd visited the previous day with Frank and
Brimley. But I pulled off to the right, and into the parking
lot for the TLAS only eight-tenths of a mile beyond the
high school.

It was still early enough that only a few had arrived.
The shelter wouldn't be officially open for hours … their
actual operating times hadn't concerned me in more than
a decade, so I went in through a back door marked DO
NOT OPEN! and was immediately greeted/assaulted by
the smell and sounds and sights (*and a few short seconds later,
the barks/meows*) of the seventy-five or so (*it varied day-to-
day, sometimes hour to hour*) cats and dogs that lived in this

shelter. A low-slung beagle/basset/boxer mix named Gwen seemed to be the appointed greeter of the day, and she *rowfed* once and then padded over, waiting for me to get down to her level for sniffs and kisses … I did.

"Hello, Gwen," I said. "How is it possible you're still working here? I was sure you'd found a home with those people I saw taking you for a walk on Tuesday."

Gwen's only answer was kisses, some accented gently with teeth, but a voice drifted up from behind/beneath the front counter, as I'd imagined it might. "We were filling out the paperwork, and they'd even picked out a new collar and leash, when they really began to understand the extent of her medical needs. We'd talked about the shots, but when I put the stuff up on the counter, they backed off and said they'd have to think about it. They might be back." Dot's voice was brave and strong, but wasn't entirely convincing, to me at least, so I tried to boost the signal with an ear and muzzle rub.

"I think they will, Gwen … they'd be fools to pass up the chance to take a sweet thing like you home, yes they would. And if it's not them, there will be someone, maybe today."

"Maybe you?" Dot asked coming out from behind the counter. "You could easily handle her, and I think Gwen could handle you. In fact, you two would be perfect for each other."

I waited a beat, to avoid responding both too quickly and too loudly, and stood up at the same time, disengaging from the love-fest with Gwen. "No, I don't think so. Sorry Gwen, sorry Dot." I turned slightly, to face Dot and away from Gwen, and spoke in a low voice. "I like her fine. She's a sweet dog, but, she's maybe a bit too much like …"

"I get that," Dot said. "I really do, but some people

like a new dog that's similar to their previous one. There's some Santa Claus looking guy out in Lake Clear who essentially keeps taking the same dog off our hands again and again. Three big black dogs he's brought home, and he swung in on the first of the month, with wet eyes and sad talk about his current big black dog slowing down, asking about who we've got in the big room or on deck."

"I'm not even sure I want to live with another dog … yet, or ever," I said. "I like coming here to walk the beasts." *(That was a double-entendre, as I like all of the beasts in the TLAS, but especially enjoy taking out the dogs that are huge/hyper/difficult/aggressive … that was how I'd met Hope, who was neither huge nor hyper, but was difficult in the extreme.)*

Dot and I had been having this conversation, about various and specific dogs, and the concept of a dog to fill the hole left in my life by Hope's general absence. Since I'd come back from the trip Hope and I took out west, by myself, just a few days before the new year, she'd been trying to set me up with all of the available dogs she knew. It was sweet, but something just wasn't clicking/working. I wasn't sure I was ready to have another dog in my life *(and was surprised by how much real estate the process of thinking about it took up in my forebrain and the other neighborhoods in my skull).*

At this point in the conversation, when Dot traditionally tends to launch into a convincing argument about how I need a dog, and that there are obviously dogs who need a person, I was thankfully rescued by a bark and shout and the pounding of feet from behind us/me. Steph Brentworth, a longtime employee of the TLAS who liked the dogs she served more than the people they sometimes went home with, ran down the hall chasing Grumpy, a smallish boxer mix puppy from a litter of *(predictably)* seven puppies that had been brought in with their mother, Snow White (*a cute, if boringly named perfectly white boxer*). They'd all been abandoned by an owner who decided they didn't really want a dog any longer, much less a litter of puppies. Grumpy pushed Gwen out of the way with a small growl, and jammed his face into mine … his name came from a pair of well-placed birthmarks/hair-patterns over his eyes that made him look perpetually angry. The other pups were similarly dwarf-named, and their care/handling/training had been Steph's project since their arrival a few days after their birth, nearly two months ago.

"Who hasn't been out in the longest. Who's full of beans and needs to be run into the ground … I feel like going off-trail with someone who requires a workout," I said, scooping up Grumpy and handing him back to Steph as I spoke to Dot. "One of your restless brutes and some time and space to think and plan, and then we can talk about that thing I sent you an email about earlier."

"That'd be Snowflake," Dot said, and even though I was trying to rub one of the wandering cats (*unsuccessfully … cats don't like me; I think they sense something missing/different in me, but I keep trying*). I could hear the smile on her face as she spoke. "He doesn't get out much. He's not much of a runner, but he's a big sniffer, definitely a brute, and he likes to explore."

"Snowflake, huh?" I said. "He's not a kitten, right?"

She started back toward the big room (*where 20-24 dogs are housed in pens for the public to wander among and fall in love*), and then took a right turn into one of the isolation rooms, calling over her shoulder before she disappeared, "It's possible one of the girls was being ironic when she named him (*which meant he came to TLAS absent a name, either abandoned or taken from the previous owner, and was named by one of the other young women who devote their lives to the dogs and cats at the shelter)."*

I heard a low rumbling sound from the back of the shelter, and a series of items crashing and getting knocked over or out of the way of something large and clumsy. In a perfect world, there would have been a glass of water on the counter next to me, so I could glance nervously at it, noting the perfect and increasingly violent rings resulting from massive impact tremors … but it's not a perfect world, so I made a note to bring/arrange just such a water glass for my next visit to the TLAS and looked down the-the hall at the land-based kraken Dot had released.

Snowflake preceded Dot out of the isolation room. For a moment, I was tricked by my brain's autocorrect (*in terms of relative/visual perspective*) into thinking that Snowflake was only massive … then Dot came out and when they were side by side, walking down the hall, I got an accurate feeling for his size. Given Dot's height, I judged Snowflake to be 37 inches at the shoulder, and guessed that he outweighed her by 70 pounds (*although I had never been told to use my carnie-like ability to judge height/weight/age on women, I kept the data in my head, in an encrypted file*). His face was wrinkled and the same size as my chest. Regarding his name, as Dot liked to say, Alanis Morissette could have cut the irony with a spoon, when she needed a knife … he was black as coal in the mine.

"Whoa there, big fella," she said. "Here he is, Tyler, please wear him out. Don't go too far, cross any roads, or let him loose. He looks enough like a bear that he might get shot." (*I'm not great with tonal variations or humor, but I don't think she was joking.*)

"What is he?" I asked, certain she (*and hoping that he*) wouldn't take offense. The advent a few years ago of genetic testing for dogs to determine their exact breed makeup by percentages fascinated me, and I constantly found myself wanting to test most of the dogs at TLAS.

"No exact idea because he obviously came without papers," Dot said, "but he looks like a Neapolitan Mastiff."

"He looks like a black lab that fell into a vat of radioactive waste and is part of the way ready to take on Mothra." I'd been working my way through a great course/collection of graphic novels and movies featuring monsters associated with the nuclear age that was being hosted/mediated by an online college.

"We'll stay in the forested square of land behind the shelter," I said, referring to an area bounded by Route 3, Lake Street, Algonquin Avenue, and Lower Saranac Lake. It was all private property, but nobody seemed to mind much, and neither Frank nor Dot had told me to stop taking dogs back there, yet.

We headed out the back door and took off at a slow jog to get clear of a minivan that was disgorging a clown-car-ian load of small children, most of whom could probably fit into Snowflake's mouth before he had to chew or swallow. We followed the trails in back of the TLAS until they ran out, and then we kept heading back and down and away … ducking and leaping and clambering and untangling as we went. I love taking the really big ones for walks in the woods, even though I get a bit torn up in the process … it's busy enough work that I can disengage from my regular thought process, and give the crew in the back of my head a chance to think about whatever I'm working on without looking at it directly, if you know what I mean.

At one point, we stopped to sit on a big glacial erratic just in view of the sparkling lake through the trees. I fished a couple of dog bones out of my jacket and asked

Snowflake to sit. He threw a mammoth paw at me, without my asking, and it thumped down on the top of my head like someone had dropped a meatloaf onto me from a second (*maybe third*) floor window. A moment later, he was looming over ... bathing me with a tongue that felt exactly like someone was rubbing my face with a flounder, occasionally taking my nose slightly inside his mouth for a surprisingly gentle gnawing. I lay there for a minute, looking up at the patterns the interlaced maple and balsam branches made, thinking about nothing and everything, got ahold of the edge of what might eventually be an idea about finding/catching the pattern killer. I grabbed Snowflakes's loose cheeks and pulled him down for a full-on-the-mouth kiss, and ran the rest of the way down the hill to the lake with him. We reached the water's edge in thick woods almost exactly midway between two big houses/boathouses, and the big dog followed me into the water. At first, he seemed a bit reluctant but then began excitedly drinking quarts of lake water once he was standing in a couple of hundred billion gallons of the stuff.

I was, as per usual for these walks, covered in spider webs and needles and sap and bugs and dirt and scratches and blood and tiny sticks and such, so I stripped off my shirt and Tevas, threw the former into a handy tree branch and the latter onto a flattish bed of moss below the shirt-branch, and waded out deeper into Lower Saranac Lake, enjoying the cool/clean/abrasive feel of the sand beneath/between my toes. Snowflake leaned slightly back and away from my direction of travel, his eyes and the folds of skin covering his skull shifted into a new configuration that I took to signify discomfort/fear/reticence.

"It's okay, big guy," I said. "I have to dive to wash off

the detritus from our walk, but you don't have to swim if you don't want to."

I pulled a coiled chunk of paracord (*about 25 feet*) from a pocket, tied one end to the loop on his leash, and made a ring at the other end that I held onto. "Just stay there, okay buddy?" I said, or asked, or begged, depending on who interpreted my tones (*but since nobody was there besides the two of us, it probably didn't matter … Snowflake didn't seem to hear/listen*).

Making a shallow dive, cognizant of my own short leash, I felt/heard, in the weird way you (*or maybe just I*) experience when swimming underwater, a crashing and tumbling and ongoing splashing/falling sound behind me. I quickly surfaced and turned, expecting to see a tree collapsing into the lake on top of Snowflake and me, and thinking about how I could drag the beast to safety against his will if I had to. (*I probably couldn't.*) The good news was there was no tree collapsing into the water on top of us, and I didn't have to rescue Snowflake; the bad news was the sound and fury I'd heard while under the water signified a massive dog launching into the lake after me, intent on rescuing me from the huge/hungry/angry drinking bowl of Lower Saranac Lake that had apparently swallowed me whole.

He was mid-leap when I surfaced, directly in his path, and both of us struggled to occupy the same space for a split second … he won, and I got knocked back into/under the water again, prompting another rescue/leap, which nearly drowned me (*since he landed on my chest, and we were both by now significantly tangled in the paracord/leash*). I relaxed and held what breath I had for a few seconds until he moved off me, and then I stood up and got us untangled. He seemed proud of saving me but kept giving me slightly scared looks until eventually he took my hand in his mouth and towed me to shore.

I retrieved my shoes and shirt, and we walked back up the hill, through the woods to the TLAS, more slowly this time … the Earth/gravity seemed to be pulling on him more than me on the way back up, and he was panting by the time we got to the back door, despite a few breaks near pretty rocks (*I'm a sucker for a good glacial erratic, and subject those around me to the tyranny of glacial deposition any time we come across a nice one*) along the way.

"Oh, great," Dot said when she saw us come in. "You guys went for a swim. I was gonna mention that he's a little scared of water, even the kiddie pool we have in back, but it seems like you … what?"

I must have leaked a smile or frown or something (*I don't emote much, but Dot knows me as well as anyone on Earth, and can pick up the tiniest things*), so I explained, "I went in the lake to wash off forest-crud, and Snowflake dove in after me to affect a rescue … he's like a hero."

"Why's he so out of breath?" she asked, using a tone that our history would indicate was her way of kidding. "Did you ride him like a horse up from the lake as punishment for swamping you during his rescue?"

I've always been left in a quandary in these situations. I was pretty sure she was kidding, but any response I attempted to give seemed to fall flat (*straight answers don't work, and I'm not good at funny ones*), so I tried answering at a tangent. "Gravity and this dog are not friends … hauling his mass up the hill was hard work for him. I expect he spends much of his time inside or nearby, not on long, or hilly, walks."

Dot crammed a handful of cookies into his gaping maw, her arm getting temporarily engulfed and wet a third of the way to her elbow, and then she took the leash from me. "Go on up front and wait for me while I get him settled back into his pen in *ISO*."

I grabbed a warm towel off the top of the dryer on my way by and made sure that I was reasonably dry before sitting in her tall chair on the far side of the front counter. My email from early this morning was open on her laptop, and a TLAS census sheet for May 2015 next to it had doodles all over it … question marks and lightning bolts and drops/droplets (*which I assumed could be, probably were, blood*) and cartoony knives and guns and a mix of happy and sad and angry faces.

Dot's confident steps in those heavy boots she favors were approaching, and without turning, I said, "If I were Meg, instead of me, I would have some questions to ask, and even some conclusions I might draw, about these pictures you made while looking at my email to you."

"But?" she said.

"Since I'm not a counselor," I said, "and may, in fact, be the opposite of one, I assume you'll tell me about any problems/questions/reservations you have about helping me, and will just say *no* if you don't want to get involved."

She smiled her *Tyler is crazy, but not entirely wrong* smile and looked up at the ceiling for a second thinking about what she was going to say next. A busy and jarring James Taylor song came on the radio, and she nodded.

"This song is titled, 'Sun on the Moon,' Tyler," she said. "It's a tune on one of the playlists I made for you. I was deep in a box of wine the other night with Lisa, talking about you. I've got a life here, and a life with Lisa, and I love 'em both. I also have a life, a history, with you. The things we do, used to do, mostly, are awesome and scary and stupid and good. I love the way I feel when I help you do something stupid, but right, and possibly illegal. Lisa's not crazy about the things we used to do (*I had a moment of nerves, wondering how much Dot had told Lisa about a few of our adventures … some of those things had no statute of limitations*), but she likes you and loves me."

I was getting impatient, but didn't want to say anything to derail, or worse, slow her down.

"You're getting impatient, but don't want to say anything to derail, or worse, slow me down," she said, smiling at my widening eyes. "I didn't read your mind, Tyler, but you've got tells. Anyway, like in the song, when he says 'the sun on the moon makes a mighty nice light' (*the song specified 'made,' but I didn't say anything, and tried to keep my face immobile*). Maybe you, maybe the stuff you do when you work a case, something anyway is like the sun, shining on the moon, which is me in this extended metaphor. I can feel it making me shine or glow or whatever, and I like it."

I nodded, ready to get to work.

But she had one more addition of the extended metaphor, "Not every time, though. Some do a better job of making me shine than others. It occurred to me, remember, I was deep in the cheap red at the time, that it was like full or crescent or new moons, related to the position of the sun and the moon and the Earth, which in my metaphor is the job you're, we're working on. Anyway," she said, with her best Vito Corleone chin-scratch and accent, "I'm drinkin' more."

I nodded, twice, hopefully signaling my understanding of both the quote and her overworked metaphor. "I get it, I really do (*I wasn't sure that I really did*). I'd like to keep you involved in ways that you want … ways that make you most shiny. Mostly with this one, I need you to provide some balance, and a sounding board for my ideas," I said. "I require help making better plans … ones that take human irrationality into account."

"Then I'm your girl," she said. "I'm irrational as they

come. But I hope I can maybe fit into this one as a bit more than *idea girl,* Tyler."

"There could definitely be more for you if you want. I just didn't want to take you, or it, for granted," I said. "For a lot of the up-front stuff, though, you can't do much, because you're so well known in the community, and my working assumption is this guy is a lifelong resident … you probably know him."

"Shit, that's creepy. "You actually think I might know the guy who killed those people on the island the other night?"

"Those people and a lot more, if I'm right," I said. "Which, you know, I am. (*I'd watched a few seasons of 'Monk' recently, and the shoe fit perfectly at this moment.*) I'm pretty sure I can find out who he is, where he's based, and how he does what he does, but I'm going to need help making my decoy/bait plan work without getting anyone we like killed. I might need you as a backup at the end, with a boom-y or flame-y diversion/show-stopper to help make sure the white hats win."

"That sounds like you've got a lot going on," she said, looking worried and dropping her eyes down to the doodles for the first time since she'd walked up a minute ago. "Can you do it all, even with me helping?"

"We can totally do it," I said (*pumping 3.8 times more confidence into my voice than I felt*). "I'll need a lot of help from you in managing the layers of this thing."

"Explain," she said.

"This investigation is going to be big and messy and have lots of moving parts. Some of those parts will be clumsy and noisy and obvious to the killer, by the very nature of the way the law enforcement agencies, especially the FBI (*I used the special, Lector-esque, emphasis again, and Dot nodded and winked at me, making me feel a bit better about it falling flat last night ... kids*) operate. Instead of trying to stop them from being clumsy and obvious, I want to incorporate their clumsiness and obviousity (*I slip fake words into conversations with Dot from time to time. It's one of the ways I do humor*) into my plans. That being the case, I need to make different layers of my plan, all of them working toward my innermost goal. The outermost is what I'll do with Agent Brimley, next layer in is the one with Frank, who knows me more and won't believe just the outer layer. Inside that will be the real meat of my plan, with John and Mark, Xander's new aide (*she nodded, which I took to mean they'd been to TLAS at some point since Mark started working with Xander*) and a female accomplice to be named later. Inside that is the plan that Edith, the kid who saw her parents killed, thinks I'm working. Finally, inside all of those layers of plan will be you and me and the real plan ... still sound shiny?"

Dot rubbed her forehead. "You'll explain it in more detail at some point, right?"

"Definitely," I said, thinking I'd probably need some poster board and markers (*and wondering if I'd need to make another whole layer to involve Meg, since she had access to that kind of supplies*). "It's a complex plan, or series of plans ... with layers."

"Like an onion," Dot said, "or an ogre, or a cake, or a parfait. Tyler, did you come up with this whole layered thing as a setup for me, as a *Shrek* joke?"

"Nope," I said, although I might have ... just a little (*she really, really likes that movie, particularly Donkey, whom she feels is her doppelganger*).

I ran outside to my Element, grabbed the donuts, and a cooler with some Cokes in it, ran back in, and helped with TLAS-stuff for a few minutes until she had some space in her schedule for 20 minutes ... then I filled her in on what I'd seen and heard and done and thought in the last 24 hours, since learning about the murders, and the presence of a pattern killer. (*She insisted on using the term serial killer, while I bounced back and forth for reasons only the gremlins in the primitive bits of my head knew.*)

When we were done, I asked if I could borrow as close to a perfect dog as she had for an hour or so, and headed off to my next meeting with sweet Sadie under my arm.

Mulflur Road, Saranac Lake, NY
Friday, 7/10/2015, 9:27 a.m.

I hadn't actually been inside the house on Mulflur on that hot Friday last August, but I had heard firsthand descriptions, and read the reports and studied the crime scene photos. I almost expected to see blood stains and spatter and gore and broken furniture when Iskra Kovac opened the door and invited me inside, but it was spotless and light and clean.

"Tyler." Iskra leaned in to hug me and kiss my cheek, missing or ignoring the body language and other signals I sent her way. "So nice to see you. Why do you make me wait so long between visits? Let me get you some coffee and baklava while I see if the boys are up yet."

"I would love some baklava, but no coffee, please," I said, looking around and listening. "I'm sorry I didn't call ahead to ask if it was okay if I came by to see Xander and Mark."

"What nonsense, call ahead," she said, clucking. "You gave me my son back. Come into the kitchen and tell me about what you've been doing to keep busy this summer."

I followed her, noting signs of renovation and addition that were in line with what I'd seen pulling up the driveway. Iskra picked up a cordless phone by the fridge and dialed a number, waiting and then smiling when a voice came on at the other end.

"Xander, it's Mommy," she said. "Mr. Cunningham is here in the kitchen. Can you and Mark come down? We'll all have baklava." She listened for a few seconds, said, "Yes, my love," hung up the phone, and started pouring coffee (*and water for me*) while she took out a huge platter of baklava and a pile of small/delicate/expensive looking plates. She must have seen me looking at the phone, or been expecting a question, because she pre-empted me. "After what happened last summer, we gutted the house, connecting the main living area to two attached living suites, one for Darko and me, one that Xander sleeps in with his aide. It's a step between how we used to live and how he'll need to live in the years to come, and now with Mark and the other one, Derek, working and staying with him alternating nights, it's better than ever."

She looked up and back toward the rear of the house and used some form of mother-radar to gauge Xander's level of preparedness/proximity.

I snaked a hand out to secure another piece of baklava, but Iskra was quicker … tapping the tip of an outstretched finger with the spatula, and scooping another hefty chunk onto my plate before she continued.

"We've got another minute or two before the boys arrive," she said. "Tell me what you've been doing to stay busy? We loved your pictures of the trip you took out west, you know, and Xander was particularly sad to hear about Hope. He did like that dog (*she couldn't keep a tone of incredulity out of her voice … Hope was not a sweet or likable dog, but she and Xander had gotten along reasonably, thanks to the power of cookies*). Have you been doing the detective thing you do? Are you helping anyone right now?"

I could hear/feel heavy footfalls coming our way, and tried to sum things up for Iskra. "I've been canoe-camping a lot since April. The trip out west was pretty and different, and Hope and I had a nice time together exploring the desert. She liked spending time with Xander too (*mostly for the cookies, but I couldn't see/think of any reason to be that honest*). I've brought a dog from the shelter for us to take for a walk once he gets down here, if he'd like to. I've been keeping busy, but not doing many actual investigations lately, although I started working on something just the other day."

Iskra crossed herself, and looked down the hallway where Xander and Mark were now approaching and quickly/quietly whispered to me, "Those poor people out on the island?"

"Yes," I whispered back, unsure of exactly why, but certain from her face it was the right thing to do. "I'm working for the daughter ... and Frank Gibson ... oh, and the FBI." (*I didn't bother with the Lector-ization at all this time.*)

"Hey, Tyler," Mark said as he followed Xander into the room. "Not so long time, no see."

Xander had moved around and past both his mother and me, making a beeline for the big tray of baklava; Iskra seemed about to say something, but Mark raised a hand out of Xander's view.

"Xander Kovac," Mark said, "can you say good morning to Mommy and Tyler?"

"Good morning, Mommy," Xander parroted, in tone and cadence. "Good morning, Mr. Cunningham. Hope is waiting in the car?"

"No, Xander, sorry, Hope's not here," I said, "but I did bring Sadie, a very nice dog, who might like to go for a walk with you and Mark and me a little later, if that's okay ... if it doesn't get in the way of your plans for the day (*I said all of this to Xander, but it was mostly directed at*

Mark, and to a lesser degree, Iskra)."

Xander stuffed the Eggo-sized piece of baklava he'd been nibbling into his mouth and headed for the front door at a high rate of speed … a hip-swinging speed-walk that I was sure had been acquired through a childhood of being told not to run.

"That sounds great, Tyler," Mark said over his shoulder as he followed the big man out of the room. "I'm with Xander for a few hours this morning, and we were planning on hiking around Dewey Mountain awhile, and then going for a swim at the end of the road down past the Trudeau Center, but we'd love to hang with you and Sadie first."

The front door opened and closed twice in quick succession, and I was left alone with Iskra again.

"I would be grateful for it if you could think of some way I could help you in looking into the death of that girl's parents," she said, and then, looking sheepish, "but you know, nothing like what you did, what happened with Cameron."

I covered my discomfort with the moment by grabbing another slab of Iskra's spectacular baklava … honey and light pastry and a few kinds of nuts, including nearly powdered pistachios. "Um, well, I can't think of anything at the moment, but thanks for the offer (*since she had just mentioned Cameron, one of Xander's aides who I had, in fact, managed to get killed during my investigations last summer, I didn't think it would be a good idea to say anything about my wanting to talk with Mark about possibly helping me with my plans to poke at a serial killer).*"

Luckily, before I was forced to respond or interact with her any further, I heard a gentle set of steps and hand on the front knob, followed by a clompier one. Mark, then Xander came back into the kitchen a moment later, each wearing a different smile. (*I'm a student of smiles, not being much of one for smiling, or much else on the emotional spectrum, myself.*)

"She's a ridiculous little thing, isn't she?" Mark asked. "But the big guy is so excited to show me his tricks and dog-wrangling expertise, I had a tough time getting him back in here. I had to promise him another piece of baklava, and told him we should bring Sadie a little bowl of water."

Xander had swung by/past us to grab a Pyrex mixing bowl that Sadie, an interesting mix of Chihuahua and dachshund and (*maybe*) pug, could, and might, sleep in without curling up into her tiniest ball shape. He plopped a pair of pastries onto a plate, took a short stack of napkins, and headed back out, certain (*correctly*) that we would follow him. I waved at Iskra miming a full mouth I didn't have. Dashing out the front entrance, I caught up to the guys at the passenger door of my Element, where they were watching, and being watched by, Sweet Sadie.

Sadie has been at the TLAS for more than a year, waiting unsuccessfully, but with much patience, for someone to claim her for their mutual forever home. The main thing standing in her way is a heart condition called Chronic Valvular Disease, which is somewhat common to small dogs … Dot has to explain it to every prospective adopter of Sadie, and to date it's been a deal-breaker. As its name suggests, CVD is chronic, and is treated, in Sadie's case, with a suite of meds that work relatively well, but cost a fair amount per month. Dot has been pushing for me to take Sadie home with me, to live at SmartPig, but although I enjoy the small and sweet dog, she just doesn't feel right to/for me. I've been toying with the idea of offering to pay for her treatment regimen for her next potential adopter, so it's not standing in the way of a forever home for her.

I opened up the door, clicked on a nine-foot lead (*most of that length was needed to deal with the height differential ... whenever I took her for a walk, it felt as though either she was standing in a hole or I was up on a ladder*), and lifted her down to the ground. Sadie could have jumped down, but I wasn't sure she'd stick the landing, and why risk embarrassing her in front of new people. She quickly found the right spot to pee, took care of her business, and then turned to meet Xander and Mark. A combination wiggle/wag/smile/moan followed, and then she flipped over to show them her perfect, if inordinately tiny, belly. (*Truly, it would be difficult to ordinate it, given the dark/dense fur covering it, moles pretending to be nipples, nipples pretending to be ticks, and a complete lack of belly-button due to a surgical scar ... all that being said, it was still a great little belly.*)

"Sadie," I said, "sit ... and shake."

She did it perfectly, and very politely accepted a tiny piece of kibble for her efforts. I ceremoniously passed a handful of the treats to Xander and told him to try.

"Sadie," he said. "To sit and shake."

She did her part, even though Xander gave her the kibble-nugget before she had finished sitting down all the way. He repeated the trick a few times, and both of them seemed happy with the burgeoning relationship. (*Xander made a happy sound each time Sadie did it, and Sadie wagged and inched closer after each iteration/repetition of one of her simplest tricks.*)

"Xander Kovac," I asked, waiting until he tore himself away from Sadie, and looked up at me, "Would you like to take Sadie for a walk around your house?"

"Take Sadie on a walk around my house," he said. "Yes."

"You did a great job at the shelter, with Dot, the last

time I saw you there," I said, "but remember to walk slowly with her. Sadie's legs are very little, and we don't want her to have to run on her walk."

He gave a single slow, definite, nod, "Walk slowly with her. Sadie's legs are little," and with that he began to walk, nearly in slow motion, around the Kovac house.

We knew he would be fine, but Mark and I watched them intently when they traversed the lawn and rounded the new addition and passed out of our vision. I sensed both of us aiming our hearing back toward the woods behind the Kovacs' house, willing things to be quiet and go smoothly.

"They'll be fine," Mark said. "Thanks for coming by with Sadie for Xander. Now, what's with the email you sent this morning at 0-dark thirty? I like what you did for Xander, and meant what I said about helping you out someday, but I know who I am. I'm a middle of the pack thinker at best, and I make up for that by working hard, always have. I'm not a genius or a detective, and I'm working on a recreational therapy degree, not criminalistics. Certainly no Clarice Starling (*it was funny that references to* Silence of the Lambs *kept sneaking into my conversations/thoughts in the last 24 hours, or maybe not ... maybe it was a common knowledge/language we all had about pattern killers*) or even Doctor Watson. I don't see how I could help, although the offer still stands, as long as it doesn't screw up my gig with the Kovacs and the big guy, or my studies at Paul Smith's."

"It's not one hundred percent yet, but I have the beginnings of a plan," I said. "I think I can feel the shape of things ... of how this guy does what he does. When I'm more sure of the way he's worked, I may need/want to set a trap, with live bait. All of my contacts in town probably know him, except for you. You're new enough, and fringe enough, to the community that he probably doesn't know you yet. That, in combination with the fact that you are a veteran of hazardous situations, and expressed a willingness to help, all worked together to bring me to ask you for your assistance ... that being said, you can, of course, say *no*. It's probably the smart thing to do."

"Sell it, Cunningham," he joked.

"I don't know if you heard what happened to Cameron?" I asked. "The guy who was working with Xander last summer, when he helped me?"

"Yeah, I did," he responded, somewhat flatly, "but why don't you take thirty seconds and tell me your version of it."

"I had a perfect plan to draw out Danica's killer, clear Xander's name, and enjoy a few days of camping back in the Saint Regis Canoe Area," I said. "Cameron was willing to help me because he was a good guy who loved Xander and believed me when I told him that nothing would go wrong."

"So what went wrong?" he asked, looking for any sign of Xander rounding the far side of the house (*not yet*).

"I didn't take into account that the person who killed Danica would be so desperate, and also, such a good shot," I said. "I watched Cameron die a few feet from me, and nearly got myself and Xander killed as well."

"Sounds like a fuck up," he said. "How you gonna avoid something like that happening this time, if I were to help you?"

"I am reasonably certain I can control the environment more effectively this time," I said, "with lines of sight and access. I would also find a way to get backup into/onto the board ahead of time, or sneak it in with you. Also, this guy is an up-close, and silent, killer ...

he's not going to take a shot with a rifle from three hundred yards in the middle of a number of occupied campsites. He takes pride in getting in and getting out again without anyone knowing about it."

"I'm in," Mark said, as Xander finally came around the corner of the house by the kitchen. (*We could see him talking with someone, I suspect his mother, through the window and gesturing to Sadie, who was following determinedly and seemed wagtastic.*)

I had expected more resistance, so wasn't entirely ready for such quick/easy capitulation; I skipped ahead in my scripted talk (*jumping my internal teleprompter down a few screens*). "Don't say *yes* yet. I'm not done ... I was hoping you might have a like-minded, or at least an equally willing/foolhardy, friend from out of town to be co-bait with you once I figure out where to tether you."

Mark tipped his head back, thinking, for a few seconds until Xander closed within shouting distance, "Need more treats for Good Girl Sadie."

I flipped back to the image I had in storage of the handful I'd passed him a few minutes ago, doubted he'd had time to have Sadie do her trick 37 times, and decided instantly that I didn't care. (*She tended toward being too thin thanks to her meds so a bit extra wouldn't hurt things at all.*) I reached into my shirt pocket, and pulled out another similarly-sized handful, and passed it to Xander as he came within range, hand out, immediately showing us the trick again.

Mark looked at me, through/across/past Xander and Sadie, and said, "Let me work on that, Tyler. I'd like to help, and not just cuz I feel like I owe you something for what you did for the Kovacs and the big guy. I'll get back to you tomorrow or the next day."

"And now Xander Kovac," he said, addressing

Xander, "let's hit the trail up on Dewey, and then I wanna go swimming down by the rocks. (*I assume he was referring to the big pile of rocks jutting out into the water at the far end of Algonquin Avenue.*) We can visit with Sadie at the shelter next week, and I'm sure we'll be seeing Mr. Cunningham before too long."

"Dewey, then swimming," Xander said, and handed Sadie's leash to me on his way back inside the house. He was done with this portion of his day … with Sadie and me.

"Thanks, Mark," I said. "I know it's a lot to ask, and I would certainly/completely understand if you decide it's not in your best interests (*correctly, it wasn't, and wouldn't ever be, in his best interests*) to help me with this."

"What were the parents' names?" he asked. "How old is the girl?"

I told him, but wasn't certain he was fully listening or had actually asked the questions as questions so much as explanation. Xander came out with a backpack which he passed to Mark before climbing into an aging (*if not aged*) Subaru station wagon and buckling his seat belt. Mark gave a tight wave and got behind the wheel and they drove away, leaving both Sadie and me wondering about the rest of the treats I'd recently given to Xander.

When I dropped Sadie off with Dot at the TLAS, I stole back one of the donuts I'd given her/them (*more than a little surprised there were a couple still in the box*), and headed out after promising to fill in Dot as things progressed … assuming they would.

Helgafel Farm, Route 86, Gabriels, NY
Friday, 7/10/2015, 11:23 a.m.

I crunched into/onto the graveled half-moon driveway by
the farm stand out by the road, about halfway between
Donnelly's Ice Cream and Moody's Tree Farm. I sat for a
minute, listening to the engine cooling and bugs making
bug noises, and a distant cow at the tree farm (*and
apparently, now, cow farm*) calling out in the still-cool
morning. When the wind shifted slightly, I could smell
the barn from up the hill behind the farm stand and
wondered if they might have a side of bacon I could take
home with me.

"The hippie kids are getting nervous," Barry said
from over by the produce display, where I noticed one of
the people working there today was getting ready to come
over and check on me.

I got out of the Element and waved to the people
manning the stand, then pantomimed that I was heading
over to the cabin nearby, but distinctly separate from the
public end of things at Helgafel Farm. I'd first come out
here nearly thirteen years ago as a part of one of my
earliest cases (*the successful resolution of which ended with me
being able to live/work in the SmartPig office*). I rubbed the
scratch John had given me yesterday and thought about
our interactions through the years.

He and his friend/boss/protectee, Nick, had moved

up here seeking anonymity from a prior life that I assumed involved some degree of illegal activity, choosing to hide and wait (*from what, for what, only they knew. I had learned/decided not to ask questions a long time ago*) on an organic farm that must have lost a fair amount of money every year ... although it/they produced some truly great bacon. Initially, we'd been forced to work together, something neither of us relished, but over the years we'd been able to help each other thanks to complementary skillsets. He'd recently been tutoring me in self-defense and unarmed combat, having noted that I seemed to end up in rough shape many times at the end my cases.

"Tyler, I thought you'd be by after lunch," John said from behind me ... neither Barry nor I had noticed/heard his approach. (*Barry is usually present when I visit with John, either because I am likely to be on edge in his presence, or as Barry suggested once because they like each other.*)

"My morning went more quickly/smoothly than anticipated," I said. "So I came out hoping you'd be available."

I have no idea what he does to keep busy on/around the farm, or what his duties are/were with regard to Nick, but I believed that if he wanted me to know, I would, so I don't ask. I know John reads a lot, as much as anyone I know (*besides me*), and likes to watch the young people Nick employs working in the barns and fields, and he enjoys the views from the farmhouse across the fields facing the High Peaks to the east (*and currently back over my left shoulder*). He has almost always simply appeared whenever I arrive and park and wait a minute; it would be disquieting if I were the type of person who alarms easily (*but I'm not, so it's not*).

"Great," he said. "Come on in. Let's talk about how I can help."

I followed him when he turned tightly on his heel and headed back to the small cabin at the border between the farm and the rest of the world in which he lives. His fancy espresso machine was gurgling and hissing and gently shrieking … getting ready for the complicated operations he would soon perform resulting in tiny mugs of vile smelling inky coffee that he drank night and day. I also spotted a bucket filled with what appeared to be tiny bottles of Mexican Coke (*which, like Canadian Coke, is made with real sugar, and is significantly better than what one can find in the United States most of the time*) and ice.

He waved a hand at the bucket, went over to the copper and brass monstrosity that had just finished warming up, and asked, "Barry can take care of his own needs, yes?"

Barry brushed past me without breeze or contact (*of course, since he's a fiction only seen by me, and sometimes acknowledged by John*), went to John's rolling bar, and turned back a moment with a tumbler filled with what looked like bourbon, three of his sausage-fingers of the stuff, poured over an ice cube.

"Not that I care," John said, looking unerringly in Barry's direction (*a trick he swears he manages by reading my body posture, rather than seeing him as I do*), "since he certainly doesn't drink me out of house and home, but did he opt for one of the Cokes, some of the bourbon he usually favors, or something else entirely?"

John's been fascinated by Barry since he first found out about him. We've talked about my lingering hallucinations growing out of some horrific things that were done to me, seen by me, and done by me, three summers ago, but interestingly enough, John hasn't completely dismissed Barry's existence (*or input*) as symptom … instead he often talks with Barry, using me as go-between.

"Tell him that, *yes*, I'm drinking his fancy bourbon before noon, an' enjoyin' it too," Barry said. "I can't see it bein' bad for me at this point, or me having to drive us back to town later, amiright? Hah!"

I started relating his answer to John, who had just sat down on a large, badly scuffed, reading chair after fiddling with the machine to his satisfaction, resulting in a four-ounce serving of espresso in a pottery cup with no handle … one the farm kids had made last winter in their new kiln.

"Why's he bother with all of that noise and fuss for a few ounces of coffee in that mug of his?" Barry asked. I tagged this onto Barry's answer about his not-really morning drinking some of John's bourbon.

"I like the crema," John said, "the foam on top, and the burning bitterness and how it scalds my tongue just a bit."

"Plus, it's really more of a beaker than a mug, Barry, since it lacks a handle."

Both John and Barry gave me essentially the same stare for a few seconds of total silence in the small cabin, then John shook his head and laughed a bit at me looking back and forth between him and my personal ghost.

"Your email said you wanted to talk with me about the killings out on Lower Saranac," John said. "I assume Gibson and those he works for asked you to help?"

"He probably would have gotten around to it, but first contact was made by Agent Brimley of the FBI (*no emphasis on it this time because John was now oozing no-nonsense, so I didn't bother*), the lead suit that was standing with him in the parking lot behind SmartPig yesterday morning."

"He's the one from the other time?" John asked. "The thing at the hospital, with the governor?"

I nodded and continued, "The victim's daughter survived the attack by diving into the lake, evading the killer, and treading water in the dark until Frank came out in a boat, responding to her screams, and fished her out of the lake. Brimley thinks the killer may have been doing this for a while up here. It seems like a pretty interesting and unique opportunity to look for/at a serial killer … and the girl's tough and brave and all alone in a newly scary world."

"Softie," Barry and John both said at the same time, smiling to themselves and at me.

"Get stuffed, both of you," I said. "I need your help *(really talking to John, now, but always willing to listen to Barry's take on things)*."

"I think Brimley is right and there may well be a serial killer operating here in the Tri-Lakes. He's gone mostly unnoticed to date because he grabs people while they're here from another state … camping out in the island campsites on Lower Saranac Lake."

Barry mouthed the words, "Fuckin' cool!"

John tilted his head back for a few seconds … thinking, then slurping the last of his espresso out of his beaker *(I thought the word beaker emphatically toward both of them)* and moved over to make some more, while saying over his shoulder, "Keep going, Tyler, I can still hear you. Oh, and tell me any thoughts either you or Barry might have about how your guy picks his victims and/or deals with getting there and away and/or the disposal of their cars and camping gear."

Justin and I used to move and dump bodies from time to time," Barry said casually. "A couple of times on the lake. As long as you're not blowing an air-horn while you're doin' it, nobody says nothing *(double negative, I thought, but didn't say, not wanting to muddy the waters or confuse either of them*)."

"I think that's going to be how we find/trip/catch our guy," I suggested. "I believe he's got a way of knowing which sites are going to be occupied, and when, by his target audience … which would seem to be out-of-state vacationers. They're not missed here, not missed immediately anywhere, and when they are and someone remembers they were vacationing up in the Adirondacks, even if the authorities are able to track them up here, all anyone up here knows is that they showed up, paid for a site, stayed and eventually/apparently left."

I filled them in a bit on what I'd gotten from my visit to the island, and talking with Frank and Brimley and Edith. Also, I told them about my layered onion plan (*editing it so as to make out as if John was the innermost layer, although I'm reasonably sure he didn't believe me*) for keeping people busy, and then started to go through the layers in more detail.

"Brimley and his minions will sift the big data and long shots like boat rentals and ATM-cams and credit card records and first-aid supplies and canvassing other people at campsites/houses around the lake and at gas stations and on the major routes into and out of town … if we're lucky, that'll eat up thousands of man-hours without them getting too horribly in our way. Frank and Brimley are already expecting me to do weird research and reading through piles of paperwork that seem pointless to them, and they've committed to helping me access data so I'm going to do that, but also focus on the site/victim selection process. Once I know how, I'll focus on who and how often (*or when, but how often seemed clearer*)."

I stopped for a moment, long enough to get another of the tiny Mexican bottles of Coke. (*I imagined that I could taste a difference, a slight improvement over the cans because of the glass container, but it was probably due to my being on the job, which always made the world and everything in it seem a shade brighter and a touch more in focus.*) Barry and John both worked on their drinks in a manner that suggested they were waiting for me to continue, so I did.

"The different people/parts of my plans should keep working independently," I said, "and while it's entirely possible that Frank Gibson or Agent Brimley will find their way to our guy, I'd be willing to bet (*if I was the kind of person who bet on things, which I'm not*) that I'll find him first."

"Why would you assume that?" Barry asked. "Besides your massive ego, I mean."

John saw my face change minutely, and asked, so I related Barry's question, to which he nodded and said, "He's got a point, Tyler, they've got lots of brains and feet to throw at this problem, and you've got you."

"First off," I said, trying a sarcasm script I'd been working up with Dot in recent months, "let me thank both of you for the vote of confidence (*it fell flat*). I think I will succeed where they will fail, or at least work slower than me because they're all approaching it as a law enforcement issue. The nature of most crimes and criminals and the very size/strength of the forces they have arrayed against this guy ends up working against them. Frank has been telling me for years that most crimes are committed by people who are drunk or angry or stupid or greedy or lazy … sometimes a combination of two or more of those things. Solving the crime and catching the bad guy is very often a matter of checking the husband or a disgruntled employee, or talking to other criminals who are eager to sell out the bad guy you're looking for … for a reduced sentence."

I stopped to take a breath and watch my small (*and partly imaginary*) audience nodding metronomically before continuing, "This guy has possibly been killing people for a decade or more without getting caught, so he's not stupid or a drunk or lazy. He isn't killing his victims for love or money or out of anger toward them. Most likely the guy isn't known by/to them so they won't find him by talking to neighbors and friends and family and coworkers of the victims. He's not making the sorts of mistakes, or even the moves, the authorities are used to … their training works against their efficiency when looking for this guy, or his patterns of behavior. The thing is, the community to which Frank and Brimley, and all the other Franks and Brimleys, belong has been trained by years of success with a more standard line of inquiry than will work with our guy. Most serial/pattern killers don't get caught through this kind of police work … they get caught by accident or dumb luck. They get pulled over for a busted tail-light with a victim in the trunk, or there's a record of a parking ticket at the murder scene, or they annoy a neighbor sufficiently with noise or smells and they call the police. From that point onward, the system works, but the initial break is mostly beyond what traditional law enforcement is capable of doing … how they're capable of thinking. I'm going to focus on site/victim selection, and that's how I'll get him … get to him before Frank and Brimley," I said.

"I follow lots of your reasoning, Tyler," John said, "but still don't know how you can know you'll find what you're looking for."

"Because if we assume he's been doing this for years without getting caught, that implies not picking the wrong spot/people, or getting picked up afterward on his way home. If that's true, then he has to have a clever/sustainable/repeatable methodology. I can find that if I look at enough paper."

"Okay," said Barry. "If we accept that, which I don't entirely, but who gives a fuck since I'm along for the ride no matter what, whadya need him for (*pointing at John with his empty, fake, bourbon tumbler*)?"

"I'm glad you asked," I said, and I was because it's hard to prove you can do something you haven't done yet (*even though I was still certain I could do it*). "When I get close to the end of this, I'll bait a trap for the killer, and John will be there to help me catch/stop him before he can kill my bait. I'm good enough with unarmed combat to know that I'm not good enough."

John ignored the fact that I'd answered a question he hadn't asked or heard ... he was used to that after a few years of dealing with me/Barry; he redirected, "It's good that you recognize your limitations, at least your physical limitations (*he smirked in Barry's direction, mouthing "am I right?" and swinging up a virtual high-five*), and, of course, I'll help you if you get things set up to snare the killer. Beyond that, I've got two questions: can we call him The Campsite Cutthroat?"

"Asshole," Barry murmured, "that's a stupid name. But can we, name him?"

I ignored Barry, focusing instead on John, "You said two questions?"

"Seriously, I follow your logic on why the LEO community can't get him as quickly as you might be able to, but why not just tell them how to do it, and let them throw all of their people at solving it?"

"I thought about it, I really did, but I'm still nearly certain that I can look at the paper differently than they can. How about if I can't find him in a week, I tell Frank and Brimley everything I've been thinking about how he does it, and let them loose on the killer?"

John nodded and stood up to start the brass and copper thing shrieking again. Barry refilled his bourbon with an ostentatiously noisily dropped ice cube and bottle gurgling (*especially given the givens of both ice and bottle being imaginary*), and I grabbed a pair of the small bottles out of the quickly emptying bucket. I kicked some thoughts about the hunt and the trap and the finale around with the two of them for another hour before my brain/belly/bladder were all sloshing and full, and I headed out in search of an ice cream cone at Donnelly's, followed by a swim at the Lake Clear Beach (*one of the Adirondack's best unkept/unkempt secrets*).

SmartPig Offices, Saranac Lake, NY
Friday, 7/10/2015, 2:18 p.m.

Because it was Friday, the flavor of the day at Donnelly's
was Strawberry (*twisted with vanilla … the only choice you get is
the size cone you want*); I got a large for myself, and nearly
ordered Hope's usual baby cone before I remembered
she wasn't waiting for me out in the Element … instead, I
sat down on the grassy hill up and behind the exit door
and watched the clouds/tourists/mountains for a while,
not thinking about missing my dog or a killer in the rye
(*filtering the occasional victim from the steady stream of visitors the
Adirondacks survives on*) or the time bomb in Mickey's head
or, eventually, where and if I fit in the world/mass of
humanity.

   I had a bag with a variety of gear and clothes in the
back of the Element, so when I pulled into the unmarked
driveway leading to the parking lot of the Lake Clear
Beach, I swung way down to the far end, opened both
driver side doors to make a changing
booth/space/alcove, and swapped my shorts for a
bathing suit before heading down to the water. (*The beach
is a long crescent of sand at the northeast end of Lake Clear and is
sandy and shallow for more than a hundred yards out.*) The state
defunded upkeep of it a few years ago, along with
hundreds/thousands of other wonderful sites, which
mostly meant someone took the sign down, they no

longer send a crew to rake the beach every once in a while, and they stopped maintaining the outhouse in the woods behind the beach. I usually like to come to this beach early in the morning or after dark or on rainy days, when other people aren't there/here, but I had missed that opportunity for today, and wanted to swim anyway.

Listening to kids splashing at the waterline, smelling Coppertone and someone smoking a cigarette, I walked out some fifty yards, feeling the rough sand and smooth/round freshwater snail shells under my feet. The water was cool down by my feet, and warmer up by my waistline, and the sun was shining hard onto my face as I looked up at the sky and felt the light breeze occasionally coming in from the far side of the lake.

I thought, as I often do when swimming/paddling the waters of the Adirondacks, about the difference between lakes and ponds … although governing bodies differ/dither, most people will lead off with size, others will talk about sunlight penetration (*with a pond being shallow/clear enough to allow sunlight to penetrate to the bottom of all portions*) or temperature and layers (*with ponds being thought of as more uniform in temperature and lacking the layers and layer-interchange found in lakes*). I lean toward size/depth, and the other considerations tend to follow those, but don't care much (*until the day 'they' ask, at which time I have a lengthy/learned treatise on the subject to deliver*).

Standing up to my waist in the water, shrieks and fun behind me, and the cold and empty depths in front, I seemed to have come to a fork in the road (*at which point, from behind me, I heard Barry do his Yogi Berra imitation, "take it!" … I only knew it was Yogi Berra because he'd told me the first time, which had given me a headache and made me consider getting an MRI/brain scan*). I knew what I had to do, and had a vague idea of how to do it. Now was the moment to start doing it and stop thinking/talking about it, so I stayed there, standing in the water for another few minutes, because that's what I do, both literally and figuratively … I stand on the brink. I hadn't made any mistakes yet, or at least none that had gotten anyone (*including myself, arguably the most important possibility*) killed yet. If I went ahead with the plan, I stood a better than even chance of making the mistakes I always made … not properly factoring in the way people react to stressful/difficult/dangerous/ challenging situations. (*I tend to assume that I act rationally and other people should as well … they don't.*)

I took a breath, blocked out the sounds of the people behind me and my imaginings of the cold water and snapping turtles and leeches ahead of me, barely beneath the surface, and dove. Swimming down and away from the light and the warm sun, I pulled as hard and as long as I could with legs and arms and lungs, keeping my eyes open to see what there was to see. I surfaced, lungs burning, spots dancing in front of my eyes, smiling and whole and perfectly (*well, reasonably*) comfortable with what was in front of me.

When swimming to shore and running the gauntlet of tinies and tiniers and people who might want to talk to me, I scooped up my stuff and jogged back through the woods to the parking lot and my Element. I called Meg Gibson, the lead counselor for the Saranac Lake Consolidated School District and Frank Gibson's wife/partner, and asked if I could stop by for lunch. (*Meg is a nurturing soul, and would feed and clothe and hug the world if it were remotely feasible, so I knew the answer before I asked … just the way I like my questions.*)

"Of course," she said. "I was planning on making up some ham salad and deviled eggs and cutting open a watermelon (*a lie, on her own she would have found something healthy/ simple in the fridge to eat, like a yogurt*), so I'll make enough for both of us."

"I mostly wanted to see you," I said, glad not to be bothered much by feelings of guilt when manipulating people. "But is there any chance of Frank coming for lunch, or afterward? I wanted to talk with him sometime today, a bit under the radar if possible." (*Meg has some idea of what I do, and how I do it, but still, I believe through sheer force of will, managed to think of me as an innocent and lucky observer who just kept being in the right place at the right time.*)

"Frank said something the other night about that man from the Albany FBI wanting to talk to you about what had happened. I assumed he wanted your help. He didn't think you had anything to do with that, what happened, did he? The Albany guy?"

I used to think that Meg was genuinely curious/ clueless from the way she asked some of her questions, but long-term exposure to those queries and follow-up questions had lead me to believe that she was playing chess with people/situations and operating a few moves ahead of most everyone else. (*I played by different rules, possibly played an entirely different game, than she was used to, so I liked to think she didn't play me as much as she did other people.*)

"Well, I think I creeped him out a dozen years ago, with the cryptography *(and bomb, but we wouldn't talk about that, and we wouldn't talk about not talking about it)* thing at AMC," I said, "and he's kept an eye on me ever since. I don't think he really thought I killed those people out on the lake, but it probably gave him an entree to talk with me from what he would perceive as a superior position."

"So are you going to be working with them, Frank and this Brimley?" she asked, not hiding the dislike in her voice. (*I appreciated the loyalty … and noted that she had, in fact, remembered his name.*)

"I think it would be more accurate," I said, "to say that I'll be working on the same investigation they're working on ... I tend to look at, and approach these things a bit differently than Agent Brimley, and even Frank, would/will/do."

"And it mostly works out okay. At least it seems to certainly work out the way it was supposed to," she said. "I'll see you whenever you get here."

I drove straight into town, opting for Forest Home Road instead of 186 and 86 because I'd spent much of my morning out that way and felt like driving the emptier/quieter route with more curves and trees and glacial erratics and fewer cars and buildings and people. I'd forgotten they were messing around with the bridge on Ampersand Avenue (*the route which would allow me to avoid the main/crowded part of Saranac Lake, and come out near the TLAS and the Gibson house*), so I ended up having to go through town anyway. I noticed while driving by the building that houses SmartPig, that a window I was reasonably certain I'd closed before leaving ... was wide open. Actually, I didn't think enough of it to stop because I wanted to get a chance to meet with Meg (*and talk with Frank*).

When I turned at the town hall 13 seconds later, and was pulling into the Gibson's driveway 138 seconds after that, I was slightly disappointed to see both Meg's car and Frank's cruiser in the driveway. Not wanting to upset their dogs (*and having been invited to do so years ago*), I just approached the house, opened the door, walked in, and made my way back to the kitchen to help Meg finish getting the lunch ready.

Toby and Lola, both formerly counted among the ranks of shelter dogs, were embarrassed and pleased (*in that order ... in rapid succession*) when I surprised them in the kitchen; they swarmed over me with kisses and bristle-pokes until I agreed to kneel and give them the attention they deserved. Both dogs were built on a basic Labrador frame. Toby had some collie mixed in, and Lola was at least half boxer; neither of them had liked Hope and the feeling was mutual. (*I once tried the pun 'mutt-ual' with Dot, and she waved it off like a bad smell.*) They could smell other dogs on me, along with the few remaining cookies in my pockets, and the greeting threatened to turn into an interrogation, so I flung the treats into a distant corner and made a break for the center island, where Meg was mixing things in big bowls.

I picked up a serious chef's knife from the cutting board and started reducing a Vidalia onion to tiny fragments of its former self. It might be surprising to some people, but I enjoy cooking with Meg, not least because she has nice kitchen equipment/gadgets, whereas I have cheap stuff that might not make the cut if I were forced to vacate SmartPig for some reason. She, in turn, enjoyed it, because her husband, Frank, had no interest in the processes by which ingredients were transformed into meals. I was continually fascinated watching this couple from the up-close-and-personal seats they'd afforded me by more than a decade of close association.

"I need most of the Vidalia in a small dice, and about a fifth in a mince," Meg said, "for the salad and then the eggs, okay?"

"Got it," I said. "I thought I saw Frank's car in the driveway."

It wasn't a question, and deliberately left entirely specious (*as Meg well knew, I saw nearly everything that passed in front of my eyes, and remembered what I saw perfectly*), but it gave her some space to craft/frame the answer she wanted to give. Meg smiled into the bowl she was working over, and nodded very slightly. She had designated/elected/appointed herself my humanity instruction professor a number of years ago, and this was one of the lessons we'd both struggled with (*me with accepting/learning/internalizing it ... her with being patient in explaining it again and again and again ... and again*), the appropriate/friendly/positive use of untruths.

"He's had a few early mornings and long days recently," she said. "So when I called him for lunch, he raced home to get a chance to run himself through the shower and put on a fresh uniform. Some grand muckety-muck from Albany is dropping in this afternoon for a progress update."

"He'll probably want me there to ..." I started to say.

"He definitely won't want you there to ... do anything," Frank said, walking into the kitchen looking crisp and clean. He smelled terrific (*something about his clean shaven, regularly shaded chin, implied aftershave*). "In fact, Tyler, it'd be better if you were out on the water, or deep in the backwoods when Commissioner LaDuke gets here. I don't wanna explain how you fit into the investigation, and I sure as shit know Brimley doesn't."

Meg made a slightly sad face while glancing down into her bowl, which by now I suspected she was done with, but using for cover ... as with me, she had designated/elected/appointed herself Frank's humanity instruction professor a few decades ago. (*It was possible she did it with everyone, or at least everyone in her inner circle/circles.*) She needn't have worried, though, as I wasn't sensitive to these kinds of slights, or perceived slights ... and as it turned out, this feeling of pressure, combined with wanting me gone, worked in my favor.

"I can arrange that without any problem," I said. "I was planning on scouting the island campsites on Lower

Saranac this afternoon, and since Commissioner LaDuke is likely a flatlander, he'll believe I'm out of cell phone range." (*Most of Lower Saranac has great reception.*) "I'll leave it on but let everything except texts from you go to message."

Stopping to let my agreement sink in for a moment, I offered up the dice to Meg for the ham salad, and to mix the mince into the deviled egg bowl myself. I tasted/tested it with a reasonably clean pinky, decided it needed a few squirts of Tabasco Chipotle sauce (*as I almost always do, with anything/everything I make*), then started scooping the mix back into the halved egg whites. Meg had paprika out for the final garnish, but I opted for seasoned pepper instead (*it adds some color as well as a bit of taste, unlike paprika, which has no taste when topping deviled eggs, at least to me*). She gave her bowl a final stir, and ladled/spread/shoveled the ham onto thick slices of a nice-looking oat-nutty bread, topped it with lettuce and tomato, and she orbited around to the fridge for drinks. Meg held out a Sam Adams Light, but Frank gave a *no* nod, and a *yes* nod when she held out a two-liter bottle of yellow cap Coke (*US bottlers produce Coke during Passover with real sugar, as designated by the yellow caps, or so they claim … it doesn't taste as good as the Canadian or Mexican Coke, but I haven't done the science, had it analyzed, yet*). She put all of the food and some plates and glasses on a tray, along with a pair of soup bones stuffed with peanut butter that she took from the freezer (*I assumed for Toby and Lola*), I grabbed the Coke and a bucket of ice … Frank held up an index finger, shook it at both of us, snaked his hand into the fridge, and pulled out a single beer for himself.

We headed downstairs and out into their fenced back yard with the dogs following me. Meg set the tray down on the picnic table and offered the bones to first Toby, and then Lola, who both squeezed themselves under the benches to take up all of the legroom under the picnic table. We ate meals together frequently enough that we all knew the routine, and nobody stood on ceremony ... within 20 seconds, we all had full plates and full mouths, and silence reigned in the Gibson back yard.

By the time I was partway through my second sandwich, Frank had finished his beer and shifted to Coke (*hiding the empty under the table seemed pointless, but appeared to make him feel better, and cost Meg and I nothing*) He was responding to Meg's gentle probes about the case with more comfortable and lengthier answers than he had initially done. The dogs were making a ridiculous amount of noise from under the table, working to gnaw and separate the bones from the peanut butter inside them, and each of us took turns listening to, and smiling at, the contented slurping and scraping, as refuge from the busy/fruitless/gory investigation that Frank detailed in the cool/green/sunny/peaceful back yard. Their son, Austin, had stayed up at Clarkson at the end of his first year, taking some summer-session classes, and working, and staying close to his *first-ever* girlfriend, who Meg wasn't entirely comfortable with, and whose appearance seemed to make Frank blush slightly and avoid eye contact when it came up in conversation. I think they had welcomed my presence in their home, especially at meals, during the last year more than ever with Austin's absence.

"I'm pretty sure from what Meg told me," Frank said, "and based on past performance, that now is the time you make a bizarre request for seemingly useless piles of paperwork that will end up cracking the case before the rest of us get a handhold."

"I was going to talk about other stuff for a while, and lead up to it," I said, "but *yes*, we've come to that time. I need to know everything there is to know about the reservation system for the campsites on Lower Saranac. Also, I need to know who else knows it, who has access to the reservations ahead of time, how they access it, and then just lots of time to look through all of the records I can get my hands on, going back ten or twenty years."

"Oh," he said, "is that all?"

"Yup," I said. "I think there's a good chance (*nearly a certainty, but I wanted to downplay it, even with Frank*) that the reservations might have something (*nearly everything, really*) to do with victim selection."

"I know one of the guys who spends his summer days checking the people into campsites at the boat launch," Frank said. "He'd have access to alla that, but sharing it with us, with you more particularly, might be a problem for him and his bosses at the DEC."

"Agent Brimley of the FBI (*finally, I got a response to the phrasing/emphasis, from Meg, who gave a slow nod/smile*) might be able to push things through if you don't have the juice."

I meant no offense, but Frank's face clouded, and Meg shook her head slightly, and even the dogs seemed to stop their excessive chewing noises from under the table for 7 long seconds of total silence. Frank didn't look at me, but he and Meg seemed to have a lengthy non-verbal discussion which ended when he pushed his plate back and stood up.

"Let's go," he said.

Meg made some generic sputtering noises, and asked about supper and looked back and forth between us. I grabbed the plates and stacked them on the tray and started gathering glasses and napkins and reached under the table for Frank's empty (*getting a couple of kisses from the dogs while I was reaching around under there*).

"Now!" he thundered, stomped off and in and up and out, with me in tow ... I assume Meg took care of clearing/cleaning, and I felt badly for leaving that to her (*and also for leaving her with this scene at the end of her lunch*). I took a few steps toward my Element, and Frank snapped and pointed to the passenger door of his cruiser.

"Buckle up," he said, once I got in. "You never know when you'll flip in a high-speed pursuit. Be safe!"

It's what he always said in the face of my refusal to use the seatbelt ... something he did as a general, really inviolable, rule. He waited me out, glaring/staring until I capitulated.

Frank drove sedately on our way out of his neighborhood, and even once we'd turned onto Route 3, toward the boat launch ... he started to speak twice before he found the words he wanted to say in the way he wanted to say them. "Tyler, you're the fifth person today who has suggested, or implied, that I'm not cop enough to get the job done finding this asshole who orphaned little Edith. Frankly, (*I refrained from a joke I'd worked out with Dot about this turn of phrase from him, sensing the timing wasn't right*) I'm really fucking tired of it."

"I'm sorry, Frank," I said. "You know I'm not good with people, in general, or managing emotions and tact ... that's not an excuse, it's a reason/statement. It's also nothing you don't know ... sorry, this isn't about me, it's about you." (*This was some of Meg's tutoring coming through/out in what I hoped was an appropriate manner because I care about Frank and his feelings, and also need his help with my investigation.*)

He smiled a tiny bit while looking straight ahead. "Sounds like my Meg talkin'. I know you're doing the best you can with what you've got, same as me, but it drives me nuts. Brimley treats me, all of us up here, like peons;

it's the same with some of the higher-ups in the troopers. This guy who's coming up this afternoon is going to be shitting on all of us for not catching the killer already, and we all gotta take a big serving and smile afterward."

"Is there anything I can do to help, make it better?" I asked.

"That," he said, "what you just did. Well, that along with finding this motherfucker for me, and I'd like to bring him in and shove him up Brimley and LaDuke's ass." (*I struggled with the concept/phrasing for a second, and then let it go … everyone has trouble with figurative language from time to time.*)

"If you can get me access to this information, I'm reasonably confident (*absolutely certain*) that I can find the pattern killer," I said, "and once I do, he's yours. I have no interest in arresting him, or bringing him in, or shoving him up anyone's ass."

"Do you need resources or manpower from Brimley or me to help you do whatever you're going to do, look for whatever you're going to look for?" he said. "Because they told us in the short-term, we've only got to ask, and it's ours."

"Ask for ground penetrating radar, a pallet of Canadian Coke, and a pair of kinkajous," I said, "and I'd like a slide from the back window of SmartPig down to the parking lot."

He started to reach for the pad that lived in his pocket, stopped himself, then started for it again, then looked away from the road for a second to check me out. "This joke thing you're trying out is … unsettling," he said.

"I wasn't joking," I said. "Well, not entirely. Saranac Lake PD and/or SmartPig could totally use a nice GPR setup, getting the right Coke is a pain sometimes, and kinkajous have prehensile tails, tongues long enough they're often responsible for pollinating flowers, and lack anal scent glands. In addition, I would think the benefits of the slide would be obvious to anyone who thinks about it for more than a second. Do you think Brimley could actually get me/you/us any of that stuff?"

"Let me start with the information about campsite reservations," he said, "and we'll go from there."

We pulled into the boat launch. It was completely transformed from the previous day's LEO-tastic chaos; today it was back to normal, with regular people and boaters and campers and fishermen and water-skiers all vying for position, shoving their boats into, and pulling the same boats out of, the water. It was somewhat organized chaos. Just outside the center of action was a small cabin that people used to check in with the DEC about reservations/availabilities for/of campsites in the Saranac chain of lakes.

Frank made eye contact with his guy, but it was a few minutes before he was able to get someone to sub in for him so he could come over to speak with us.

"Frank," he said, "I'm assuming this is about …"

"Yup, Gerald, it is," Frank said. "This is Tyler Cunningham, and he's helping SLPD and the FBI figure out what happened. He's got questions I think you can help us with, and instead of filtering them through me, an' screwing up, he's just gonna ask you directly, okay?"

Gerald nodded, shook my hand, and looked expectantly at me.

"I need to know how people make reservations for the campsites," I said. "Who has access to that information? Then, I need you to give me access to as many of the reservations as possible, going back twenty years."

He looked up into the trees for a few seconds, then refocused directly on Frank. "I can't do that. You know I can't do that, Frank. That's all proprietary information. Heck, I don't even know if we own that data."

"This guy cut open the parents of a little girl," Frank said, "no older than your Marta, and she hid in the water, screamin' until I fished her out. I don't wanna hear any more about can't, or proprietary. And what do you mean, you don't know if you own the data? You're the ones who make the reservations for the campsites."

"Nope," Gerald said, warming up and getting rolling a bit, perhaps wanting to distract angry-Frank. "America Camping is the company that's been doing all of the reservations since about 2000. Everybody makes their reservations online, or by phone ahead of time, using the company website. Even walk-ins, people who drive up to the cabin asking if we've got a campsite for the night, have to go through the system. We either tell them to do it or help them do it with our own terminal. It's slow as hell when they do it that way."

"And you've been doing it like that since the millennium?" Frank asked, " I thought it was all still paper and checkmarks on maps."

"That's how the rangers do it when they're checking on site usage and such," Gerald said. "But yeah, Saranac Lake was one of the first places to go online. We helped America Camping develop and test the software."

My mind was racing, exploring the possibilities and implications of what he'd said.

"Were you here back when they set it up, Gerald?" I asked, hoping against hope.

"Nope, sorry," he said. "None of the DEC people who worked with the development team from America Camping are still working here, or even for the DEC anymore, now that I think about it. Bob and Frank and Taylor were, but they were the last, and they've been gone for years. Why?"

"Any of the original team might have access to the raw data, or know someone who does," I said, "and that would streamline getting at the information I need, and maybe speed things up a lot."

Gerald hung his head briefly, then it shot up hopefully. "The username and password have been the same since I got here, and were laminated into the book back then. Maybe it can give you whachur looking for."

"Let's go take a look," Frank said/commanded, and walked off, forcing Gerald and me to follow.

The cabin was crowded with people eager to get out to their campsites, people with random questions for the guys in green and tan uniforms, and now, us. Gerald shoved the intern behind the computer out of the way to pull out a drawer, grab a grimy three-ring binder that had been repaired with duct tape at least twice, and lead us to a tiny desk in the back of the cabin. He had flipped through a number of plastic-laminated sheets and sleeves before finding the one he was looking for ... it was an old piece of lined paper, torn out of a notebook, had some hand-scrawled notes on it. He pointed to a username and password at the top of the page:

username: ranger
password: saranac891

"That's what I've been using since I started here," Gerald said, "and it gets me everywhere on the AC website I need to go. What do you think?"

"That it brings some serious weaksauce in terms of security," I said, "but beyond that, I don't think it will allow me to drill down to the level of data access I'll need. American Camping wouldn't want rangers checking campers in their system to have access to deeper stuff that they could screw up … it'd be an *admin* account of some sort."

Gerald gave an excited squeak, flipped the page over, and looked with some confusion at the back which was unlined paper and showed a map apparently detailing proposed new and retired campsites … he looked at the paper for a few seconds, then reached into the top of the plastic sleeve and pulled out the lined sheet we'd been looking at before. Scattered across the back were phone numbers and names of people and email addresses of people in the America Camping hierarchy, along with another username/password, which he proudly poked with a stubby index finger:

username: sladmin
password: C1u3L355

"Frank," I said, "bring me home."

"Why?" Frank asked. "What's wrong?"

"Nothing," I said. "I think that's exactly what I need, and want to get to work."

"Wait, wait," Gerald said, "I'm not even sure it's okay for you to see this stuff, or look at the customer information until I check with the AC head office."

"Okay, Gerald," Frank said. "No problem. If you say wait, we'll wait. But can you send a request in today?"

"And you guys'll wait until I hear back?" Gerald asked.

I was taking mental snapshots of everything on this page and flipped it back over to the side we'd originally looked at to see if there was anything else that could possibly be useful … by the time Gerald noticed what I was doing, and gently took the paper out of my hand and slid it back into the sleeve, I had memorized a mixed bag of names and numbers and URLs and email addresses and phone numbers along with some keywords and login routes/routines.

"Sure," I said, trying to put a convincing tone into my voice and look on my face. "We'll wait until Frank hears back from you."

I started retracing our route back out of the tiny cabin and back to Frank's cruiser, not really listening/hearing the closing of the discussion/interview between Frank and Gerald. I was sitting in the front seat with the door propped open to avoid roasting when Frank got there 94 seconds later.

"I guess the second thingy was good news," he said.

"The username and password were promising for a number of reasons," I said, looking at him for a second before continuing, "that you don't care about, so I won't bore you with them."

"Gerald's gonna get in touch with whoever at the camping website, but it'll prolly take some time for it to turn around, either way," he said. "He wants to believe you're gonna wait to take a look under the skirts of the website, or database, or whatever. I assume you're not gonna wait?"

"That's a dumb question, Frank," I said, "since you likely already know the answer to it, and in any case you don't want to know the answer to it. Let me say unequivocally that I am not going to do anything illegal/immoral/ill-advised with whatever information we may, or may not, have gained from our talk with your friend Gerald (*the upside of lacking social/emotional software that most everyone else comes equipped with from the factory is that I am an utterly convincing liar*)."

"Exactly what I thought," Frank said, smiling a bit. "What's your next step, or steps?"

"First, I'll see if I can get in using the stuff we saw/learned," I said. "The next thing, at least as important is to find a way to, independent of the America Camping data, reduce my search field/parameters ... if I can get in at all, there will instantly be far too much data for me to manage/sift, so I need to find some ways to cut the amount or paper (*or screens*) that I need to look at. I've got some ideas, first among them is in line with your earlier request that I get out into the field, away from easy contact/summoning by your Mr. LaDuke."

"What should I tell him, and Brimley when they ask about what you're doing?" he asked.

"Tell them the truth," I said. "Tell them I'm working on something having to do with the campsites and victim selection, that it's computer-y, that it looks/sounds boring, and that you don't know any more than that."

"Sounds good," he said. "They'll believe alla that, from you and from me. Thank goodness for low expectations. Here we are."

I got out and nearly jogged to the Element, waving over my shoulder in response to whatever it was that Frank said as I dashed out of his car, then driveway, then neighborhood. I made a beeline for SmartPig, intent on ascertaining if I had access to the data I needed, and then hitting the lake for a few hours to eliminate campsites from the list of queries I'd drop into the America Camping system.

At first, I didn't notice anything out of place until I reached for the doorknob and saw the frame was splintered and a few significant pieces of the locking mechanism were on the floor, both outside and inside my once-secure offices. I had substantial security measures that rendered the door very secure once I was inside, but when leaving SmartPig, it was mostly a couple of good locks (*which was more than anyone else in Saranac Lake, but entirely insufficient when facing a sledgehammer, which is what my intruder appeared to have used to gain entry to my bat cave*). Everything inside my offices had been explored/damaged/violated by someone both curious and angry, as well as creative and energetic (*except, I noticed in a distant corner, on the top of a bookshelf, a small and old and scuffed wooden box I'd brought back with me from my trip to the Southwest last winter ... if I was the type to breathe a sigh of relief, I might have done so at that moment*). I looked around the room and thought and wondered for 13 seconds (*glad for the first time that Hope wasn't alive. She might have been here and exposed to this, only with more dire consequences than was possible with just stuff*), before turning around and heading to the library for their computers and a chance to think.

Downtown Saranac Lake, night to morning to midday

Vanilla had been driving around most of the night, restless and wired, pacing in his huge cage and rattling the bars. He drove out on Route 3 to Star Lake then back and down to Newcomb, then over and up to Plattsburgh before returning down Route 3 to Saranac Lake as the sky grew light again. He spent the night driving and thinking, fuming at both the fact that he'd taken the foolish chance in the hospital … and had failed. Pulling over occasionally at rest stops and parking lots, he would walk and stomp and cry to the heavens at his bad luck and curse the stupid girl. He talked, sometimes shouted to himself and Beast as they drove, pounding the wheel in frustration and crying at times, but never swerved across the yellow lines or onto the shoulder.

As always, Vanilla paid cash when he stopped for gas or food, and talked just enough to avoid piquing anyone's interest. He was medium everything: height, weight, tonal range, hair color, and length. None of his clothes had names or brands or places printed on them, and they were all in darkish earth tones. If he stopped moving or talking to you, your eyes would have trouble holding onto him.

Vanilla drove a dark blue pickup with an aftermarket cover on the back, just old enough that nobody could remember having seen it, or even whether it was a Ford or Dodge. The miles rolled by under his watchful eyes, steady hands, and measured foot on the gas, always five miles an hour under the limit. Like everything in his life, he maintained the truck perfectly, much of the work done himself in the workshop side of his big garage. Every time he stopped for gas or food or the bathroom, he walked around the truck, kicking the tires and checking the lights. He never drove farther than his mailbox without two spare tires, extra fuses and bulbs for every system, and a few thousand dollars in twenties and fifties stitched into a repaired seam in the driver's seat.

Vanilla had finished the long and quiet run through the empty woods between Cadyville and Vermontville with a mostly full tank of gas, but achy and stiff, in need of coffee and donuts, so he passed the turnoff that would have taken him home, and went through town to wait in the parking lot for Dunkin' Donuts to open. The truck that supplied the Saranac Lake DD rolled up at around half-past four, the same time a few employees started arriving, rubbing sleep out of their eyes and stretching in the cool, quiet air.

Even though it was past five by his watch when the kid unlocked the front door, Vanilla had forced himself not to be waiting by the door, as someone might remember a person who wanted coffee and donuts that badly. He was, however, their first customer of the day, and was walking out with an extra large coffee and a pair of plain donuts when the second customer walked in. Vanilla strolled by the man entering without focusing on his face. Instead, he dug for keys and looked out to the parking lot, and affected a bored and busy attitude. It was only when he sat in his truck, parked a row back from the front for security, that he realized it was Tyler Cunningham.

Vanilla had read and heard plenty about Cunningham in the last two years. People said he knew things nobody else knew and could figure out a person's secrets just by reading about him. It was for that reason that Vanilla and Beast had made it their business to stay clear of him, and never talk about him, just listen, and watch. Cunningham had purchased a big box of donuts, and was sitting at one of the tables, obviously waiting for a couple of people; Vanilla decided to wait and watch, at Beast's request.

Vanilla started his truck and drove around the parking lot, all the way over to the Advance Auto Parts, where he usually went to get the parts and supplies needed to maintain his truck. He parked for a minute, then drove back, this time with parking lights instead of headlamps, parking a few spaces over from his previous spot, and at an angle he hoped would change the profile of his truck to someone looking out the window of the donut shop. He turned off the engine and the lights after cracking the windows and settled down to wait and watch and drink coffee and eat donuts. He was good at waiting, had practiced over the years, could have waited in the truck, in the parking lot, for hours if need be. He didn't have a very long wait.

A quarter hour after Vanilla moved to his new blind, two cars pulled into the Saranac Plaza, and then into the slots closest to the front door of Dunkin' Donuts: an SLPD cruiser and a dark colored sedan with too many antennas on the roof to be civilian. Frank Gibson got out of the cruiser, looking like a bear stuffed into the uniform. A slick guy in a suit got out of the unmarked car, moving as though he'd already had his morning coffee. They both went in and sat down with Cunningham. A moment later, after what must have been greetings, both new men got up and went to the counter to order coffee and donuts.

It was impossible to tell what they were talking about, but Vanilla had to assume they were talking about him, and his work, his recent failure with that tiny bitch. They all looked to be on an even footing in the discussion, and before too long the meeting, or whatever it was, broke up and they went their separate ways. Vanilla had no idea which one, if any, to follow, so he listened to Beast's advice to follow Cunningham, curious when he saw him circle back for even more donuts.

Cunningham drove through town and pulled in at the animal shelter. Vanilla had heard he worked there sometimes, so he kept driving by, and looped back a few times, hoping to see Cunningham.

On his second pass, Tyler came out being towed behind what looked in the early morning light to be a black bear, disappearing into the woods as Vanilla drove around the turn and out of view. Beast was howling that they should take him, but Vanilla had a better idea.

They went home and spent a few hours hauling trophies out of hidey holes Vanilla had found or made in the old house over the years: a penknife from his first, shoelaces from a couple who had lived in Boston, a locket of hair from a child on his first camping trip, and so on. He also ripped out the carpeting of the barge he'd used the other night and burned some items in the huge metal gridwork box he used from time to time for burning garbage. The rest he double-bagged in giant, thick, contractor trash bags, which he shoved into the back of his truck. He then filled a squeegee bottle with Clorox and sprayed down everything he might have touched the other night, and any places he had stored trophies over the years. He had read that bleach destroyed DNA evidence, and even if it didn't, the caustic, clean bite in his nose and throat felt and smelled like safety to him.

Vanilla drove out of town on Route 86, decided he would treat himself to an ice cream cone at Donnelly's after visiting the dump in Lake Clear, briefly wondering what the flavor would be today, before turning west onto Route 186, in the general direction of the dump. He pulled in, waited his turn for the before/after scales, avoided eye contact and conversation with the guy in the shack at the scales, although they'd been in school together for 13 years, and threw the big bags into the huge container. When they hit bottom, a hanging cliff of crap was dislodged and buried his treasures, and he sensed Beast stretching and straining at his daylight bonds, grinding his teeth and hungry for Cunningham's blood.

After deep breathing for a minute and soaking up cool from his air-conditioned truck, Vanilla drove back around and paid for the loss of weight in those bags, and headed back out to the road with songs of vengeance in his heart and thoughts of ice cream in his head. All thoughts, vengeful or otherwise, fell out of his head when he pulled out onto Route 30, and was face to face with Cunningham driving his black Element toward Paul Smiths. It appeared Cunningham hadn't seen him, wasn't looking at him.

Vanilla drove two hundred yards or so, to the wide spot in the road next to the small cemetery, and pulled a U-turn, speeding a bit to try and catch up with Cunningham, maybe to see if he pulled his own to follow Vanilla. Coming around the turn just past the dump, Vanilla could see Cunningham's brake lights and turn signal as he pulled into the Lake Clear Beach parking lot. Vanilla followed him in, bringing Beast to the forefront now, ready to take Cunningham if the opportunity presented itself. It didn't.

Cunningham changed into swim trunks and brought a towel with him down to the water. There were dozens of people at the beach, based on the number of cars in the parking lot, so Vanilla went back up, hauling Beast away from the brink of action. Beast shouted out a counter-proposal that made some sense to Vanilla, although seeming ridiculously bold. They talked it out as they drove back into town and parked at the far end of the lot back behind Main Street, near the building where the old man Maurice rented space to Cunningham.

Beast took the reins and walked up the narrow stairs, feeling strong and scared and as though he was on the cusp of some new greatness, or disaster. He had always operated in darkness before, but here he was walking among regular people, ready to attack his enemies in their own homes. Necessity had diminished his options, and although desperate, he realized the power in his new position in the world. His only choice was forward, bold. It was now Beast's world. The time for calm and cautious and careful Vanilla has passed.

A flush spread across his face and chest. Adrenaline flooded his limbs. His eyes and ears grew more keen with every passing second, mounted step. He didn't even stop at the top of the stairs, just raise his heavy, booted foot, and kicked out at the door like a battering ram. The door was solid, but apparently just on the latch-lock, and flew open when it flexed inwards under the pressure of his full body weight and a second kick right next to the knob. He strode in, pulling on the gloves Vanilla had insisted upon and began to savage the world headquarters of SmartPig.

He wasn't searching for secrets so much as counting coup on an enemy who had filled him, briefly, with fear and uncertainty. As Beast tore and tossed and kicked and upset and sacked and ransacked the large single room, more and more of Cunningham's strength transferred to him, in much the same way it felt when he tasted his victims' blood in the woods, in the night, off his knife. Vanilla had cautioned him to be quiet, but Beast let loose a roar, daring someone, anyone, to come. He would take them, in broad daylight, in Cunningham's home, and paint the walls with their blood… bathe in it. Beast found nothing of use to him in figuring out what Cunningham was doing, or looking for, but before they left, Beast listened to Vanilla and opened cans of soda he found in the huge refrigerator and poured their contents into the guts of every piece of electronic equipment he could find, also on books and papers and clothes and paintings. Beast kicked over the fish tanks, glass and pebbles and water flooding across the floor, and stomped the flopping fish. He left only when the room was a shambles and his rage and fear at Cunningham was exhausted. Beast shrunk back into, inside Vanilla and made his way down to the parking lot, to his truck. All the way back home unseen, as always.

Lower Saranac Lake, NY
Friday. 7/10/2015, 6:27 p.m.

The landing outside of SmartPig felt too hot and stuffy to
bear, so I fled down the stairs and out into the alley
leading to Main Street. The ferocity of the attack on my
office, on my stuff, on me, was stunning and heady and
unnerving to a degree that shocked me. Getting up on the
busier street, with more people felt good, and I turned
left and crossed at the spot where Main Street and
Broadway part, continuing to the library to sit and think
and read and plan and, eventually, win.

"He knows you," Barry said from beside me, "and he
hates you. He wasn't just tossing your place, wasn't just
sending a message. He wants to kill you, wants to destroy
you. Justin and I didn't have anything like that going for
us when we went up against you. If we had, we might
have beaten you."

"Thanks, Barry," I said, ignoring the curious stare
from an elderly woman I passed coming out of the door
of the Community Store. "That helps ... really makes me
feel better about the way things are going, puts me at
ease."

"That wasn't my intent, Tyler," he said, missing my
labored efforts at sarcasm somehow (*even though he was
definitely/definitively on the inside*). "I'm trying to warn you to
be careful with this guy because the inside of your melon

159

is the only place I exist anymore."

I nodded and walked into the library.

It was shocking to me that I could walk past people who knew me, had seen or talked to me before, without them seeing/knowing the level of violation I was carrying/managing. I sat on one of the comfy couches in the library magazine room for a slow count of 307 seconds (*307 seemed appropriate, being both a prime and the HTTP status code calling for a temporary redirect*), breathing slowly and evenly and letting my brain feel around for what I'd lost, what it would cost me, what it would cost any progress in the short term. Everything I needed most was in my brain and on the America Camping files, so that wasn't a significant problem. The killer obviously knew I was involved now and looking for him (*might think, in fact, I was actually looking at him*), so my approach and visible role from this point on would have to change.

Before I could do anything else, I needed to verify that Frank and I had found something useful in talking with Gerald and that I had the pertinent access pathways in my head. I signed up on the clipboard sheet for some time on one of the public computers and resolved before I was done filling out the request that I would need better resources than the library could offer me. I estimated a 20-minute wait before I would sit at the keyboard, so I stepped out to make a trio of quick calls.

"Dot, I have a pair of favors to ask," I said once I got ahold of her at the TLAS. "I ran into a bit of trouble and need to buy the computer I helped you pick out for Lisa's birthday from you. I'll replace it with an identical one I'll express from Amazon. Also, I need the number for your friend Mona, who you said works for that company that does extreme cleaning."

"What the hell happened?" she asked. "Are you

okay?"

"I'm fine (*which wasn't necessarily a given because I'd been injured in the performance of my duties as a consulting detective in the Adirondacks in the past*). The killer must have found out somehow that I'm involved in the investigation, got into, and trashed, SmartPig, and I'm left without my tech or a place to sleep."

"I'll bring the computer by ASAP, I assume you need it now," she said, "and I feel really bad, but I can't offer you our couch. You know how Lisa feels about this sort of thing, me too I guess (*things had changed a bit after the previous winter when Dot was nearly beaten to death during an investigation*) when you come right down to it."

"No worries, Dot, seriously," I said. "I understand. I'd like to be a bit further back from all of this stuff too. I don't generally creep out, but SmartPig looks like a pack of wild dogs was turned loose in it, which brings me to my other point, Mona."

Dot gave me Mona's full name and number and promised to meet me outside the library in ten minutes with Lisa's/my new laptop; we hung up and I dialed Mona.

"Hi, Mona," I said. "My name is Tyler Cunningham, and you don't know me, but we have a friend (*I don't know that Dot is exactly a friend, but calling her one makes for a quicker explanation*) in common, Dorothy. She told me about what you do for …"

"Clean-Tech, yeah," Mona said, "and Dot's told me about you (*she chuckled a bit under her breath, which made me wonder what, and how much, Dot had told her … but that was a problem for another day*). What can I do for you?"

"I need your professional services," I said. "My office was broken into, the door is broken, doorframe is badly damaged, and everything in the space has been destroyed/vandalized. I'd like Clean-Tech to clean it to the paint on the walls, and varnish on the floor, and cart everything else away; if you have a person that you work with who can repair the damage to the door and frame and any other damage, that'd be great."

"Sure, yeah, we can do that," she said. "There's a guy in Saranac Lake we work with who does general contracting and painting, as needed. It's not cheap, though, did Dot tell you?"

"I have more money than anything else in the world, Mona," I said, the pathetic nature of that truth creeping into my voice a bit … I felt tired. "I'd be more than willing, enthusiastic even, to pay extra if you and Clean-Tech could postpone any current jobs you're on and bump me and my home (*I noted that I didn't call it SmartPig or my office*) to the top/front of the list. If Dot told you what I do, then you might appreciate that I'll owe you a favor if you can make this happen (*everybody has bad luck, bad days, and I'm pretty good bad luck/day insurance if I do say so myself*)."

She took a few seconds to think, possibly picturing their workload in the coming days, and said, "I'll be down with a Clean-Tech crew tomorrow morning at seven. If you can meet me at your office with a two-thousand-dollar deposit, we'll get started and work things out from there. Cash is better than a check for us."

"I've always felt the same way, Mona," I said. "It smooths out life's bumpy road like a heavy earth-moving machine. (*My use of figurative language was improving, but it was still admittedly a work in progress.*) I'll be there before seven with a short-stack of cash for you (*now I was thinking about pancakes*) … thank you."

As soon as we'd hung up, I dialed Meg's number. She picked up only after the machine had already answered the phone *(indicating to me that she'd been out back with the dogs).*

"Meg," I said. "Tyler. I'm sorry to bug you again so soon, but I'm wondering if I could sleep in Austin's room tonight, and possibly tomorrow night?"

"Of course," she said. "As long as you need. What's wrong? What's happened? Are you all right? Did you call Frank? Should I call Frank?"

"Breathe, Meg," I said. "That's a lot of questions. Their answers are: nothing major, someone broke into SmartPig, I'm fine, no, and no, you shouldn't call him."

I didn't do that just to be obnoxious … Meg has an orderly mind, and this forced her to replay her tape and compare it to my responses, defusing her, at least partly.

"Tyler, is there a reason you don't want to tell Frank?" she asked. "There might be clues, or DNA, or a witness, or something."

"It's possible, Meg. But I don't think so. More importantly, I don't want what is probably minor league vandalism to distract Frank and company from the important parts of the investigation. My bet is that nobody saw or heard anything useful. Beyond that, I don't want Frank's, and especially Agent Brimley's attention to shift from what they're doing toward me and my break-in." (*I wanted to stay below everyone's radar until I had a better picture of the killer's methodology and systems, and could put some plans of my own in place.*) "It's likely (*not very*) that the break-in had nothing to do with the killer we're looking for, and, in that case, I wouldn't want them to divert resources from the real investigation."

"Well," she said, uncertainly, "what do we, do I, tell Frank? I'm not going to lie to him about important stuff. We don't do that." (*I assumed that she meant she didn't lie to Frank because I did, all the time.*)

"Tell him that I was a little scared to sleep alone in SmartPig or in the woods while all of this was going on, which is the truth. If you're going to feel uncomfortable about this, I can find somewhere else to stay, Meg (*now slightly worried about not being able to get out of this at all, and wishing I'd just stayed at a hotel with wireless, which was no longer an option*)."

"No, Tyler," she said, with a sigh. "We'll make it work." (*I resolved to drive in loops and park some distance away from their house each time I went there, or anywhere else peopled with those I care about until this business was finished.*)

"Meg," I said, "thanks a ton, but Dot's here and I've got to go, but I'll see you later."

I hung up and waved, in case Dot hadn't yet seen me. She flashed her headlights and pulled over beside the Element.

"Hey there, stranger," she said. "Wanna buy a laptop?"

The laptop I'd helped her pick out for Lisa's approaching birthday was sitting on the passenger seat, wrapped, with a bow and a card ... I felt guilty/angry/sad (*or at least my best approximations of these emotions*). She followed my glance and nodded.

"It's not a problem, Tyler, it really isn't," she said. "As long as you have a replacement for this one wrapped and ready to go before the twenty-fourth. How bad is SmartPig?"

"Bad," I said, the depth of feeling in my answer surprised me ... it was just a place, just stuff, but the violation felt bigger than that, somehow. "Really Bad."

"Mona called a few minutes ago," she said. "Must have been right after she got off the phone with you. She asked if you had the green to pay for a rush job, along with some repairs and repainting. I told her you were good for it."

"Thanks," I said, "for everything. Can you pull three-thousand dollars from the cash cache I've got not-so-hidden in the ceiling above your bathroom? (*I'd asked her years ago for permission to use her apartment as a remote storage facility for money, and I'd ended up needing it a few times over the years.*) "Would you mind bringing it with you to the shelter tomorrow morning? ... I'll swing by and pick it up on my way to meet with Mona."

She nodded. I reached into the open window, grabbed the present, pulled it back out and started ripping/pulling the paper off. Dot made a face.

"I gotta head back to the shelter," she said. "Call me when you make a breakthrough with this guy. I still wanna help you if I can, without, you know."

Of course, I knew and nodded, "Thanks so much, Dot. You always come to my rescue ... I wish I was more ... better at being a friend."

I finished unwrapping my present (*since I had it, it was mine ... logic!*) inside the library, mostly filling one of their ridiculously tiny trash cans with the paper and leaning the box against the can. Plastic and bubble-wrap and another box and some Styrofoam later, I had a laptop and plugged it into the wall to build up a bit of a charge before I began.

Giving it a minute, I opened up the browser, navigating to the America Camping website, thinking about (*and rejecting the idea/concept of*) crossing my fingers before I tried the ancient admin username and password we'd found earlier. It worked. The screen that loaded was not the pretty consumer-side thing meant for customers, but the utilitarian interface that programmers designed for other programmers. I dropped down through some menu options to explore my access to current and past reservations, to see how the data was organized, and how searchable it was. Just to see if I could, I did a historical search of campsite #35 (*the Richardses' campsite*) for this year, eliminating all people registered for the campsite with New York license plates (*they had to register an address, automobile information, number of tents/boats/people in their party, as well as payment/contact info*) ... a second later I had 37 results (*37 is the 12th prime, and is permutable with 73, the 21st prime; 12 and 21 are also permutable ... I viewed this as auspicious, and a sign of great things/data to come*).

Once I had proven both I could access the data on camping reservations and sort the mountains of data within the America Camping system, I had to do a bit of leg (*really paddle*) work to develop a smaller sample-size of possible sites to work with before I could really begin to crunch the data.

I left the library, laptop and cord under my arm, and headed back through the busy part of town, looking around only when I started to head down the alley that would bring me back to my Element. The perpetrator had followed me at some point and also gained access to SmartPig. (*I had briefly chastised myself for not engaging/using all of my security measures ... it had simply not occurred to me that I might need to, that he would engage me so soon, if at all.*) Also, I couldn't help feeling exposed in the backstreets and away from the press of people. I quickly pulled my Hornbeck canoe from the shed where I kept it most of the time, strapped it onto the roof of the Element, and drove away. Although I wanted to stop at Meg's, to drop off the laptop and get it plugged in and charging, first I navigated a series of loops through/around town. No way anybody could have followed me unless they had a helicopter or satellite devoted to the task (*or a GPS tracker, but I was willing to assume our guy didn't have access to any of these things*), so I felt reasonably safe parking for a minute to run in, plug in the laptop, say a quick hi to Meg, and run back out, promising to tell her everything (*patently a lie, I never tell anyone everything*) when I returned in a few hours.

I drove more loops on my way out of town, eventually finding my way out onto Route 3, heading toward the state boat launch and beyond that, Tupper Lake. I overshot the turnoff for Crescent Bay Marina, and pulled a U-turn just past their big steel shed, keeping an eye out for anyone hitting their brakes or seeming interested in me. It occurred to me, as it often has before, that the Adirondacks is an easy place to follow someone and a tough place to lose them ... we just don't have many roads up here to get from any one place to any other place. Given the givens, though, I felt somewhat safe pulling down to the water and launching my canoe into the calm afternoon waters of Lower Saranac (*despite the fact that Crescent Bay is a private, not a public, launch ... one of the owners owes me a favor from last winter, and I was sure she'd recognize my car and not tow or hassle me*).

Layers of worry/stress/paranoia (*I hadn't been fully aware of*) fell away as I took the first few strokes out into the protected waters of the eponymous Crescent Bay, then turned to the right/west, and around Eagle Island, which had the first five campsites I wanted to put eyes on. From the map I had, campsite #1 appeared a likely contender, but the ground truth on site was different ... it included a DEC dock and station (*possibly maintenance supplies for all of the campsites*) directly across from the campsite, and only a hundred and fifty yards away. Campsite #2 had seemed on the map as though it might be too exposed via sightlines to other nearby campsites, but it really wasn't ... I marked it as viable.

I spent the next 187 minutes looping my way through

the most likely islands and campsites I'd marked on my map of Lower Saranac Lake, eliminating some, adding a few, and at the end I had a list of nine campsites (*out of the sixty campsites on this lake*) that seemed reasonable options if I had been a serial killer who wanted/needed to kill people and get away with it. It was certainly possible that he had some on his list that I did not, and vice versa ... but the odds were good there would be significant overlap. I had cut the number of possible sites by 85 percent, which would result in an 85 percent reduction in the number of records I'd need to look through to find my/his possible victims.

Quite an odd contrast, paddling in my beautiful boat on a lovely lake on a gorgeous day, trying to deconstruct horrible murders committed by a terrible human. I found I was able to focus on the good things about what I was doing, and drop the bad things into a box I shuffled to the back of my brain. By the time I pulled my Hornbeck boat from the water, strapped it to the roof, pulled back up and out on Route 3, and looped my way back into Frank and Meg's neighborhood, I had a sunburn. I parked at the Algonquin Apartments, waited a full ten minutes in the car to see if anyone took any interest in me, and then went cross-country (*through woods and people's yards in a way that had to throw off anyone following me in a car*) before arriving at Casa Gibson, hopefully in time for some dinner before I got down to large piles of paperwork (*even though it would likely be digital paperwork, which sounds oxymoronic, but isn't*).

Casa Gibson, Saranac Lake, NY
Friday, 7/10/2015, 11:53 p.m.

"Tyler," Meg called out from the kitchen as I walked in, "come back here and tell me about your afternoon."

I returned to the kitchen fending off leaps from the excited dogs on my way back … Toby and Lola weren't used to seeing so much of me and were letting me know they were happy about it (*besides loving me, they approve of the fact that I am much less concerned about feeding dogs people-food than Meg and Frank, which they're definitely in favor of*). Meg was in the midst of chopping and prepping for a huge salad (*she seems to forget that she and Frank are just two people when she makes meals … three with me as a guest, but still*). Based on the foodstuffs covering most of the available counter space, it looked like a variation on a Caesar salad, with more summer vegetables (*and fruit, if you count tomatoes and other turncoat salad fixings as fruit, which I don't … I'm looking at you, avocados and cucumbers*), and lots of tastes/textures/colors. I helped myself to a knife and cutting board and started halving/seeding/peeling/cubing avocados (*because I enjoy working with avocados … the textural contrast between skin and seed and flesh intrigues me*).

"I paddled all around Lower Saranac, looking at campsites," I said, "trying to decide which ones I'd use to kill people, if I was so inclined."

She scraped a knuckle with the carrot peeler she was

using … I'd likely distracted her (I *never peel carrots because I like the way the skin tastes*). "Shit, Tyler!" she said and jammed the offended/offending finger into her mouth. After sucking on the injured knuckle for a few seconds, she continued, "And of what benefit will your field trip be in your further investigations?"

"I eliminated most of the campsites as likely places our bad guy would select to kill people, due to proximity and sightline issues. All told, I think there are nine possible/likely campsites, out of sixty. Out of a possible nine thousand records per year, my field trip eliminated 7,650."

"And how many years of records are you going to look at?" she asked.

"Probably the last decade, so call it thirteen thousand records," I said. "But of those, I can probably eliminate about nearly a third because they'll be in-state, which I think he avoids. That takes us down to about eight thousand, and I bet half of those are groups too big for him to try … you can see how it goes. I have a long night ahead of me, but I should have something to talk with Frank and Agent Brimley tomorrow or the next day."

"Does it creep you out?" Meg asked, and then looked away, embarrassed (*I couldn't see why she would be, but assumed she'd explain it to me*). "Climbing inside this guy's head, all of these people's heads that you figure out, being so good at it?"

"Not really," I said. "It's just something I can do. I find it more interesting than painting Jack Miller's house, so I do it."

She was concentrating too hard on cutting little coins from the carrots she'd peeled and stayed doing that for nineteen seconds, before turning her face up to look at me again, a bit of guilt/sorrow in the arrangement of facial muscles and eyes. "I'm sorry, Tyler, I didn't mean anything."

"Meg, what on Earth could you have to be sorry for?" I asked. "You didn't say anything to feel bad about."

"No," she said, "but I feel as though I implied you're like them, and that makes me feel like I betrayed you, a little."

"I am like them," I said. "Not in the important ways, not in the worst ways ... but like those old Apple ads, I *think different*. It makes me useful in trying to figure out, understand, people like this guy, or Steve Street or Petr Edelmann (*naming a few she knew, and leaving out some names she didn't know about, people who'd met with messy ends because of my ability to think, and act, different than normal*). I'm not them, not this guy I'm helping Frank look for, but I get what you mean, and maybe why you felt bad.

"Don't though," I continued, "feel bad. Don't worry, don't feel sad/bad for me. I like who I am, and where I am ... you and Frank, and Toby and Lola (*I added, scratching ears with one hand while passing out some avocado with the other*), Dot and John, and the rest of the people in my life up here, and all of those from before, all together made/make me who/what I am. I don't know if that makes sense."

She put down her chopping knife, wiped off her hands on a dish towel over her left shoulder, and came over to grab my face with both hands and give me a kiss on my cheek. "It makes sense, and finally, after nearly thirteen years, you are starting to make sense," she said, eyes shinier than normal. "Promise to be careful. It would be a horrible waste to let yourself get killed by this asshole after finally finding out who you are, and where you fit in the world, and how."

Frank came through the front door like an angry/

tired/sweaty rhino, and the dogs ran out to check on him; seventeen seconds later, he stomped into the kitchen, nodding at the two of us, uniform shirt already unbuttoned and trailing him like a rumpled/sweat-stained flag or cape. He grabbed two beers in a dexterous paw and sat down in a kitchen chair with a crash and the look of a deflating balloon.

"Fucking suits," he said. "They could mess up a cold beer!"

Toby and Lola sat and wagged, looking sorry/sad/ashamed for whatever they'd done, and were so perfectly earnest that halfway through a long tilt of beer, Frank started to smile around the bottle, leaning forward to let both of them cover his face with kisses. Meg relaxed next to me, letting out a breath she'd been holding, perhaps waiting to see which way Frank was going to go.

"Why don't you go and wash the day off, sweety, and we can talk about how the suits make your life, and job, more difficult when you're in your comfies," Meg said. "Tyler's joining us for supper, and spending the night in Austin's room. After your shower, he can fill you in on how his largely suitless investigation is going while we eat."

Frank came back into cop-focus for a moment, looking at me from flip-flops to earlobes for … something (*only he knew what, and whether or not he found it*); he nearly asked a question, but chose not to for some reason. Instead, he finished the first beer and dropped the empty in the recycling tub next to the fridge, swerving back by the table on his way out of the room to grab the second bottle before clomping upstairs, followed by the dogs.

"You remember the renovations we did to the upstairs last year, Tyler?" Meg asked.

I nodded, keeping eye contact, but mostly wondering about how much trouble I'd be in if I grabbed a couple of slices of American cheese from the fridge to help me survive until dinner.

"One of the things we did was put in a new shower stall," she continued, "a huge thing that Frank gave me no end of grief about. It's four by eight, and has multiple shower heads and a bench and sauna capability."

I nodded, sliding around the rim of the room slowly, reaching into the fridge for another Coke, and then back in and feeling for the cheese; Meg extended a graceful leg and foot out, and with just the toe, kicked the door closed, with a definitive shake of her head.

"Anyway, if you listen in about a minute, you'll hear Frank singing," she said. "Austin and I have assured him we can't hear it, or he'd stop. If you went up and could get into the bathroom without Frank shooting you, you'd see Toby and Lola standing in the shower with him while he sings to them, sometimes with them."

I looked up at the ceiling where I knew their bathroom was, could hear some singing (*Springsteen, I thought*), and now was powerless not to picture Frank and Toby and Lola singing a trio in the shower.

"The singing, and music, in general, helps him disconnect from the stress of his work, and to refocus his mind," she said, pointedly (*although I was certainly missing the point*). "I've been thinking more about your playlists project, and wondering about bringing it into my work at the school."

Meg and Frank had both given me their playlists shortly after I mentioned the concept one night when they had me over for shepherd's pie (*not my favorite of her meals, but edible*).

"This shower routine is better than therapy or beer or

talking over supper or watching Jon Stewart," she said, and looking ahead through her cute story, I thought I could see where she was going. "He's better at his job, better with Austin and me, and in a better place because of that shower, and most especially, those dogs."

"I'm not ready for another dog," I said, pre-empting. "I go to the shelter, and walk these dogs and just don't feel the connection I had with … her. Someday I might, but it'll have to be the right dog. I just haven't met him or her yet."

Meg went back to chopping for a carrot's length of time, then turned back to face me, making her point with the knife tip.

"I wasn't talking about you," she said. "Well, not entirely. I was talking about Frank being more than the man you know. Working together on this case could be good for both of you if you can stretch your definitions of, and comfort with, each other."

"Agreed," I surprised myself slightly by saying, "and I think that's why we're both doing it … that and Edith, the girl. She got to both of us. The thing is, Meg, we both also need to be careful. I'm not a cop, and the things I sometimes do (*oops, edging too far into truthiness*), the way I do things, could pollute the way Frank, a cop, does things, or the outcomes, legal and otherwise. Similarly, although using the resources available to Frank, and the FBI, is a massive temptation, it comes with a big price tag … greater scrutiny, and possibly massive legal trouble and/or jail time."

Meg made a face indicating she was about to laugh/scoff, so I cut her off, wanting to finish before Frank got back down to the kitchen (*and I could hear him thumping around in other parts of the upstairs now*). "Think about the outcomes of the thing with Xander as compared with the couple out in Onchiota."

"You saved Xander's life and figured out who the bad guy was. He fled the Adirondacks (*actually, he's buried in a shallow grave near the south end of Fish Pond, which is a part of my point, but a difficult point to make to a cop's wife, in their home*), and Xander was cleared of his sister's murder," she said. "And I never heard of the couple you helped out up in Onchi."

"My point exactly," I said. "The thing with Xander and his bad guy was big, had lots of moving parts, including the police, and I think I took my eye off the ball a bit (*nice use of figurative language there to clarify/make my point, though, if I do say so myself, my speech therapist would have been proud*), and Cameron (*a guy who could have grown to be a friend of sorts*) got killed. The thing in Onchiota was below the radar of the law enforcement community, but had the potential to be just as nasty/messy/bloody, but I made it work because I kept all of the parts/pieces under control."

"Cut to the summary statement, Tyler," she said, with a little growl in her tone, "and in a way that doesn't make it sound like it's Frank's fault that that sweet Cameron is dead."

"I don't in any way think/feel/believe that Frank was in any way to blame for Cameron's death," I said, looking her right in the eyes (*but also, wondering if I could get away with eating a few quick slices of bread … I literally felt as though I was starving to death waiting for Frank to come back down*). "It's entirely on me. I'm able to figure things out and make plans, but they tend not to work as planned because I don't take the human element into account effectively/efficiently. It seems to get worse when I have standard humans on both sides of the equation/solution to work with, and I guess I'm worried that might be what happens with this thing about Edith and her parents and the serial killer. There are so many moving parts, and it's so complex, I worry that I'll make the same mistakes I normally do, and someone will get hurt or killed because of me."

"You're an asshole," Frank said, coming back into the room with Toby and Lola (*both of whom were noticeably damp to the touch, but to a uniform degree which implied, to me at least, they had been towel-dried*). "We've talked about this before, Tyler. You're one of the good guys. Weird as hell, and you certainly work outside of standard police procedures, but you get the job done and this corner of the world is better for having you in it. If you hadn't stepped in, Xander might be inside that hospital up near P-burgh, Steve Street would still be walking around town (*his eyes shifted away from mine when he said this, and I wondered briefly how much he knew, or suspected about what happened back in the woods of the Saint Regis Canoe Wilderness, between the carries*), and he might have killed Cameron or Xander or the parents or someone else anyway. An' if you think we don't know about the Turners, an' what happened with Mitch up in Onchi, then you mebbe aren't as smart as we all hope you are."

"It sounded like Toby was barking at something upstairs while you were in the shower," Meg said, with a rigidly composed face, but sparkling eyes. "Was he upset that you locked him out?"

Frank went to the fridge for another beer, this one a Sam Adams Light, ignoring her question/redirect and turned back to me after opening it. "I think that fucking Brimley and the suit I wasted my afternoon with, have an idea of what you're gonna be doing for us to help us catch the guy. I see it a little differently, knowing you a bit, and having worked with, or at least near you, in the past. I'm happy to do my thing, and let you do yours, and if you get to the finish line first, help out if I can."

"That sounds reasonable," I said.

"Yup," Frank said. "And continuing along that reasonable track (*he said as Meg carried a tray of things for supper down and out to their back yard, leaving us briefly alone in the kitchen*), I would be very happy if at the end of all of this you and I were able to cuff and bring in this guy, alive, so he can stand trial. It has not escaped my notice that both George Sears and Steve Street hit the road and were never seen or heard from again, by anyone, after tangling with you. Guys like them generally don't disappear as thoroughly or effectively as George and Steve did, just sayin' is all."

I felt myself straightening slightly, and preparing a deflection/rebuttal, but it apparently wasn't needed.

"Shut up," he said before I could even begin to speak. "I don't want to hear it, don't want to talk about it, don't even really want to think about it."

At that point, Meg reappeared from the pantry and Frank seamlessly (*possibly seamlessly I wondered, as he didn't seem to change anything, but …*) shifted gears.

"Here, honey," he said, in a lighter tone. "Let me get the salad, and Tyler can haul the drinks down."

Dinner was fantastic, and for the next twelve minutes, nobody said anything outside of making yum noises. Meg then talked a bit about the summer sessions she was running: a social group for some kids who struggled forming and maintaining functional social relationships, with whom she cooked and played games and took trips out into the community; and an intro to psychology course for some high school students who were packing their transcripts prior to college visits in the coming year. Meg got Frank talking about the afternoon meeting with

LaDuke, but he started to redden after two minutes, and she redirected to my afternoon in the boat, and how that was going to dovetail with the info we'd gotten access to thanks to Gerald at the boat launch.

"You sure you don't need someone to help you wade through all of those records?" Frank asked. "The Feebs love that shit."

"Thanks," I said. "But I don't need/want help, and if I did, it wouldn't be someone from the FBI. Whispering my results in Brimley's ears is in no way what I'm looking for. Besides, you remember we can't actually use or look at this data until America Camping gives us permission, which smart money says they won't."

"Why not?" Meg asked, "Surely they'd want to help out with stopping a murderer."

"Any big company finds it much easier to say *no* than *yes*, honey, to anything," Frank answered, although she'd asked me. "That, and even if they wanted to help, their legal department exists to help them avoid liability and exposure to lawsuits. If it turns out Tyler is right and the killer picked his victims using their data, their website, they'll be sued forever and for everything by everyone."

"So what's the point?" Meg asked. "What good will it do to find out how he chose his victims?"

"More information is more better," I said. "Every little bit we know about this guy and how he works will help us find and trap him ... and even if we can't legally acknowledge/use the America Camping data, once we know who the guy is, the FBI will be able to build a case from the sheer amount of evidence they'll gather from his home and friends and neighbors and coworkers and people he went to grade school with and going through his garbage ... that's what they do, what they excel at."

"So say tonight goes perfectly, and you sift through

thousands, or tens of thousands of records of people who've been camping on Lower Saranac for the last twenty years," Frank said, warming to the subject (*which had an inversely chilling effect on me, as we neared the outer boundary of his onion layer, and I mentally scrambled for a reasonable distraction/diversion*), "and come up with a list of likely victims ... what's next?"

"It's a little tricky," I admitted. "I'll have to bring my list of names to Brimley for him to compare with the list he's generated since he started keeping an eye on me, twelve and a quarter years ago ... the bomb in the hospital thing. Then he can ... no, wait. You can run the names I come up with against a list of missing people, even in other states, right?"

"Yup," Frank nodded. "If I don't run it through the FBI databases, they might not even notice, or at least not for a while. Why?"

"The less he knows about what I'm doing, the better," I said, "because we're (*I was careful to stress 'we're'*) going to use the FBI to help us build a trap, allowing you to put the guy in cuffs and stuff him in the back of your cruiser."

"How?" Frank and Meg asked (*and it looked like Toby and Lola also wondered, because they gazed at me when their parents did ... I reached down and gave each of them a chin scratch and a piece of chicken from the salad ... Toby and Lola that is, not Meg and Frank*).

"I'm not one hundred percent on that yet," I said. "More like forty-seven percent, but it's coming, and I'm confident I'll have something by morning, or at the latest the next day ... my plan is to get this guy in the next few days."

"No fuggin' way," Frank said. "We're weeks, or months, maybe years, away from catching this guy. I'd bet you a Benjamin there's no chance we have him before the end of July (*he seemed confident of this, but his confidence might have come from knowing I don't make wagers*)."

"I'll take that bet, sweet-cheeks," Meg said. "But instead of money, I'll bet you our spring vacation. If you and Tyler get this guy by July thirty-first, we go to Santa Fe. If you don't have him by close of business August first, we'll go to Cape Canaveral. Deal?"

Frank looked over at me, appraisingly/thoughtfully/anxiously, for a few moments before he nodded. He seemed genuinely torn when he reached across the table to shake on it with Meg. (*I didn't point out the seventeen-hour dead zone in the proposal she'd put forward … it didn't seem germane.*)

We cleared the remnants of supper up and into the kitchen, and ate ice cream sandwiches standing around the kitchen. (*I broke one in half and gave the bits to the dogs, under the scornful, but eventually accepting, stares of Meg and Frank.*) Frank did dishes, as he always does, and I excused myself to go up to Austin's room to start working, looking at records on my/Lisa's computer.

Once I got the hang of how the America Camping systems worked, I was able to search each of my nine favored campsites for the five-month season of each year for occupancy by less than three people, from out of state. I eliminated people who indicated they were bringing a pet (*on the assumption that pets would be too tricky for our guy to try sneaking up on*). After some time spent exploring and familiarizing myself with the system, I was able to generate a folder with only 1260 records, somewhat less than I had expected.

I thought 1260 was an interesting number for a couple of reasons. First, it is the smallest of the vampire numbers … which is most interesting simply for its name (*so feel free to ignore what follows if you wish*). Second, it is the sixteenth smallest of the highly composite numbers, which means it has more divisors than any smaller positive integer. Although credit for the term was given to Srinivasa Ramanujan in 1915, Plato made use of the concept numerous times more than two thousand years earlier when describing the optimum number of citizens for a city (*Plato referenced the number 5040, because of its highly divisible nature, suggesting that being able to divide a given population into the maximum number of groups/combinations was advantageous*). I wondered/wandered for a few minutes, trying to imagine, envision how the number of possible victims could possibly be related to the killer or victims or the community of campsites on Lower Saranac Lake before a loud/chainsaw/fake snoring sound from the bed behind me pulled me back from the sea of numbers in which I was swimming.

"Jesus, Tyler," Barry said. "You are the most boring person alive or dead, on this planet. How the hell did I end up stuck in your head?"

"Barry," I said, "what do you want? Why are you here?"

"I don't know why I'm here," he said, in a flat/tired voice. "I really don't. You should ask Gibson's wife, she's the head-shrinker."

While I had debated talking with Meg about Barry a number of times in the years since he came into my life/head/consciousness, there was/is/would be too much about our relationship that I wouldn't feel comfortable/safe going into, which seemed a self-defeating start to any work with a counselor ... so I'd limited my discussion/reflection about the nature of my haunting by Barry to talks with John, although Dot knew about him (*Dot knows pretty much everything about me, but it's*

one of the things we don't talk about much … that and Bronsen,
the man who very nearly killed her two winters ago), or at least
knew of his existence.

"I think you're here because I'm nervous about
screwing up at finding and trying to beat this guy, worried
that I'm not smart/strong/resourceful enough to beat
him *and* outsmart the cops and the FBI at the same time,"
I said. "I can't worry about that now. I need a list of
possible victims so I can see if my theory is right, and
from there tighten up my partial plan for catching this
guy."

"So do it," Barry said. "Who's stopping you?"

He tipped a trucker cap down over his eyes and went
back to sleep on the only bed in the room. It would be
better for me if he left before I decided to get some sleep,
so I didn't embarrass myself by sleeping on the floor or
on a couch downstairs (*Barry guffawed at this, and then left me*
to my work after murmuring, "fuggin' Plato an' compostable
numbers").

I divided the list of records/possibles into singletons
and pairs and then started googling them along with their
listed state of residence at the time of their visit to the
Adirondacks. Lots of people don't leave much of a mark
on the world by dint of their passage through it, but most
unavoidably leave some traces on Google or Facebook.
By the time I was out of Cokes and almost ready to take a
nap, I had a list of 34 of the singletons, and 78 people
from the list of pairs/couples that might be missing. I
couldn't imagine that the Lower Saranac Lake Campsite
Killer (*way too long/cumbersome … it'd need some work*) had
killed 112 people (*not counting the people I had likely missed*),
but I was willing to bet he'd killed some of them.

Sneaking downstairs as quietly as was possible for me
(*and Toby and Lola, who were delighted to show me where*

everything in the kitchen was, especially the treats and kibble ... in her excitement Lola tripped on her food dish, and the stainless steel bowl skittering all over the floor was quite possibly the noisiest thing I had heard in years), I grabbed a cooler from the stairs down to the basement that I filled with Cokes and cheese slices ... think-fuel for the next couple of hours.

Something about the still-echoing clatter of Lola's food-dish, in combination with sneaking (*perhaps pointlessly*) back up the stairs like a ninja, gave me a peek at the tiniest edge of an idea. I drained a quick Coke, fought off the cold headache that wanted to split my skull, went back down the hall to the bathroom (*unaccustomed, after years of sleeping outside or in SmartPig, to the feel of deep carpeting under my toes in the nighttime darkness*) to splash my face and let the idea germinate and sprout while I pretended to do other things.

Once more fully formed, I spun the nascent plan around in my head, trying to see it from every angle.

"Ooof," Barry said, from his brain's eye view. He was the first person besides myself (*if he was to be counted as such, and for my money, he was*) exposed to it. "That's a doozy, even for you, Tyler. There is no way for that pile of steaming crap of a plan to work out like you're hoping, without getting someone on *Team White Hat* killed."

"I admit, it probably needs some tweaking," I said. "But given the crowded field of play, and the urgency on both sides of the equation, I can't help but think it's got some merit. To shore it up a bit, I'll need to talk with someone, or a couple of someones, outside of my skull to poke holes in my thinking, and try to patch them. But before that, I need to extend my look at the America Camping data back a few more years, and broaden it to make sure I'm not missing anything ... or any campsites."

Going back to my original search parameters, I

extended them back to 1998, the first year America
Camping had online operations (*or at least records in their
system*). Following that, I did a search of the entire span
for another five campsites on Lower Saranac that our
killer might have used. I didn't think any of them were
nearly as likely as the original nine I'd identified, but I
didn't want to miss anything. After my 'Elimination by
Google' method (*patent pending*) of winnowing down the
possible suspects, I had another 137 possible … making a
total of 249 potentially missing/dead persons spread out
among the fourteen campsites over seventeen years,
which was a strangely huge number, although less than I
had originally suspected I would find (*I was of the opinion,
based on what I'd read over the years, that there was no way this
guy had killed 249 people … that would place him in a top ten slot
for serial killers worldwide, but I would be very surprised if the final
number didn't turn out to be more than ten, given the givens, and
the laws of probability*).

All those people, all those bodies, all without
him/them being seen or found. I wondered where all of
those bodies had ended up. How had they moved from
campsites to their final resting place (*which reads as more
ecumenical than I meant/mean it to be*)? I flashed back to
Edith's memory of the boat/barge, and another piece fell
into place. The data and images of the maps and the
names of people swirled around in my head … one
moment I didn't know, and the next I did. It was like a
lightning strike in my consciousness. He lived, or at least
had a private dock, at the end of the lake by Ampersand
Bay … it's the only way it could have worked so well for
so long. He used a boat, or barge, to move the bodies and
gear from the kill sites to his base of operations for
disposal. It was brilliant … and disappointing. Finding
him would be a boring search of houses and properties

and people living along the shore of Lower Saranac Lake. Now, it would take time and warrants and door-knocking and lots of other standard police stuff that I didn't know/care about. Once I told Frank and Brimley about this, they'd get him. Surely just a matter of time. It was exactly the sort of thing the cops and FBI were better suited for than me. If Frank and the FBI got ahold of that, they'd shunt me off to the side, and simply grind away at the problem through standard methods and catch him in short order.

A moment after all those thoughts ran through my head, they were followed by another … I didn't want that outcome. I wanted to catch him, directly and not through drudgework, but trickery. That would require a plan, so I could catch him quickly enough that one of the myriad drones didn't figure out the simple (*if slow*) solution to our mutual problem before I could work my mojo. I started making and discarding plans until I came up with the bare bones of one less stupid and dangerous than the others.

Barry was luckily/logically nowhere to be seen, so I fell onto the bed, and slept for a few hours, then went downstairs to take the dogs out and wait for Frank to wake up.

SmartPig Offices, Saranac Lake, NY
Saturday, 7/11/2015, 6:53 a.m.

Frank came down the stairs at three minutes after six like one of the walking dead, shambling and groaning, hands held out in front of him, blinking in surprise when he came into his normally dark and empty morning kitchen to make coffee, only to find it well-lit and filled with the aroma of a fresh-brewed carafe.

"You don't even drink coffee, Tyler," he said, taking the first cup from me, black, and downing the scalding bitter potion. (*Meg had told me lately he's been drinking his first cup straight, and then sugaring/creaming the subsequent one.*)

"No, but you do, and I need you able to use your brain before I explain what I've got. Besides, I need to be gone in forty minutes," I said. "Also Toby and Lola have been fed and walked, no matter what they tell you."

"Oh, God, that's good," Frank said, slurping the last inch out of the mug. "How long can you stay? Although what the hell was that noise in the middle of the night? It sounded like you were trying, unsuccessfully, to juggle flugelhorns."

"Lola got excited during a late-night Coke-run," I said, "and tripped over her own bowl … if it seemed loud from your bedroom, you should have heard it while trying to sneak through the kitchen."

Frank nodded and ruffled Lola's ears on his way over

186

to refill his mug, this time adding a lot of cream and sugar. "After we got upstairs and in bed last night, Meg tol' me about what happened to your office," Frank said. "I'm sorry, don't be mad at her, you hadda know she was gonna tell me, although I get why you didn't raise an alarm, even if it was just for insurance paperwork purposes. (*Frank seemed unconcerned that my break-in coincided with our investigation into a serial killer, so who was I to mess that up with facts and truth and logic.*) But if there is a burglar or vandal in the area we should be on the lookout. Was there a possibility of any fingerprints or whatever that we could have collected?

"Nope," I said. "He just hosed everything down with Canadian Coke, which is, sadly, nearly perfect for trashing electronics and books. I've got a person coming by this morning to clean the space and fix the door and repaint if/where needed. I'm just glad Maurice, or the new renters from downstairs, didn't walk in on whoever it was."

"Okay," Frank said. "I assume you bein' here waiting for me, with coffee for me an' the dogs fed and walked, means you had some luck last night with your sneak and peek under America Camping's skirts?"

"I've got 249 names for you to run," I said. "Are you awake? This is important."

He frowned at me, and drank the rest of his second mug, went to refill, and grabbed a pad and pen from the crap drawer under the coffee machine once he'd appropriately doctored his coffee, then sat at the table and scowled at me.

"Yup," he said. "I'm awake. Gimme."

"I found 249 names from the various campsites around Lower Saranac Lake who may have gone missing at some point since 1998. I added five more campsites

187

and pushed the search back to the beginning of their recordkeeping, which was 1998. I'm sorry, I know it's a lot of names, but I couldn't restrict the search more without running the risk of missing names/people/victims."

He nodded. "You get me the list, an' I can get started on it first thing. Mebbe get Weinstein on it once I get pulled for other stuff. Jim is a good guy, and he knows how to keep his mouth shut. What happens next?"

"What do you mean?" I asked. "I'm going over to SmartPig to give this woman, Mona …"

"Tyler," Frank said, "do *you* need some coffee? I meant what happens once we run this list. What do you do with the names I'm gonna give you later today?"

"It partly depends on who went missing, and where/when," I said. "If the pattern killer took his victims from the campsites I think he used, and at the rate I'm guessing, I may have a plan that might stand a good chance of catching him, although we'll have to use Agent Brimley in a manner that he'll resent after the fact." I thought for a minute, debated something Barry had suggested, and decided to give it a try. "Frank, it's just possible this guy uses a Whaler or a barge to transport bodies and gear from the campsites to his base of operations or a deep spot where he dumps things … this could be the kind of thing that could be a semi-useful tip for you to filter to the FBI/Brimley, and soften the blow from our using/tricking him, if you're worried about it."

"I got no problem using that skid mark any way we need to," Frank said, "but if my ears are working, I heard an 'I think,' an 'I'm guessing,' an 'I may,' 'might.' and a 'good chance' when you were describing your master plan. Is there any way we can tighten that up a bit before we take chances with a serial killer who may have been killing people in my town for as much as twenty years without getting caught, or us even knowin' about him?"

"I'll work on it," I said. "You've already got the list. I sent it to you last night. Some of the names are in groups of two ... if one of the names, but not the other, is missing, it's just a coincidence, not the killer."

Frank stood up part way through my talking and shuffled out to the living room to scoop up his laptop, and go through the steps to bring up his browser and email. Two minutes later he had a hard copy in his hand and was writing GIBSON & WEINSTEIN EYES ONLY across the top of each sheet with a red Sharpie.

"Jesus, Tyler, you don't think ..." he paused.

"No, Frank," I said. "I'd be very surprised if there were more than twenty or thirty names from that list that actually ran into our guy. I think it's likely I ran too big a net through the data, and am wasting a bunch of your time."

"Twenty or thirty names of who?" said Meg as she walked in stretching and bee-lining for the coffee carafe. (*It was beginning to look like I was going to have to make a new carafe before I headed out.*) "G'morning all."

Frank gave me a cutting look, and even with my poor people-reading skills, I translated it to mean he didn't want me to say anything about my/our list to Meg ... I gave him a slight nod and stuck my head in the fridge to poke around for a bite of something before heading out to meet Dot and then Mona.

"Just something Tyler's worked up for the case," Frank said. "It may be nothing. I'll check it out later."

Through some impressive (*for Frank, and for a bit after six in the morning*) legerdemain, the sheets listing the possible victims had disappeared from the table, and into the waistband of his pajamas. Meg seemed momentarily aware that something had changed in the room, but couldn't quite place it, and when Lola sat down next to her, farted loudly, and turned quickly to look for the perpetrator, the moment passed. Frank started her talking about her classes/sessions for the day while they enjoyed their coffee together. (*Contemporaneously, I enjoyed a Coke and six slices of bologna, splitting the final one between the dogs, who also enjoyed it.*)

I dashed out the door and retraced my circuitous route through the neighborhood back to the Element at the Algonquin Apartments. While waiting a minute for the car to warm up, I peered around to see if anyone was watching me, before I looped my way around, and eventually to the TLAS. I parked the Element at the far end of the lot, behind their dumpster and the big dog run fence (*hoping to make it at least harder for someone to find/track me*) ran in and hunted around for Dot, who, it turned out was doing something down in the basement involving water dripping from a new wet spot in the ceiling/floor (*depending on your location/perspective*). She held out a hand in a gesture that either meant *wait* or *stay the hell back* … since they both amounted to roughly the same thing, I turned around and went upstairs to experiment on kittens for a minute.

That sounds worse than the reality of what I was doing. I have always found that dogs like me, and cats hate/fear me. I have a theory that it has to do with my emotional wiring being different than most people's. Recently, Dot talked me into helping with a litter of orphaned kittens … bottle-feeding mainly, and they hadn't seemed to mind me as much as older cats did (*it might have been due to the bottle of replacement mother's milk, hence my experiments*). I walked into one of the rooms that was lined from wall to wall and floor to ceiling with cat cages, and could literally see the cats move back/away from the doors as I passed (*nossir, they didn't do it figuratively, they actually moved back*). At the end of the room was a large playpen filled with kittens (*not my bottle fed litter, but one slightly older*). They piled over each other to sample my fingers with mouths and paws (*with implied, and delivered, teeth and claws, but little ones*), made little squeaking noises at me, and seemed receptive to my ear-scratching and tummy-rubbing.

"It's taken care of for the moment," Dot said to my back. "Come up to the desk, and I'll give you that thing."

I bid the kittens adieu, walked past rows/columns of suspicious cats to the door, and turned left toward the front desk.

"They don't flee in terror in the face of your obvious soullessness?" Dot asked.

I used to theorize, when in a dramatic mood, that dogs like me because they want to, and cats hate me because I don't have a soul. (*I don't know that I believe other people have a soul either, in the sense that most people mean, but I have/can/will feel a difference between other people in our spiritual makeups and me, and needed to assign it a name.*) Dot has opined that I put out some pheromone that freaks cats out.

"Strangely, no," I said. "Four-week-old kittens don't fear/hate me ... it must come later. I'll be interested to see when."

"Whatever," she said. "Maybe you're changing and the other cats are just used to hating you, and all cats that meet you from now on will love you, and name you their king."

I didn't think it was likely, but after a moment discerned that she didn't think it was either, so I just held my hand out. Dot reached under the counter, pulled out a thick envelope, and passed it to me.

"She's charging you three grand to clean your place?" Dot asked, "What the fuck did this guy do to SmartPig?"

"It's a mess," I said. "Lots of broken and trashed stuff to cart away, dead fish and smeared walls, some stuff to repair/replace/repaint, and I don't want her to get hung up or stop because of money. This is more than she asked for, but I assume that if she doesn't spend it all, I'll get something back."

"First world problems," she said. "Say *hi* to Mona for me when you see her."

"I will," I said. "Thanks, Dot, and good luck with the water in the basement."

She nodded, and said, in a low voice that likely (*hopefully*) only I could hear. "Thanks, Tyler, and good luck fooling the cops and the FBI and the serial killer. Have fun storming the castle!"

I winked in her direction to acknowledge receipt of the message and snuck out the back door before looping and pausing and eventually parking in front of the bank next to the building SmartPig was housed in. Once up the stairs and at the front entrance, I was surprised/pleased to find Mona and some minions already at work, battling the chaos/mess/damage the killer had wrought in his frustration. (*I hated to think he would do all of this while in a good mood, and doubted he could have remained hidden for so long if that had been the case.*)

"You must be Tyler," she said, smiling. "I'm Mona, and I'm both happy and sad to meet you."

Dot must have explained something about me because she didn't extend a hand to shake as a part of her greeting.

"Thanks for doing this on such short notice, Mona," I said. "I'm grateful. Do you have any questions for me before I give you a bunch of money and leave again?"

"Which of your belongings do you want us to salvage, or clean, or trash?" she said.

"Everything broken/ripped/fried (*gesturing to the electronics the killer had doused in Coke*) should be trashed. Clothes that can be washed can be put in a bag for me to take care of later unless that's something you do (*she nodded that it was*). Books that have been stained or torn can go out. Same with my camping gear and pictures and such (*I felt lucky that I had a small safe that he hadn't been able to open/damage, that contained my few important documents and irreplaceable pictures and family items*). Beyond that, if there is such, I trust your judgment. I want a new door like the old one, solid wood, and fitted with the Fox bar hardware (*which, if I'd had it in place, would have kept this guy, along with the 10th Mountain Division if they cared to break into my place, out in the hall*) from the old door. I'd like any repainting you need to do to be as close to the old colors as is possible, but I understand if you can't do an exact match."

"That all sounds good," she said in a tone that suggested that what she said next wouldn't be good news. "Dot said you're some sorta detective, and that your place was vandalized by the guy who killed that family out at the campground on the lake the other day."

Instead of answering, I handed her the envelope. She flexed it in practiced fingers, and looked up at me, somehow aware that it was too much money ... I decided to press a perceived advantage.

"There's three thousand dollars in there," I said, "in case you run over. I didn't want you to have to stop and wait for a resupply. Besides speed and quality, I hope I'm paying for discretion. I'd like whatever Dot told you about me and/or what I'm working on now to just stay between you and her … and me, if you have questions about it. Since you're literally (*again, not figuratively*) in the middle of this mess, you have the right to some basic information. I am a sort of detective and am working with the police and the FBI (*no tone necessary/used*), and this damage was, in fact, most likely caused by the person who killed two people on one of the island campsites on Lower Saranac Lake a few days ago. You shouldn't be at risk, since he would appear to be mad at me, and would have no reason to be upset with you. That being said, nobody ever regretted being too careful when possibly dealing with a serial killer, so I would recommend you always work in teams of three, leave the windows open, and call the SLPD if you hear/see/smell/feel anything that gives you the wiggins. (*Dot and I had recently watched a few seasons of "Buffy the Vampire Slayer," and it felt like a reasonable reference to attach my message to or vice versa*)."

She looked back over her shoulder at her minions, who were industriously cleaning and sorting, and nodded at me. "Got it."

I turned and headed back out and away from what had essentially been my home for the last decade and a quarter, I could hear Barry stomping and muttering his way down the stairs behind me, something about picking your battles and sissies.

Dunkin' Donuts Parking Lot, Saranac Lake, NY
Saturday, 7/11/2015, 8:03 a.m.

I started looping on my drive out of town, and then it
occurred to me that I wasn't going anywhere too secret or
dangerous and had no reason to punish the planet by
burning so much fossil fuel, so I drove straight out to the
Saranac Lake Plaza, ran the drive-through at Dunkin'
Donuts for a perfect dozen, and parked in the middle of
the lot ... in plain view of serial killers and everyone else
in Saranac Lake (*almost all of them, almost certainly not serial
killers ... I may have been a bit short on certainty, but I had more
than a pound of donuts and some warm cans of Coke from the back
of my Element, which made up for a lot*).

While I ate and thought and drank and wondered
when Frank would call for clarification on the list, I
decided to call Mickey.

"Hey, kiddo," Mickey said when he picked up. I
wasn't worried about waking him up, calling so early ...
he got up bright and early every morning, even on
weekends.

"Hey, Mickey," I said. "How're things?"

"I just heard a tiny popping sound from the back of
my head," he said, and he must have heard, or imagined
my grimace. "C'mon Ty, I'm fine. My neurologist said the
thing looks better than it did, and that I could live with it
for the rest of my life. They're still knocking around

195

which treatment they prefer, but it seems as though smart money is on it being sixes. But I'm sure you know all of that, and probably more, from everything you've been reading. Dr. Patil's office manager said you've been sending him a steady stream of journal articles. Kiddo, you're going to have to control that urge if you don't want to alienate him. He's a good guy, and the team he's assembled is the best you can find without flying for six hours east or west."

"I know, Mick," I said, "but I keep finding these articles with new stats and treatments and drugs."

"Enough about me," he said with finality. "I feel great today and don't want to obsess about this thing in my melon, Ty. Tell me what's new since we talked."

"Well," I said, "we've actually had some big, and grisly news up here. What may be a serial killer who's been operating in the area for a while, killed a couple of people out on one of the island campsites on Lower Saranac Lake. We paddled on it last summer with Anne and the girls, remember? The one with all the little islands. Remember? We ate lunch watching those kids jump off the big cliff (*on Eagle Island, but he didn't need that information*)."

"No shit?" he said. "Yeah, I remember. Well, I guess they have to be somewhere … serial killers, I mean. Are you involved?"

"Yup," I said, loving to hear the enthusiasm and excitement in his voice, and the sharpness and smooth flow of his words and thought process. "Frank Gibson and an agent from the FBI came by the other day to ask me to help out." (*I didn't explain that part of the reason I was on Brimley's radar was that he initially suspected I might have been the killer.*)

"That's great, Ty," Mickey said. "You be careful. I'm

not going to tell Anne or the girls. It'd just worry them about you, and scare Anne enough that we'd never come back up to see you."

My phone buzzed in my hand, and I pulled it from my ear and noticed it was Frank's cell calling me.

"Mickey," I said, "I've got to take a call from Frank. I'll call you later today or tomorrow to set up my visit, okay?"

"Sounds great, kiddo," Mickey said. "Be safe. Love you!"

"Love you too, Mickey," I said, and then took Frank's call.

"What's up Frank?" I asked, still seventy-three percent thinking about Mickey.

"First name I ran, Susan Burke, came up as reported missing in 2001," Frank said. (*I wondered briefly why she was the first name he ran, since she wasn't the first name alphabetically or chronologically on the list, but I dismissed my worry and went back to listening to him.*) "It blew my mind, Tyler, this is real. He grabbed all of these people, some guy living in my town."

Lost in my own thoughts I answered Frank's news with silence.

"I'm calling with good news, sorta, and you sound subdued, even for you," Frank said. "What's up?"

"Sorry," I said. "I was on the phone with Mickey when you called."

"Sure, yeah, no worries," Frank said quickly, knowing something about both Mickey's problems, and my complex relationship with both Mickey and death.

"Anyway," Frank said, "are you gonna need the whole jacket, case file, on her, and any other we find?"

"Nope," I said. "Sorry, I didn't say so before. I/we just need to know that they're actually missing, and I assume, never been found, mostly to confirm that it's a serial killer and not just bad luck and coincidence." (*As well to confirm which sites were most in use by this guy as kill sites.*)

"That'll speed things up," Frank said. "I'll let you go. Sorry to bust in on your call with Mr. Schwarz. How's he doin' anyway?"

"He sounds good, sounds strong," I said. "Thanks for asking. I'll talk to you later. Call me when you finish going through the list, okay?"

"Yup," said Frank, "back to the grindstone. Later, Tyler."

Now I had nothing to do for a while, and nowhere to do it … it was maddening. The killer had trashed my bat cave and I had to assume he was watching me, intent on interfering with, or harming me; I was safe enough parked in the middle of this stupid parking lot, but if I went to see/visit/talk to Meg or Dot or Snowflake or John or Mark and Xander, I could expose any/all of them to risk from an unpredictable/unstable person who was mad he hadn't been able to kill everyone he wanted to murder this week, and seemed upset with me for doing my job (*or more properly the job of the cops and the FBI*). I could go for a paddle on Lower Saranac, or on any of the hundreds of lakes and ponds within an hour of my current location, but I was ready to push this thing through to the end and didn't want to be out of cell phone range or too far from Frank if/when he finished working his way through the list. Lacking anything more productive to do, I finished my box of donuts, four warm Cokes, stared at my phone and started thinking about going for a swim, to stretch out some kinks, and work off some of the junk food I'd eaten in the last few days.

Roaming Saranac Lake, daytime

Beast was driving through the Tri-Lakes in great, looping circles, trying to catch Cunningham's scent. He swung by the boat launches looking for that stupid toaster of a car that he drove. He drove by the cop Gibson's house, saw the wife's car was still there, and thought about stopping in to have a talk with her about her friend Cunningham. He drove by and saw the dog-lady out front of the TLAS, working with a ridiculously large black dog on a short lead. The size of the dog put him off, but Beast knew she was friends with Tyler and wanted to lash out and hurt someone, something, to ease his own pain. Driving and muttering and smacking the steering wheel and imagining the sweet release he wanted to find, to feel, to trade the pain for power.

As a child in his mother's house, pain had found him early and often. She had told Vanilla whatever man she was currently with didn't mean anything by the way they treated her or him. Their actions were how they showed love or concern, or they'd had a tough day at work. She told him, taught him, to smile through the pain and sadness and being scared, and hold that pain and fear for the person who gave it to him. He gathered, hoarded the pain and fear for years, smiling at the torment until his face hurt from the smiling and he thought his head might split open and spill his brains all over the floor from the pressure of holding it all in.

One September morning, at his grandfather's cabin on Franklin Falls Pond, he had been judged old enough and tasked with the trash fire, and everything changed for Vanilla, for the first time. The orange flames bloomed, and while he felt the heat on his cheeks and saw the smoke rising toward a heaven he already doubted, his personal load of pain and fear temporarily lessened. Not by much, but enough. Enough to let Vanilla realize the way to let go of everything he'd been holding inside his eight-year-old head and heart. He started a regular routine of burnings at camp and at home, everywhere really. He stole a Zippo lighter from his grandfather that fall, and, although Vanilla never became a smoker, he always carried the lighter.

Vanilla didn't meet Beast until the following summer, again out at his grandfather's camp. He was playing mumbly peg with a scout knife the old man had given him when a huge toad hopped out from under the cabin, near where Vanilla sat. Surprised and somewhat scared by the unexpected appearance at his elbow, Vanilla drove the knife into the middle of the toad's back, pinning it to the earth. The small croaking scream and wriggling legs heralded the birth of Beast. Scared and sad and smiling ... Vanilla was gone ... replaced by strong, sure, and savage Beast who sat on the ground in his place. He had become a master of life and death, stronger than the parade of losers his mother sheltered, and sheltered with, from a world for which they were ill-equipped. Beast was a god. He twisted the knife, watching the toad jerk like a puppet. Everything had changed, and would never, could never, be the same again.

His mother was first to notice the change when he came back from the weekend out at camp, she said something about him looked taller, and how grown-up his voice seemed. That night, taking a bath to wash off a long weekend of fish scales and smoke and barefoot running, Beast was thinking about the toad when Eric came in for the last time. His mother's apartment had only one bathroom, so everyone had to share, but Eric always seemed to need to pee when Vanilla was bathing or showering. Eric pushed the door open and started in. Beast surfaced and roared.

"Get out," he said. "I'll be done in a minute."

"I just gotta take a piss, little man," Eric replied, angry at being challenged, but also unaccustomed to Vanilla talking back. "Just take a sec."

"Grandpa said it's not right," Vanilla deflected, seeing the bulk of Eric filling the door. "He said bathroom stuff is private and only deviants come in when other people are using the bathroom."

"Your grandpa is a crazy old drunk, who never had to share nothing his whole life, cuz he din't have nobody," Eric said, looming over the tub and boy.

"You don't talk about my grandpa like that," Beast returned in a foolhardy rush, flailing and splashing his way up and out of the bath, "and you don't get to see me naked no more, pervert."

Eric cuffed Beast, spinning him around and back down into the water. When his mother came in to see what the noise was a few seconds later, Eric was holding her boy's head under the water; she kicked her boyfriend until he released the boy.

That night, Eric left and never came back, and spent the next year finding regularly flattened tires on any vehicle he drove ... until he got the message and left the region. The boy never took a bath again, didn't much like swimming either, certainly not swimming underwater. His mom kept up her steady stream of loser boyfriends, but locked doors became a house policy, and she made sure the men who shared her bed were distinct, and distant, from her son, who was himself distinct and distant, and growing more so every day, from everybody.

The night Eric shoved Vanilla under the surface of the bath water marked the beginning of an ongoing pattern of the disappearance of small animals in the area around Beast's home. Over the years, when he and his mom moved from time to time, the disappearances followed. Beast and Vanilla faced the challenges an unfair world served up through a slowly, but steadily, increasing worship of fire and pain inflicted on others. He first tasted the blood of a victim by accident, licking a squirrel's blood that dribbled down the blade onto his wrist, but it soon became a necessary part of the ritual. The deeper the patterns of behaviors were that seemed to save him, the more distant he became from the rest of humanity, although he never lost the easy, comforting, and fake smile his mother had taught him.

As his grandfather aged, Beast's mother, and the increasingly strange and distant boy, moved back in with him into the small house at the north end of Lower Saranac Lake. One day, in his grandfather's study, on a dusty old PC, he discovered his next source of power, of importance. The boy found computers in his first year of high school, and never looked back. He was better than other people at using and understanding the technology, and those who knew him could feel it without his having to brag or offer; they always asked for his help. His power extended beyond the other kids, to adults too. The power of owed favors and respect and paid jobs working at troubleshooting computers and networks gave him access.

The boy met Jecinda in his junior year, and it seemed as though she was all of the things he had been missing. The Beast, and the fires, and the small tortured animals, all went away for a few happy years. The boy and Jecinda were married soon after they graduated from high school, and he kept working with computers, and everyone needed and respected him. He was happy. He worked for local companies and individuals, helping a variety of people in the community with computer resources and needs; none of them suspected the quiet and confident young man was mining and finding and hoarding their secrets. His life was better and happier than he had thought possible ten years earlier ... until he came home one day to find Jecinda packing liquor store boxes with her belongings into the Camry he'd given her.

"I just don't know you anymore," she'd said. "I thought you were more than other people ... more exciting, more smarter, more interesting, but you're not. You're empty and boring. You're vanilla, and I want flavors in my life."

She drove away, down the driveway to the rest of the world, leaving the boy with his drunk mother and dying grandfather in the old house. Beast flared back up from some dusty corner of the boy's soul and cried out for blood and flames until the boy went into the woods and gave the Beast what it wanted. He raged and roared at the injustice of it all, arguing with his absent wife that vanilla was a flavor ... he knew it to be true. Vanilla beans grew from exotic orchids from the other side of the world, and they took years to flower and must be pollinated within hours or die, and the beans have to be cured for months in a tricky process. The complex smells and tastes of vanilla derive from hundreds of chemicals that affect the human senses and brain in varied and interesting ways.

When the boy came out of the woods the next morning, he carried the stinck of fire and blood, and happy to secretly think of himself as Vanilla, but with Beast, and the knife, in his back pocket.

Vanilla smiled now, ignoring Beast screaming down the walls of the prison he was relegated to when out in public, forced to behave like a human. He had swung through Lake Placid and back, looking for Cunningham, spotting him when Vanilla pulled in for donuts and coffee. Cunningham sat there, mocking him. Vanilla did drive through, suffering the incredibly slow woman who had to ask three times what kind of glazed he wanted, smiling through the window at her, and assuring her it was no problem.

He briefly considered grabbing her hand when she passed him his donuts and pulling her out, to drag her and dump her at high speed in front of the state troopers' barracks in Raybrook. Vanilla and Beast each vied for control.

What happened, or rather didn't happen, with Edith Richards out on Saranac Lake had changed the rules, changed everything, for Beast and Vanilla. He, sometimes they, knew their game was over. Their plans were coming apart, and he was coming apart, the wall between his two personages degrading hour by hour. He had wanted to take Edith, drink her blood from his blade, hoping it would heal what was wrong with him and his world; the heavy police coverage on her had made it impossible, and now she was gone, whisked away from him in the darkness.

He wanted for it, for him, for his life, to mean something, to make them understand who he was, and why he was Vanilla and Beast, but nobody would listen, or care. Going back now wasn't an option. He could only go forward, and although it was new and scary to the little boy who still lived inside the towering haunted house that was Beast, it was exhilarating too. He had nothing to lose anymore. They would get him now, and while he couldn't control that, he didn't have to sit and wait. Beast ordered Vanilla to find a campsite for tonight or tomorrow, and at the same time, Vanilla ran around in small and tight, angry and excited circles thinking about how he could slow them down, throw them off his trail for a few hours.

Vanilla stuffed Beast back down through the trapdoor and parked fifty yards from Cunningham, both of them eating and thinking.

Beast had a wonderful and horrible idea he believed would at once ease his, and Vanilla's, pain, distract those hunting him, and hopefully allow him to play his game one more time. Sitting in the truck a short distance from a man he didn't know, but who in his mind was assuming characteristics of the Eric and every other bully Vanilla and Beast had known in their angry and brutal life, Beast's smile grew similar to the Grinch's in a barely remembered memory from one happy Christmas with his mother. Vanilla went through the plan with Beast. They tweaked it here and there, toning down the bloodshed in exchange for an increase in the likelihood of escape to fight another day. Five minutes later they drove away.

The hunting rifle was in its hard case in the back of the truck, but too rifle-like to take out in town, so Vanilla drove out to a quiet spot on the edge of Moody Pond. Beast retrieved it, loaded the magazine, wrapped it in a sleeping bag they kept in the back of the truck for road trips that ended with sleeping by the side of the road, and carried the rifle to the cab. He drove back into town, quickly scouted the two locations he had in mind, and returned to his first target, preparing to shoot a person for the first time in his life.

Beast pulled the truck as far up into the driveway of the newly renovated Dewey Mountain Recreation area that would still allow him an unobstructed view of the animal shelter. No movement around Dewey as yet and only intermittent traffic passed on Route 3. He jockeyed the truck around until it was facing back down the hill where he could see the shelter through his passenger window. He estimated he was 250 yards from the building, too far for a dependable shot from him, and the piece of crap rifle he'd inherited from grandpa. The 3x scope wasn't much help, as excited as Beast was, it was jumping all over the place when he sighted in, even leaning the front end on the passenger door frame. A woman walked out with some mutt, and Beast aimed for center mass and slowly pulled in the slack on the trigger until the shot surprised him.

Beast watched the woman and dog spin and fall, not knowing or caring which he'd hit, he leaned the rifle butt down on the floor, against the seat, started the truck and drove to his second planned target. Sirens blared behind him as he drove away, well below the speed limit, and he headed for the Gibson house.

The wife, or at least her car, was still there when Vanilla stopped the truck across the street from the house. He left the vehicle running, not wanting to risk a screw-up in Beast's excitement to get away after the shooting. Spotting a shadow moving briefly between a gap in the curtains of what Beast assumed was their living room, he raised the rifle and steadied it against the passenger doorframe, waiting. She, Beast assumed, passed by the gap again a half-minute later, and Beast yanked the trigger in blind reaction. The noisy blast from the rifle preceded the collapse of the big picture window by only an instant. When the loud echoes and breaking glass sounds had died off, Vanilla was driving down the street and thinking about what he would eat for lunch while he made plans for playing the final game tomorrow night.

Gibson House, Saranac Lake, NY
Saturday, 7/11/2015, 11:18 a.m.

I was still in the parking lot, finishing the last donut in the
box, along with my sixth decidedly too-warm Coke, and
wondering where I should head for a swim and to find a
private enough place to pee, when I heard the first sirens
from the SLPD a mile and a quarter to the northwest … I
ignored them, as I generally do. Police are often in a
hurry, right or wrong, and it generally wasn't anything to
do with me. When a trio of vehicles from the state
trooper headquarters in Raybrook (*barely more than three
miles to the southeast of my current location in Saranac Lake, for
those readers who are building their own maps in their own heads*),
rocketed by in close formation with light bars blazing but
no sirens, I became more interested … interested enough
that I started up the Element and was about to start
rolling toward the noise. My next thoughts included
wondering if they'd caught my guy through something
like a traffic stop or a flat tire with a body in the back.
Then Frank called.

"Frank," I said. "Did you manage to finish going
through the list already? I had it figured as taking another
hour and a …"

"Tyler!" Frank shouted into his, and subsequently my,
end of the phone. "Shut the fuck up and get your brain in
gear. Someone just shot a dog and one of the employees

at the TLAS, and also put a round through the big picture window in my house."

He stopped talking and I had/heard nothing but the minute hum/buzz of cell phone telephony … I had waited for a punchline or similar for a foolish second and a half before I was able to get my brain in gear.

"Who got shot at the shelter?" I asked, "and which dog? You just said a window at your house … is Meg all right? Was she home? I assume it's our guy, but why would he do that? Why those two things/places … what do they have in common?"

I knew the answers to my last three questions (*and also had time to feel bad, hoping the person and dog shot at the shelter weren't Dot and Snowflake or Gwen or Sadie*) before Frank sorted out all of my questions and decided which ones to answer. In that moment I worried that our killer seemed to be unraveling, which often signaled an endgame of some sort, but also heralded less predictability and more random danger to those in the area of the investigation (*which could screw up my plans, such as they were*).

"Steph Brentworth was hit in the leg after the bullet passed through the abdomen of a boxer-mix puppy (*which had to make it one of the seven dwarfs*)," Frank said. "Steph'll be okay. Dot's not sure about the dog. Meg was home, but in another room. She's freaked out and I told her to cancel classes today. I wanna send her to stay with family in Tupper until this is over. As to the other thing, I got no earthly idea how this whack-a-mole connected the dots in a way that it made sense to shoot up my house and a fuggin' dog walker."

"You gotta tell him, Sport," Barry said from beside me. "He'll figure it out before long, and could be pissed you din't tell him."

I hate it when my imaginary friend is smarter than me,

but when you're right, you're right.

"Frank," I said, "the only logical/rational connection is me. I stayed with you guys last night because I do think it was him who trashed SmartPig and I was (*scared*) … I didn't want to be alone. I could tell the damage done was more than kid vandalism. There was a violence to it … but I could also see there was nothing to be gained by treating my office as a crime scene because it would just slow down the investigation. I'm not sure if he's devolving or trying to distract me or both, but I think he somehow found out that I was helping, and he's lashing out at people/places I care about in an attempt to mess with me."

There was silence, except for the aforementioned hum, from the cell phone.

"I'm sorry, Frank," I said, "I'm so, so sorry, I didn't mean for anyone to get hurt. After SmartPig, I just figured that I could hide from him until we finished all this."

"Yeah," Frank said, "I kinda wish you'd told me about what happened at SmartPig sooner, but you still woulda spent the night, an' I probably wouldna done anything different. You got nothing to be sorry about for any of this Tyler, batshit-crazy killer is batshit-crazy. I gotta get into this, I'll talk to you later."

"Wait, Frank," I said. "I get that you want to be on the ground looking at the scene, but if you're not going to keep pushing on the list, you have to find someone else to do it. At the very least, it's possible he's not batshit-crazy, or not *just* batshit-crazy. The guy might have done this with an eye to throwing off our pursuit of him. If you stop working the list, then he wins."

"Yeah," Frank said. "I guess. You might be right. All the people gettin' thrown at this, I s'pose I can leave

Weinstein working the computer and phone on your list. I gotta tell you, Tyler, when we got the first calls about the shootings—Jesus, shootings in Saranac Lake—I already had seven confirmed missing people and was only through the first fifty-some names on the list. If it sticks at that rate through the rest of the names, we'll have …"

"Thirty-two, possibly more," I said. "Which is why you need to keep Weinstein working the list. You also need to make sure he keeps what he finds to himself until he can hand it off to you."

"If by doing that you mean I'll get a chance to take this guy down," Frank said, "instead of Brimley and the windbreakers, then I can guaran-damn-tee he'll keep quiet. He shot my house, Tyler, mighta been trying to kill my wife, coulda killed her. Poor Lola still won't come out from under the fuggin' bed."

"Before you go," I said, "do they have any information about the shooting/shooter?"

"Nothing useful," Frank answered. "Usual witness stuff. People mighta seen a van or a truck leaving our neighborhood after the shot was fired, but nothing for sure, and nobody saw anything at the shelter before or after. Meg and some people from around the neighborhood, and also near the shelter, are pretty sure it was a rifle and not a handgun, but that already seemed likely. I gotta go, Tyler. I'll have Weinstein cc you when he tells me he's finished the list. Where'll you be?"

I wasn't aware of my thought process until I'd already answered. "Your house. I'll be at your house with Meg and the dogs."

Seemed to me, I could probably help out with Meg and Toby and Lola, and there'd be a ton of cops there for the rest of the day, so our bad guy wouldn't likely return.

I dialed Dot's cell number and it went to message

twice before she picked up, "What?"

"Dot," I said, "I just got off the phone with Frank. I heard about Steph and one of the dogs."

"It was Sleepy," Dot said, gasping and huffing and crying into the phone. "There's so much blood, like a lake of it on the ground around them. I can't talk. Can you come?"

"I'll be by as soon as I can," I said. She had started to speak, but I just rode over her with volume and insistence. "He also shot at Frank and Meg's house ... it sounds like nobody there was hit, but I told Frank I'd head over to help out with Meg and Lola."

"Motherfucker," she said with a vehemence that took my breath away. "Give them my love, and stay safe. I'll see you later. Gently!" (*This last bit sounded as though it was spoken to someone else, and then she hung up.*)

I called the Good Chinese place to get a mess of food ... enough for Meg and me along with the local cops and the staties and the windbreakers who would be working through their lunches, and then I drove over to pick it up, along with a mixed case of cold drinks from their fridge.

When I rolled into the Gibson house driveway, I'd arrived in time to see a couple of guys screwing a large rectangle of plywood over the hole that used to house their big picture window. As I climbed out of my car, I was addressed loudly/sternly and was told to stay where I was, by two giant state troopers who didn't know me (*and vice versa*). They had hands on unsnapped holsters, and I stayed very still until one of the SLPD guys told them who I was and helped me unload enough of the food and drinks to feed Meg and me. I left the rear gate open (*the Chinese place had given me a couple of bags of plates and napkins and utensils and sauce packets when I told them what I was doing with my larger than ordinary order*) and waved the assorted

LEOs to help themselves to the food and drinks.

Meg was sitting in the kitchen, telling the story in a bored tone that implied she'd been through it a number of times already. She looked up and smiled weakly when I came in, nodding and mouthing a *thank you* when she saw the food and drinks. She reached down into her lap and scratched Toby's chin and picked up the story where she'd left off.

"Lola?" I asked, not caring that I interrupted, or minding the glare of the trooper too much.

The cop looked at me as though I was crazy. (*I assume because a friend had been shot at, and I hadn't asked how she was ... Meg knew I would have already known she was okay, and had heard, and was concerned about Lola, and that I knew she'd be concerned about her too, but couldn't get away to deal with it just yet.*) Meg just pointed up through the ceiling to their bedroom, where Lola always hid from storms and thunder, and sometimes the UPS guy.

I swung by the fridge for a slice of cheese, grabbed that and a hot dog as well, and headed back out and up to the bedroom. Not wanting to surprise or scare her further, I spoke softly while entering the room.

"Hey there Lola-girl," I said. "I heard you had a rough morning and just wanted to check in and see how you're doing."

I figured she didn't understand what I was saying but was positive she appreciated my manner of talking with her. I lay down next to the bed on the far side from the door, Meg's side, and looked under. Lola's face was inches from mine, eyes bugged in fear, lips pulled back from her teeth and panting ... I wasn't positive she recognized me, so I didn't want to risk a hand or fingers yet.

"Sweet girl, I know," I said in my lowest, most

soothing voice (*patently false, but practiced over years of shelter visits under Dot's tutelage*). "This morning sucked. Gunshots are loud and scary, and the glass breaking must have made it even worse, but it's over now, and I've got cheese."

I ripped off a small piece of cheese and tossed it near, but not at her. She flinched when my hand moved, but seemed interested once she smelled my bribe in the confined space under the bed. A few seconds later, her nose stretched slowly across the gap between cheese and dog, and a pinkness of tongue snaked out to sample, then snag, it. I tossed another piece, talking the whole time, and she didn't flinch that time, getting the treat almost before it landed on the carpet.

A few minutes later, Lola was working on the last nibble of hot dog, leaning against me, shivering, and making contrasting/conflicting little noises ... happy moans about hot dog, cheese, and having her belly scratched while leaning against a friend with sad little indictments about people who would shoot her house and break her windows and scare her mommy. I completely agreed and thought fully unkind thoughts toward the serial killer who had made the mistake of scaring my friend, Lola-dog.

Still holding onto Lola, I pulled out my cell phone and called John and Mark to escalate events moving toward the final stage of my plan/trap. John had some ideas to refine our strategy which I generally liked. Mark asked permission to bring in a girl friend. He worked really hard to assure me she wasn't a girlfriend but was a girl friend, and I felt as though I was caught in an Abbot and Costello loop for nearly a minute, until I told him I didn't care which/who she was, but that she'd be a welcome addition, as long as she knew what she was getting herself into … he mentioned she was an MP they'd met 'over there' and that she was a significantly bigger badass than him (*which forced me into picturing some form of lady-Reacher*). I got off the phone nine minutes later and offered to split my Hunan shrimp with Lola. She seemed agreeable, and we headed downstairs to have lunch with Meg.

Gibson House, Saranac Lake, NY
Saturday, 7/11/2015, 4:07 p.m.

The police and FBI and staties kept tromping in and out
of the house during the next few hours ... measuring and
scraping and swabbing things, as well as talking to Meg,
asking her an endless loop of the same six questions. Lola
hated all the intruders, growling and muttering and giving
me looks while asking why I kept letting these potential
murderers into her house; Toby mostly slept, although he
kept opening a single eye to check/certify the locations of
both Lola and Meg. Meg was thoughtful and distant and
restless. After they'd finished retrieving the bullet from
the wall (*where it had ruined itself as useful evidence slamming into
one of the studs ... what would seem to be roughly a 1-in-8 chance*),
she wandered over a number of times to stick her pinky
into the hole and look at the plywood, imaging the spot
outside where the gunman had been lying in wait, trying
to kill her.

　　I kept her fed and watered, and tried to casually track
her pulse and color for possible shock. (*Since I don't
generally touch people, she busted me after my second attempt at
subtlety.*) She smiled sweetly/genuinely and threatened to
break my fingers if I tried to take her pulse again, but I
was able to watch the slight throb on her neck and temple
and keep time while holding up my end of whatever
conversation we were having throughout the afternoon.
Whenever possible, she made a point of not/never

talking about the serial killer, what Frank and I were doing, and how we were obviously being pushed around by this guy. Once we had demolished the Chinese food and drinks and I'd made her a few cups of tea and checked on the food/drink supply outside (*I may have jogged from the house to my Element, and it may have been a slightly serpentine track, but I didn't actually scream or dive under the car when a car door slammed, which I considered a victory*), Meg suggested I could go. She insisted they'd be fine, but something in her eyes suggested otherwise, however slightly. I stayed.

Although I didn't know what to do (*something of a rarity for me*), I had a generalized feeling this was something I *should* be doing, and for one of the few times in my life, especially when dealing with people and emotionally charged moments, I felt as though this was exactly where I should be.

I took Toby and Lola for a walk in the fenced back yard after lunch, when the activity level of the representatives of the law enforcement community had died down some. The dogs frolicked in the kiddie pool biting water and splashing and leaping and rolling around and eventually mostly emptying the pool through their efforts/play. (*Confucius said, "Choose a job you love, and you will never have to work a day in your life." The sentiment was certainly true for these dogs.*) I mistakenly sat down on the grass to watch them play, which they took as a signal to include me in their wrestling, and I was soon soaked and covered in cut grass and drool. It was a wonderful distraction from waiting and worrying about details out of my control. When Meg came out the back door carrying my cell phone in front of her as if it might bite (*or had already bitten*), I told the dogs that playtime was over, took the phone, and turned my back on the three of them.

Wandering to the far corner of the fenced backyard enclosure, I leaned into the ninety-degree angle of corner, enjoying the feel of the pressure on my shoulders from both sides, and told Frank he could speak now.

"Thirty-seven people on the list you gave me are actually missing, as declared by family or friends of landlords since the first one, Nell Tidwell of Quonochontaug, *I shit you not*, Rhode Island, in 1999," he said. "It's more than you thought, more that I could have imagined in my worst nightmares (*I doubted that, but said nothing*). It's fifteen percent of the list, Tyler, he took, killed, nearly forty people!"

"It's only a hair over fourteen percent, Frank," I said, "and the percentage, even the number isn't important … at least not at this moment. I need you to send me the list and let me cross-reference it with the campsites to see which ones he took them from. And I need you to set up a meeting between you and me and Agent Brimley, and then to distance yourself a bit from me before and during the meeting."

"Why would I do that, Tyler?" Frank asked. "Much as I hate to admit it, you saw through the knocking on doors and hoping the guy gets drunk and turns hisself in, and skipped ahead to nearly the end of the game, like taking the slide in Candyland (*a reference that was lost on me, but I made a noise of affirmation*). I want everyone to know how much you helped, and have no desire to minimize or distract from it, much less build distance between you an' me."

"Frank," I said slowly, and deliberately, possibly insultingly (*based on past experience when I speak extra slowly/carefully for regular-speed humans*), "I'm going to lie to Brimley, and set him up to be obvious and brutish and overbearing and then clumsily reveal his cards (*all strengths of the FBI)* to our killer, while we pull a shitty (*Dot assured me this was an actual term, meaning a sneaky and underhanded trick*) on both him and the killer, resulting in the bad guy's capture. I'm eighty-three percent sure it will work, but there is a near certainty that at the end of the day, he'll know exactly what I/we did, and how we did it. That being the case, I'd prefer he thought of me pulling a shitty on him, not coming from the both of us."

"Tyler, that's sweet and all," Frank said, "but I understood your plan the first time you explained it (*the portion/layer I explained to him I thought, a bit guiltily*), and I get that it'll step on Brimley's toes, but I wanna get this fucker. He shot my wife, well, at my wife, and scared the crap out my Lola-dog (*truer than he knew, but Lola and I had cleaned up and nobody else had to know*). I'm all in."

"Frank, we're not going to catch him *more* because you risk your job/pension/standing in the LEO community," I said. "Let me carry this part of it, and trust me when I say there will plenty left over for you to do later on."

He grumbled a while but capitulated quickly enough that I wondered how much convincing I'd actually done. The air on our conversation went dead for twenty-seven seconds, and then he told me that the file I wanted was waiting for me in my inbox and that he'd set up a meeting with Brimley for 5 p.m. at the SLPD. I hung up and ran inside to look at a long list of dead people.

The killer favored a few campsites above all others, and had only used one of the five late addition sites ... and that one only once. Campsite #35 was his clear favorite, having been the location of choice for eleven of his victims over the years. Campsites #2/#4/#5, on Eagle Island, were his next favorites, each having served up six victims over the years. #10, on Knobby Island, had been the short-term home to four victims. That only left two each for campsites #60 (*the only landlocked campsite he'd killed at, at the mouth of Lonesome Bay*) and #13 (*on Green Island*). Seven of the campsites I'd considered possibles, he had never tapped (*which led me to believe that he saw them as less desirable for killing grounds for some reason that I'd missed, or he'd made up*). It was just barely possible that I had missed a victim/campsite, but I tended to doubt it … 37 seemed a reasonable number, and I had trouble imagining him reaching beyond my fourteen possible campsites in site selection. (*Any I hadn't included posed serious problems of exposure/getaway/proximity/density, and he appeared to agree, based on his usage of the ones at the top of my list.*) I tossed thoughts along those lines around for another minute before chucking them, assuming they were based on my worry at the number of people involved in various layers of the onion plan (*which I had begun thinking of as Plan Parfait, because of the layers, not it's perfection … or Frenchness*)

I dove into the active reservations on the America Camping website and looked to see which of the guy's kill sites were currently in use, and which ones would be tomorrow. Six were currently occupied, with #35, the Richardses' old site, still cordoned off with tape and festooned with evidence flags, the only exception. Five of them were due to receive new tenants as of tomorrow, #2/#5/#10/#60/#13, while campsite #4 was registered to stay for another two days (*I hadn't included #35 in my peek, thinking it moot as I assumed it would be closed for the rest of the summer, for all intents and purposes*). Sometimes, as Mickey has often said, "It is better to be lucky than good," and this would appear to be one of those times.

I checked to make sure Austin's printer had paper in it, that my laptop could find it wirelessly (*it did, and it could … different 'it' in each case, but you know what I mean*), and printed out a fresh map of the campsites on Lower Saranac Lake (*using the DEC's pdf map, not America Camping's … I didn't want to give Brimley too much, too quickly*). I circled 13 of the campsites from my research/ guesswork, leaving out #60 (*which was the only non-island campsite among the kill sites, so it lent itself to my deception quite handily*). I rewrote the notes I'd taken/based on the America Camping website data, but altered it to leave out mention of my thoughts/suspicions that Campsite #60 might be amenable to our killer. At the end of my work, I had a nice, convincingly scribbly/messy/inspired looking stack of documents, that I then spent a few seconds crumpling slightly.

I dialed Frank's cell. He picked up on the first ring. "What's up? Everything okay?"

"Everything and everybody is fine (*except for the thirty-seven people our guy had killed during nearly two decades, plus Angela and Keith Richards, bringing his total to thirty-nine, which was still nearly everybody being fine, if you looked at it from far enough away, and over a large enough timescale, and also didn't include Sleepy the dog and Stephie the shot shelter worker*)," I said. "I just had a thought that might prime the guy's pump a little and push him in the direction of … the thing I'm working (*Frank would know most of it soon enough, but at this stage, less was more, or smarter, or better, at least for me, for my layer of the onion*), we're working. Has anyone connected the shootings with the killings on the lake?"

"I've gotten a gazillion calls and emails today asking me about a connection, but I've been ignoring them all," he said. "Been kinda busy. Why dya ask?"

"Could you call a few local news sources/outlets and do a *deep background* or *unnamed source* thing?" I asked. "I want you to tell them three things, and make sure they all get each one, okay? First, that the SLPD is pursuing some fresh leads, and is confident that a person of interest will be in custody soon. Second that a steady stream of support and manpower is coming in from Raybrook and Plattsburgh and Malone. Third, that a number of island campsites on Lower Saranac Lake are being closed pending further investigation into the killer's methods and victims."

"Okay. I think I get what you're doing, Tyler," he said, "but I gotta ask, how do you know you're not pushing him too hard, or that he'll jump the way you want him to if I dump this stuff into some reporters' laps?"

"I don't and I don't," I admitted. "But assuming my brain isn't serving up the good stuff does me no good. I've read a lot of books and articles and stories about serial/pattern killers, and this should work. Anyway, it's what I've got … thoughts?"

"Nope," Frank said. "I'll do it, and we can all just keep our fingers crossed. I'll see you in about an hour at The Lodge (*for some reason, SLPD called the ugly building they operate out of 'The Lodge' … go figure … I found that I liked being included in the crowd by Frank and that it bothered me slightly, liking it*)."

"See you," I said and hung up.

Another phone call. "Hi Mark, I think we're a *go* for tomorrow. Can your friend, who is a girl (*I emphasized my order choice so as to avoid another lengthy discussion about the intensity/flavor of their relationship*), make it up here sometime tonight? I'm only asking because if she can't, my plan can't possibly work, and my actions in the last few days/hours may prove to have pushed him toward a totally avoidable killing spree."

"But no pressure, right?" he said. "She can be here four hours after I call her, but you'll have to fill her in on the details of the mission once she gets here. I hinted to the Kovacs that I was helping you with this thing, and Iskra took the next week off from the restaurant. They really like you, think you're like a god."

"Yup, no pressure," I said. "Pack a bag with a few days of clothes for camping on the lake, and tell your friend, who's a girl, to do the same. The Soffermans will be coming from Vermont, via Route 3 out of Plattsburgh, so we should meet out that way to talk about what's going to happen in the next forty-eight hours or so."

"Should I know that name, Tyler?" Mark asked. "Did you mention them before, the Soffermans?"

"No, I didn't," I said, more than a bit nervous at having leaked that in semi-casual conversation. My brain/plans/thoughts were moving fast, and there were lots of moving parts to these nested strategies. "I'll fill you in later ... let's say nine o'clock at the big gas station that serves food in Redford, nearly twenty-nine miles past Saranac Lake along Route 3. Tell her to drive straight through without stopping in Saranac Lake. I'll pick you up at 8:10 at the Kovac's house, okay?"

He affirmed that it was, and I hung up so I could call John.

"Tyler," he said when our cell phones connected, "were those shootings about you, or this guy, and is everyone all right?"

"Meg is fine," I said. "One of the shots went into the Gibson's house. The other went into one of the employees and a dog at the shelter, which reminds me I need to talk with/check in with Dot to see how she's doing. (*I felt badly for not doing that earlier, and, interestingly, also for not feeling worse about not checking back in sooner.*) Absent definitive proof either way, I'm nearly certain it was our guy. (*A growing awareness in me indicated we really needed a cool name for him … in all of the books I'd read about serial/pattern killers, they would have already had a really special name for him; maybe Dot would have something.*) His actions and our responses are coming to a head, and my/our/the plan should be in place by tomorrow. I need you to be ready to spend some time in the woods on the QT (*I had become familiar with this term through reading over the years, but never able to find a trustworthy etymology/origin, so was always slightly nervous when/while using it*), and to meet Mark Devlin and a friend of his, who are helping us out. The friend is also a girl. (*I was severely conscious of the way I referred to her now and was growing nervous about meeting/speaking with her in a few hours, not because I would be putting her life at risk, but for fear I might mislabel her relationship with Mark … stupid.*) They'll join us at the gas station in Redford at nine p.m."

"No problem," he said. I waited for more, but there wasn't any.

"Great. I've been looping and swirling when driving around the last day or so, to avoid and/or identify anyone tailing me. You might want to do the same just in case you've made it onto his radar."

"Got it," he said.

I hung up (*out minimalism-ing John, mostly because we were done, and somewhat because I now felt a driving need to talk with, and see, Dot and the staff and beasts at the shelter*). I threw myself in the upstairs shower, put on a cleaner (*if not entirely clean*) set of clothes, grabbed the sets of papers I'd prepared for Agent Brimley, and headed out after giving kisses and hugs to Meg and Lola and Toby (*the latter thought I was pushy and a bit dramatic, giving me looks that suggested some degree of unwanted touching*). Meg had decided to stay in Saranac Lake despite Frank's offer, but she'd agreed to them keeping SLPD cars in the neighborhood to ward off evil-doers.

The Lodge, SLPD Building, Saranac Lake, NY
Saturday, 7/11/2015, 5:47 p.m.

I looped out and away from Casa Gibson, stretching my
awareness as far as was possible in all directions, feeling
for someone paying attention to me ... nothing
registered, even with paranoia set to 11 (*a Dot-ism ... the
11, not the paranoia*). I pulled all the way around the back at
TLAS, hiding my Element behind the dumpster and
fence, even going so far as to pull onto the grass to try
and increase my level of cover from all road sightlines.

"We're gonna kill this fucker, right?" Dot whispered
fiercely into my right ear when she pulled me in for a hug.
(*It was something she wouldn't ordinarily do, knowing my preference
for minimal physical contact with humans, but I assume it was a
piece of theater to cover the interrogatory in the middle of a crowd ...
and maybe because she was having a really bad day.*) "Tell me
we're going to kill him, Tyler. Stephie will be on crutches
and in PT for a coupla months, and that rat-bastard killed
my fucking dog. He killed Sleepy!"

She was shouting by the end of this statement
(*thankfully no longer in my ear, as she'd backed off after her follow-
up question*), but nobody seemed to mind/notice ... Dot
thinks of all the staff and residents of the TLAS as her
family, and the violation visited upon them today was not
the sort of thing she could/would forgive. I didn't know
Steph very well, but, of course, I hadn't wanted her (*or*

225

anyone) shot (*or even shot at, I mentally added, thinking of Meg and Lola, and Toby-dog ... although he hadn't seemed to notice*). Sleepy was a cute and goofy little dog who would have made a sweet companion for some lucky family; I had taken her for walks a few times, and could clearly picture the white muzzle/bristles at the front of an otherwise black head (*as though she'd dipped her nose into a bucket of white paint*).

"The plan is still in flux," I said in a quiet tone that I was reasonably sure would only reach her ears (*and those of Simon, the one-eyed and three-legged cat who lived most of his life on the counter. Even though he was a cat, I was pretty sure I could trust in his discretion*), "but if it goes even somewhat according to our layer of the plan's intent, he'll be dead or in some scientist's bug-box by the end of business tomorrow."

"I was gonna go over and visit with Meg and Lola this afternoon," she said, "but things here were crazy, and I spent a lot of time bouncing back and forth between TLAS and AMC and the vet's."

Tears started leaking from her eyes. Her mouth and chin set in a serious expression that I wouldn't want aimed at me (*although it was, so ... more properly/accurately, wouldn't want it composed with me in mind*). "Sleepy was such a sweet girl, and that family from Bloomingdale was thinking about taking her home and she gave my hand a fucking kiss as she bled all over the place while I drove her to the vet at what must have been a hundred fucking miles an hour. Steph, poor thing, insisted I take care of Sleepy while she waited for the ambulance, and wouldn't tell me about her leg until I gave her the bad news about Sleepy when I visited her at the hospital."

"Can I swing by your place tonight?" I asked. "I've got a couple of secret, and a few not so secret, meetings to take care of first, but then I can tell you about your job if you're still up for it."

"I'll leave the light on for you, and won't sleep until I know how I can help kill this fucker," Dot said. "Seriously, Tyler, he needs to be deceased when this is done, even if I have to do it myself. Don't worry," she said, simultaneously reading my mind and asking the impossible. "Lisa's spending the night at Steph's to help out. She doesn't need to know a thing about any of this, or about my helping, ever."

I nodded, grimly (*because that was the only flavor of nod called for/permissible in this situation*) and headed back out to my car and the meeting with Frank and Brimley.

"What the hell are you talking about, Cunningham?" Frank seemed to be laying the disdain/disrespect on a bit thick, although Agent Brimley was enjoying the temporary and grudging role of *good cop*. "I'm glad you're getting paid out of someone else's budget for this (*he was waving the thin sheaf of doctored papers around*). You're saying the killer is taking people off of the islands on Lower Saranac? There must be thirty islands, you want us to guard them all?"

"There are twenty-seven islands, and not all of them have campsites on them, Officer Gibson," I said. "Also, you missed, or are just ignoring, my point. Looking back through the records, there appear to be six campsites that he's been active at in the last decade and a half ... those are the ones you should warn/check."

"Okay, Tyler, okay, Frank, let's everyone take a minute and just breathe," Agent Brimley said. "I know the shootings, which remember, may or may not be related to the killings on Saranac Lake (*Lower Saranac Lake, I thought, but didn't say, willing him on*) have everyone a little ragged. I think you both made some valid points in the last ten minutes, but you're maybe both too close to this. Let me walk us all through what information we have, and then we can talk about logical and measured responses. Okay?"

Frank and I nodded, avoiding eye contact with each other as Brimley continued.

"Tyler has some information which may, or may not, prove out to be useful and/or usable in moving our investigation forward," he said. "We'll talk more later, the three of us, about how he got the information, and what action should be taken if it proves to be through illegal means. A number of the names associated with Tyler's research (*I had noticed he only referred to me by my first name while expecting me to address him as Agent Brimley ... I assumed he had a first name and guessed it wasn't Agent, but didn't feel it was important/advisable to ask/rock the boat at this point*) are also on the original list of names I had gathered mining the data stream (*mixed metaphor*). I think at this point, regardless of how anything else plays out, we have a responsibility to warn people staying at these sites that they may be in danger."

He stretched and puffed a bit before continuing, "To that end, the calls I made ten minutes ago were to pass the new information up and down the chain, and to get some of my men riding with DEC personnel in their boats to warn each island campsite on the lake. I've already sent and received emails and texts with some pushback from two opposing schools of thought in Albany. Starting within a few minutes—one wants me to clear all of the islands and other campsites in the area—another wants to avoid panicking tourism dollars and to just put some decoy teams out in the most probable spots to try and catch this guy."

Frank looked scared for a second as though he might

say something stupid, so I jumped in, "Agent Brimley, there are thousands of people camping in the Adirondacks in mid-July and simply no way to get them all out of the woods. With the other thing, trying to trap the guy, I think it's a good idea, but you have a responsibility to warn people in those hotspots now, if they could be in any danger. How long would it take you to set up something like that decoy trap plan in those six campsites?"

"Assuming I could get approval from the people I need it from," he said, "and funding and gear and people. Probably a few days, maybe a week to set it up right, and not scare this guy off. (*Meanwhile, I thought, you've got a bunch of windbreakers racing around the lake, obvious as all get out, pushing him straight into my trap ... thanks FBI!*)

"The bigger problem, though, at the moment," Brimley said, "is a leak in your department, Frank (*who I see now got the first name treatment as well*). In the last hour, a number of local news outlets have been running or prepping a story that a 'source close to the investigation' says we're on the verge of picking up a person of interest for questioning, that we're closing campsites on the lake, and manpower is coming in to reinforce us from Malone and Plattsburgh and Raybrook. What the hell, Frank?" He was obviously exasperated. "That's exactly the opposite of the low profile we're looking for. You need to get a message to whoever is leaking this shit that it's absolutely got to stop, and that if I find out who's been talking to the press without going through my press liaison, I'll have his badge." (*This was an exciting moment for me, although I didn't let it show... I'd only ever heard that phrase in movies before.*)

"I'll spread the word," Frank said. "Cunningham, walk with me."

We left the little conference room and walked out talking for any audience we might have, about further research and sharing my sources and being careful not to cross any lines … until we were alone in the entryway.

"Do I wanna know what's happening next?" he asked.

"You really don't," I said, "but you shouldn't make any plans for tomorrow afternoon and evening if you can avoid it. I think you might want to polish those fancy chromed handcuffs Meg gave you for your last promotion (*he didn't think anyone knew about that/them, and tried to keep his face still*), and work on your 'I can't give you much in the way of details yet, but we're a team and everybody worked really hard to keep the people visiting and living in the Adirondacks safe' sound bite, for when you perp-walk him in past Brimley and the other suits." (*Dot had used the term once, and I liked it, although when she used it, she was referring to me being "perp-walked" at the only somewhat successful completion of one of our adventures.*)

"That'd be nice," Frank said, "but I'd settle for the guy getting caught, or killed, or just your plan not going tits up."

"If things go badly tomorrow night, or even just significantly sideways," I said, not wanting to acknowledge the possibility, but now imagining a few worst (*and then some even worst-er*) case scenarios. "Meg and Dot both have an email from me with the contact information for Kitty Crocker's flesh-eating legal team … even dead, she still has considerable reach in the higher planes of government/society, she and Mike. Also, Dot has access to a couple of caches of my money, which might help. (*I've seldom run into a problem that couldn't be solved, or at least nudged toward a solution by the judicious application of a few thousand dollars.*)

"Was all that supposed to make me feel better, Tyler?" Frank said. "Cuz it didn't."

"I think it's all going to go off without any major hitches tomorrow night," I said. "But I keep trying to remind myself that this guy has literally gotten away with vicious/bloody murders since before I moved up with impunity ... he's either lucky or good, or both."

"Comforting," he said. "Call me if you need anything. My phone's staying with me, with the ringer on from now until this is done. (*Frank had once famously switched off his phone, and left his walkie in the cruiser, and missed the closure of a major case we had partly colluded on, and Meg and Dot gave him flack for it at every opportunity.*)

I walked out of the police station, suddenly feeling a cold spot hovering over my chest. Glancing around for the obvious sniper, I began moving in random jerks and fits outside to my Element; nobody shot me, so either it worked or I was a paranoid muttonhead ... I found that I could live with both options. I looped my way out and up and around the middle school and the HHott house (*a garden center where Xander worked twelve to fifteen hours every week, and I made a point of shopping there whenever I could rationalize buying plants for people*), and then eventually back down Main Street, pulling a U-turn in front of the library. Parking directly in front of the Good Chinese place to eat made sense to sit and think and drink for a bit before the next phase of the plan commenced (*mindful of the lack of good shooting positions for the killer to take advantage of and any hope of getting away afterward*).

Afternoon, Saranac to Tupper to Paul Smiths to Placid
and back again

Vanilla and Beast seemed to be sharing the same
time/space more and more often as their situation
continued to fall apart. He'd been listening to the radio all
day while driving big and pointless loops through the Tri-
Lakes, bouncing back and forth between WNBZ and
NCPR, and was shocked to hear them talking about him
as the afternoon wore on. They didn't talk about him
exactly, didn't know who he was, yet; but it sounded as
though they might be getting close. He turned the nose of
his truck back toward home, rolled up and into his garage
using the opener to minimize exposure, pulled all the
shades and hid in the basement while packing and
repacking his kit.

The announcers on both stations broke in to say the
authorities expected to have a person of interest in
custody soon. This had to mean they had found
something to push them in his direction. It had to be
Cunningham, the cops couldn't move so fast without
outside help. But then the guys on the radio said there
was help coming down from Malone and Plattsburgh,
and in from Raybrook; Vanilla felt their presence pushing
on him from that direction and fought the urge to flee
through Tupper and escape either south or to the west
into the empty wilderness of trees past the old logging
town in either direction. The radio also said the FBI was
closing the island campsites to help keep people safe

from the killer.

Vanilla scrambled up the stairs and ran over to the window to peer out between the blinds with his grandfather's 10x60 binoculars. Bracing them against the window frame to reduce the shaking of the powerful magnification, he watched DEC boats crisscrossing his end of the lake from island to island. Every boat had at least one guy in the recognizable dark blue windbreaker with big yellow letters on the back, FBI. They spent a few minutes on each island, before moving onto the next. It seemed that some people left and some people stayed, so maybe they weren't ordering people to go, but they certainly appeared to be warning them about him. He went back downstairs fuming and scared, with Beast whispering something in his ear.

It came to him eventually, the radio mentioned islands, but not campsites on land, like #60. Beast had taken two campers from campsite #60 over the years, a friendly and trusting middle-aged lady in 2001, and a divorced fireman in 2007. The FBI didn't know about them, didn't know about site #60, Beast insisted to Vanilla excitedly. This could be their final and glorious Fuck You! Vanilla started up his desktop computer, climbing the stairs again, while it booted up, to make himself a plate of sliced cheese and ham. He opened an anonymizer on his browser and logged into the camping website and database he'd helped build years ago. Vanilla looked through upcoming reservations and saw that a couple from Vermont was checking in for campsite #60 tomorrow. Beast and Vanilla conferred for a minute before deciding they would pay the Soffermans a visit tomorrow night.

Feeling better, stronger, calmer, Vanilla pulled the shades letting in the late afternoon light. The boats with the FBI people seemed to have gone, and he got the idea to go out for a ride, to look at campsite #60 for himself. It had been years since he'd visited the location, and Beast agreed it was a good idea. They wouldn't bring any of their tools, maybe just a cooler and picnic dinner and a fishing pole, blending in with the other boats rounding out another vacation day.

A few minutes later, Vanilla untied his small Whaler and puttered south and east through the waters and islands he and Beast had roamed as an apex predator for years, a wolf in sheep's clothing then as now. As he motored between Eagle and Knobby Islands, thinking about the people he'd taken from each over the years, he continued to feel more and more confidence flowing through him, swelling him after the cowering fear he'd swum in during the last few days. The boats and FBI agents that zipped by him while he rounded Sable Island, heading toward Lonesome Bay and campsite #60, robbed him of some of it, and he felt himself partly deflate, felt Beast retreat deep inside as Vanilla forced a friendly, but definitely not beckoning, wave in their direction.

The campsite was as he remembered, isolated and way out on the end of the peninsula that extended partway into, and through Lonesome Bay. Vanilla motored into, then back out of, the bay, noting the landing spots on both sides of the campsite, but also keenly aware of the boats buzzing across the water behind him, watching, or at least aware, of him. They headed back in the general direction of his dock, Beast and Vanilla talking and arguing, then talking again, about how to take the couple who would be arriving at campsite #60 tomorrow. By the time Vanilla tied the Whaler to the cleats on his dock, they had worked out what seemed a good way to play the game one last time.

Mobil Gas Station, Redford, NY
Saturday, 7/11/2015, 9:39 p.m.

When I'd driven past SmartPig, I'd seen lights and
shadows suggesting movement/people/activity, and
wondered briefly what they could still be doing up there
… I forced the thoughts out of my mind, with the help of
heaping plates of greasy and spicy pork and shrimp and
noodles and fried rices and dumplings and four bottles of
(*clearly inferior*) American Coke. I pulled out my Kindle
Paperwhite and bounced around between the five books I
was currently reading, restless but eager to distract myself
with a good story (*with a happy ending for the good guys,
hopefully*). Lawrence Block kept serving up good stuff, and
I was happily buzzing through his latest classic noir book.
I was also feeling my way through a Travis McGee novel
I'd read a few times before, loving the feral evil and
emptiness of his villains, as always. I had been reading
chunks of a fun book about an astronaut stranded on
Mars that Dot had told me about (*she was excited about the
movie, which was already in production, and teased that she couldn't
understand why I'd read the book when I could get it done in two
hours later this year*). I'd just started going through a series
of mysteries set in the Adirondacks, written by a local
author who I'd seen walking dogs a few times at the
shelter with his son … Santa Claus and a mini-him, Dot
called them, but I enjoyed the books (*they had a nice feeling*

of place, and I liked the place). I rounded out my current
reading diet with a tech-thriller about brain implants and
the scientists who love/fear/implant them, a fun read
with some frightening implications for humanity. (*It was
an interesting story, but every time I read a chunk of it, I drifted to
thoughts of Mickey, and got sad and distracted, so it was getting less
eye-time than it otherwise warranted.*)

I ate and read, ordered more food, then ate and read
some more. Halfway through my second supper, I snuck
back through the kitchen to the tiny hidden bathroom for
customers, wondered if I could just stay there (*either in the
bathroom or the Chinese place*) for a hopeful/foolish instant
before discarding the idea. I finished the food, and read
for another 47 minutes (*because 47 is an awesome number for
lots of reasons*) before heading out to loop around the town
a bit (*I was getting used to this mode of travel, and wondered if I
would have to, be able to, break the habit when/if this was all over*)
before swinging by the Kovac house to pick up Mark. He
was waiting in the driveway in the partial darkness with a
backpack and duffel. When I pulled up, he walked around
my Element, opened the hatch and threw his bags in
back.

"Kimmy texted me when she passed through Tupper
Lake a few minutes ago, so she'll probably get to Redford
around the same time as us," he said. "She asked me to
ask you about our rules of engagement."

Thankfully, I'd read the term in a book, so I didn't
have to ask him what it meant. "I'll explain it to everyone
(*Mark's head came up when I said that … he was possibly
expecting this meeting, and maybe tomorrow at the campsite, to just
be the three of us*) over Cokes at the Mobil station."

I drove out of town, not Redford and Plattsburgh on
Route 3, but on Route 86, toward Paul Smiths, cutting off
a few miles before Paul Smith's College onto Route 60 in

Gabriels which would take me up through Rainbow Lake and Onchiota before joining Route 3 for the final 14.4 miles up to the Mobil in Redford. I could see the whole region on a map projected inside of my skull, and tried to think of chokepoints for the killer to be observing/ following from, along with how to defeat/evade them. I pulled into the Buck Pond Campsite Road, turned around and parked with lights extinguished for a full five minutes to see if anyone was following. A trio of cars passed by on Route 60 while I waited, but I recognized the cars, and could eliminate each of the drivers as the potential serial killer *(one little old lady who needed help getting her cats to the vet, one high school aged boy whose arm had been in a cast for six weeks, and a Vietnam vet with chronic obstructive pulmonary disease who I knew had an oxygen tank next to him in the car)*. Once they passed, and I had waited another sixty seconds, I pulled out and continued driving to the meeting. We turned into the Mobil station at 8:53, and I took the extra time to fill up my gas tank and keep an eye on the road from both directions.

Taking another minute while we were waiting, I explained my playlist study to Mark and asked if he would like to participate. He smiled and nodded and said that he would start working on it, talking about local music he had found since moving to the Tri-Lakes; he mentioned something about proposing a similar project with some of Xander's service providers, and asked me about participant debrief/explanations regarding their music *(pulling me further into a self-examination loop I had no wish to enter, especially at this moment)*. I looked desperately down the road toward Saranac Lake, hoping for someone, anyone to come and disrupt this line of talking/reasoning.

At 8:56, John pulled in, gave me a nod through his windshield as he pulled in, parked at the far end, and

walked into the large building (*it's probably 40 by 120 feet,
with a deli counter and nice bathrooms and even some tables down
at the end farthest away from the cashiers, all of which are reasons I
picked it as a meeting spot*) just ahead of Mark and me. A tall,
athletic looking woman walked out of the bathroom
when we entered the big space. She saw Mark and started
in our direction. She leaned in for a kiss on the mouth
and an involved hug that seemed more than friendly to
my untrained/inexperienced eye. Mark turned to face me
with a slightly reddened face and neck and dilated pupils
and increased respiration rate/depth.

"Tyler Cunningham, this is my friend Kimmy
Garber," he said, making the standard hand gestures back
and forth. "Kimmy, this is Tyler. He's my ... the guy I
told you about."

I spoke up first, keeping hands/arms at my sides, to
avoid handshaking, or hugging (*if she was a hugger*). Both
activities I dislike, especially with unfamiliar people. "It's
a pleasure to meet you, Ms. Garber, thanks for coming."

"It's important to Mark, and that's enough to get me
on the road," she said. "It all sounds a little sketchy,
which is okay, to a point. I'm hoping you can explain it
further, so it makes enough sense. I wouldn't want to
have to let Marky down."

"Let's grab some drinks, or snacks if you're hungry
and sit down to talk awhile," I said. "My treat." She
snorted at that, but headed back to the long line of
display fridges across the back wall, selecting a few drinks
and a bag of chips before meeting us up at the register.

I paid for her stuff, mine, and the things Mark picked
out, and also pointed at John as he walked up to join us.
"Him, too." Then we all took a seat at one of the tables at
the far end of the building.

"I suppose you're all wondering why I've called you

here," I said. "No, not really, I just like saying that. If you're all willing to take what I think is a calculated/controlled risk, I think we can catch, and put a stop to a serial killer who's been working the Tri-Lakes since the end of the last millennium."

First, I went through how I'd been pulled into the investigation by Frank and Brimley, and what I'd learned/suspected from my visit to the crime scene and interview with Edith. I then expanded into my research and sneaking into the CA website/database (*leaving out Frank's help/involvement, to contain/isolate different elements/layers of the plan from each other*), and the findings and numbers over the years. Then I outlined how I'd used the media and the FBI to hopefully push our killer toward campsite #60 (*not mentioning the push for an escape route through Tupper, as that wasn't likely to be needed, and in any case wasn't their layer*), which brought us to the Soffermans.

"I called them earlier, having found their information on the Camping America reservation page, and explained how they could help the FBI with a sting operation by not canceling their reservation, but not keeping it either. We'll be meeting them up in Plattsburgh early tomorrow morning, and setting them up in a hotel for the next few days where they'll lay low. We'll swap cars with them and you two (*pointing to Mark and Kimmy*) will continue on to Saranac Lake, check in at the boat launch, paddle out to campsite #60, set up camp, and act like Soffermans on vacation for as long as it takes."

"As long as what takes?" Kimmy asked.

"For the killer to feel secure enough with your cover to move in and try and kill the two of you," I said, "but we don't want that to happen … the last part."

"That's a relief, Tyler," she said. "How are we going to stop him from doing that? Killing Mark and me?"

"John will drive back down tonight," I said, gesturing to John, "and hike out to the woods near that particular campsite and keep a low profile while watching the site, and you guys, and the killer as he approaches. The killer favors a knife, so he'll have to get in close, and we won't let him. I'll head back down after we intercept the Soffermans tomorrow morning and find my way back into the woods somewhere near the campsite, hopefully not too near John's hiding place. Once we see the killer tie up his boat at one of the landing points along the peninsula near the campsite, John and I will signal you that he's in the vicinity, and as soon as he gets close to your campsite, and we see that he's armed, we'll announce our presence and cable-tie him for the police, who I'll call."

"That's great if everything goes according to plan," Mark said, "but back there (*he pointed vaguely east-south-east, I'm assuming toward Afghanistan, where he and Kimmy had met and served*) we said that a plan never survives first contact with the enemy. So what's plan B?"

"I figure that whichever of us is closer to where he lands can disable his engine, or just untie and push off his boat, so if we spook him without catching him, he'll still be trapped, and we can call in the cavalry."

John raised his hand, which struck me as a little funny (*or it might have been the stress leaking out in unexpected ways*) … I pointed my Twinkie in his direction, indicating he should feel free to speak.

"No offense, Tyler," he said (*in my experience, that always precedes something offensive to the person being spoken to*), "but that's defensive and reactive and likely to be noisy and expose one of us, or the whole plan, to this guy before he gets to the site. Back in the eighties, I was posted here and there around the globe, once with a young Marine, James Mattis, who went on to great things in his day. Even back then, he was quite a wordsmith, and my favorite of his sayings has always been, '*Be polite, be professional, but have a plan to kill everybody you meet.*' I always took it to mean that you need to be ready to go all the way before anything starts. If you are, sometimes you won't have to kill everyone in the room."

"I don't have a gun," I said, "don't want a gun. I don't want to kill this guy. If we come to that, we screwed up."

"Be that as it may be, Mr. Cunningham," Kim said, "I'm up here to help him (*pointing at Mark*) help you, but I'm fully invested in the two of us coming home in one piece after your little adventure. So I'm with John here, and will be ready to do what I have to … to punch out at the end of the shift."

Mark nodded, looking at the two of them and then me. I agreed, but didn't want him dead if it was at all avoidable (*and it has always seemed to me that if you go into something with a plan in place for things to end in a certain way, it usually ends up happening like that*), but of all the blood I didn't want on my hands, theirs was more important than the killer's.

"I think we let him know he's surrounded and outnumbered, that he's brought a knife to a gunfight and we're happy to turn him into the authorities with whatever level of damage is required," John said. "If we don't get close or make noise until he's boxed in and giving up, it should go smoothly. If things do go sideways, our priorities should be to get clear of the hazard, and let our backup, I assume Gibson, with a boat at the end of the lake, reacquire and take him."

"Frank will be standing by at a friend's house on the lake, off-duty and borrowing a personal boat, not his (*I'd briefed him on this idea at the end of our meeting with Brimley, and Frank liked it, the casual feel),*" I said, "similar to how this thing started. There's some symmetry to it, but more importantly, it hopefully makes everything seem more casual, less planned. Whichever way it goes, John will sneak back into the woods after, and I just came in response to a phone call from a friend attacked while camping with a girlfriend … friend who's a girl, not dating, just friends, but maybe more, I don't know."

Kim smiled a bit, looking down at her hands on the table.

"Thanks, Tyler," Mark said. "That was great. Not awkward at all."

"Moving on," John said, smiling at me, enjoying the tension that I didn't understand, for reasons I also didn't understand. "You two will have to spend the whole day at the site just enjoying the outdoors and each other. Assume our guy is watching, either close-up or from a distance with optics. Talk normally. Do what you'd normally do while camping. You can whisper to each other in a closed tent, but outside of that, be in character every second. What are their names, Tyler?"

"Tom and Florence Sofferman, from Milton, Vermont, just north of Burlington," I said.

"We'll meet them tomorrow morning about ten at the Days Inn," I said. "They already believe the story, wanted to, having heard the news, and they jumped at the chance to help out the FBI joint task force. I've got some convincing-enough paperwork for them to sign *(reminiscent of the pile that Brimley had me sign a few days ago),* and we'll give them their room keys, rental car, and some cash for incidentals in exchange for their cell phones and car, loaded with camping gear and canoe. They agreed not to call/tell/talk to anyone about how they're helping us until ninety days after the end of the operation."

The people running the gas station were making exaggerated cleaning motions and stage-whispering about having to close soon, so I asked if anyone had questions.

"I think we get the basic shape of it," Mark said. "Pretend to be Tom and Florence Sofferman on a camping vacation, lure a killer into camp with water fights and grab-ass and hobo stew, surround and disarm and zip-tie the fucker to a tree and wait for off-duty Officer Gibson of the SLPD to come by and pick him up. Easy as cake."

"Pie," Kim said. "Easy as pie (*in a tone that made me wonder if it was a set piece between the two of them*)."

"Everybody, make sure your phones are charged tomorrow for updates via text, and turn off the sound now, so you don't forget," I said, and did it with mine, just to make the point.

We got up and I drove at the front of our two-car parade to the Days Inn at the mall-y edge of Plattsburgh, while John made his way back to the Tri-Lakes to prepare (*in his own way*) for his part in the coming adventure.

Days Inn & Suites, Plattsburgh, NY
Saturday, 7/11/2015, 10:17 p.m.

I walked into the Days Inn to check on the reservations
I'd made: two rooms (*for Kim, and Mark*) for tonight and
one room for the following four nights (*for the Soffermans*).
I'd booked it all with the SmartPig corporate card, on the
assumption that if Brimley was in a mood to follow
things back from campsite #60 after what happened,
happened, he'd be able to do so, no matter what
impediments/ruses/multi-colored-herrings I threw in
his/their path.

"Two rooms," Mark asked/commented/noted, as I
handed the key cards to him and Kim … smiling.

"We don't need two rooms, Tyler," Kim said. "We're
getting into character."

I felt awkward and blushed and stammered my way
through a few different parts of an explanation of why I'd
gotten them each a room.

Mark laughed, and held out a hand to me to stop,
"It's okay, Tyler, she's just messing with you. It's possible
I exaggerated the *friend, not girlfriend* nature of our
relationship. What? (*said to Kim*) I wasn't sure, what with
how we'd left things, and that time you mentioned a guy
you'd gone out to dinner with a couple of times."

She grabbed his hand and dragged him down the hall
toward the elevators. I was left there holding the spare

244

room key card in my hand. I called after them that I'd see them around eight in the morning. After a few seconds, I shoved the card into my pocket (*thinking vaguely that I might shower and dress nicely for my part in tomorrow's performance*), turned, and headed back out to my Element, for the drive back down to my scheduled/planned talk with Dot.

Dot and Lisa's Apartment, Saranac Lake, NY
Saturday, 7/11/2015, 11:29 p.m.

I clomped up the stairs to give the cats time to hide from me, and to make sure I didn't surprise Dot when I knocked on the door. The experiences of the last few years, most notably related to my kind of adventuring/investigations had, on occasion, given her cause to be nervous, so I did what I could to reduce it where/when I could.

   Dot opened the door before I could reach out to knock on it; she'd obviously been waiting for me to come and made a complicated set of gestures with her hands and face and mouthed, "Lisa's here." I nodded, followed her back to the kitchen and apologized to both her and Lisa for the lateness of the hour. Lisa got out a yellow cap two-liter bottle of Coke (*which gave me some indication of her positive and supportive mood/inclination toward me*) out of the ancient fridge which took up a fair portion of their kitchen's square footage, and poured me a glass over a few ice cubes (*I don't like it watered down by melting ice, and don't like the feel of ice touching my lips, but said nothing*). I sat down on the long side of the kitchen table, with each of them on one of the shorter ends, and the wall opposite me. Directly in front of me, hanging on the wall, was the huge/heavy cast-iron frying pan I'd used two winters ago to smash the hands of a man who had grievously injured

246

Dot when she'd tried her hand at my style of investigation/direct-action without me.

"Dot tells me she's helping you with this, but in a pretty out of the way and low-risk capacity, Tyler," Lisa stated, looking me straight in the eye from eighteen inches away, and holding my eyes with hers. "I made a point of being back so I could hear you say it to me yourself."

Her love for Dot is a fierce and jealous thing, big enough to drown in, or be washed away by. If I was capable of jealousy, I might be envious of what Dot and Lisa have, but I'm not, so I'm not, but I do feel a hole inside me, where something is missing (*maybe a number of somethings are missing*).

"She tells you correctly, Lisa," I said. "She'll be miles away from where we'll be … doing what we're doing, and her role is to be plan-G, only called into action if plans A through F don't work. She likely won't get within miles of the guy, but even if everything goes splat, she'll never be within one hundred yards of him."

Lisa looked slightly suspicious while Dot seemed a little glum and disappointed … if I was reading their expressions correctly, it was the best I could hope for, given the givens.

"That sounds a little thin, Tyler," Dot said. "This guy shot up my shelter, one of my people, and killed one of my dogs. I want a piece of him, not from a mile away, not as your twenty-seventh backup plan. I want to spit in his face and see his eyes get weepy and wet when we beat him."

"You'll take the deal Tyler's offering, my love," Lisa said, in a tone that brooked no debate, "or you'll take a pillow and blanket and your smelly damn cats, and find someplace else to sleep tonight, and forever. I came closer to losing you, playing cops and robbers with him (*without me really, which was the problem, but I held my tongue*), than I ever want to have happen again. You choose right now, with him an' me in the room: are you his sidekick, or are you my wife?"

Dot stood up and walked around me, around the table, and bent from the waist to kiss the top of Lisa's head and encircle her with her arms. "You're my wife, my only love, and I choose you this time and every time, but I'm also going to help Tyler put this asshole in a box. Picture Sleepy's sweet face, and imagine for a second those bristles and the way her kisses felt, or sounded when she planted one in your ear."

One of the reasons I like spending time with Dot and Lisa is to watch the rapid cycling of emotions they exhibit … in the last few minutes I'd seen fear and guilt and suspicion and anger and love and heartbreak and hope and hopelessness. They were both a bit teary now, and each looked at me with their own complex mix of thoughts/feelings on their faces.

"Okay," Lisa said, facing both of us. "You can help (*talking to Dot*), but you (*turning to me*) have to keep her out of the middle of things and get her home to me in one piece, even if it means screwing up your plans, or getting in trouble with Frank, or putting that miserable fuck in a hole in the woods. (*I couldn't help darting a quick/nervous/ guilty glance at Dot since she knew that I'd done exactly that, more than once, and hoped she hadn't told Lisa … Dot gave a careful three-millimeter negative shake of her head.*)

"Now," she said, "I assume you two want to talk about things I shouldn't, and don't want to, hear, so I'm going to go to bed, and expect Dot to join me in ten minutes, Tyler."

We both nodded, and watched/waited while she

strode out of the room.

"Give," Dot said.

I told her everything I'd been doing and planned to do tomorrow, in a three-minute precis. She nodded because she'd heard much of it earlier.

"Where am I while you guys are in the woods suckering the Lower Lake Killer?" she asked, looking at me for approval about her proposed name for the guy … I gave a small, but definite shake. (*It was a terrible name.*)

"You'll be down on Route 3, about halfway from Wawbeek Junction (*the way we referred to the junction of Routes 30 and 3 near where the Wawbeek, an old resort/restaurant down near the bottom of Upper Saranac Lake, used to be*) and Tupper," I said. "At the start of the marshes near the oxbow pond about a half mile past the fishing/boat launch on the Raquette."

"And what on Earth, of use, could I possibly be doing there?" she asked (*which was/is a fair question … it's on the outskirts of nowhere*).

"You remember the heavy/clanky/awkward duffel bag I hauled up the stairs after the thing out on Floodwood Road last fall?" I asked … this was how we referred to things she'd helped me with when Lisa was in the house, possibly within earshot. She'd helped me move a dead man's car to confuse those who might/would be looking for him, namely the entire law enforcement community of northern New York. I'd come up with an idea for a SmartPig purchase after that series of events as well as watching an episode of *The Walking Dead* with her and Lisa. The duffel, more specifically its contents, had been expensive, but I hoped it would pay off if things went that far sideways where Dot's help was needed.

I'll bring it downstairs tonight, and dump it in the back of your car," I said. "You need to take off from work a little early and head down to spend a few buggy, hopefully, pointless hours at the edge of the swamp, and wait for my phone call or text for one of two directives."

Continuing my explanation of her possible duties took another couple of minutes, at which point Lisa began coughing ostentatiously from the bedroom, and we wrapped things up. Dot assured me not only that she understood her place/job in the plan, but she hoped we'd need to make use of her ... and the duffel.

I found the duffel in the back/bottom of their front hall closet, with a strip of duct-tape labelling it TYLER, tore off the tape, said/yelled "goodnight," hauled the clanking/heavy/awkward bag back downstairs, and threw it into the back of Dot's car after checking that the device and the road flares were in there and seemed intact. I sat in my Element for a few minutes checking for any signs of movement/lights/life, and then headed out for one of my favorite remote/wild spots to hang and hide ... an abandoned/closed bridge just to the north of Lake Kushaqua.

Underside of a bridge, north of Lake Kushaqua, NY
Sunday, 7/12/2015, 4:32 a.m.

The township in which my home for the night resided
was debated *(not hotly, but debated, nonetheless)* among people
who appreciated such things as hanging a hammock
underneath a bridge that the rest of the world has
forgotten. It might be in Vermontville, it might be in
Onchiota, nobody wanted the bridge so nobody claimed
it *(but neither did they argue too strongly against it, as that might
have drawn as much attention … everyone seemed to feel that
disinterest was the best policy)*.

I had found it ten years ago, while exploring and
expanding my internal map of the world *(as I'm nearly
always doing … it's part of how I cope with a big and uncertain
world)*, and taken shelter under it one rainy afternoon
when I didn't want to go all the way back to town *(and
SmartPig)*. I'd set up the tarp I use over my camping
hammocks to keep the weather off since the bridge was
no longer watertight. The increased visibility and feeling
of solidity and the sound and vibrations of the wind
against the bridge, when the storm intensified later, was
wonderful, and I'd often returned to this spot in the
intervening years.

Nobody finds themselves at the north end of Lake
Kushaqua by accident … it's more than four miles of
significantly rough dirt road to get there from the middle

of nowhere at the sleepy intersection in Onchiota. If you do pass someone on the way to or from this spot, they've nearly always already turned around or are about to turn around and admit they're lost while heading back toward a more civilized kind of wilderness. All manner of signs along the way warn people away from the bridge, lest they be foolish enough to want to try and cross it (*I did, on foot, and didn't fall through/down*), but you can still find your way off the main dirt road, and onto a spur, dirt(*-ier*) track that brings the occasional fisherman out to the water/bridge.

It was down this very track that I pulled my Element, running it up into a thick cluster of raspberries and maple saplings that closed behind my car … hiding it as if it had never been. I pulled the small go-bag I always, thankfully, given the last day, keep in my car, complete with a lightweight hammock for just such an emergency. And I slipped a headlamp over my forehead, and waited two full minutes in the dark for the sounds or lights of pursuit before flipping it onto the dimmest setting. I hung the hammock from metal braces I could easily reach (*I'd been more ambitious/foolhardy in past visits, hanging the hammock from higher and climbing down into the hammock to swing twenty feet above the water burbling its way toward Loon Lake*) and climbed up into my aerie to think about the day behind, as well as the one ahead.

I tried to feel my way through the necessary exchanges and interactions that tomorrow would bring, but as always, human dynamics required more finesse to manage/control/compute than those of math or space or physics or cooking, and I kept running into my own uncertainty before I got too far down any particular path of possibilities. After a fruitless/frustrating 17 minutes, I switched to listening to the sounds the forest and river and bridge all made in their ongoing and complex interactions with each other. I fell asleep thinking about ecosystems and edge-effects and the symbiotic relationships all humans choose and understand, and respect. *(Everyone else seems to know their way around these relationships as naturally as squirrels understand trees and hawks, and I never seem to learn how to gather food and/or avoid predation. I jammed myself awkwardly into that metaphor ... sorry.)*

I woke up when a large something crunched through the gravel up on the roadbed above me, but whatever it was, it got scared by some noise I must have made, and crashed off and into the woods, which meant it likely wasn't my serial killer. A few minutes later, I got up and made some breakfast and eventually pointed my car in a vaguely northeast direction to make the drive up to Plattsburgh, thinking of the Dunkin' Donuts near the SUNY Plattsburgh campus as an optimal spot to wait for everyone else to wake up and for the day to begin. I had a feeling it would become fast and violent and end badly for some, if not all, of the people involved in my layered trickery *(but that could have just been pessimism born of sleeping slightly cold and in my boots ... time would tell).*

Days Inn & Suites, Plattsburgh, NY
Sunday, 7/12/2015, 8:13 a.m.

I eased the Element down a series of tiny, and ill-repaired,
dirt roads/tracks/paths up and down hills in the back of
beyond, north of Kushaqua, until the wheels finally
touched tarmac again (*cracked though it was*); it felt like a
superhighway. Following my GPS's compass as much as
possible (*since there were no roads as far as she, the Teutonic and
bossy voice had earned her the name Helga early in our relationship,
was concerned*), I took northerly and/or easterly choices
when they came up. I found a series of bigger and more
civilized roads when I climbed up and out of the forest
primeval, eventually finding Route 3, and sped my way up
toward donuts and Coke and Mark and Kim (*which I will
admit, patient reader, was a list in descending order of importance at
that point in my life/day/plan*).

I got two boxes from the DD near SUNY
Plattsburgh, each containing a perfect dozen, assured
them once again that, *no*, I didn't want/need coffee. I
always pass the Dunkin' Donuts that was/is closer to the
hotel where I assume Mark and Kim still slept, based on
repeated results from my cruller test. Crullers are not a
favored donut of mine, but they do generally have the
shortest effective shelf-life, so when exploring/expanding
my world for donut suppliers, I will always order a cruller
to determine freshness. There are six Dunkin' Donuts in

254

the greater metropolitan Plattsburgh area, and in repeated samplings of all six at different times of the day and year, the store closest to the university consistently had the freshest crullers (*the DD in SL would fail the cruller-test, except for the crucial/critical fact that there are no other options within 50 miles, which necessitates the introduction of a curve in the grading scale*). Donuts safely planted on the passenger floor beside me, I drove out to the spot where the ferry to Vermont launches from, stopped at a convenience store on the way to top up my gas tank, offloaded some liquids and solids I had no further use for, picked up a couple of cold six-packs of Coke, and then headed out to watch waves and big boats and noisy white birds for 53 minutes, while I ate and thought and again tried to reach through time to shape the events of today/tonight in the ways I wanted things to go.

While poking along on the way back to town and to the Days Inn, I explored some new roads/neighborhoods to expand my internal map of Plattsburgh. At seventeen minutes to eight, I pulled in the parking lot, regardless and instead of waiting, snuck in and up to rap on their door. For a few years, I've been refusing to stop in at front desks, preferring/insisting on either walking or sneaking into the hotel to accomplish my business without seeking the approval of the sleepy functionaries behind the desk … walking in past the desk requires/demands the correct level/appearance of confidence, without being boisterous or haughty, while, in other cases, it's entirely possible to get inside without having to run the gauntlet. In this case, with this hotel, I was able to walk around the outside and spy an exit door that had a shim jammed into it to prevent full closure … I was able to walk in and up to Mark and Kim's room without seeing another person. I knocked, waited, knocked louder, waited, and knocked still louder before I heard movement from within … a tremendous crash, loud male cursing, louder female laughing, and finally a voice from the other side of the door.

"Tyler?" Mark asked. "That had better be you, and someone had better be on fire since you're early."

I heard/felt a thump through the door, someone being shoved aside, the chain being pulled from the latch, and Kim opened the door and waved me in. They both had towels covering external genitals but were soaking/dripping wet. Mark was rubbing an elbow and the wet floor tiles just outside the bathroom and overturned end table between the bed and bathroom were enough to help me make some assumptions about the crashing/cursing/laughing I'd heard moments ago.

"How nice," I said. "I didn't know the rooms had two showers."

Mark looked awkward, Kim giggled into a hand unsuccessfully covering her smile, and I figured this was another relationship thing I'd have to ask Dot to explain to me. (*I couldn't imagine why people would want to do that stuff in a place meant for getting clean, as well as run the risk of injury with all of those hard/slippery surfaces nearby.*) I pulled a box of donuts out from behind my back, and the moment was forgotten, or at least behind us (*is there anything donuts can't fix?*). Kim ran around the room picking up a few things before dashing into the bathroom. Mark dropped his towel and started getting dressed in front of me. (*I turned and looked out the window, wishing I'd grabbed a donut before the naked-time had commenced, unable to find one now.*)

An entirely donut-free two minutes and 27 seconds later, I heard the bathroom door open and Kim yelled at Mark, "For Christ's sake, Mark, don't make him wait. Tyler, you can turn around, Mark's fully dressed."

I did as she suggested, and they were, in fact, both dressed and less drippy than before … also plowing through the donuts in a way that made me glad I'd gotten my own box.

"Uh," Kim began, "we can pass as LEOs posing as Tom and Flo Sofferman, but you need a little … sprucing up."

"What do you mean?" I asked.

"If you're going to sell them on your story, all that paperwork and the badge you showed us last night are a good start, but we need to get you cleaned up and dressed a bit better. Hop in the shower to scrub off the woods a bit, and then we can find some khakis and a white dress shirt and a blue or black windbreaker somewhere. Sound good?"

I decided/admitted that she had a point and I could use a shower, so I nodded and went across the hall to the other hotel room I had rented to shower. Then we headed over to the local Walmart to find all of the clothes necessary for my Fed-costume (*thankfully, I'm an easy size to shop for*) and a huge bag of heavy-duty cable ties. We were back in time to meet the Soffermans when they arrived a few minutes after ten.

Days Inn & Suites parking lot, Plattsburgh, NY
Sunday, 7/12/2015, 10:14 a.m.

My new clothes felt stiff/shiny/obvious, but I think that
worked in my favor when the Soffermans drove up; they
saw the three of us waiting at one end of the parking lot,
and made straight for us. Kim and Mark had suggested
they stand close behind, and to one side of, me, holding
papers and room key and cash and big Ziploc bags …
waiting for my signal to approach. The Soffermans
stepped out of their Subaru wagon, loaded with gear
inside and a canoe on the roof.

   "Good morning," I said. "Thanks for coming.
Thanks for helping us. I'm Special Agent Astucia, Jamon
Astucia (*I felt like I was bonding up my fake name as I stuck my
hand out, but that's how my two assistants this morning insisted it
was done … it occurred to me as I shook first Tom's, then
Florence's, hands, that maybe they were setting me up to look silly,
but there was nothing I could do at that point*)."

   "Excuse me, Agent Astucia," Florence said. "Can you
say your first name again?"

   I was already regretting the clever name (*would Bill
Smith have killed me?*), "Jamon, ma'am," I said, "like Jame-
On … my father was born in Belize (*God help me, I couldn't
stop with pointless backstory details*)."

   "Uh, okay," she said. "So, I guess you can't tell us a
lot about what's going on, but…"

   "We've reached a point in our investigation where the
higher-ups feel that having some undercover assets would
be beneficial to us, and safer to the general public … that

258

being you," I said. "These agents (*I waved a hand back at Mark and Kim*) will be filling in for you on your camping trip on Lower Saranac Lake for the next few days while you stay here in Plattsburgh on the government's dime. We've arranged for a suite for you, a rental car, and some spending money so you can stay off the credit card radar."

"What are we supposed to do, or not do?" Tom Sofferman asked.

"That's a great question, Tom," I said. "I see you packed the car as if for a camping trip which is great. Did you also pack a bag for each of you during your stay? (*nods*) Great. Can you get them out now, so we don't forget in a few minutes when the agents take off for their/your camping trip? This car (*I pointed out a rental sedan I'd arranged for them*) is yours until the sixteenth, as is the hotel room (*handing Tom the room key*)," I said. "Both are paid for, and this (*I felt Agent Kim tap me on the shoulder with a thickly stuffed envelope, which I took and passed to Tom*) should keep you fed and watered until we see you on Thursday. There's enough to pay for meals out and whatever else you might feel like doing while you're our guests (*Kim had told me to pitch my voice slightly here to creepy it up a bit, insisting that a Fed would*). Which brings us to (*Agent Mark stepped forward with labeled Ziploc bags for each of them*) … cell phones and credit cards please (*I had thought we might have trouble at this stage, but Mark had told me that once they had three-quarters of an inch of government cash in hand, we could have taken their clothes without hearing a peep*). We need you to stay off the radar for the next few days because we're unsure of just how tech-savvy the alleged perpetrator is … we'll monitor your phones, and if there's an emergency, one of my tech-support people will get in touch with you through the hotel."

They both seemed uncomfortable having given us their phones and cards, but the final piece of the hustle seemed to do the trick.

"I have a few forms for you to sign," I said in my best officialdom tone. "Confidentiality, indemnity, insurance, per-diem, and such ... feel free to read it before signing (*which, in combination with the thickness of the packet, almost guaranteed they wouldn't give it more than a cursory glance ... they didn't*). Sign every place you see a yellow flag ... and date it there, great. Agent Todd can serve as witness as called for at the bottom there (*I wasn't positive if Todd was supposed to be his first or last name and didn't think Mark knew either, but a series of bumps and squiggles later, I had the thick sheaf of documents in my hand*) ... super, thanks so much."

"Any questions?" I asked. It appeared not. "Great. Remember, please, no calls to family and friends. My direct line number is at the top of the front sheet on the packet Agent Sigrid gave you, please call at any time, day or night, if you have questions or concerns, and either I, or one of my people (*another suggestion from Kim, just the right/expected touch of superciliousness*) will do whatever we can to help. Again, thank you so much for your help in this matter." (*I shook both of their hands, for the second time in ten minutes, despite my discomfort with the Locardian practice. Mark and Kim had both insisted it was necessary, so I capitulated.*)

"We're happy to do it," Tom said, putting his arm around his wife. "Happy to help."

Florence looked a bit nervous/excited/giddy as she said, "It's just exciting to think we're a part of all this, part of a real-life criminal case. Imagine."

Tom had the envelope of cash in hand, and Florence had the rental car keys and the key card to the hotel suite, and we had everything we needed ... so we left as quickly as seemed polite/plausible.

Mobil Gas Station, Redford NY,
Sunday, 7/12/2015, 10:33 a.m.

Mark and Kim (*now Tom and Flo*) were following me on
my way back down toward Saranac Lake, but I thought
we should pull in for a second to catch up before they
walked onto the next stage. I signaled a right-hand turn
and pulled up at the far end of the parking lot, away from
pumps/market/free-air and waited for them to pull in
beside me.

"I think that went well enough anyway," I said.
"Enough to give us the window of opportunity we need
to play our game down at campsite number sixty. You
guys should poke around in the back of the Subaru for a
minute and play with the roof-rack to make sure you can
find and work everything when you get to the boat
launch. From here on out, you need to be Tom and
Florence Sofferman."

"They're sweet," Kim said, smiling. "They left a note
for us with the receipt for the campsite and a little map of
how to get to the boat launch and to the campsite, and a
list of all the gear they packed for us, including a cooler
stuffed with food and non-alcoholic beer, which is just
about the cutest thing ever."

"So, once you two are comfortable with the
Sofferman camping kit, I'll head out and down and make
my way over to the woods nearby that campsite," I said,

261

"where I'm sure John is also, by now. Don't look for either of us or the killer ... we'll be there and hopefully impossible for you or him to spot, and you should count on the fact that he'll be watching from the moment you get to the boat launch until we take him (*or he takes you, a grim minion in the back of my melon piped up*)."

Mark yanked on the tie-downs for the heavy-looking Old Town canoe up on the roof, and Kim swung the hatch open and started to move stuff around, unloading and reloading things a bit (*everyone loads a car differently ... everyone*). They seemed intent on their job and ready to go ... no questions.

"I don't entirely understand why you two are doing this," I said. "I'm doing it because it's what I do, how I fit in this world, but there's still time for one or both of you to come to your senses. If so, we can drive back up to P-burgh and call the cops and FBI (*I'd apparently given up on the special emphasis thing*) and tell them everything, and let them do what they do."

"He's here because of what you did for his new best friend," Kim said, pointing with an elbow toward Mark, "and also trying to be a big damn hero. (*I gave her an acknowledging nod for the Firefly reference.*) I'm here because I like him an awful lot, and once he told me about things, I worried he might not be able to manage without me. Besides, I want to see how it turns out, this thing, and ... us. I can't want to do that without him."

Mark leaned over and kissed her on the top of her head, and I felt a momentary certainty that I was sentencing a perfectly formed/fit couple to death at the hands of a hugely successful and long-running serial killer ... thankfully, I don't do facial expressions unless I try to, so they couldn't read me in this instance.

"Well," I said. "Good luck, be careful, and if someone

tries to kill you, you kill 'em right back (*paraphrasing Mal a bit, but Kim got it and returned the smile*). I'll be there when he's about to make his move … don't kill him if you don't have to, but if you're unsure, kill him a lot, and we'll clean up afterward. I want to get to know both of you better (*thinking briefly of Cameron from last summer, whom I would never get to know any better*)."

That seemed to kill the mood a bit, and I didn't know how to fix things, so I left.

State Boat Launch, daytime

Vanilla had arrived, with donuts and coffee, shortly
before the guys in the shed would be there. He parked far
enough away that he'd blend in, wearing a big hat and
bigger sunglasses so nobody'd recognize him. With a view
of the entrance off Route 3, and of the shed, Vanilla was
sure he wouldn't miss the Soffermans when they arrived,
and he didn't. It was an extended wait, and he'd long-
finished his donuts and coffee, and was thinking about
sneaking into the woods for a pee when the red Subaru
station wagon with the right Vermont tags turned in and
pulled up and parked in front of the shed.

   The couple got out with some papers in hand, and
Tom Sofferman entered while Florence leaned against the
car and looked at the ramp leading down into the water.
Beast rolled down the window a few inches and breathed
deeply, imagining he could smell her across the
impossible distance; he shifted uncomfortably, adjusting
his pants, and continued watching. She looked at the
shed, seemed to think about joining her husband inside,
but instead, walked down to the water and stuck a teva'd
toe in to feel the temperature. Walking back up the ramp,
she seemed to be glancing around, beyond the shed and
their car, but Vanilla was back and knew he was far
enough that she'd only see a parked truck and windshield,
not him.

Tom Sofferman came out a minute later, said something to her, and he drove the car down to the water's edge while she followed on foot. Together, they unstrapped and carried the canoe to the paddler's dock. The couple began unloading their camping gear and hauled it down to drop it beside the boat. Partway through the process, Tom stayed and started loading the boat in what appeared a practiced manner, while his wife kept shuttling back and forth, bringing bags and boxes of stuff from the car to the boat. She was too pretty for Tom, but that happened sometimes. Beast howled for her blood, desperate to taste her, and him, the husband. Vanilla counseled patience, preaching the hunt and reminding Beast of games played, and enjoyed, in the dark woods, on previous nights.

In a compromise, they started the truck and drove out past the couple, mere feet away. Beast rolled down his window and snuffled in huge lungsful of air she'd moved through, while Vanilla noted they both seemed in good shape. He hoped that Beast would be able to take them both later, by the light of their campfire when they were tired after a day of sun and fun. Vanilla drove up and out of the boat launch area, to his lair, for a few hours of preparation before heading out to watch and wait and eventually take their prey. Play the game, win the day, and drink their blood from the blade of his knife (*and maybe directly from her neck or breasts, depending on how things went*).

Woods near campsite #60, Saranac Lake, NY
Sunday, 7/12/2015, 8:23 p.m.

As I drove away from Mark and Kim at the Mobil station, I didn't look for them in my rearview again, trying to get my head in the game … this serious game we were playing with the killer (*for whom, it occurred to me, we still didn't have a good name*). I turned off Route 3 for my Onchiota cutoff again, this time driving out to Paul Smiths and taking Route 30 towards 186 (*where they met in Lake Clear*) and then continuing on Route 30 all the way out to the far end of Upper Saranac, heading back in the direction of Saranac Lake on Route 3. My routing was far from the shortest/quickest way from point Redford to campsite #60, but it kept me out of Saranac Lake completely, and hopefully off the killer's radar (*and out of his vision*).

I could sense campsite #60 off to my left through the woods as I drove along Route 3, and felt some pull to park by the side of the road and walk the shortest distance to it. Instead, I resisted and drove another half mile along the road, then pulled on the right and drove around a few turns on West Lake Shore Road until my Element would be impossible to see from Route 3. I grabbed my resupplied and augmented go-bag, and headed back to Route 3, waiting until I could neither see nor hear traffic in either direction. Sprinting across the road, from woods to woods, I disappeared into the thick forest adjacent to Lonesome Bay.

Heading west until I could see the water, I turned left to follow the shore down to the next bay, and eventually up the peninsula, at the tip of which campsite #60 was located. No human path existed from where I was to where I wanted to be, but there were almost always animal tracks/trails near the water, so I was able to make pretty good headway with a minimum of noise once I found a small and ill-used deer-trail. Twice I stopped to listen and look, either for people behind or ahead/around me; I stopped walking and leaned against a tree for a few minutes, waiting for the noises of the forest to resurface, for the beasties to forget/forgive my intrusion. The sound of boats echoed on the lake to my right, cars on Route 3 to my left, and once, a helicopter moving northeast to southwest, above the lake, (*possibly looking for a boat, or simply traveling along a reasonably direct route from Saranac Lake to Tupper Lake on a medevac flight*) but I didn't hear/see/sense any other people in the woods within the limits of my sensory package. I continued moving through the woods as quietly as I could and soon turned back north and east up the peninsula.

Campsites #58 and #59 were both also on the peninsula with #60, and were obviously occupied (*#58 was quieter than #59, but I spotted bright tent fabric through the woods, and smelled breakfast/morning fire smoke from one or both of them*). I was able to pass by both without anyone in either camp noting my passing and moved much more slowly now, choosing the spot on the ground each foot went, to avoid snapping sticks. Being extra cautious at this point, I paused regularly to listen and look around for signs of life. I didn't see John, but I assumed/trusted that I had passed him (*or at least near him*) at some point in my slow progress up the narrowing peninsula. When I spotted the end of the land, I cut over and away (*to the south/right*) to look for a hide/blind.

A car-sized boulder, with a fallen tree leaned up against it, was perfect and I nestled into the space between the two, wrapping myself in a big camo fleece blanket. I imagined I would be essentially invisible to anyone who wasn't specifically looking for me, and even then someone would have to be close/lucky to spot me. I'd filled my hydration sleeve in the hotel, and took a long drink now (*disappointed, as always, with the chlorine taste of city water when in the woods*), then ate some jerky and a handful of gummy worms before closing my eyes for a nap, certain I'd wake up before anything happened, or anybody killed anyone else.

Awakened a short while later (*not wanting to look at my watch/phone, I guessed more than 20 minutes, but less than 60, based on the dryness of my mouth and stiffness of my joints*), I could see and hear Mark/Tom and Kim/Flo landing and unpacking the canoe, hauling stuff up from the water to the campsite, pitching the tent, and eventually setting up an early lunch on the picnic table. They laughed and joked and talked about non-existent jobs and pets and a roofer … I was impressed. In the afternoon, they went for a swim and gathered firewood for the evening, and if Kim noticed me when she passed nearby during wood gathering, she was polite/smart/cagey enough not to say anything, or break character. I was getting quite stiff and itchy (*and I don't even want to talk about peeing in situ … in fact, forget I said anything and we'll all try to put it behind us*) and wishing for a fast-forward button as the afternoon stretched on into early evening. They swam and read and at one point retired into their tent for a noisy bout of sex that seemed to be taking the performance a bit too far. As the sun started easing down out of the sky, Kim and Mark started a small fire. I could see them prepping and cooking tinfoil stew packets ... the smell made me hungry in a way that the jerky and gummy worms in my pack didn't help.

I kept my eyes and ears open, searching for any sign of another boat coming into range of *our* campsite. It wasn't until the sun had started to approach the treeline on the far shore that I heard one too many repetitions of a non-woodsy noise from somewhere behind me that it occurred to me that both John and I had walked cross-country to get here ... there was no good reason the killer had to come in by boat (*although he had in all of his previous outings*). Suddenly, I felt a weight drop on me ... the possibility of a monumental screw-up/miscalculation, an assumption on my part that could put everybody on the ground here at extreme (*mortal*) risk.

The shootings, trashing SmartPig, going after Edith in the hospital ... all of these things spoke to the killer devolving. I'd ignored the clues, intent on finding my way to the quick solution. The realization smacked me like a thunderclap in my hide/side/brain, and I felt a desperate desire to stand up and shout, calling the whole thing off. Luckily, I rode over that desire and spent a second adjusting my plan minutely instead.

Having figured all of that out in a horrible instant, I soon realized there was next to nothing I could do to remedy my oversight. I sent out a text message to John/Mark/Kim (*killer could have walked overland instead of boat, he could be here already ... stay the course or abort?*), but had no way to know if they got, or understood it. We were all already to some degree committed but could probably figure out some way to redirect or escape the situation if Mark and Kim wanted to do either. I saw Kim lean in to give Mark a kiss by his ear that lingered slightly too long for a simple kiss/nuzzle, and then got messages back from both John and Kim a minute or so later … both said to go ahead with our plan, so I checked in with Dot to make sure she was in place for her role in tonight's drama. She must have been waiting/watching to hear from me because I got thumbs up text inside a minute. I began to run new scenarios in my head to try and predict whatever was going to happen next.

"The good news is that it's gonna happen," said Barry, beside me, under a monstrous camo blanket, "and soon. The bad news is that it's not gonna go down at all the way you were hoping it would happen."

I couldn't help but agree with his logic, and quickly dashed off a text to Frank saying the killer had come in overland and that Frank should get to campsite number sixty ASAP. He sent a reply within thirty seconds saying he was on his way, maybe eight to ten minutes away; I settled down into my warm/private/snug/hide next to wait for the cavalry to arrive and take this situation from a dangerous level of chaos to a safer, if less satisfying, state of control.

When I heard the shouting down the slight hill in the campsite a few seconds later, I knew we didn't even have the time it would take for Frank to get there from his friend's camp/dock.

Sundown, Lower Saranac

Vanilla parked in one of the spaces by the side of the road just past Lonesome Bay and walked as quietly as Beast was able along the shore toward the campsite. His backpack was heavy and swayed from side to side. Thankfully, the sweatshirt he wrapped around the bone saw and spare blades prevented any clanking. Quiet gurgling of Gatorade in bottles was comforting to both Vanilla and Beast as they found killing, and especially dismembering the bodies afterward, to be thirsty work. They hated the headaches that had accompanied dehydration in earlier games when Vanilla hadn't planned ahead.

When he got to the base of the finger of land sticking up and into Lower Saranac, Vanilla called a rest break for five minutes before the slow walk up the narrow wedge of land to the end, where the Soffermans were waiting for him. Once his breathing wasn't so labored and the beating of his heart stopped hammering in his head, Beast's ears picked up noises from nearby campsites #58 and #59. Not a lot, and not specific words or even voices, but the sounds of human activity in the woods, by water, were unmistakable. Vanilla remembered watching a movie years ago where the hero confused a giant worm by moving in a pattern that was unlike those heard, or seen, in human movement; he tried to convey the essence of it to Beast but was unsure if the suggestion found purchase on his alter-ego's blood-drunk consciousness.

Beast finished the liter bottle of purple Gatorade and uncomfortably left the bottle on the ground next to his resting spot. He and Vanilla never littered, hated litter and litterers, but, in this case, they didn't want to run the risk of loud empty-bottle crunchy noises. He peed against the rock he'd been sitting on, vaguely aware of marking his territory, and set off toward campsite #60.

As Beast got closer, he began to block out the sounds from the campsites behind him and focus on the sensory input he was getting from the space in front of him. He heard woodland noises, rabbits and squirrels making sounds from small movements. The smell of fire giving off both spicy pine and sharp birch smoke, and beneath it the odor of onions and butter and beef, maybe hobo stew. He could see the couple Vanilla had spotted at the boat launch, hours ago, watched them talking and laughing, once ducking into the big dome tent for some enthusiastic sex, and checking phones a couple times, but otherwise just enjoying the woods and water and being on vacation.

Beast and Vanilla both watched the scene with a delight they hadn't felt since the early rounds of the game. Something terrifying and exhilarating and freeing about the feeling, the knowledge, that this was the last game, peaked their senses. After tonight, win or lose, there would be no going back to the mildewed house and musty memories of hiding and pretending and crying in the darkness with his secret victories and secret trophies to ward off old ghosts and fears. After tonight, win or lose, they would be something new, something the world had never seen. Beast smiled at the thought of bathing in the blood and fear of his victims again and again, until he lost, tonight or a thousand nights from now. Vanilla could natter at him with his cautionary advice, as had forever been his way, but Beast was finally in charge. He was determined to paint the woods red, and fill the lakes with blood, to remake the Adirondacks in his image, a dark place, wet and sticky and filled with whispers and screams and pleas and denials, and above all, the blood of his victims.

He rose from behind the rock where he had paused and walked down into campsite #60 like a king or god, parading among his lessers. The Soffermans seemed stunned, but not as surprised as Beast had hoped they would be when he walked out of the woods and into the clearing filled with their gear and smells and noise.

"Good evening folks," Vanilla said, at Beast's invitation. "We're doing some spot checks at campsites around the lake, after the recent unpleasantness. Do you have some ID and the paperwork you'd have gotten from the rangers when you checked in for the campsite?"

Something was wrong. Beast didn't know what, but the sensory input felt different than it should have been. The Soffermans didn't seem either scared or cowering. Both Tom and Flo had big loose shirts untucked and seemed to have altered their posture slightly, and moved their hands slightly toward similar spots at the small of their backs. Instead of turning toward their tent, or just subconsciously shrinking away from him, a stranger, they had spread out and away from each other by a few feet, and then taken several steps closer. Beast found himself taking a step back to maintain distance and reaching to his side for the big and sturdy Buck knife he'd brought for tonight.

"Don't," said a deep and rasping voice from behind him, where Beast thought there'd been only rocks and trees. "We've got you, son. It's over and done."

"It can't be over," Beast said, quietly, almost to himself. "There's no over. No done."

Beast turned his head slowly until he could see the old man stepping out of the brush with a pistol pointed at the center of his forehead. He heard more noise from the woods, and that fucking Cunningham stepped out, with a handful of cable ties, reminding Beast momentarily of when Vanilla's mom used to make spaghetti for supper. Tom and Flo Sofferman, or whoever, whatever, they were, both had handguns out and pointed in his direction. Beast noted coolly, more so than he felt, that all three armed individuals had fingers outside the trigger-guards of their guns. If he could bring them in close enough, if their guns made them brave, he might get at least one. Adrenaline roared through his body like a tsunami down an alley, blood hyper-oxygenating, muscles flexing, senses sharpening; everything in front of him, nothing and nobody behind.

Woods near campsite #60, Saranac Lake, NY
Sunday, 7/12/2015, 8:41 p.m.

I stood up from my hide and moved as quickly as I could through the darkening woods, to the campsite. The killer was standing in front of me, facing Mark and Kim, having just finished saying something, and John was eight feet behind him, pointing the pistol he'd had the other day at the killer's head. Kim and Mark now had their own handguns out, but not fully trained on him (*aimed at the ground between themselves and the killer*).

"Don't shoot him unless you have to," I said, stepping into the campsite clearing, and gesturing to everyone (*him included*) with my cable ties. "Frank will be here in a minute, and it'd be better for lots of people if this guy is in shape to answer questions."

"Fine," John said. "So long as he doesn't force the issue."

"Tyler," Kim said, "move slowly to within six feet of him and wait for him to turn sideways to me and put his hands behind his back for you. If he doesn't do that, I'll shoot him in the knee, and we'll figure out some other way to do it (*we both followed her directions ... I moved in, and the guy turned around and put his hands as far behind his back as was possible with his bulky backpack somewhat in the way*)."

Emboldened by his cooperation, everyone took a relaxing breath.

"Cross your wrists behind your back, and let Tyler loop the tie over your hands," Kim continued. "Tyler, make sure you feed the strip in the right way and then pull it as tight as you can. It'll hurt, but he's not gonna have them on long enough to do permanent damage. They're temporary restraints."

He held out his hands for me, not quite meeting, behind his back, and with the large-sized tie in hand (*I shoved the rest into my belt to free my hands*), I moved in to secure the serial killer.

As soon as he felt my fingers close around one hand, he spun around and before I knew it, he and I were at one point of a trapezoid, the other three being John and Kim and Mark. I thought (*possibly pointlessly*) that the shape was more trapezium than trapezoid, and it occurred to me that the word might have jumped into my head because the killer was manhandling the trapezium bone in my right hand, which could lead to an increased risk of arthritis in this already prone area. The thought was nearly forced from my head by the feeling of a knife blade against my throat, and everyone shouting in quick succession (*nearly simultaneously*).

"I'll open him up and drain him in the dirt if you three don't throw your guns in the fire in the next five seconds!" the killer screamed, and I could feel a small rivulet of blood start down my neck and into my shirt.

"How about we don't throw explosives into the fire while you're jumpy as a cat and have a knife at our friend's throat, shithead?" John asked. (*I wasn't crazy about the challenging tone, but assumed/hoped he knew what he was doing*).

"Why'n't you tell 'em all that shit about the two different uses of the word trapezium, Tyler?" Barry said from over next to John. "Especially the stuff about the guy who's gonna kill you with a huge knife mebbe increasing your risk of arthritis thirty years from now? If you're lucky, the one with the knife might fall asleep from boredom, and then you could tie him up like you were supposed to."

"Drop it," Kim said, finger inside the trigger guard now, and gun aimed at his center mass. "Drop the knife or I will kill you!"

"Let him go, and I'm sure we can work something out," Mark said.

"If you're not going to make a productive suggestion, maybe you could just shut up for now, Barry," I said. "Things are tricky enough right at this moment without smartassery."

Everyone real looked momentarily confused, and then John smiled fractionally and gave me a tiny wink.

"In the lake, then," the killer said. "Everyone chuck their gun into the lake or Cunningham dies!"

"I cannot for the fucking life of me imagine why this shit always happens, and people chuck a perfectly good weapon into the lake," Barry said. "Just you watch, in a few seconds, they'll be tossing perfectly good guns into the water, an' he's still gonna kill you. Because, why wouldn't he, once everyone has disarmed themselves?"

John must have been watching me very carefully, because he cut me off before I could speak to answer Barry, "Tyler, that's not going to help anything, please just be quiet while we work this out. Trust me."

Mark broke first (*as I had suspected he would*), and threw his gun into the lake underhand … it landed with a splash like a fish jumping. Listening in that direction, I thought I heard the sound a motorboat approaching, dopplering in as it came our way. The killer's eyes/head turned and followed Mark's gun arcing out and into the water, and saw that John and Kim seemed to have noticed the new sound also. Kim and John appeared to be trying to send messages through the ether for a few seconds until the killer jerked the knife at my throat for emphasis (*I will always regret that I made a small and pathetic sad/scared noise when the blood flow increased down onto my chest, as it clearly forced the next actions/reactions*).

"Okay, okay," Kim yelled, at least partly to get his attention, and distract him from John (*who must have won their argument of shrugs and eyebrow-tilting*). "He'll make a piss-poor hostage if he bleeds out in your arms. See, I'm tossing it into the water."

She did toss her gun into the lake, but just barely, and it banged/clanged off some rocks at the water's edge; the killer's eyes/ears/attention were drawn to the spinning/sparkling metal and noisy entry into the water.

It was at that moment John shot him … and me.

Woods near campsite #60, Saranac Lake, NY
Sunday, 7/12/2015, 8:47 p.m.

In the strictest sense, John didn't shoot me. The killer had
turned marginally at the noise of Kim's gun entering the
water, and John had scooted sideways a few feet to get a
better angle on the bad guy. His aim was good, he
hit/broke the guy's ulna, a fragment of which
punched/blew into the heavy trapezius muscle at the top
of my right shoulder (*"Don't you fucking start!" Barry
cautioned me forcefully as I thought this*).

The killer dropped the knife and shoved me into John
before he could get off another shot. I tripped midway
across the distance between us, my head and injured
shoulder rammed into John's stomach, pushing all of the
air from his lungs in a giant WHOOF." From behind us,
a feral scream echoed as the killer scooped up the knife,
and dove on top of us.

I heard the knife rip through shirt and skin and flesh
three times; each time I wondered if he'd stabbed me or
someone/something else in the tangle of limbs and
trunks that we three presented, rolling around the ground,
or if I was just in shock and hadn't realized the damage
yet. John's final groaning exhalation told me everything I
needed to know, and more (*at least about this particular stage
of this particular encounter ... there were a nearly infinite amount of
things that I wanted to know nearly an infinite amount about*).

279

Suddenly, I was able to disengage from the pig pile I'd been a part of ... and rolled clear.

"All of you stop moving, stop even thinking about moving!" the killer screamed.

John was still moving, but his formerly grey T-shirt and khaki pants were now mostly black with blood. Mark started in John's direction, and the serial killer stopped him with a shot that twanged off a boulder next to Mark. (*I'm not sure if he missed, or if it was a warning. I lean toward the former, as I can't imagine why he would give any of us a warning at this point. I've had no luck hitting anything more than a few feet away the few times I've tried to shoot a handgun, despite what TV teaches us.*) I could definitely hear a motorboat getting close, and it should have been slowing by now, but wasn't ... Frank?

I turned to face John and started to take a step in his direction when the killer logic-ed me to a standstill.

"He's dead, Cunningham," he said. "His brain and nerves just haven't finished shutting down yet. I'm pretty sure I got him in the liver, maybe in the abdominal aorta, look at all that blood pouring out of him. If he was on a table at AMC right now, he'd still prolly die, but out here it's a done deal. If you go to him, I'll shoot you, and kill you. If you don't, I won't shoot you and might screw up in a minute and one of you could take advantage of it."

That's when Frank ran his friend's Whaler into/onto the shore, and everything shifted sideways ... again. Frank seemed to have braced himself adequately just before the impact because he wasn't tossed ashore along with the cooler that was resting on the front bench of the boat, which clattered loudly onto the land (*in a messy display of inertia's longstanding promise to moving objects*), spilling a mix of beers and sodas, both full and empty. He walked the length of the grounded boat with exaggerated care, warranted by both the situation on shore and the shotgun he was holding at his shoulder. As he stepped ashore, he slid a finger of his forward hand up an inch or so to turn on the light mounted under the barrel.

"I'm not gonna rack a round into the chamber," Frank said, "like they do on TV because I've already got one there, and I don't want to waste it just so I can scare you. I don't wanna kill you, but if you don't first lower and then drop the gun in your hands, I will shoot you. And my gun's bigger."

Frank didn't have great positioning for getting off a clean shot at the guy; the killer had partially shifted behind Kim while Frank was exiting the boat, and now the killer moved closer still. The bad guy's gun (*really John's gun, but I didn't want to think about that/him, not yet*) was already raised and he walked it in until he was able to make his point effectively by jamming the barrel into Kim's cheek hard enough that I was certain it would leave a bruise (*if he didn't decide to blow a hole in the side of her face in the coming seconds/minutes, which would leave a hole, making a bruise irrelevant*).

"Fuck you, Frank," he said.

Frank looked at the killer's face more closely than he had seconds earlier, during his amphibious landing. "Holy crap, Bernie, Bernie Longwater? Howzat possible? We went to school, played ball, dated a few of the same girls. You're not a ..." Frank ran out of words.

"I guess we both know I am," Bernie said, "now, anyway. Listen up, Frank, I'm going to take your boat, and this young lady is gonna come with me to ensure none of you do anything stupid like try to rush me or call the rest of the cops before I get down the road a piece."

"Fuck that, Bernie." Frank spat. "An' fuck you. You know me like forty years. What do you think the chances are I let a guy who's killed people in my town, my goddamned town, get away from me? Much less take a hostage?"

Frank hesitated for a second, and then looked at me. I imagined his thought process, cutting and pasting things from the last few days together, and remembering that I'm often (*always, really, but there's such a thing as too honest*) the smartest guy in the room. Assuming I had a plan underneath this botched mess that had only played a plan in crappy summer theater … I nodded very slightly.

"I've got a counterproposal for you, Bern," Frank said, "an' it's the best deal you're gonna get tonight. Most other options involve you shooting that pretty girl a half second before I end you with this 870. You an' I get into the boat and these folks shove us off. When we're fifty feet away, I'll drop the 870 into the lake, and you've got me as a hostage in case your day continues as shitty as it has been so far. Sound good?"

"How do I know they don't call the cops the second we leave?" Bernie (*wisely*) asked.

"We might," I said, watching Frank wince, but I needed to help/push them in the right direction and wasn't sure Frank had that much of the picture figured out. "But it doesn't matter because everyone will be coming in from Raybrook and Malone and Plattsburgh by now anyway. When I called/signaled Frank, it went out to all of them too, so your world and chance of escape is getting smaller by the second."

I thought I saw a glint of understanding in Frank's eye as he put it at least partway together, but it could have been the firelight. Bernie thought for seven full seconds before he agreed. Thirty-nine seconds later, I was gauging how far from shore they had to be before I took off.

"Buckle up and be safe!" I yelled into the darkness, as

the boat floated away, hoping Frank would understand/ remember.

"Tell me one of you, or the Soffermans brought a headlamp?" I asked, "Mine got broken at some point in the last few minutes, and I have a feeling I'm going to need it running through the woods."

Mark pulled one out of his pack and tossed it to me; I caught it with my injured arm, which hurt a lot, but was at the same time heartening (*in that I could use it somewhat normally*). Both Kim and Mark started asking what they could do. I broke their hearts.

"You two need to start making phone calls to the cops and fire department. Stay here with John," I said. "Someone will need to explain a safe/sanitized version of what happened here to the authorities, and someone has to stay with John to make sure that nobody drops him in the bottom of a boat or drags him along the ground like a bag of garbage. I wish I could stay and call, but I can't do either. I have to see if I can catch up with Frank and Bernie and find some balance/closure to this whole thing."

While I'd been talking, I'd dashed out a text to Dot.

> **Black hat in 20 mins, I'm right behind him**
> **I'll flash headlights as we come up on your position.**

I snapped on the headlamp and was running through the woods as fast I could without dying, 23 seconds later.

Route 3 between Saranac Lake and Tupper Lake, NY
Sunday, 7/12/2015, 9:12 p.m.

I could feel/smell/hear the lake behind me, and I ran
directly away from the vastness of water, and toward the
road and Route 3. Even though I have an exquisite sense
of direction, and extensive internal maps of this area, I
was a bit worried about getting turned around in the dark
with all the adrenaline in my system, while running at top
speed. So I forced myself to run in a straight line, not
taking the easier route when it presented itself through
the rolling topography of these woods. I ended up
running up and down more hills than I would have
ordinarily. The branches and trees littering the woods
were thick enough that I had to proceed with a hand in
front of my face or risk losing my eyes every few seconds.
My legs and arms were quickly scored by scratches, both
deep and solid (*anyone who says that forest fire prevention is a
universal good is ignorant of nutrient cycling and forest succession, as
well as the dangers of high-speed runs through ancient forests in the
dark when the life of someone you care about hangs in the balance*).

   After only a few minutes of racing against time, my
throat was burning, my lungs ached, I had cramps in my
sides, and my legs felt wooden and undependable when
dealing with the vast and constantly changing fields of
data/input I was able to glean from the too-short cone of
light Mark's headlamp gave me. (*I wasn't sure I could make*

284

it, but I had to, so I did … somehow.) The good news was that the neck wound Bernie had given me would be indistinguishable from the hundreds of other cuts and scrapes crisscrossing all of my exposed skin … the bad news was that by the time I exited the woods and turned back to the left to find West Lake Shore Road (*and my Element*) I was so covered in dirt/bark/blood that I appeared to have clawed my way out of a shallow grave in the woods, and would definitely have trouble making any useful point if stopped by a cop between here and (*hopefully*) catching up to Frank and Bernie.

I had maintained a heads-up map/display of my progress through the woods, as compared to Bernie and Frank in the Whaler. I assumed a three-minute run to the end of Lonesome Bay (*where I assumed his car was stashed either by the road or in the trail leading to a campsite on the north side of the bay*), and another three minutes manhandling a handcuffed Frank up to Bernie's vehicle. (*I refused to allow for the possibility of Frank's being dead in the bottom of the boat, as it would have sped Bernie up too much, and also left me a horrible admission of failure speech with Meg.*) Then they would hit the road south and west toward Tupper Lake. I assumed Bernie would head that way because local news outlets and I had hammered on the forces of good coming to affect our rescue (*and his doom*) from all other possible outlets from the Tri-Lakes: Plattsburgh, Raybrook, and Malone. By the time I slammed the door of my Element (*key already in hand*), I had pictured myself and Bernie on my map of the area as being barely more than six minutes apart at rational driving speeds … more information flooded my brain/consciousness that was in my favor (*for a change of pace this evening*). Bernie would want to drive safely, even sedately, to avoid the attention of the notoriously summer-stop-happy police in and around

Tupper Lake; I had no such desire/inhibition.

"Too Fucking Right!" Barry said from his copilot seat, next to me, "Let's ride, Tyler. You know what I want!"

My mental map/math placed Bernie/Frank on Route 3, roughly 6.5 miles ahead of us, still two miles from the South Creek boat launch onto Middle Saranac Lake at Marcy's Bridge (*which Dot insisted was named after a dog, despite what the plaque on a rock near the bridge said*). I pulled out onto Route 3, flipped the high beams on, turned overdrive off (*a marginal difference in power/acceleration to be sure, but I wanted every possible advantage*) stomped the gas pedal to the floor, and hit my iPhone's play button on what I consider to be Barry's playlist.

AC/DC's "Thunderstruck" is, I'm told (*by an admittedly incorporeal/imaginary/biased source*), the ultimate example of classic hard rock … perfect guitar opening, banging drums, and an energy that builds and builds throughout the entirety of its 4:54 (*which by the way, is a Smith number, meaning that the sum of its digits is equal to the sum of the digits in its prime factorization … I love Smith numbers, not least because they were discovered/named by Albert Wilansky, not someone named Smith, whose brother-in-law Harold Smith, had a phone number that Wilansky figured out was one of these numbers*). The opening guitar solo lasted 29 seconds, by which time the Element and I (*and Barry*) were going faster than 80 miles an hour, at which speed I could assume Barry and I were closing on Bernie/Frank at a rate of one mile every three minutes, meaning we should catch them in 18 minutes (*more or less … there were lots of variables on the map and in my head, very few of them solid/stable, or in my control*), by which time they would have already passed through Tupper, and either continued on Route 3 toward Watertown, or turned south heading to Long

Lake … unacceptable. I stepped up our speed to 90mph, and adjusted the map based on the new differentials (*and assuming I didn't end up a bloody mess after pasting a deer with my slow car, driving too fast*). At this speed, my Element handled like it had a brick wall up on the roof rack.

If I could maintain this speed (*which I couldn't, but neither would they be going a constant 55-60, there were turns and slower spots on their way, as well*), I should theoretically catch up to them as they came abreast of Dot at her appointed spot half a mile past the fishing launch roughly midway between the intersection of Route 30 and 3. I couldn't afford to take my eyes off the road for long enough to send Dot a text to make certain she was in place and ready to go (*nor should I micro-minion her, as it could undermine confidence in her abilities and worth to me, one of the creatures living in the back of my skull offered*). As I was thinking all of this, and picturing an Indiana Jones-esque map with the two cars on it, I swung out to pass a cautious traveler, and had to swing back in when I spotted the glowing eyes of a deer emerging from the woods and guardedly stepping onto the far-side shoulder of the road.

"Micro-minion. I like that," Barry said. "Say, Tyler, not for nothing, but it'd be awesome if you didn't get us killed trying to save Gibson. Whack as you are, you're prolly better than simply not being anything, anywhere, anymore. Besides that, despite bein' 5-0, Frank is an okay guy, an' that wife of his is all right, reminds me of my mom a bit. You an' him dyin' the same night might be too much for her to handle. So how about you stop doing math and maps and coming up with clever terms and shit, and just focus on driving."

"Got it," I said, as I slalomed around a fat raccoon gnawing at some roadkill in the middle of my lane. "Shut up now, please."

The song ended (*I saw Barry reach up to hit the back button, and then shake his head sadly*), and we rolled on down the road to a wildly misogynistic song by Aerosmith that I'd never listened to before … it occurred to me I should dump the song before Dot found it while scrolling through my iPhone someday.

"Buddy-whipped," Barry stage-whispered, "An' if you really listen to the…"

"Shut up, Barry, please," I said.

Luckily there wasn't a lot of traffic between Tupper and Saranac at nearly nine o'clock on a Sunday evening, so I didn't have to scare too many people (*just the one I'd already passed going in my direction, and one coming from the other direction, if you were interested*) with my impression of a low-flying plane. We came to the intersection of Routes 30 and 3 just as the Aerosmith song ended. I felt a micro-gravity disturbance in my gut when we went over the bump right before the big downhill, and for the first time in minutes I could see a pair of taillights in the distance, down the hill after the intersection and way down the straightaway heading on the final run toward Tupper; it felt right, and as though it would be them. (*If it wasn't, Dot and I would owe whoever it was a pretty huge apology, but I chose not to dwell on that possibility, for a number of reasons.*)

"Too fucking right," Barry mumbled just at the edge of audibility … I let it pass. As we got closer, I could see the configuration of the taillights matched my memory of Bernie's truck (*now that I knew who he was, I was able to place him in my world, and remembered the exact shape/color/intensity of his headlights and taillights*). I considered trying to text Dot the information about his headlight configuration, but discarded the plan even before Barry could speak up, on account of danger, due to our high rate of speed, and the likelihood that Dot wouldn't understand my text about

Bernie's headlights anyway.

The next song began, one by Dropkick Murphys that I (*until tonight*) always associated with a Boston/cop/ Wahlberg/Sheen movie that Dot and I had watched a few years ago, that had ended with almost everyone in the cast getting shot in the head in a too-long scene in an abandoned building near the Boston Waterfront (*spoiler apology … and Dot insists I'm bad with spoilers and apologies*). The Element and Barry and I fell/rolled down the long hill picking up speed and my roof rack began to whistle as some degree of cross-breeze hit it. We closed the gap still further/faster.

I reached forward along the map in my head and could see/feel the spot where Dot was hiding, probably cramped and stretching and sweating and wondering if I was crazy, if the headlights she could just make out were the right ones, and she should really do what I'd sent her there to do. Trying to feel my way into the truck with Frank and Bernie (*desperately hoping Frank was buckled into the passenger seat, and not just in the bed of the truck*). These three dots, two moving and one stationary, were all coming together near a bridge by a swampy pond/bog alongside the Raquette River in the next 90 seconds or so (*"Before the end of the song," Barry murmured from beside me*); there was nothing to do but drive the rest of the way to my appointment with luck/destiny/karma (*mine, Bernie's, Frank's … I wasn't sure which/whose*). When I got to a spot where my internal mapmakers/mapkeepers assured me Dot would be able to see me, I began to flash my headlights, alternating between rapid and slow flashes until I saw a road flare blaze into its eerie red life, and could tell there was no further need for signals.

I was just driving by the fishing boat launch (*called The Crusher for reasons neither Dot nor Frank could explain to me …*

Meg probably could, being from Tupper, but I never asked; I made a note to do so, when appropriate) when I saw the headlights of the vehicle now only 1000 feet in front of me swerve and shudder, then flip and fly off the roadbed, to the right, into the sphagnum flats and swamp and oxbow left from some earlier iteration of the Raquette River. I started working my brakes as hard as was possible without my tires losing touch with the road surface.

"He didn't slow down," Dot yelled as I rolled up on her with my windows open, and music turned down. "You said when he saw the flare he'd stop for sure. Are you positive that's the right guy? Why didn't he stop, Tyler?"

"Because I was chasing him, Dot," I answered. "He must have thought you were just a motorist in trouble, and there's no way he was going to stop for that while I was after him."

I parked on the side of the road, scooped up and threw the flare into the water beside the bridge, helped Dot finish rolling up the Stopper Strip (*a thing like a runner carpet made of steel spikes, designed to stop cars in high-speed pursuits*) and shoved her across the bridge (*dragging the heavy bag as quickly as she could jog*) toward her car on the far side of the bridge/causeway spanning the swamp so she could put/hide the bag in the back of her car … I sent her on her way back to Saranac Lake (*despite continued shouted/urgent questions and protests*) with a final yell of thanks and a reminder of what we'd talked about earlier, and then stalked carefully down to Bernie's truck with my headlamp ready but turned off, an aluminum baseball bat (*that had never seen the inside of a baseball diamond*) in my left hand, and my favorite knife, a CRKT folder, in the other hand and at the ready.

Night, somewhere near Tupper

Everything went wrong, but not at first, and even then, not without some upside. Beast had enjoyed the feeling of taking the old man, tasting his blood and watching him bleed out in the middle of his friends, in the middle of their trap. The feeling of power he exercised over the three fakers was wonderful, and Beast had planned a long night of playing with his food, a cat among baby birds. Then Gibson had come, and everything went bad. His armor vanished the second he was recognized, and in a blink, his night of fun and blood and the sharp and bloody edge was over; instead Vanilla was running for his life with an anchor around his neck, slowing him down.

He had considered killing and dumping Frank as soon as they reached the far end of Lonesome Bay, but thoughts of roadblocks and standoffs filled his head and he forced the handcuffed policeman to stagger and jog in front of him all the way to the truck, threatening to shoot him in his belly if he tripped or tried anything. Bernie had laughed when Frank insisted on Bernie buckling him into his seatbelt, but had relented when Frank whined about a lifetime of safety talks at school, and not wanting to be liar at the end; Bernie had buckled first Frank, then himself in, *for safety*, with a smile. Bernie remembered the radio and Cunningham talking about cops coming from Malone and Plattsburgh and Raybrook, and could really only head out and away from them, toward Tupper Lake and the big empty spaces of the deep wildernesses of the park. They drove away from pursuit, Bernie now intent on filling his car with gas and supplies at the Long Lake Stewart's, and then disappearing into the deepest, darkest corner of the park to dump Frank's body, and hide, and think.

He'd seen the headlights closing on him too fast in his rearview during the run from Lower Saranac to Tupper, but hadn't been able to think of anything he could do but keep on driving away, planning to stop on the far side of Tupper, in the big empty between Tupper and Long Lake. He'd leave a clubbed Frank on the road next to the car, and shoot Cunningham when he came to check on him. Bernie was smiling at the thought of tasting Cunningham's blood, maybe taking a finger or an ear from his fallen enemy, when he saw flashing in his rearview mirror and a flood, a river, of sparkles cross the road a hundred yards in front of him by the glow of a road flare. Then everything was noise and spinning and broken glass and slamming into things and crashing and rolling and vomit and pain.

Bernie came back to himself shortly thereafter, hanging upside down from his seat, feeling pain everywhere but especially in his head and neck. His glasses had flown off during the spinning, twirling, thumping, bumping crash, and he had no idea where they were, so everything was blurry and one eye was swelling shut. He heard a sound from outside of the car that his brain eventually processed as a voice, and he saw a flashlight shining in through the passenger door, and focused hard on making sense of the sounds and what he was seeing.

"... can crawl out if I cut the seatbelt," Cunningham

said. "I'll try to catch some of your weight as you fall. Your hands are still cuffed, and I don't have a key here … do you have a spare?"

Frank was apparently incapable of a coherent answer, so Cunningham sliced through Frank's seatbelt and used his hands to try and slow the big man's fall down onto the dented roof of the truck. Bernie was surprised to hear a splash when Frank landed, but it seemed to wake Frank up and he inch-wormed awkwardly out through the opened passenger door. He mumbled something to Cunningham, who seemed to stand and bounce on his feet for a few seconds before answering.

"Yes, Frank," he said. "The truck's settling into the sphagnum bog. We're a little lucky that it didn't just rip through and sink to the bottom. Let's get you up to the roadside, and I'll dig a cuff key out of my backpack."

He walked over to the truck and leaned down and spoke through the hole at Bernie, "I'll be back for you in a minute, don't go anywhere, okay?"

Bernie swung his head around wildly to look for Cunningham to shout his objections, and the top of his head splashed through a half-inch of water that hadn't been that high 20 seconds ago. Bernie started screaming and thrashing, but a broken right wrist stopped him being able to manipulate the seatbelt release.

Route 3 between Saranac Lake and Tupper Lake, NY
Sunday, 7/12/2015, 9:23 p.m.

I jogged down through the spongy sphagnum, amazed at
how far the vehicle had flown/skidded/rolled/slid before
coming to a stop ... I don't pray (*I've always thought it was
roughly the same thing as shouting or whispering at the rain, so
couldn't see the point*), but I did feel myself pointedly hoping
that Frank was okay. It looked as though every window in
Bernie's truck had broken during the rolling/bouncing/
sliding impact, and it was all spread out in a sparkly
comet-trail behind the truck dimly/occasionally reflected
in light from my blinking hazard lights and Mark's
headlamp. I wrenched open the passenger-side door, and
bent down, unaware until a bit later that I'd been holding
my breath.

I slapped my hand across Frank's neck and felt a
strong pulse and could also hear his steady respiration
sawing in and out, sounding a bit congested. (*He suffers
from summer allergies and often forgets to take his meds when
working hard/long hours, as he had been recently.*) While gently
calling his name, I slapped his left cheek lightly (*it was
easier to reach with the inside/palm side of my hand, and I didn't
want to backhand him*).

"Frank," I said, "It's Tyler. You're safe now, and this
is almost over. Do you think you can crawl out if I cut the
seatbelt? I'll try to catch some of your weight as you fall,

your hands are still cuffed, and I don't have a key here ... do you have a spare?"

He was somewhat awake, but essentially non-responsive; I wanted to move him away from the car for a number of vaguely connected reasons, even if it was a medically questionable decision. It seemed as though I was standing in a few inches of water that hadn't been there a minute ago (*which brought me back to sparring with John in that bog near Upper Saranac at the beginning of all of this ... thinking about John made me sad and angry, both unusual/uncomfortable feelings for me*). Bernie was starting to wake up, and I wanted Frank clear of him before I rendered aid to his old school friend. It was also possible that the truck could catch fire (*as upside-down is not conducive to gasoline staying in fuel tanks/fuel-lines/engines, and sparks/flames happen in and around crashes all the time*).

I cut the seatbelt with my folder, and tried to catch Frank as he fell into the water pooling in the roof of Bernie's truck; it seemed to make him more alert, and he hunched his way out of the truck with my help. When I dragged him a few feet farther away, I saw Bernie start to wriggle a bit more (*the bizarre angle of his seatbelt-side wrist suggested he'd be waiting for my help before freeing himself*). Frank mumbled something unintelligible, but I took advantage of the moment to drop a little psyops on Bernie.

"Yes, Frank," I said, "The truck's settling into the sphagnum bog. We're lucky it didn't just rip through and sink to the bottom. Let's get you up to the roadside, and I'll dig a cuff key out of my backpack."

I waited a beat, and then walked over to the passenger window (*not wanting to get in range of a lucky swipe of Bernie's knife if he had somehow managed to hold on to it*), and bent in to speak to him. "I'll be back for you in a minute, don't go anywhere, okay?"

Frank was scrabbling like a squashed bug, and while he lacked the coordination/strength to get mobile/upright on his own, I was able to convince him to lean on me and use me as a cane. In this way, we were able to hobble over to the side of the road where I dropped/deposited him onto the gravel. After digging a universal cuff key out of my Element's emergency kit ... clicking off the hazards first to stop the annoying blinking ... I unlocked him and then spoke right into his face.

"Frank, it's Tyler," I said. "Do you know where you are and what's been happening?"

"Tyler," he said. "Is everybody okay? I remember the campsite, and getting into Bernie's truck, but nothing else."

"You and I are bit the worse for wear," I said, "and John's worse off than that, but I think the situation has stabilized. Can you sit here for a few minutes before I take you to the hospital?"

He turned his head slightly to the side and threw up on his chest/lap/hip. When he was done heaving, he wiped his mouth with the back of his hand like a drunk, and looked up at me blearily and nodded, but with lots of questions in his punch-drunk eyes.

"Bernie?" he asked, part question, part statement, part pointless self-condemnation.

I looked up and down the visible length of Route 3, turned back to Frank and answered in a flat tone, "It looks as though he must have died in the crash, Frank. I'm sorry. Sit here, and I'll be back in a few minutes. If you think you're going to throw up again, please lie down on your side, not your back."

Frank looked both shocked and in shock and as though he had something to say/ask/demand, but there wasn't anything I could (*or wanted to*) tell him right now, so

296

I turned and walked back to Bernie's truck.

The water was almost up to my knees when I got to what I now thought of as Frank's door, and bent over to peer inside. Murky water would have been up to Bernie's nose if he kept his head held down, but he was craning it way over to one side to keep nose and mouth and one eye out of the deepening seepage. His eye was huge and bright with a primal fear; panic made his voice high and hoarse.

"Jesus, Cunningham," he said, "I thought you'd gone for good. Come around and help me get out of this truck before I fucking drown. I've got a bag full of money in the back. If you let me go, it's yours."

"We can talk about that in a minute, Bernie, but first, show me your hands," I said, noting that he was somehow less intimidating with a name (*maybe/ especially/ particularly with the name Bernie*). "I don't much fancy you finishing the job you started over on Lower Saranac (*I rubbed the cut he'd given me, in case he'd forgotten, what with all the fear of drowning while being helplessly pinned in place*)."

He swung his arms wildly so I could see both hands were empty; the pain of moving his right arm distracted him momentarily, and his head flopped down into the rising water ... now up to his ears. He inhaled, the sputtered and screamed and blew out a lungful/mouthful of water mixed with snot and blood.

"Okay," I said, and walked around the truck, slowly.

"You're a cruel fuck, Tyler," Barry said, suddenly next to me as I rounded the truck. "You don't have to do this. Just like you didn't have to do what you did to me."

I wished that Barry wasn't here for this and would have liked for this next thing to be mine alone, but Barry came and went according to his own rules (*or more properly those of whatever part of my consciousness he comes from, or answers to*).

"If you knew me a little better, Barry," I said, looking him straight in the eye. Below me and to just to my left, Bernie was emitting a continuous and incoherent whistling/burbling/retching scream, "you'd know that this *is*, in point of fact, something I have to do, just like you and Justin and the mineshaft were things I had to do. I don't ask, have never asked, to be pushed into a corner, but sometimes it happens, and this is apparently what I do to get out of corners."

"Nobody puts Baby in the corner," Barry said, nodding … it was a passable Patrick Swayze imitation.

I bent down, pulled Bernie's door open, and knelt down in the cold and mossy water seeping up and out of the bog as the truck slowly sank into the sphagnum. Bernie's eyes were so wide I thought he might have popped something in his head, and he seemed beyond coherent/cogent speech … he was just making vowel sounds, with the occasional "ch" and "ck" mixed in.

"Okay, Bernie," I said, using the same tones I use when dealing with scared dogs at the shelter, "just relax, I'll have you out of there in a sec."

He craned his neck nearly perpendicular to his left shoulder, breathed in deeply, and then relaxed in the seatbelt. I reached in, found where the belt crossed his shoulder, then his neck, and grabbed the hair at the top of his head. I pulled down and held him in place. For a few seconds he must have convinced himself that I was holding him out of the way so I could cut the seatbelt without putting him at risk. Then the burning started in his lungs, and I wouldn't let him move/breathe. He thrashed and jerked for 23 seconds before a cough betrayed him; he inhaled the scummy water and started drowning. I held him for another minute, until well after he'd stopped moving altogether and waited by the truck for another full minute after that before slamming the door and walking up to the road to check on Frank.

He was asleep/unconscious on his side, and I sat down next him and started calling people.

Adirondack Medical Center, Saranac Lake, NY
Monday, 7/13/2015, 12:43 a.m.

"Agent Brimley," I said. "It's Tyler Cunningham. I'm on the side of Route 3 about three miles east of Tupper Lake. Frank Gibson is unconscious and needs medical attention. The killer, Bernie Longwater, is dead in his vehicle about a hundred yards from my position. If you haven't already heard, he attacked a group of campers and killed someone at a campsite on Lower Saranac Lake earlier this evening."

"Cunningham!" he shouted in my ear. "What are you talking about? What happened? How did this happen? Why are you—?"

I interrupted him at this point.

"Agent Brimley," I said in what I hoped was a calming voice. "I will tell you everything, and answer all your questions to the best of my ability (*these would be only the first of many, many, lies that I would tell him during what would turn out to be a very long night*), but I need you to get an ambulance on the way for Frank … Officer Gibson, right this second. Also, I need to know that you are rendering appropriate aid to the people at the campsite on Lower Saranac Lake. To repeat, Officer Gibson and I are located on the side of Route 3 roughly three miles east of Tupper Lake. The campsite where the incident, and murder, took place is campsite #60. Can you repeat that information

300

and then get off the phone to make the calls you need to make?"

He did, then he did, and then I assume that he did because the first of many vehicles topped with flashers began arriving nine minutes later. Before they arrived, though, I made another few calls.

"Dot," I said when she picked up, "tell me you made it home without stopping, or being stopped, and have hidden the thing somewhere not your car or house or the shelter."

"I did," she said, "and I wasn't, and I did (*she likes to play Tyler, especially when we're working together*). That thing worked on his truck like a catapult or something. It was like magic. Was the miserable fuck who shot Steph and Sleepy in that truck? I hope so, and I hope he broke everything."

"He was," I answered, "and so was Frank."

"Holy shit, Tyler!" she interrupted. "I didn't know. Oh, my God! How could I know? Is he okay (*I rightly assumed she meant Frank, not Bernie*)?"

"You had no way of knowing," I said (*I didn't tell you because I couldn't trust that you wouldn't hesitate to use the stopper strip, a nasty sheet of spikes that would flatten the tires of any vehicle that crossed it*). "I'm with Frank now, and I'm pretty sure he's just shaken up ... I patted him down a second ago, and couldn't find any signs of breaks or internal bleeding, and his pupil response seems fine, as does his heart rate and respiration."

"And the guy," she asked, soberly, quietly, "the killer?"

"He's dead," I said, "It would appear he drowned after the crash when the car settled into the bog."

"Did you ...?" she began.

"Our cell phones are essentially walkie-talkies, Dot," I

said. "I'll stop by later when I'm done at the hospital, and make another stop or two. (*I was thinking about Nick, John's employer and longtime friend, as well as Meg and Mark and Kim.*) I have to call Meg now, and let her know Frank's okay (*more or less*)."

"G'bye Tyler," Dot said, "and, thanks for, y'know (*I didn't*)."

I closed the connection, sighed, and reached over to pat Frank on a giant and clammy/clumpy shoulder (*he'd apparently had some peach/blueberry pie while waiting at his friend's camp for my phone call*), and dialed his wife as I became aware of flashers approaching from both directions.

"Tyler, Jesus Christ, tell me what's happening," Meg said after picking up on the first ring. "It sounds like every emergency response vehicle in town headed over toward Tupper in the last few minutes. They also sent Tiny Tim over to babysit me (*Tiny Tim was a huge SLPD officer, who while not the smartest or fastest tool in their drawer, was known for his people skills, and for, by dint of his size and reassuring voice, making people feel comfortable after horrible things happened to them*), and he just poured me a milk glass full of Evan Williams."

"First things first," I said, "Frank's gonna be okay. He was in a car accident (*I didn't/wouldn't mention that I had essentially caused the accident*) with the serial killer, who it turns out Frank knows from school … someone named Bernie. Frank seems mostly shaken up as a result of the accident (*possibly a lie, but I didn't see an up side of being a slave to the truth in this instance*). He saved lives tonight, mine included, and he'll probably be home with you tonight, but if you and Tim (*I had trouble, for some reason, using the nickname*) head over to the hospital in a bit, I'm sure they'll want to check Frank out before sending him home." (*I was sure there would also be interviews and paperwork, and possibly an overnight observation given his groggy and vomit-y state, but why spoil Meg's imagined perfect ending.*)

"I have to go now," I lied, "as everyone with a flashing bar on the roof of their vehicle seems to be pulling up to Frank and me. We'll see you at the hospital."

It was too late to call Mickey, although that was my next impulse. Instead, I sent a brief email telling him that I had news and an interesting story to share and that it looked as though I should be able to head down for a visit tomorrow or the next day. I hit the *send* button as the overlapping flashers of a half-dozen emergency vehicles threatened to send me into a seizure, and an ostentatiously unmarked (*yet unmistakably cop-esque*) car pulled up next to Frank and me sitting on the shoulder of Route 3, Brimley's bumper/grill, hot and bug-coated, a foot from my face.

"Tyler," Agent Brimley stomped up to me shouting even before he was out from behind the wheel. "How the hell did this happen? And how did you and Gibson end up in the middle of it all?"

Frank started to try and sit up and made some proto-speech noises, but I pushed him gently back down to the gravel.

"I'll tell you everything, I promise (*a lie, but experience has taught me that it's the one people want to hear, even if they don't believe it from the outset*)," I said, "but Frank's in no shape to give a statement now, he needs medical attention, and I'm not going to say another word until the ambulance pulls away, with him in it."

I emphasized my micro-soliloquy by making the motion of turning a key to lock my lips shut ... I'd seen Dot do this with Lisa a number of times under similar-ish circumstances. It seemed to infuriate Brimley, and for a second, his hand slid minutely up toward the shoulder holster under his left armpit. A moment's pause later, he waved the waiting EMTs in, and I gave them a precis of what had happened, what I'd observed of Frank since the accident, and a report of his vitals when I'd first pulled him out as well as just a minute ago. They slid a backboard under him, fit a collar around his neck, team-hefted him onto a stretcher and carted him away to the waiting ambulance (*I have never understood the policy of leaving an ambulance running at all times when on-scene, as it adds noise and smog to what is already, by definition, a bad place to be*), and drove off heading to Saranac Lake and Meg.

Brimley watched the lights of Frank's ambulance fade into the night, then turned his attention to the upside-down truck settling slowly into the bog, and finally looked over at me.

"So the guy, our guy, is out there, dead?" he asked, and then ticking off questions on his fingers, continued, "How'd he get that way? How'd Frank get into whatever shape he's in? How did you and he get involved without my knowing about any of this? Who's the dead guy at the campsite on Lower Saranac Lake? And lastly (*a word I intensely dislike and judge people for using*), did you shit the bed, and how badly?"

"Those are six great questions," I said, "and I'm going to answer all of them, but in a slightly different order than you asked them. okay?" (*I didn't actually care, or need to adjust the order of his questions, but my study of the psychology of this sort of situation suggested that appearing to be agreeable and obsequious would put Brimley in a better frame of mind to accept my story. I waited for a moment, giving him a combination of my smiles, #s 2/3/8, and finally getting a nod.*)

"I did, if I understand the metaphor correctly, shit the

bed, and quite badly," I said. "The person who the serial killer murdered at campsite #60 tonight is ... was, John Heimdall, a local, and a friend of mine (*to the degree I have friends, John was one, and Brimley would want a pigeonhole for our relationship*). I took another look at the data I got over to you earlier and found another possible campsite that the killer might have been using through the years. I wasn't sure, but I didn't want to leave anyone exposed to possible risk, so I hiked in from the road, taking along John as my backup in case things went badly. They did, and I called Officer Gibson on my cell phone, but while waiting for him to arrive, while trying to de-escalate the situation, John was repeatedly stabbed by the killer."

"Officer Gibson came by boat," I said, "and arrived shortly after the killer stabbed John to death, to find the killer, who he recognized as Bernie Longwater, holding the campers and myself at gunpoint. Gibson was able to calm the killer down enough to not shoot any of us, and the two of them left in what would best be termed a hostage situation.

"I ran through the woods back to the road and followed in my car (*skimming over how I knew which direction to follow in, as that implied/admitted more manipulation and pre-planning than my current story called for*), and caught up to Longwater and Gibson here, where they apparently went off the road for reasons unknown to me (*a blatant lie, but it might leave room for Frank wrestling the wheel to the right, or some similar story*). I ran out to the truck, which was already settling into the water under the bog, and was able to cut Officer Gibson free, and drag him from the vehicle. By the time I got him a safe distance from the truck and made sure that he wasn't too bleeding/broken, the truck had settled farther down into the water. Longwater hadn't been responsive when I first went to the vehicle, and when I went back to free him, he was dead, either drowned or dead in the crash, I don't know."

I made a show of ticking/counting off six fingers, and then looking up at Brimley. "I think that's all of your questions answered ... I wish I had better answers and hadn't screwed up."

He appeared to be tossing my words, and the answers preceding them around in his head, looking for easy ways to trip me up, and (*thankfully*) finding none. If Frank and Mark and Kim stuck to the script we'd talked about, and nobody reported having seen Dot hanging around at what would coincidentally turn out to be the scene of a fortuitous accident (*not to mention someone/anyone noticing how intensely/uniformly Bernie's tires were shredded*), we would seem to have a chance of getting away with the admittedly shaky story. I was bolstered by what Frank had told me time and again (*and my experience had shown to be true*): if the LEO community had to choose between a neat package that was easy to explain to their superiors, delivered a bad guy, as well as making them look good ... or a messy tangle that made it look as though they'd all been used/fooled by a homeless half-assed detective, they would pick the easy (*and mediapathic*) story every single time. (*This had been true a few years ago when I'd killed Barry and Justin and their boss, George, and I hoped it would hold true in this instance.*)

"You'll probably spend the next few days telling your side of things a bunch of times to a bunch of people in a bunch of neutral-colored rooms with bad lighting, but assuming your story can hold its mud (*a metaphor/image I didn't/couldn't follow, but I nodded slightly anyway, since he seemed to be looking/waiting for some degree of affirmation*), we should be good."

"Great," I said, done with him and Bernie and this

swamp most of the way to Tupper. "Can I go and check in on Frank and John now?"

I turned when he said, "Yes, but we're nowhere near done yet, Cunningham, so don't even think ..." and climbed into the Element without hearing the rest (*doubtless something about making myself available for further questioning, and/or not leaving the area without his permission*).

When I pulled into the parking lot of the Adirondack Medical Center, I noted it contained about ten cars more than would be expected at this time of day, at this time of year ... many of them cop cars parked seemingly wherever they felt like stopping. (*It's possible there was more thought involved, but then again, maybe not.*) I recognized Meg's car, still running and with hazards flashing, in front of the main entrance, and Dot's car parked way down the second tier of spots (*possibly hiding, just in case*). I considered briefly (*as I always do*) parking in one of the eight unoccupied handicapped parking spots, dismissing it (*again, as I always do*) not because of legalities, but thinking how badly I'd feel for that eighth legitimately handicapped driver to roll up after a rush on the spots and see no space for themselves. I parked down near Dot's car and walked in through the hissing main double doors.

Meg and Dot were sitting on one of the couches at the far end of the big waiting room (*closest to the hallway that would lead to the room where Frank was being seen/helped, I assumed*), huddled against cold or fear or both, possibly something else entirely that I didn't/couldn't understand. All of Meg's attention was focused on the hallway in front of her, willing a smiling doctor to come out and lead her back to her husband, with reassuring news and comforting pats all the way. Dot must have heard the hissing of the doors, or my footsteps approaching because she turned and smiled, then gave me a guarded/coded look that might impart some meaning to others, but meant nothing to me. She leaned even closer to Meg, gave her a squeeze on her shoulder, and whispered something to her.

"Tyler, oh my, God, Tyler," Meg exclaimed, turning and then jumping up and running over to me. I forced myself to keep my pace and forward momentum steady, even though I wasn't sure if she was going to kiss or curse, hug or hit, me. *(It turns out that I'd get a mix of everything from her ... she feels, a lot.)*

She swept me into her arms and then pushed me back out to arm's length a moment later.

"Sweet, merciful Jesus, you look like you've been through a leaf shredder," she said. "Do you need a doctor yourself?"

"I'm fine," I said. "I just got a bunch of scratches from running through the woods. How's Frank?"

She slapped me. "You said, 'mostly shook up.' He is decidedly more than shook up. They're deciding now whether to splint or cast various parts of both of his arms, and they've had him in both an MRI and an X-ray looking at his skull and brain. He was mumbling about coming home tonight, but the doctors all want him to stay for at least one night. I would be even angrier with you if Terry, one of the EMTs, hadn't told me that you pulled him out of the truck before he drowned, which that goddamned Bernie, *it's too goddamned good for him*, did."

"I told you I'd look out for him, Meg," I said, "I just wish I'd done a better job of it. He saved my life tonight ... saved a couple of lives."

"Tell me everything," she said, settling back onto the couch, and pulling me down next to her.

I did, but I told her a safe version of the story that

was very similar to the one I'd told Brimley but casting Frank as much the hero as I thought I could get away with ... Dot followed along and when I started through it a second time (*at Meg's urging*) she disappeared briefly, returning a few minutes later with an armload of Cokes for me and a ginger ale for Meg. We spent the next few hours mostly waiting, sometimes talking with a series of doctors all of whom were engaged in checking Frank out. When we finally went back to see him in his room, he looked more bruised and scratched than I remembered, but essentially fit; he had three fingers splinted, and his right arm in a sling, but no casts.

Meg rushed over and then stopped an inch short and air-hugged him. He reached around her clumsily with the arm not in a sling and patted her back. He looked at Dot over Meg's shoulder and gave her a wink and a nod (*I stink at unspoken communication, but I interpreted the way he looked at miserable Dot and the way she relaxed somewhat, as meaning that he either had seen her, or just knew/guessed what she'd done out there on Route 3, and understood*), then turned to me.

"Tyler, I," he said, "I don't remember a lot about what happened tonight. Brimley asked, but ..."

"I'm sure he can wait until tomorrow," I said. "Spend a few minutes with your wife, right now, and then try and get a good night's sleep. Tomorrow, go home, kiss your dogs, sleep all day on the couch, take fistfuls of Advil, don't set the alarm or answer the phone, and when you're ready, you can tell Brimley what happened. We shouldn't talk about it, but anyone would be expected to talk with his wife." (*I winked and nodded, and was trying to beam to him the message that I had told Meg the safe version a few times, so she should be able to feed it to him*) As I said this, I noticed Meg turn from her injured husband to give me a careful/

studious/weighty look she'd never cast in my direction before, and it occurred to me that she might not be done with me.

Frank nodded and asked if I was going to see a doctor before heading out as well. Now that the action had stopped and the extra adrenaline had run through my system, I could feel every scratch and cut, and especially the uncomfortable lump of Bernie-bone in my upper arm; I would have loved to sink into a deep sleep and let doctors make it all better, but I had miles to go before I slept ... seriously, miles to go. It must have taken longer than it felt like, because Dot poked me in the side, and Frank repeated his question.

"If you don't mind doing me a small favor before I leave," I said to Frank. I could see/feel all three of them wince a little as I said it, but I pressed on (*the way you do, when it's important*), "could you talk to someone about me getting in to say goodbye to John?"

The three faces made an interesting study, and I took a mental snapshot of them while Frank thought for a second; he then smiled and nodded slightly. Meg looked shocked and confused and then finally, possibly, a bit ill. Dot gasped and greyed and turned and vomited, and looked up at me to confirm what she had already, but just, figured out. We'd talked around it for hours, focusing mostly on Frank or Stephie or the surprise of Bernie Longwater being a killer; a few people, one of the doctors or an EMT or cop, had mentioned a final victim a few times as the evening wore on, but neither Dot or Meg pursued it, and I had left it alone ... until now.

"John's dead," I said, confirmed, "and I'd like to see him if you can arrange it."

Frank nodded and gestured over to the phone a few feet away. Meg handed it to him and he talked to a series of someones for a pair of minutes before handing it back to Meg to replace on the faux woodgrain bedside table.

"Can you find your way down?" Frank asked. "They'll be expecting you. I said it was a part of the investigation, which I guess it is, in a way."

I thanked him, let Meg hug me, and tapped my watch in Dot's direction to let her know that I'd be by to talk with her later. Making my way back into the hospital proper, I walked through the pale halls that smelled of sick and dying people and medicine and antiseptic and loss and fear, losing my way twice, but finally finding my way back to where they were keeping John's body.

Navigating through the labyrinth of halls leading from the living (*and dying*) to the dead, I heard a pair of running feet coming up behind me, and turned to face the person I'd been waiting for (*and dreading*) for the last few hours … Agent Brimley of the FBI (*I put the emphasis in, internally, without meaning to*).

"I must have just missed you in Officer Gibson's room," he said, panting slightly, and looking at me for some reply (*there was none I wanted to give him*).

"Yes," I said. "He seems largely intact … lucky."

He nodded and gave me a cynical stare for a full five-count before saying anything. "Yeah, lucky. People seem to have all sorts of luck when you're around. Good luck and bad luck, depending on where they stand in your judgment."

Again, he looked at me for an answer … I glanced down at my watch, and leaned infinitesimally down the hall as if ready to go, prompting him to continue (*despite his obvious desire for me to answer one of many unasked and nebulous questions*).

"Bernie Longwater, for example," he began, "had some extremely bad luck tonight. After years, decades, of literally getting away with murder, he kidnaps a friend of yours (*also an officer of the law, but I didn't point this out*), and miraculously suffers four explosive flat tires at precisely the right moment, when you happened to be in pursuit."

Again, there was no question, and again I kept my silence … he looked as though he wanted to punch me (*whether for my silence or my actions or the luck he was questioning, I couldn't say/guess*).

"There was also a fair amount of luck involved with the outcome of that crash," he said. "Officer Gibson and Mr. Longwater both had seatbelts on, both received similar injuries, but Gibson could probably go home tonight, and Longwater's on a slab downstairs somewhere (*which prompted a movement from me, in the direction of the morgue … not to flee Brimley's questions, as he possibly surmised, but because I could feel the pull of wanting to say my goodbyes to John*).

He waited a shorter period of time after his last musing on the nature of the luck of people around me, seemingly comfortable with my silence now.

"I don't want to look this gift horse too closely in the mouth, Cunningham (*a small segment of my brain wondered if the cop-diminutive use of my last name was due to his suspicions about my manipulation of chance, because he didn't like me, or some form of acceptance of me into the brotherhood*). I don't like you. We'll never be friends, and I don't trust you (*question somewhat answered*), but this worked out reasonably well for me, so as long as Gibson's story is fairly close to yours, I'm not going to question any of the luck, and this case goes down as a win for me and Gibson and you (*not so much for Bernie or John, or the other 39 victims, I thought*). I still think you're some kind of bug," he said, "and I'm going to keep an eye on you and this part of the world from my vantage point at the data center in Albany, but knowing that I'm doing that, I'd bet you'll be careful enough to avoid drawing much attention."

Nodding my head didn't seem to satisfy his desire for more than that, and I wanted to get going, so I said, "I think I understand what you're saying, and implying, and agree that things worked out nearly as well as they could have for nearly everyone involved. I'll be available by phone or email if you have further questions, but I'm going to be heading out of town to visit a sick friend in the next few days, so I'll be hard to reach for a face to face talk."

This seemed almost a relief to him, and since he didn't say anything else, I continued down to the morgue.

Adirondack Medical Center Morgue, Saranac Lake, NY
Monday, 7/13/2015, 12:58 a.m.

I walked in through one of the double swinging doors to
the morgue and was assaulted by the mix of smells
waiting in the cold room … formalin, alcohol, shit, stale
blood, raw meat, bone-dust, rot … and paperwork. The
attendant was tall and thin and had an expression on his
face as though he thought he was in trouble.

"He's still in the bag," he said. "Do you think you
could help me transfer him onto the table?"

"No problem," I said. "Gloves?"

He pointed out a box, and I slid on a pair of blue
nitrile gloves, thinking as I always do, of *Firefly*. We
moved the gurney holding John's bag, and John, over
next to the primary worktable … I took the head-end, he
took the feet, and on three we grunted/lifted/slid the bag
over and onto the table. The contents of the body bag felt
heavy and loose, not as though they had anything in
common with the agile and strong and sprightly man I'd
been sparring with just a few days earlier. I signed
something on a clipboard when the attendant held it in
front of me, without looking, and then unzipped the bag.

The smell of blood and meat and the woods came up
at me violently from the inside of the bag, and I peeled
the stiff vinyl bag away from the face of the man, maybe a
friend, I'd known for more than a decade. I looked across

314

the table at the attendant and asked in my flattest tone if he could give me a few minutes of privacy. I don't know what Frank had told him, what he thought I was going to do, or actually/actively care about any of that. The guy stared at me for a few moments, told me not to take or leave or change anything with the body, then slid from the room, like a slightly creepy egg out of an equally creepy frying pan.

I felt embarrassed and lost for a second, not sure why I'd come, what I wanted from this visit ... then while thinking about it, my unconscious took over, and I pulled off the right glove and reached into the bag to stroke his cheek.

"I'm so sorry, John," I said. "I did my *Tyler Thing* and got the job done, but left someone else to pay the bill, as I tend to do, and, in this case, it was you."

"Not for nothin', Tyler," Barry said, unexpectedly next to me, in ridiculously large surgical scrubs, "but that's just about the creepiest thing I've ever seen, which is sayin' something."

"Creepier than talking to one dead guy while hallucinating another dead guy?" I asked, wondering what Meg would have to say about this ... or Dot.

"Mebbe," he said, nodding. "Yup, your gentle caress is creeping me right the fuck out. I'm dead and I've got fuckin' goosebumps."

"Go away," I pleaded, and this time, he did, then I turned back to John's cold and grey and already stiffening face.

"If you could, you'd tell me that you knew what you signed up for, and likely say something about luck, and point out that if you hadn't done your bit tonight (*last night I corrected myself internally, which almost threw me off stride, but I kept going*) there would have been more dead bodies

... maybe all of us."

He just lay there. I slid my fingers up through his thinning (*no longer thinning, I corrected, just thin*) hair, and cupped my fingers around his skull, feeling/imagining inside for any lingering electrical impulses in his brain, finding none.

"I'm not good with thanks or regrets or loss or death, and I think that I should be, maybe somewhere inside am, feeling these things," I said. "You helped me with this, along with dozens of other things, large and small, dangerous and tedious, and now you're just aging/ spoiling meat on a table. I can't thank you, or tell you to be careful, or ask you why I get to talk with Barry but not you (*John had helped me understand my PTSD, or whatever I was living with, having Barry in my life/brain, and dealing with anger/fear associated with some nasty events in my recent past*), or ever get to honestly best/beat you in one of our sparring matches."

"I keeping losing people," I said. "It's as if we're all slogging upstream against a current, and they keep getting swept away, leaving me ... sometimes because I tripped them or didn't help them when I should have, sometimes because angry/hateful men fly planes into buildings. I'm tired, John, tired of losing people I care about, just plain tired of losing."

I stood over John for another minute, thinking about what I still had to do before I could sleep, then what I'd have to do during the next few days, and humming a tune John favored when sparring ... then I zipped the bag shut, threw my gloves into the biohazard bag by the door, and headed out into the night.

Dot and Lisa's Apartment, Saranac Lake, NY
Monday, 7/13/2015, 2:27 a.m.

I tromped up the stairs to their door loudly, so as not to
surprise Dot, and also to give the cats a chance to flee the
front room with dignity. Dot's cats (*all cats, really, but hers
in particular*) hate/fear/shun me, and it just seems polite to
give them some warning so they don't have to pop their
eyes, and slip on fuzzy paws and run into things on their
way to the bathroom (*the spot they generally choose to hide from
me, which is awkward when/if I have to use the bathroom, and the
reason I generally pee in the woods surrounding the parking spots
outside of the house Dot and Lisa share with another set of tenants
I've never seen*).

Dot opened the door and ushered me in, pressing a
small bottle of Mexican Coke into my hand as we sat
down at the kitchen table. I drank straight from the
bottle. She sipped from a jelly jar filled with what smelled
like bourbon and an ice cube and a few drops of the
bitters I'd made her (*and a few other people in my world,
including John, and Frank, and Mickey*) for Christmas last
year. We both drank in quiet and more than a bit of
awkwardness for nearly a minute before she spoke.

"Lisa's spending the night with Stephie," she said,
"whose leg hurts, but I think Lisa wanted to be gone
when you showed up anyway. I wanna hear it all, but
before that ... you have to shower. You look like

something out of a horror movie. Go (*gesturing down the hall to the cats' hiding spot*)."

I showered quickly, bleeding slightly onto the white floor of the shower stall, and into their fluffy guest towel (*sorry Lisa*), and then returned to the kitchen in time for more Coke for me, and bourbon/bitters for her. Dot waited three seconds for me to start talking, took a gulp, and then dove right in.

"I heard the guy was dead from the initial impact, that he died in the crash," she said. "Is that true, did I kill him with that carpet of nails that I rolled out for him?"

Looking across the table at Dot, perhaps my closest friend, or confidante, on Earth, I paused, soaking in her expression/emotions. (*I'm always amazed, always learning, from her.*) A part of her was horrified at the idea, and a part of her wanted to be the agent of Bernie's death. I didn't know which she would prefer, didn't know how to ask, so I did something that perhaps demonstrated/proved the depth/reality of our friendship … I told her the truth (*something I don't/won't/couldn't do with most people*).

"No," I said. "He seemed fine, outside of a broken wrist, after the crash. I got Frank clear, and went back to the truck for Bernie as you drove away. He was still very much alive at that point in time and was pretty much fine until I killed him, drowned him, to be more precise (*and why not be*). I can't fully explain why, but I just didn't want him in the world, my world, our world, anymore. It might have been John, maybe the knife he held at my neck, possibly the fact that he would have probably killed Frank, or maybe my promise to Edith Richards … I honestly don't know."

She took another swallow of her drink and grabbed another Coke for me, then gestured for me to continue.

"He offered me money," I said, not knowing where I

was going with that line of thought/conversation, but wanting to spill everything to/on Dot. "At the end, he was scared, and I lied to him to calm him down enough to allow me to grab his hair and hold his mouth and nose below the water level in the truck and drown him."

Dot took a long pull from her glass, swirled it around and looked at the waves of refracting light given off as melting ice mixed with Evan Williams (*her 'house' bourbon ... and also apparently Meg's, something I didn't need to know, certainly didn't need to think about, but somehow couldn't help doing*), and looked up at the ceiling, then turned back to look at me.

"I'm glad that fucker's dead," she said. "Glad, but then also, somewhere down inside me there's a stain of relief that I didn't do it. Does that make me a coward?"

"I couldn't say," I said, "but I don't think so. I think it makes you a person, a good person. Sleepy and Steph made you mad, but you're not a killer ... thankfully. That's something you don't have to carry."

She started to say something, stopped herself, nearly said it again, and then washed the thought and words down with a large gulp of bourbon.

"I know what you're thinking, what you mean (*maybe I did, or maybe she was going to talk about doing a load of laundry, or hating the Twilight series, both are things that have come up during previous late nights with Dot*), and I have some degree of concern about all of this," I said, waving behind me to indicate the lake and the road to Tupper, but also the past, and my past crimes and killings. "Not that Brimley or Frank will catch me, or figure out what really happened out there tonight. They may know, or think they know what happened, or may come to know some or all of it in the days and weeks to follow ... but they don't really want to know. This worked out as well as it could have for everyone … except John, that is."

Dot got up for a handful of ice cubes for her drink from the freezer, and pulled a pair of the Cokes out of the fridge for me as well.

"No," I continued, "What I'm concerned about is that I may be a *Bad Guy*. I've killed people, ended them, taken them out of play, out of the world, and it doesn't really make me feel much of anything one way or another. I think I do it because it's the right thing to do … Brimley might disagree (*Dot held in a smile for reasons that escaped me, she later told me it had to do with another person named Brimley, and oatmeal, but I never understood the humor in it*). I wonder if he might think I'm some slightly less evil, somewhat less random, version of Bernie."

Dot held up a finger, indicating I should wait a minute (*I think … once she did this, and I reached across the table to pull it, as a childhood acquaintance, Niko, had taught me, and she had looked horrified for a second before she started giggling uncontrollably*), and got up to make a new drink for herself, putting both more bourbon and more of the homemade bitters into it than I generally see her do.

"Fuck that shit, Tyler," she said as she settled back in at the table. "You're not him. He was a monster, literally a menace to society. In solving dozens of cases, helping at least that many people over the course of more than a decade, you've been forced to kill (*I could have argued her word choice, but obviously didn't*) five people. Not innocents either, those five people tried to kill you and the people around you who you care about (*'whom,' I thought, or 'that,' to avoid the difficulty altogether … but I didn't say anything, as Dot might throw something at me*). You're not roaming the streets or woods looking for people to kill. In a couple of cases, you've been forced to do it in order to stay alive or keep your world running along on an even keel."

I wasn't sure I agreed with her logic, but since it was well-meaning and allowed for rationalizations that would make it okay for me to stay on the streets/woods, not find a place for me to hide from future possible victims, I was willing to embrace it as truth, or near-truth (*or at least a convenient and comfortable lie*).

She continued talking/convincing, and I stayed long enough for us to enjoy another few Mexican Cokes, and for Dot to work her way through a few more of the drinks, that she began referring to as 'Dots,' and we talked about all sorts of things. I told her I was planning on heading out of town for a while to get clear of the closing of the investigation, and to visit Mickey. (*I also had in mind to visit Edith, but didn't mention this to Dot because I thought her vision of me as knight in shining armor might tarnish slightly if she knew more about my promise to the young lady, and recent orphan, to kill the man who'd killed her parents, and my plans to tell her the truth about it.*).

She told me she'd spoken to Lisa, assured me effusively that she'd never tell her everything about our shared adventures (*I don't know if that's true, or even important, since Lisa and I have a different relationship the last few years, and I believe what Meg has said numerous times about secrets being bad for the soul. Luckily, I don't believe that I have a soul*), and that she would be coming home in the morning. Dot spoke about love and loss and Lisa and Mickey and John and Meg and Frank and the dog (*Sleepy*) that had been shot by Bernie (*"that miserable fuck" is how she referred to him, preferring, it seemed, not to name him*), and then, as her conversation ran down, she looked up at me with soggy eyes and said, "Every time I walk into the isolation room, Snowflake looks hopefully up at me, sniffs hard at the hall behind me, and then hangs his head."

I had no idea what she was talking about, or why, but

we moved on to other considerations, now this chapter was coming to an end. Because I needed to debrief Mark and Kim, and get the Soffermans back on track to their real life in Vermont, neither of these chores would be odious, but I wasn't in a mood to deal with that level of details (*although obviously I would have to*). I made a note to deal with those two calls in the morning, before anything else.

What I wanted to do more than make calls to Mark and Kim and the Soffermans and check in on Edith Richards was head down to spend as much time with Mickey as I could before he went in for whichever surgery he and his team chose. We talked and drank for another hour and then Dot threw a guest pillow and blanket on the couch for me, without even asking, and stumbled off to bed, yelling over her shoulder at me as she disappeared into the bedroom, "Have you talked to whatshisname? Nick. The guy that John works, worked, for? You need to do that before sleep tonight, you know." She stumbled off to bed followed by the cats (*which was a relief, because by that time, I really needed to use the bathroom and didn't want to head outside to pee. The couch was looking good*).

I'd been hoping to put the call off, hoping possibly not to do it at all. But Nick was an old man now, and he'd lost more tonight than I had, in losing John. I pulled my cell phone out of my jacket pocket to call the number I'd seen John dialing once, barely more than eight years ago. That was when I saw the text from Meg.

Tyler, call me—Doesn't matter what time

She'd sent it more than an hour ago, and it was getting to be really late, but her message left little room for interpretation ... so I put off calling Nick and punched in the numbers for Meg's cell. She picked up on the first ring.

"Tyler," she said. "I'm glad you called. I wanted to talk with you before you head out of town, as you tend to do when things like what happened tonight happen."

Something in her word choice and tone signaled a radical departure from her usual mothering/comforting approach to me.

"Is Frank okay?" I asked. "Are you? What's up?"

"Frank, finally, has fallen asleep," she answered. "I've been watching him all night, and he couldn't sleep, couldn't get comfortable for hours, then they turned up the pain meds, and he was finally able to relax and just fell asleep."

"I'm glad to hear he's getting some rest," I said, lacking anything better, but feeling I should stick some words into the silence she left dangling there.

"Brimley came by, and tried to talk with Frank about what happened again, but they'd just upped the medicine, so he talked with me instead."

I felt a cold spot develop along the length of my spine and up the back of my skull when the words left her mouth ... and waited for what came next.

"He talked about how lucky Frank was tonight (*last night, I internally corrected, while cursing my seemingly failing luck at the same time*)," she said, then rolling on like German tanks across French borders (*really, anyone's tanks across French borders ... I took the time to distract myself from wondering how screwed I was if Meg was smarter and more aware than I had given her credit for by admiring my use of metaphor*). "He talked about the luck you seem to bring to these *cases* of yours. Good or bad, he seems to think you make the luck. I think that although I don't like the man, I agree with him."

This seemed like a perfect moment to stick with a thoughtful silence, so that's what I did.

"I've liked you since the first time I saw you walking a dog at the shelter years ago," she said once it became clear to her that I wasn't going to say anything. "A small and sad and strange little boy, utterly alone in the world, at once too smart and too stupid to really make it in the world he found himself wandering through. It's possible I've mothered more and counseled less than I should have. I hope you can forgive me my failings in this."

"There's nothing to forgive," I said. "I have never sought your help … in fact, I've actively avoided it whenever you pushed at all."

"Be that as it may," Meg sighed into the phone, "I had a job to do and have been shirking it for years. The mind wanders and makes connections. We don't always fully understand the leaps our brain takes, the conclusions we reach, and we certainly don't say everything that comes to mind (*I hoped that she was both coming to a point, and talking about herself, as otherwise, I was well and truly lost*), but I know what I know, and I chose, for better or ill, not to say anything. Until now.

"While Frank was tossing and turning and fighting his way into sleep, through his pain and whatever demons he's battling tonight, I started to fall asleep myself," Meg said. "I had one of those waking dreams about a storm swirling around all of us … Frank and me and Lola and Steph and John and that young lady whose parents got killed."

I made an un-huh noise, mostly because I felt I'd been quiet for too long.

"We were all getting blown around by the storm," she continued, "and I wondered where you were, and how you'd fix things? Then it occurred to me that you *were* the storm, or might be the storm. Then I woke up, and you called."

"Crazy dream, huh?" I said, for lack of anything better, and hoped fruitlessly that my iPhone's battery might be about to die.

"You're not the storm, Tyler," she said, and then breathed out in a way that suggested she'd wait for me to say something more substantial than my recent contributions.

"Maybe I'm a lightning rod," I offered, mostly to fill conversational space, like a picture filling a blank wall.

"Exactly!" she said. "I think you're the lightning rod, Tyler, I really do. But I got to thinking that lightning rods, while useful, undeniably draw lightning strikes, and even though they ostensibly help people get through dangerous storms, they often result in barns burning down … even though the lightning rods tend to be fine."

"We've talked about this before, Meg," I said. "You and me and Frank and John and Dot and Mickey … sometimes (*like tonight, I thought, but didn't say*) it seems/feels like the only thing we talk about … how my being a consulting detective puts the people I care about, and me, in harm's way."

"Shut up, I'm not talking about that, not exactly," she said, in a tone I'd never heard from her lips before. "The dream, or whatever, made me think about, wonder, if a lightning rod—fuck it—if you, have been struck enough times that you're used to it, like it, maybe even need it. Need the lightning to, I don't know, exist. I wonder if you're becoming a lightning, or storm, or chaos and violence junkie?"

"I don't think that's—" I started to say.

"I'm not done, Tyler," she said. "In talking with

Frank and Brimley and you about what happened, about how you set things up, it feels like you could have helped them catch 'that fucking Bernie' without the shit-show out at the campsite on the lake, or through whatever happened out on the road to Tupper. I think you could have made it less tricky and less dangerous, but it would have pulled you out of the center of the game you were playing with 'that fucking Bernie' (*which was a name that would seem to be sticking, at least in the short term*)."

"So now you think I killed John, and nearly killed Frank?" I asked, hot wet tears burning down my cheeks for reasons I didn't/couldn't understand. "Is that what you're saying, Meg?"

"No, Tyler, not exactly," she said, with an even/careful tone that I'd heard her use at the school, with students/clients, the few times I'd gone there to meet her, or pick her up. "Bernie did all of the killing (*not all of it, but she didn't know that, wouldn't ever know it if I could help it*), all of the kidnapping. But you acted the way you did for reasons that need to be examined, looked at, thought about, talked about. I'd like to help."

I sat and looked at the wall, at the frying pan, and thought about how that adventure, that misadventure, had gone, and how it could have gone better/differently ... how many/all of my investigations might have ended differently. As tempting as it was to take her up on her offer and spill my secrets in exchange for absolution, for being fixed ... I wouldn't/couldn't let it happen. I couldn't tell her everything, no matter how much she suspected; it would be different if she knew (*if she saw*) the true me. Still, it would probably do me some good to talk with someone about some portion, some of the layers, of my life ... especially now that John was gone.

"I'd like that," I said. "I'd like your help ... like to

talk. If you're still interested/willing when I get back, I'll stop by the house and we can do that."

"How about you call when you're on your way back up," she said, "and we'll make sure to set up a time, but let's make it at my office, okay?"

That last bit freaked me out for a couple of reasons, on a number of levels that I wasn't ready to think about, so I mumbled something somewhat committal and hung up.

I thought about how much I had counted on John in the last few years, as a way to debrief after something like this (*either Campsite #60, or the road near Tupper, or my talk with Meg … you choose*) had happened, but that was no longer an option, and I felt the hole, the space, in my life, glowing in the dark all around me. Shaking my head, I tried to clear it some after a long day, and the last few minutes, and dialed the last number of the day … Nick picked up before the end of the first ring.

"Tyler," he said in a dry and papery voice, "I thought I'd be hearing from you or John before now. I was hoping it'd be John."

"Me too," I said, "I assume you know something about what he was helping me with the last few days?"

"Yes," he said. "I assume he made a mistake of some sort, and that's why you're calling me so late in the evening."

"The big mistake I'd pin on him, Nick, was him trying to help me," I said. "He was brave and glorious and saved a bunch of lives tonight, including, maybe especially, mine, and helped put an end to a series of murders going back nearly twenty years. He was only a half-step slower than the other guy, but that was enough (*more than enough really, but exactitude can be overrated at times like this*). He's dead, and his body is at the AMC. Is there anybody else I should call?"

"Ach, lad," he said (*a few times in our lengthy acquaintance, he'd let his Irish slip to the forefront, normally when he'd been drinking late with John … I extrapolated that he might have been drinking with John in spirit before I'd called*), "he's got a pair of brothers downstate, and boatloads of family back there (*I could picture Nick, and John, pointing vaguely toward Ireland, as they'd done many times in the past, when referring to the ancestral homeland*). John loved playing at hero with you, and talking about your imaginary friend, Bailey (*I didn't correct him*). It was no mistake, him helping you tonight. Doing exactly this is exactly how he would have wanted to go … not an old man sitting on the porch, like me. I'll see him again soon, and tell him you loved him in your way, as he did you. When you've got the time, I'd like to see you, and talk with you about John and some of the things we shared in our time together."

"I'll do that," I said, thinking that John would have appreciated it if I could look in on the old man for him, and talk with him about their *good old days*, and some of the adventures John and I had shared over the years.

Barry chimed in from the back of my head, "Yeah, who's he gonna tell anyways?"

I hung up after a lengthy silence on both ends of the phone call/line. Despite the late-night caffeine loading, I had no trouble falling asleep as soon as I got horizontal on the couch.

Edith's Aunt's House, Moosic, PA
Monday, 7/13/2015, 5:32 p.m.

I woke up as the light poured into the big window facing
east, and heard padded, silent, and tiny feet running away
from me as I sat up and looked around and rubbed my
face/eyes/head/hair/shoulder/neck wound. I could
smell coffee, and wandered into the kitchen, nodding to a
still sleep-doped Dot hunched over what appeared to be
her first cup of coffee. Leaning into the 1950s era fridge
that took up a huge amount of space in the smallish
room, I grabbed two of the small glass bottles of Coke
and opened them both with the church key hung by a
string on the fridge door handle.

"Give me twenty minutes, and then come over and
help me open up the shelter before you hit the road," Dot
said, "okay?"

I nodded and finished the first bottle, dropping it into
the blue recycling container in the corner before
taking/peeling/eating a slightly under ripe banana (*which is
exactly how I like my bananas, thank you very much*), and Dot
shuffled off into the bathroom to shower and hopefully
wake up a bit.

Half an hour later, we opened the back door to the
TLAS, the first ones there, and the smell/sound of
roughly a hundred dogs and cats (*along with a few rabbits …
but they don't smell much or make much noise*) rushed out to
greet me, warm and moist and surrounding/engulfing us.
I hadn't thought that Dot would need help, but she

reminded me that Steph was out of action for a few days and mornings were generally Steph's bailiwick (*which might have been the first time outside of BBC that I had heard someone use the word … should have tipped me off that something was coming*). Before anything else, she reminded me about my Bernie-bone, and spent a few minutes removing the chips from my tender, but essentially functional shoulder muscle; she'd done similar minor surgeries a couple of times over the years, and passed me a pair of bottles (*one filled with dog antibiotics, the other with 800mg ibuprofens … she told me to drink plenty of water, and take one of each of the pills four times a day until I ran out*). She understood why I hadn't wanted to get the Bernie-bone looked at, and fixed, at the hospital … less attention paid to me in connection with the already messy ending of this affair would be better.

Once she'd finished taping me up, we worked together to check on the rest of the animals needing morning medical attention, then fed and watered everyone and started the endless job of cleaning the shelter and doing laundry. When we'd gotten the morning started, and Jen showed up to help move things along toward readiness for the ten o'clock opening of the shelter to the public, Dot asked me to walk a couple of the dogs who hadn't gotten out the previous day, starting with the ones in the isolation room … I should have seen it coming, but didn't.

"We've got some live ones coming in today, and it'd be super if the dogs in the back room could have some of their wiggles and jumps out before they scare off the civilians," Dot said. "I know you want to hit the road, Tyler, but if you could walk a couple of them before you go, it could really help them find a forever home."

I entered the back isolation room and was actually surprised to find just a single occupant, already out of his cage. (*Dot had pulled a 'shitty' on me.*) I was looking straight into the face/eyes/soul (*I may not think I have a soul, but firmly believe that every dog I've ever met does … go figure*) of Snowflake, the ginormous Neapolitan Mastiff I'd walked, what seemed like, a lifetime ago. Dot must have snuck back in here earlier and released the hound from his enclosure. He was just sitting there waiting for me, leash on, tongue hanging out the side of his mouth. Something clunked, deep in my head/heart, like an old-fashioned wooden puzzle piece slipping into the correct place, or a heavy oaken door closing/latching perfectly (*or the sound of distant thunder giving you a heads up*). I sat on the floor and he padded over, impact tremors keeping tempo with my morning-slow heart rate (*still no glass of water for optimum effect, I'd have to work on that*).

He stopped about two inches from me and sat with a thud, his chest even with my eyes; I leaned slowly forward into his warm, thick, doggy fur, and he leaned into me. I felt his turkey-sized head come to rest on the top of my skull and a long and deep breath rattle out of his throat thanks to the nerve endings in my nose and eyelids. I wrapped my arms around his bulk and pulled him closer still; he resisted minutely, and then snuggled in so near I had to turn my head slightly to avoid being pushed back/over. Snowflake sighed and settled down on his butt and farted and groaned and shifted slightly to lick first an ear, then my neck, and finally my throat, where Bernie had almost let all my blood out.

His tongue was rough and broad and hot and wet, and it hurt, but also felt cleansing and somehow necessary. He pushed me over, and I let him; I lay down on the slightly sticky linoleum, and he repositioned his paws on my chest, almost crushing the breath out of me but leaving me with a feeling of being surrounded by, buried under, love and safety and security (*that I happily chose over comfortable breathing*). He began to chew some fleas that I may or may not have had on my skull, behind an ear, and then down on my chest. That was when Dot came in.

"Tyler, are you under that thing?" she asked. "Kim's on the phone for you. She and Mark headed up to P-burgh this morning and wanted to check some details with you. Your phone was off, so they called around until they got me on the TLAS main line."

I loosened my arms from around Snowflake, and dug a hand out from under his bulk, and held it out and up. Dot put the cordless into my palm and backed out of the room without another word.

"Kim, how are you and Mark doing?" I asked, "What's going on up in Plattsburgh this morning?"

"Hi, Tyler," she said. "How are you today? We heard all sorts of stuff last night. What's up?"

I told her a slightly cleaned up version of what had happened last night, and we felt our way through how messed up it all was. The road was calling to me. She passed the phone to Mark.

"Tyler, my man," he said, and I could hear Kim in the background asking where her underwear had gotten to. (*I was less and less convinced by the 'girl who is a friend' argument with the passage of time.*) "We wanted to get out of town as soon as possible, and we're going to see the real Soffermans for an early lunch. I just wanted to check in with you about what, if anything, we should tell them."

"Nothing," I said, "and less than that if you can get away with it ... 'grateful nation' and 'please keep your role in this to yourselves,' ... stuff like that, if you two feel comfortable standing in for me. I need to head down to the city to visit a sick friend, but I'd like to catch up with you both after I get back and figure out a real way to thank you for everything."

He started to say something about how they'd handle it, when Snowflake took the phone from my hand with his mouth very gently, and tossed it against the wall much less gently. I laughed and pulled him down on top of me again, and started laughing and crying into his fur, leaving both of us wet/confused/embarrassed. Dot came in a few minutes later, laughed at the sight of us still on the floor and handed me some paperwork to sign; I apparently had a new dog.

"You'll need the forms all filled out if you two are going to leave to see Edith and Mickey this morning." She smiled again at the two of us on the floor. "I took care of his final shots and checkup and got everything in order after your first visit with him. You love to think you don't emote, but the two of you were obviously made for each other."

I nodded, thanked her, signed where she told me, and made out a check to the TLAS, while asking if she needed a hand with anything else in the shelter's morning routine.

"Nope, you have to get going," she said. "Say *hi* to Mickey when you see him, and tell him I'm on the committee designing this year's ice castle. I expect him to come up at the end of January to check it out."

Snowflake and I were on the road out of town less than an hour later. He was a huge and mobile/animated presence in my passenger seat, especially after Hope (*who was a tiny fraction of his size, and tended to do her imitation of a furry donut whenever she got in the car*). His head scraped the roof of the Element and his eyes were constantly on a swivel, watching everything around him. We were headed west on Route 3 (*past the scene of last night's excitement, although Snowflake didn't give the spot a glance as we cruised by, so neither did I*), and then eventually south on Route 81, to Moosic, the town in Pennsylvania where Edith's aunt had taken her. (*I got an address/number from Frank on my way out of town, and planned to call once I was too close to refuse or turn away.*)

Snowflake and I stopped briefly at the McDonald's in Tupper Lake for a mess of sandwiches from the dollar menu, and I had to work hard to convince him to wait for me to unwrap them before he swallowed his way through most of the bag. (*I would have to pick up a better quality of food for him, and possibly for me as well, at some point, but for now it worked for both of us.*) Every few hours I would stop to stretch and we'd both take care of business, input and output. I rolled up to the house shortly after five in the afternoon and was heartened to see a pair of cars in the driveway (*and a blatantly marked cruiser parked across the street*). I pulled just past, and dialed the aunt's number, not wanting to upset or scare the occupants of the house, or alarm the police keeping an eye on them by just showing up.

"Hello," I said to the anxious/nervous-sounding woman who answered. "This is Tyler Cunningham, one of the investigators involved in the events with Edith and her parents in upstate New York a few days ago. I'd like to ask her a few follow-up questions (*not exactly true, but it might be closer to what they'd expect, and/or be comfortable with than the truth*)."

"I don't think that would be possible right now, and especially not over the phone," the woman said. "She's been so upset, and we're going to sit down to supper in a few minutes."

"If you wouldn't mind," I said, "I promise to be brief and to try not to upset her. I've driven a long way, you see, and am just outside your house. In the interests of supporting her healing process, I've come with a therapy dog (*I smiled across at Snowflake, who had burped and farted a moment earlier, the combination of which almost knocked me out of the car, and made it hard to speak in a normal voice, possibly due to a lack of usable oxygen in the Element's interior*), and I really just need to check a couple of details. I could be in and out of your hair in ten minutes."

Looking in the rearview, I watched the curtains in the big picture window flutter open, and a woman's face pressed against the window for a second ... I tapped my brakes briefly so she'd see us ... and waited.

"I suppose you can come in for a few minutes," she said. "My husband is allergic to animal dander, though, the dog you've got with you isn't by chance hypo-allergenic, is it?"

"Quite the opposite, I'm afraid," I said, looking at my constantly off-gassing, and likely hyper-allergenic, behemoth/companion. "Perhaps we could avoid troubling you and your husband by having me come in initially, and then Edith and I could take the dog for a walk on your lovely lawn (*I was nearly positive that mentioning the dog's name wouldn't help things*) while we talk."

"That sounds ... acceptable," she said, not entirely convincingly; I hung up before she could change her mind, or place any restrictions on our contact/conduct.

I got out of the car after opening the windows a few inches, promised a sad-faced Snowflake I'd be back in just a minute, and walked to the house, the front door of which opened before I reached the front stoop. Edith's aunt looked me up and down and didn't seem impressed.

"You're sure you're an investigator," she said, "and not some sort of reporter or something."

I was rescued from explaining my consultant status by Edith who shoved her way past the woman.

"Aunt Peggy," she said, "I know him. He interviewed me before when I was in the hospital before you picked me up. He's the one who's helping the police and FBI guys find the man who ..."

She faltered there and started to breathe heavily and make odd sounds in her throat. I momentarily felt like a monster, but then she turned her head toward me and winked with the eye hidden from her aunt. "It'll be fine, really. I'll talk with him and pet the dog, and wash my hands after, so Unca Don doesn't get sick."

Edith scampered halfway to my Element and turned to wait for me without giving her aunt the chance to say anything; the woman lingered uncertainly in the open door for a moment and only closed it after murmuring something about dinner being ready soon.

We walked the rest of the way to the Element, and I released the beast/hound/kraken, grabbing the end of the leash as it whipped past me. Edith giggled when Snowflake pulled me over to a fire hydrant that he towered over and hosed down ... perhaps the first he'd ever seen (*suburbs are fancy like that. Snowflake, I thought ... stick with me and I'll show you all the good stuff*).

"What is that thing?" she asked. "It looks like a bear, or like someone inflated and then partly melted a Labrador. Why on earth would you bring it with you to talk with me? It's not really a therapy dog is it?"

"I'm told he's a Neapolitan Mastiff," I said, "although it's possible there's some bear or giant ground sloth genetic material in there as well ... and no, he's not a therapy dog. Although I do find spending time with him to be therapeutic."

Edith took the leash from me (*causing me to wonder what would happen if Snowflake decided to take off running, with this waif a third of his weight attached to him ... nothing good, but it was out of my control, so I put it out of my mind as well*), and walked around the back of the house, leaving me no choice but to follow. "Do you really have more questions for me?"

"No," I said, sitting on a wrought-iron bench under a Japanese maple at the far end of the back yard. "I just wanted to keep my promise and tell you what happened ... if you still want to hear it."

She sat on the grass in front of me, with her back to the house, after first waving to her aunt and uncle who were watching from their kitchen, and nodded seriously.

"With the help of some friends, I figured out some things about the man who killed your parents," I said, looking into her eyes to see how my word affected her. "Together, we set a trap for him and ended up catching him. He ended up dying, rather than being taken into custody."

"Did you ...?" she (*sort of*) asked. "Were you there, at the end, when he ..."

I had wondered what I do, what I would say, at this point, if we got to this place in our conversation and was about to find out.

"He was alive and helpless, and I probably could have held him until the police got there, but, yes, I killed him," I said, and watched her face change, thunderstruck at the enormity of my words, and then sadden immensely ... Snowflake leaned down and covered her whole face with his tongue, a couple of times until she pushed him back so she could breathe.

"Did you?" she asked, "was it because of me, for me, that you ...?"

Again, I wasn't sure of what I would say until I had said it, "No. I told you I would, but I killed him because he'd killed a friend of mine, and tried to kill me, and I was pretty sure he would try to kill me again so he could escape, so I just took the easiest way out of the situation. I wanted to tell you in person that the man who killed your parents is dead, but just as importantly, maybe more importantly, that you, and your anger from the other day, had nothing to do with why he's dead."

It might even have been true, I don't know, but it seemed to lighten her load, and that was reason enough, regardless of what the truth is/was/will be.

Snowflake spent the next few minutes cleaning the tears from her face (*happy, sad, I can never tell the difference, and Snowflake thought they all tasted good*), soaking her from ear to ear until she began to laugh. "He really is a therapy dog."

They all are.

I walked her up the path to the back door, and her aunt again opened the door before we got there. I told her, and Uncle Don (*who lingered a safe distance from the door, and me, and most especially Snowflake*) that Edith would likely be called on by other representatives of the law enforcement community in the coming weeks, and/but if they, or she, needed to get in touch with me, I could be reached via email or phone as per my card (*I gave them the plain/boring one, with just my name and contact information*). Edith turned to pat Snowflake and (*earning a final lick, which soaked her arm from wrist to elbow*) and then surprised me with a hug (*which I endured without flinching or pulling back, just like a real person might do*).

As I drove away from their house, I was quite certain (*rightly*) I would never see/hear from her again. Snowflake and I drove east and a bit south toward the Delaware Water Gap National Recreation Area, to find a place to sleep for a few hours before heading into Manhattan to visit with Mickey.

Mickey Schwarz's Apartment, Manhattan, NY
Tuesday, 7/14/2015, 5:28 a.m.

I rang the buzzer nearly twelve hours after leaving Edith's
new home/life/world in my rearview, with a small duffle
bag in one hand, and possibly the biggest dog ever to
enter a Manhattan apartment building in the other. The
night-duty doorman came up to unlock the big front
door, and actually took a step back when he saw
Snowflake; a moment later, he opened the door and asked
me what (*and presumably who*) I wanted.

"Doctor Schwarz," I said (*'Mickey' seemed a little
casual/informal when talking to a man dressed like a Guatemalan
Admiral in the early hours of the morning in the city that
supposedly never sleeps, but does a fair imitation at 5:30 a.m.*).
"He'll be expecting me and should be awake by now (*I'd
arrived before four and waited until I was sure he'd be up and
about*)."

The doorman seemed momentarily unsure, but I'd
angled my voice toward the haughty end of polite, nearly
commanding, and a few short seconds later he moped
back to the intercom and buzzed up for Mickey. A couple
of seconds after that he was pointing us back to the
elevator and reminding me that they lived on the
fourteenth floor (*which was actually the thirteenth floor, although
I didn't point this out to the doorman ... it's an artifact of
superstition, and something Mickey and I actually enjoyed about*

their new place).

Mickey was waiting in the hallway on the 13th/14th floor, looking too skinny and older, wearing the fleece bathrobe and slippers I'd given him for his birthday. Snowflake got away from me and ran over to give him some love as soon as we cleared the elevator (*which had seemed awfully small with the two of us in it, and the upward movement had seemed to freak Snowflake out a bit in what he must have thought was a small waiting room*). I almost got ahold of the leash as it slipped through my fingers, and Mickey staggered back a half-step as the tsunami of black fur and muscles and teeth and claws rushed inexorably toward him (*there was no possible way I could 'exorable' Snowflake at this juncture, so I simply hurried to try and minimize the aftereffects*).

When Snowflake crested over Mickey and they both settled on the carpeted floor in a slow motion crash that took my breath away, I heard a scream from just inside the apartment.

"Mickey!" Anne shrieked. "Get off him, you horrible beast!"

Anne waded out into the pile of dog and husband filling the hallway, in a silky dressing gown which was open and revealing a revealing negligee, launching fierce kicks and determined punches at Snowflake (*somewhere between Miss Piggy and Jet-li in her ferocity and intensity*), trying to dislodge him from Mickey. I got there a half second later and pulled the dog back and off Mickey, who was making a series of odd noises. Anne kept screaming and kicking, and even giving chase in defense of her husband while Snowflake and I backed down the hall; I tried to look past her to see how badly Mickey was damaged.

Both of us seemed to realize at the same moment that Mickey was laughing so hard he couldn't breathe properly, and it made his laughter sound odd. I whacked

Snowflake on his bottom and he dropped his backend down with a deep thud (*again, no glass of water in sight, although a vase of flowers on a table nearby rattled ominously, which was better than nothing*), and we all turned to see Mickey struggle slowly to his feet.

"Good morning, Tyler, and welcome!" he said when he got his breath back. "What the hell is that thing?"

"It's a duffel," I said, dropping my overnight bag ... Dot has often said that tense moments can often be diffused by humor, and based on years of study, this should have been funny.

"Seriously, Tyler," Anne wheezed, still blocking the hallway, red and apparently thinking about attacking Snowflake (*based on a foot drawn back, and a hand raised in classic 'judo-chop' position*), "now you grow a sense of humor? Why on Earth would you bring that yeti to our tiny apartment to attack Mickey? Are you trying to kill him?"

We both looked at Mickey and simultaneously started to ask him if he was okay ... he chopped off the line of questioning with a slashing hand.

"I'm fine," he said. "It's actually the first time in months I haven't been listening, or feeling, for my brain to try and kill me. I thought Tyler's new friend might do it instead."

He shuffled down the hall and thumped the top of Snowflake's head with a too-frail hand ... Snowflake fell in love (*something I've since learned that he does quickly/easily, with the right people, which Mickey most certainly is*), and started licking the air in Mickey's direction.

"Mickey and Anne," I said, "this is Snowflake. Snowflake, this is Mickey and Anne."

"Snowflake, no shit?" Mickey said. "Didja see Anne go after Snowflake a minute ago? Is he gonna be okay,

Tyler?"

"I think so," I said, "I don't think Anne damaged him. He's quite a big dog, and tough."

Mickey actually giggled, and after a red-faced and angry moment, Anne did too.

"Let's get out of the hall before our neighbors call the police," Mickey said. "I just made a pot of Bustello (*the acrid and sludgy coffee that Mickey drinks all day, every day*), and Anne was proud of finding a few bottles of yellow-cap Coke the other day, and it's in the fridge. You can tell us about how you two met, what you've been up to (*he pointed at the knife-wound on my throat*), and what's new with you."

He seemed happy and strong, and for a minute had forgotten the bomb ticking in his skull, and, perhaps because of (*or despite, I couldn't be sure*) my unusual entry, Anne leaned across the hallway and gave me an unexpected kiss on the cheek.

"Yes," she said, taking my arm and scooping up my duffel on her way back down the hallway, "let's go in and talk a bit."

I was suddenly struck by a feeling/tone of hope in her voice. In the hallway, the day seemed brighter, and anything seemed possible.

We went in and had a nice morning and visit.

Tyler Cunningham

The Playlists from Tyler's Circle

Barry: "Barry's Chase Mix"
1. *Thunderstruck*, AC/DC
2. *Rag Doll*, Aerosmith
3. *I'm Shipping up to Boston*, Dropkick Murphys
4. *Welcome to the Jungle*, Guns N' Roses
5. *Closer*, Nine Inch Nails
6. *Smells Like Teen Spirit*, Nirvana
7. *Enter Sandman*, Metallica
8. *Alive*, Pearl Jam
9. *Good Riddance*, Green Day
10. *Crazy Train*, Ozzy Osbourne

Dot: "Dancin' in Footie Pajamas Mix"
1. *What Would You Say*, Dave Matthews Band
2. *What Makes You Beautiful*, One Direction
3. *Long Time Gone*, Dixie Chicks
4. *Closer to Fine*, Indigo Girls
5. *Rumor Has It*, Adele
6. *You Oughta Know*, Alanis Morissette
7. *Somebody To Love*, Queen
8. *Alleluia*, Dar Williams
9. *Galileo*, Indigo Girls
10. *Don't Stop Believin'*, Journey
11. *Love Shack*, The B-52's
12. *Uptown Funk*, Mark Ronson, Bruno Mars
13. *Raise Your Glass*, Pink
14. *I'm The Only One*, Melissa Etheridge
15. *Firework*, Katy Perry

Meg: "Music for a Rainy Sunday Afternoon Mix"

1. *Shut Up and Kiss Me*, Mary Chapin Carpenter
2. *Moondance*, Van Morrison
3. *Satellite of Love*, Lou Reed
4. *Jersey Girl*, Holly Cole
5. *Angel*, Sarah McLachlan
6. *Diamonds and Rust*, Joan Baez
7. *Round Here*, Counting Crows
8. *Fields of Gold*, Sting
9. *Angel From Montgomery*, Bonnie Raitt
10. *Just Like a Woman*, Richie Havens
11. *A Case of You*, Joni Mitchell
12. *Romeo and Juliet*, Dire Straits
13. *Don't Let the Sun Catch You Crying*, Rickie Lee Jones
14. *Come Away With Me*, Norah Jones
15. *Hallelujah*, K.D. Lang

Frank: "Drinking with Lola in the Backyard Mix"

1. *New York State of Mind*, Billy Joel
2. *Rosalita (Come Out Tonight)*, Bruce Springsteen
3. *Authority Song*, John Mellencamp
4. *Bad Reputation*, Joan Jett
5. *Up On Cripple Creek*, The Band
6. *Friends in Low Places*, Garth Brooks
7. *Southern Cross*, Crosby, Stills, and Nash
8. *Crazy*, Patsy Cline
9. *Gold Dust Woman*, Fleetwood Mac
10. *You Wreck Me*, Tom Petty
11. *Sultans of Swing*, Dire Straits
12. *Harvest Moon*, Neil Young
13. *Thing Called Love*, Bonnie Raitt
14. *Bad Moon Rising*, Creedence Clearwater Revival
15. *It's My Life*, Bon Jovi

John: "Music from the Old Country"
1. *The Irish Rover,* The Dubliners
2. *Ríl Liatroma/The Green Cockade/The Mourne Mountains,* Téada
3. *The Fairy Reel / The Old Torn Petticoat / Our House at Home,* Danu
4. *The Musical Priest/The Blackthorn Stick,* The Dubliners
5. *Cooley's/The Cup of Tea/The Wise Maid (Reels),* Tulla Céilí Band
6. *The Walls of Liscarroll Jig,* The Chieftains
7. *My Love is in America,* Martin Hayes
8. *An Paistin Fionn (The Fair-Haired Boy)/The Flowers of Munster,* Chulrua
9. *Whiskey in the Jar,* The Dubliners
10. *Dowd's Reel - The Musical Priest/Scotch Mary,* Jordi Savall/Andrew Lawrence-King

Mark: "Mark's Local Music Mix"
1. *Dead Heads and Suckers,* The Wompers
2. *Round and Round,* George Bailey Trio
3. *Hopeful Landscape,* Celia Evans
4. *Coal Tattoo,* Upnorth String Band
5. *Snowed In,* Curt Stager
6. *Brown Eyed September,* Adrenaline Hayride
7. *Holy Waters,* Rebecca Sutter
8. *Naked Trees,* Mark Jennings
9. *Sailing into Walpole's Marsh,* Gretchen and Rebecca Koehler
10. *The Water is Wide,* Ray Agnew

Mickey: "Music for Relaxation"
"I don't do playlists, Ty. I listen to *Mozart at Midnight*"

ACKNOWLEDGMENTS/EXPLANATIONS
{Excuses}

The idea for Thunderstruck has been in mind for years, waiting for the right time and place to come out and play, and this year was apparently the time and place. I'm intrigued by the concept of serial/pattern killers operating nearly in the open, but unseen and unsuspected by the world and people around them. It seemed impossible to me that one could operate in my neck of the woods until this idea came to me, and then it just wouldn't let go.

I feel as though Tyler Cunningham and I have mostly completed our journey together at this point, although I can still feel a few minor stories kicking around in the nooks and crannies at the back of my skull. Getting to know him, and the people and places that inhabit his world, has been a metric crap-ton of fun, and I had a great time in the spring of 2015 looking back through the novels and novellas to feel my way through the arc of his life since 9/11, and the events that gave birth to his Adirondack incarnation.

Having published four books (and perhaps more importantly, eight stories in this series) I felt confident coming into the writing stage of Thunderstruck. I'm a big fan and believer in the NaNoWriMo writing sprint model of generating a first draft. The need for speed and lack of concern with getting it "right" the first time really works for me. There were some new challenges in writing this book (which I'm grateful for, after the fact … upping the challenge forces us to grow and change). During August of 2015. My wife and I took a trip to France right before I was going to start writing, and I interrupted the writing sprint a few times for family stuff and a writing conference, so that it was less a continuous sprint this year than in years past. I also changed up the narrative style for this book, adding some scenes from an alternate point of view for fun (and hopefully some effect).

Amazon's self-publishing services, through CreateSpace and Kindle Desktop Publishing (KDP), continue to provide me with not only the means to publish this book, but also an abundance of useful information and resources that made it much easier to do so.

The Adirondack Park was, and is, both an inspiration for, and a character in, this book. The natural beauty and open space and peace that the Park, and especially the Tri-Lakes region, provide makes for a perfect setting for my life, and for Tyler's.

The people in my life, both private and professional, provide ideas and inspiration for my writing, and for that I'm very grateful. Although I'm often asked who the characters in my books are based on, there's no easy (one person) answer. The people living in my books and head are amalgams of many people I know and have known (and sometimes people I imagine).

The Tri-Lakes Humane Society (TLHS) is a massive force for good in the Adirondack Park, and an inspiration to me as a writer and a human being. The Tri-Lakes Animal Shelter (TLAS) in my books is loosely based on the TLHS … everything good about it is true, any illegal activities were, of course, entirely made up. We've brought four dogs home from the TLHS to live with us, and all of them were instrumental in helping me write the book in one way or another.

Origin Coffee, in Saranac Lake, was the location at which I wrote the lion's share of this novel. I would show up every morning at (or slightly before) the appointed hour, set up my work station in the back of the place, and drink coffee while banging out thousands of words each day for a month or so. Great people serving great coffee in a great location made it a wonderful experience, and I look forward to writing more stories at Origin in the future.

The Adirondack Writers Guild, a newly formed learning community and support group for writers in the Adirondacks, has also been incredibly useful in helping me to continue to grow as a writer in the last year, and I'm grateful to the people who make it up.

Friends and family have inspired and supported me throughout the writing and editing process, and I can't thank them enough. My parents (Jim and Jill Sheffield), sister (Sarah Sheffield), wonderful son (Ben), and wife (Gail Gibson Sheffield) all gave me the time and space and loving support that I needed to follow this dream, and their love gave me the courage to try, again. Some crazy camping friends: Rick Schott, Bryce Fortran, Derek Murawsky, Kevin Curdgel, and Stephen Carvalho, have helped me expand my map of the world through their friendship while camping in all seasons through the years. Countless other friends have also offered encouragement, giving me support and positive vibes during the writing and editing process.

Over the past four years I have enjoyed an incredible outpouring of support from readers of *Here Be Monsters*, *Caretakers*, and *Between the Carries*, as well as *Mickey Slips*,

Bound for Home,Fair Play, and *Promises to Keep* (the short novellas in the Tyler Cunningham series, collectively published under the title *The Weaving*), and most recently *Speaking in Code* (another Tyler Cunningham novella). It is one thing to put creative ideas on paper, a completely different thing to know those ideas are being read and accepted by people all over the world. It is that acceptance and encouragement that moved me from being someone who writes, to being a writer. That is what made *Thunderstuck* possible ... thank you all for that.

A big shout out to the entire staff at SmartPig Publishing for their tireless efforts throughout the process! We were joined once again by Superstar Editor, Kathy LaPeyre (although she didn't read this, so please excuse any errors in the front and back matter). Kathy has done a fantastic job helping to polish my fourth novel in a thoroughly amazing way, and I'm tremendously grateful to her for all of her help.

While I couldn't have done it without any of you, any errors or omissions are all mine.

Jamie Sheffield
January 10, 2016
Lake Clear, NY

ABOUT THE AUTHOR

Jamie Sheffield lives in the Adirondack Park with his wife, Gail Gibson Sheffield, and son, Benjamin, and two dogs, Miles and Puck. When he's not writing mysteries, he's probably camping or exploring the last great wilderness in the Northeast. He has been a Special Education Teacher in the Lake Placid Central School District for the last 18 years. Besides writing, Jamie loves cooking and reading and dogs and all manner of outdoor pursuits.

"Thunderstruck" is his fourth novel.

Follow the ongoing adventures of Tyler Cunningham:

"Here Be Monsters"
"Caretakers"
"The Weaving"
"Between the Carries"

and read other works by the author.

Visit Jamie Sheffield's website:

www.jamiesheffield.com

THE TRAEGER GRILL COOKBOOK FOR BEGINNERS

THE TRAEGER GRILL

COOKBOOK

FOR BEGINNERS

90 RECIPES FOR YOUR WOOD PELLET SMOKER

CHERI RENEÉ

PHOTOGRAPHY BY DARREN MUIR

ROCKRIDGE
PRESS

I would love to

DEDICATE

this book

TO MY HUSBAND, SHANNON.

Not only is he my

BIGGEST SUPPORTER

in life, it was his brilliant idea to get our first

TRAEGER GRILL, which

started my LOVE of

WOOD-FIRED COOKING.

Cooking and Carving Directions

Bagged Giblets for Easy Removal

Roasted Turkey Nutrition Information Inside.

GLUTEN FREE

Premium Young Turkey

No Artificial Ingredients • Minimally Processed

**Federal regulations do not permit the use of hormones in poultry

Premium
*all natural**
Butterball

TURKEY RAISED WITHOUT
HORMONES OR STEROIDS**

BUTTERBALL®

SAFE HANDLING INSTRUCTIONS

THIS PRODUCT WAS PREPARED FROM INSPECTED AND PASSED MEAT AND/OR POULTRY. SOME FOOD PRODUCTS MAY CONTAIN BACTERIA THAT COULD CAUSE ILLNESS IF THE PRODUCT IS MISHANDLED OR COOKED IMPROPERLY. FOR YOUR PROTECTION, FOLLOW THESE SAFE HANDLING INSTRUCTIONS.

KEEP REFRIGERATED OR FROZEN. THAW IN REFRIGERATOR OR MICROWAVE.

KEEP RAW MEAT AND POULTRY SEPARATE FROM OTHER FOODS. WASH WORKING SURFACES (INCLUDING CUTTING BOARDS), UTENSILS, AND HANDS AFTER TOUCHING RAW MEAT OR POULTRY.

COOK THOROUGHLY.

KEEP HOT FOODS HOT. REFRIGERATE LEFTOVERS IMMEDIATELY OR DISCARD.

Nutrition Facts

Serving Size 4 oz. (112g)
Servings Per Container Varied

Amount Per Serving	
Calories 170	
Calories from Fat	80

	% Daily Value*
Total Fat 9g	15%
Saturated Fat 2.5g	13%
Trans Fat 0g	
Cholesterol 65mg	22%
Sodium 200mg	9%
Total Carbohydrate 0g	0%
Protein 21g	42%

Iron 10%

Not a significant source of dietary fiber, sugars, vitamin A, vitamin C and calcium.

*Percent Daily Values (DV) are based on a 2,000 calorie diet.

BUTTERBALL®

Butterball brings people together.

By turning everyday moments into simple celebrations with family and friends, Butterball gives you tender, delicious turkey options that fit your life today.

Every Meal Becomes Special with Butterball

Roasted White Turkey**

Nutrition Facts

Serving Size 3 oz. (85g)
Servings Per Container Varied

Amount Per Serving	
Calories	160
Calories from Fat	60

	% Daily Value*
Total Fat 7g	10%
Saturated Fat 2g	9%
Trans Fat 0g	
Cholesterol 60mg	20%
Sodium 170mg	7%
Total Carbohydrate 0g	0%
Protein 22g	44%

Iron 6%

Not a significant source of dietary fiber, sugars, vitamin A, vitamin C and calcium.

*Percent Daily Values (DV) are based on a 2,000 calorie diet.

Roasted Dark Turkey**

Nutrition Facts

Serving Size 3 oz. (85g)
Servings Per Container Varied

Amount Per Serving	
Calories	170
Calories from Fat	80

	% Daily Value*
Total Fat 9g	14%
Saturated Fat 2.5g	14%
Trans Fat 0g	
Cholesterol 70mg	23%
Sodium 180mg	7%
Total Carbohydrate 0g	0%
Protein 22g	44%

Calcium 2% • Iron 10%

Not a significant source of dietary fiber, sugars, vitamin A, vitamin C and calcium.

*Percent Daily Values (DV) are based on a 2,000 calorie diet.

**(Excluding Neck & Giblets)

BUTTERBALL®

BREAKFAST
SANDWICHES
GRILLING

Visit Butterball.com for coupons & recipes

Try these other Butterball® products today!

Butterball Whole Turkeys

Butterball Ground Turkey

Butterball Deli Meats

Butterball Dinner Sausages

Butterball Turkey Bacon

Butterball Turkey Burgers

Butterball Fully Cooked Breakfast Sausage

LEFTOVER TURKEY CRESCENT BAKE

Servings 6	Prep Time 10 Minutes	Total Time <45 Minutes

Ingredients

- 2 cups stuffing mix, any flavor
- 1 ½ cups cubed cooked leftover Butterball® Turkey
- ½ cup turkey gravy
- 1 can (8 oz.) crescent rolls
- 1 cup cranberry sauce

Directions

1. Preheat oven to 375°F.
2. Combine stuffing, turkey and gravy in 3-quart saucepan. Bring to boil on medium-high heat, stirring occasionally.
3. Spoon mixture into ungreased 3-quart baking dish.
4. Separate or cut dough into 4 long rectangles. Place rectangles over stuffing mixture, leaving space between for steam to escape.
5. Bake 20 to 25 minutes or until dough is golden and stuffing mixture is hot and bubbly. Top with cranberry sauce and serve.

PER SERVING: Calories 430 • Fat 17g • Cholesterol 45mg • Protein 19g

BUTTERBALL®
Preparing Your Butterball Turkey

Size	Approximate Thawing Time		Approximate Roasting Time* Roast in Conventional Oven, Shallow Pan, 325°F	
	In Refrigerator	In Cold Water	Unstuffed	Stuffed
10 to 18 lbs.	3 to 4 days	5 to 9 hrs.	3 to 3½ hrs.	3¾ to 4½ hrs.
18 to 22 lbs.	4 to 5 days	9 to 11 hrs.	3½ to 4 hrs.	4½ to 5 hrs.
22 to 24 lbs.	5 to 6 days	11 to 12 hrs.	4 to 4½ hrs.	5 to 5½ hrs.
24 to 30 lbs.	6 to 7 days	12 to 15 hrs.	4½ to 5 hrs.	5½ to 6¼ hrs.

*If turkey is covered or placed in an oven cooking bag, cook time will vary.

1. THAW

Refrigerator
Allow at least 24 hours for every 4 pounds

- Place unopened turkey, breast side up, on a tray in refrigerator following above guidelines, or until thawed.

Quick Thaw - *Cold Water*
Allow 30 minutes per pound

- Place unopened turkey, breast down, in sink filled with cold tap water. Change water every 30 minutes.
- Once thawed, keep in refrigerator until ready to cook.

2. PREPARE

1 Remove Packaging
- Remove Turkey from wrapper. Take out the neck and giblets from the two body cavities.
- Drain juices and pat turkey with paper towels.

2 Stuff Turkey - *If Desired*
- Stuff turkey just before roasting.
- Lightly fill neck cavity; turn wings back to hold neck skin in place.
- Stuff body cavity and lightly return legs to tucked position. No trussing is necessary.

3. ROAST
For directions on grilling, frying or other cooking methods, visit Butterball.com

1. Preheat oven to 325°F.
2. Place turkey, breast side up, on flat roasting rack in 2" deep open roasting pan, Brush or spray skin with vegetable oil.
3. Roast according to time guidelines above*.
4. To prevent overcooking, loosely cover breast with lightweight foil when about two-thirds done.

5. To check for doneness, temperature on a meat thermometer should be 165°F in the breast/180°F in the thigh. However, Butterball recommends that the temperature in the breast reach 170°F for best eating experience. If the turkey is stuffed, the temperature in the center of the stuffing should be 165°F. ** Double check temperature for food safety.
6. Let turkey stand 15 minutes before carving.

**NOTE: When the thigh muscle is pierced deeply with a fork, juices should be clear and no longer reddish pink.

MEAT THERMOMETER DIRECTIONS

An oven safe (leave-in) thermometer can be inserted into the thigh before cooking. The thermometer should be placed into the thick part of thigh without touching the bone. Remove turkey from oven when it reaches 180°F. The breast should reach 170°F and if the turkey is stuffed, the center of the stuffing should be 165°F. If you don't have a leave-in thermometer, check the turkey with an instant read thermometer 30-60 minutes before the estimated finish time, then every 15 minutes thereafter.

CARVING DIRECTIONS

1 Remove Drumstick
- Cut entire leg off by holding drumstick and cutting through skin all the way to the joint.
- Remove by pulling out and back using point of knife to disjoint it. Separate thigh and drumstick at joint.

2 Horizontal Cut
- Insert fork in upper wing to steady turkey.
- Make a long horizontal cut above wing joint through to body frame.

3 Slicing
- Beginning halfway up breast, cut thin slice. When knife reaches horizontal cut, slice will fall free.
- Continue slicing, starting cut at a higher point each time.

TURKEY GRAVY

- Pan drippings
- Turkey or chicken broth
- 1/2 cup all-purpose flour
- Salt and pepper
- Cooked giblets, chopped fine (optional)

- Pour drippings from roasting pan into 4-cup measure.
- Remove 1/4 cup fat from drippings and place in saucepan. Discard remaining fat from drippings. Add broth to drippings to make 4 cups.
- Stir flour into fat in saucepan until smooth. Gradually blend in drippings.
- Cook and stir until gravy comes to a boil and thickens over medium heat.
- Continue cooking 3 to 5 minutes.

Season with salt and pepper. Add giblets, if desired. **Makes 4 cups**

STORAGE OF LEFTOVERS

- Refrigerate leftovers within 2 hours after heating. Carve turkey into pieces to speed cooling.
- Use leftover turkey within 3 days.

Questions or Comments?
Visit Butterball.com
Call 1-800-BUTTERBALL (1-800-288-8372) or
text 1-844-877-3456. Standard text messaging rates apply.
Visit us at Butterball.com for delicious recipes.

**For expert turkey advice, call the Butterball Turkey Talk-Line®
during November and December.**

CONTENTS

Chili-Rubbed Porterhouse Steak, page 47

INTRODUCTION

First of all, congratulations on your brand new Traeger Grill! My name is Cheri and in addition to being a food blogger and recipe developer at CooksWellWithOthers.com, I am also a teacher. In this book I combine my experience teaching with my passion for food to show you everything you need to know with easy step-by-step directions.

Over the years, I have had several different Traeger models and have been impressed with each one. I'm excited to show you what your new Traeger Grill is truly capable of! If you're new to grilling, it can feel overwhelming at first, but no worries. I will be with you every step of the way, and you'll be a Traeger pro in no time.

I have owned just about every type of grill and smoker you can imagine. When my husband suggested getting a Traeger a few years ago I sort of rolled my eyes, like we really needed another outdoor cooking appliance. But let me tell you—my first Traeger changed my life. That may sound a bit overdramatic, but Traeger really is wood-fired cooking at its finest.

I used to save grills and smokers for special occasions because the previous ones I owned just weren't very user-friendly. But the Traeger is so simple that, paired with the easy-to-follow instructions in this book, it can easily be used every day. Soon you'll be on your way to making yummy tried-and-true recipes, most of which even can be cooked quickly on busy weeknights. You'll also find low-and-slow recipes for when you have more time on your hands. Sitting outside with friends and family when the smoke starts rolling is one of my family's favorite weekend activities.

Many of the recipes in this book are for large cuts of meat like pulled pork, rack of lamb, whole chicken, and ribs. But anything you can cook in the oven, you can grill on the Traeger. It adds more flavor and that amazing kiss of wood-fired smoke to all of your food. As you'll see, many of these recipes are for meals that you might not think of when you think of smoked food—lasagna, calzones, and even soup! You can do it all thanks to the Traeger being so easy to set and regulate for perfect results every time, from quickly smoking a chicken to slow-roasting a brisket.

Traeger, the original wood-fired grill, has perfected the art of wood-fired cooking over the past 30 years. There is a reason they are the world's number-one-selling wood-fired grill, and you're about to find out why. Let's get started!

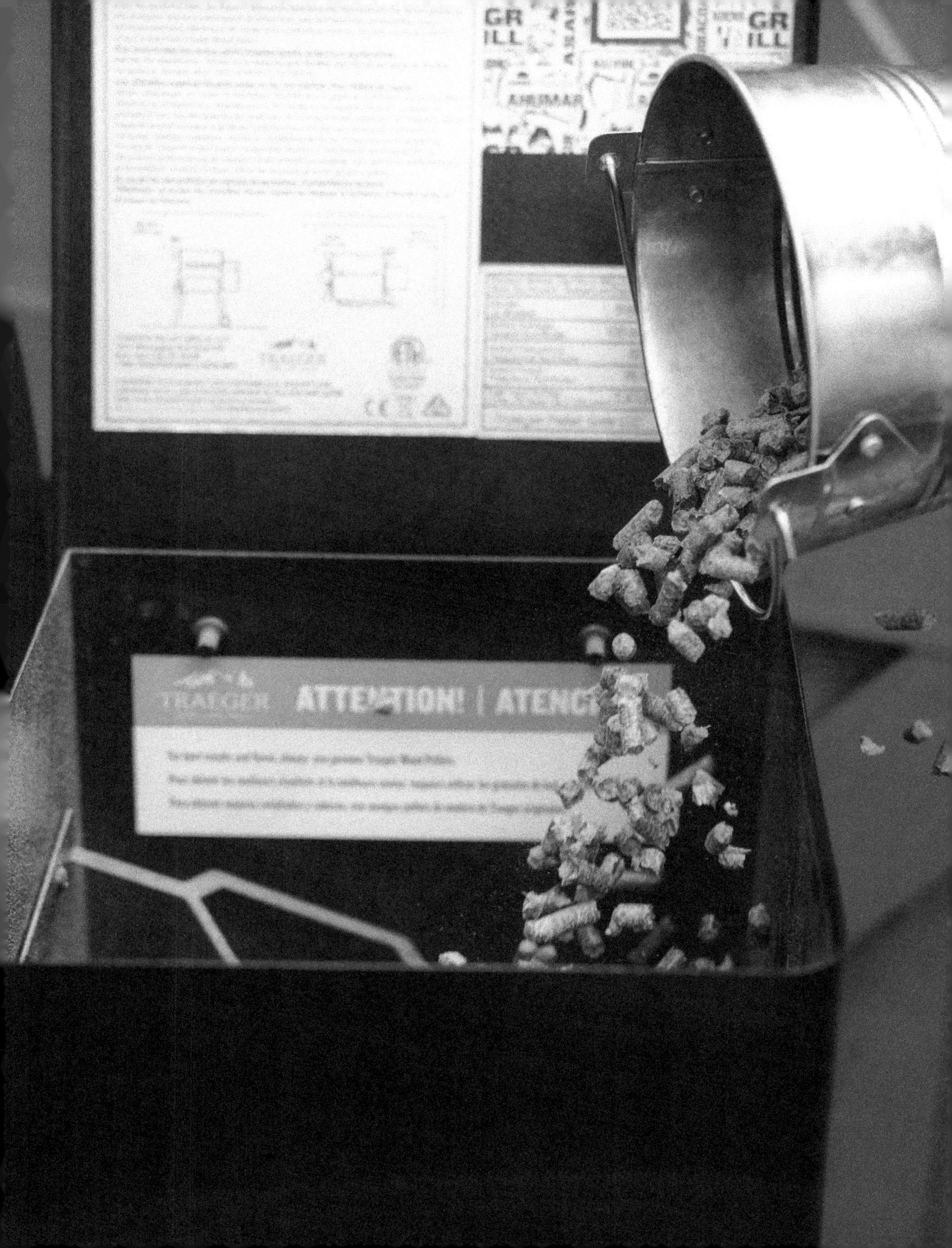

CHAPTER 1

Getting Started with Your Traeger Grill

In this chapter, we will cover the basics of getting your Traeger Grill up and running. Once you understand how your grill works and the basics of starting it up and shutting it down, you'll be grilling stress-free in no time.

How Your Traeger Grill Works

A Traeger uses hardwood pellets that come in different flavors. To get started, you'll fill the hopper with the pellet flavor of your choice. Once you turn the grill on using the controller, the pellets are moved from the hopper to the firepot by the rotation of an auger.

Once the pellets are ignited by the ignition rod in the firepot, the smoke starts rolling. The smoke created by the pellets is what gives your food that unique, incredible smoky flavor. The conduction fan circulates the smoke, distributing the heat evenly and cooking your food to perfection.

You might be asking yourself, "Is my Traeger a grill or a smoker?" Well, in my opinion, the answer is both. You have the ability to cook at a lower temperature or on a dedicated smoke setting that smokes your food low and slow. You also have the option to crank that heat up to 500°F for more of a quick, grilled meal.

Set the temperature easily with the dial and, once your grill reaches the desired temperature, simply place your food on the grill grate. Grill grates vary in size and number depending on the model you have, and you can rearrange them according to your needs for a particular recipe.

The drip pan under the grate serves a few purposes. It is positioned at an angle to catch any juices or grease that may drip from the food as it cooks. Those juices run out into a grease can, helping prevent flare-ups. You can purchase disposable foil liners for both the drip pan and grease can to make cleanup super quick and easy. The drip pan along with the heat baffle, or shield, also helps with indirect cooking—meaning the food is never actually directly exposed to flames and comes out evenly cooked every time.

One of my favorite things about the Traeger is how easy it is to start. It's literally as easy to turn on as my oven, starting in just a few seconds. You can also download a smartphone app to monitor both the grill temperature and the temperature of your food from your phone. Once your food is on the Traeger, you can walk away—no need to stand around and babysit it (although it does give off the most amazing aromas, so you may want to stick around for that). The app regulates the grill's temperature beautifully, which results in consistently delicious food each and every time. It's a nice option to be able to go inside to relax or get stuff done in the kitchen and feel confident that your Traeger doesn't need constant supervision.

A QUICK GUIDE TO THE TRAEGER MODELS

There are currently three series of wood pellet grills offered by Traeger, each with special features and size options. There is a fourth series made by Traeger, but sold only at Costco stores; however, for the purposes of this book, we'll focus on the three main series. Most of the current lines come with a Wi-Fi-powered remote as well as a built-in meat probe.

Each of the three series comes in a few different model types. The numbers that follow the model name indicate how many square inches of cooking space the grill offers—for example, the Ironwood 885 has 885 square inches of space with its two grates. (However, the Pro 22 and 34 are exceptions to this.)

Pro Series: The grills in this series are the smallest Traeger offers, but they also are the most budget-friendly. These models are perfect for smaller groups, and some can even be transported for camping or tailgating. Pro Series grills come with a smoke stack, whereas the other lines have a more advanced downdraft exhaust system. Two models in this series have a controller with a digital screen, but the others simply have a dial to manually control the temperature without additional features such as Wi-Fi and turbo temp.

Ironwood Series: This series offers all the same features as the Pro Series plus many more: super smoke mode, a pellet dump lid, a side shelf with hooks for storing cooking utensils, wood pellet sensor, a keep warm setting, and adjustable grates. Ironwood Series grills are bigger than most of the Pro Series models, which is handy if you are feeding more people. They are also double insulated, making the temperature even easier to regulate, especially when using the grill during colder temperatures.

Timberline Series: The biggest of the three series for those who enjoy big cooks. Timberline Series grills offer all the features of the Ironwood Series plus more, including an extra grate, increased hopper capacity, concealed grease pan, stainless steel front shelf, and a magnetic bamboo cutting board. Both the Ironwood and the Timberline series are equipped with a more advanced downdraft exhaust system that recirculates the smoke during cooking, resulting in a more even cook and smokier flavor.

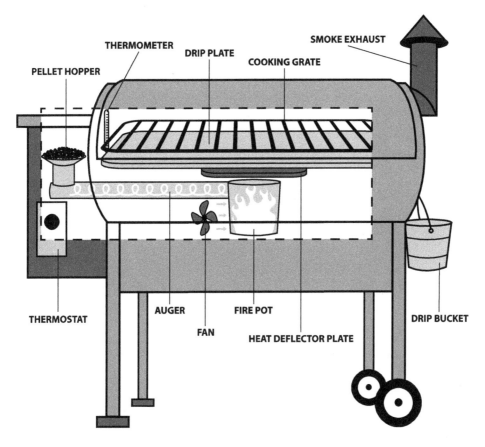

PELLET HOPPER   THERMOMETER   DRIP PLATE   COOKING GRATE   SMOKE EXHAUST

THERMOSTAT   AUGER   FAN   FIRE POT   HEAT DEFLECTOR PLATE   DRIP BUCKET

Firing It Up and Cooling It Down

Turning your new grill on and off will soon become second nature. Here you'll find easy-to-follow, step-by-step directions for your first few times using the grill. Before starting it, always make sure your Traeger is in a dry outdoor location, close to a grounded electrical outlet, and away from anything combustible.

The Pro 22 and 34 models are started and shut down in a similar way, but they come only with a dial and not some of the additional buttons and digital screen, so I have included directions for these models separately.

YOUR FIRST TIME: SEASONING THE GRILL

This is an important step to take before using your grill, because this one-time seasoning burns off any chemical residue on the grill from the manufacturing process. It also prepares your Traeger for top performance—don't skip it! Follow these steps to get started.

Pro 575, Pro 780, and all Ironwood, Silverton, and Timberline Models

1. Plug in the grill and fill the hopper with pellets.

2. Remove the bottom grate, drip pan, and heat baffle or shield so you can see the firepot.

3. Flip the switch (located in the rear of the grill) to "on" and turn on the controller by pressing the standby button.

4. Hit the menu button on the controller, then use the dial to select "auger" and then "prime auger." After two minutes, you will see the pellets dropping into the firepot.

5. Put the heat baffle/shield, drip pan, and bottom grate back in place.

6. Dial the temperature to 350°F, press the center of the dial to set it, and hit the red ignite button. Close the lid and leave it at 350°F for 20 minutes. It takes 5 to 10 minutes for the grill to fully ignite.

7. After 20 minutes at 350°F, dial the temperature to 500°F for an additional 30 minutes.

8. Press the standby button and hold for 3 seconds until the screen says "shut down cycle," then open the grill lid. It will count down on the screen. Once finished, flip the switch to "off," close the lid, and unplug the grill.

Pro 22 and 34 Models

1. Remove the grill grate, drip pan, and heat baffle.

2. Plug in the grill, flip the switch to "on," and turn the dial to "smoke" with the lid open.

3. Look in the empty hopper and make sure you see the auger turning and that there is air coming from the fan by the firepot (do not touch, as it may be hot).

4. Turn the dial to "shut down mode."

5. Put the grill grate, drip pan, and heat baffle back into place. Fill the hopper with the wood pellets of your choice.

6. Turn the dial to "smoke" for 2 minutes with the lid open. Then close the lid and turn the dial to "high" for 45 minutes.

7. After 45 minutes, open the lid and turn the dial to "shut down mode" for 10 minutes with the lid open. After 10 minutes, close the lid, flip the switch to "off," and unplug the grill.

USING YOUR TRAEGER GRILL

This is the process you will follow each time you turn your grill on and off. I prefer setting the temperature for each cook manually, and that is how the recipes are written in this book. You can also link your Traeger to Wi-Fi and set up custom cook cycles by following the prompts on the screen.

I have included two sets of directions, depending on the Traeger model you may have.

Pro 575, Pro 780, and all Ironwood, Silverton, and Timberline Models

1. Plug in the grill and press the "standby" button.

2. Hit "menu," dial to the desired temperature, and press the center of the dial to set it. Or if using a preset custom cook cycle, hit the menu button, then "cook cycle." Use the dial to select the cycle you want, then press the center dial to set it.

3. With the lid closed, hit the red ignite button.

4. Once the grill is preheated, add your food to the grates.

5. When finished, press the standby button for 3 seconds—until the screen says "shut down cycle"—and open the lid. It will count down on the screen. Once finished, flip the switch to "off," close the lid, and unplug the grill.

Pro 22 and 34 Models

1. Plug in the grill and flip the switch to "on."

2. Turn the dial to "smoke" with the lid open for 2 minutes.

3. After 2 minutes, close the lid and set the dial to the desired temperature.

4. Once the grill is preheated, add your food to the grates.

5. When finished, turn the dial to "shut down mode" for 10 minutes with the lid open. After 10 minutes, close the lid, flip the switch to "off," and unplug the grill.

REMOVING LEFTOVER PELLETS FROM THE HOPPER

Most models have a hopper cleanout, a small door toward the bottom of the hopper in the back of the grill, that's useful for when you are ready to switch up the flavor of wood pellets. Set a bucket or container underneath the door, open it, and let the pellets fall right in. You can use your hand to scoop out any remaining pellets, but a few left behind won't hurt.

If your model doesn't have a hopper cleanout door, just use a cup or a scoop to get out as many as you can. You will only remove pellets from the actual hopper, and not the auger. The pellets in the auger will be burned up by the time your grill is preheated for your next cook.

Master of the Grill

By now you know all about the range of temperatures your grill is capable of, from effortlessly smoking food low and slow to cranking up that heat for easy and quick everyday grilling. Here I will go over some features and cooking techniques that will turn you into a Traeger master!

TESTING FOR HOT AND COLD SPOTS

Yes, yes, I know I just went on and on about how the Traeger cooks food evenly and consistently. However, all grills have some spots that are naturally hotter than others. If you become familiar with your particular grill's hot spots, you can use them to your advantage when cooking. For example, if you want gorgeous grill marks, you'll want to place the meat on the hottest part of the grill. Or if something is cooking faster than you would like, simply move it to a cooler part of the grill.

Here is a fun project that my family and I do together each time we purchase a new grill, after we season it and before our first cook. Our secret is to use bread! With the grill off, place slices of bread side to side on the grill, covering as much

surface area as you can. Then set the temperature to 250°F using the startup directions for the model Traeger you have. Once the grill reaches 250°F, wait a few minutes, then flip each piece of bread over to see which is the most toasted. Any charred, burnt, or dark brown parts of the bread indicate the hottest spots on your grill. The ones that are lightly browned or barely toasted indicate the cooler spots. Pretty neat trick, huh?

I have found with my Traeger grills that the middle of the grill has pretty consistent heat, and the outer edges tend to be the hottest spots. And as I stated earlier, it comes in very handy knowing these hot and cool spots and being able to use them to your advantage.

SEARING

Searing is a technique in which food is cooked at a very high temperature to achieve a flavorful brown crust or grill marks. Traeger grills are wonderful for searing, especially the models that go up to 500°F. Grill grates can also be purchased to get an even darker sear, but they are not a necessity.

Searing is typically a quick process, which is why very high heat is important. Start by letting your meat come to room temperature, usually about a half hour for most cuts. At room temperature, as opposed to right out of the refrigerator, the meat will be more tender and cook faster. Season it with your favorite rub, or use one of the rubs from chapter 8.

Fire up your grill to the highest heat setting, either 450 or 500°F. If you are using grill grates, make sure you place them on the grill prior to firing it up.

Place the meat on the grate and cook for 4 to 6 minutes per side, depending on the cut and type of meat and how done you like your steak. If you want crossed hash marks, rotate the meat 90 degrees sideways after 2 to 3 minutes per side. Flip the steak and repeat on the other side. I don't prefer a cross sear because each time you open the grill, you lose heat, which may not allow you to get as dark of a sear.

Once you pull the meat off the grill, let it rest for 5 to 10 minutes to let those juices redistribute, making for an extra succulent cut of meat.

REVERSE SEARING

Reverse searing is, well, exactly the opposite of searing. Instead of cooking your food quickly at a very high temperature, reverse searing cooks it at a very low temperature for longer, usually 45 minutes to an hour. After cooking at the low

temperature, you'll remove the meat from the Traeger and turn the heat up to the highest setting, 450°F to 500°F, depending on your model.

Once it's preheated to that super high temperature, the meat goes on the grates for 1 to 1½ minutes per side. This finish at high heat creates that gorgeous, brown, flavorful crust and locks in all the juices, making for an extremely tender cut of meat. With reverse-seared meat there is no need to let it rest, but a minute or two of resting wouldn't hurt.

Reverse searing should only be used for thick cuts of meat, like 1½- to 2-inch-thick pork chops, a thick-cut rib eye, or filet mignon. Otherwise, you run the risk of overcooking.

GETTING MAXIMUM SMOKE

You are going to get a smoky flavor every time you cook anything on the Traeger. How much smoked flavor you get will be determined by the time and temperature at which you cook. If you are cooking quickly at a higher temperature, you won't get as much smoked flavor. When cooking at a lower temperature for a longer period of time, you'll get much more smoked flavor.

Any time you want more of this smoky flavor, I recommend starting your cook on the smoke setting. The smoke setting will run at a low temperature, usually around 180°F. It will allow more time for your food to soak up all the delicious smokiness of the wood pellets without fully cooking the food. After some time, increase the heat to finish cooking.

SUPER SMOKE

The Pro Series offers a smoke setting, but the Ironwood and Timberline Series offer a super smoke setting. In general, Ironwood and Timberline grills will give increased smoke flavor because they are more insulated and come equipped with the advanced downdraft exhaust system, which circulates the smoke around your food and gives it that extra smoke flavor. Using the super smoke setting blasts your food with even more smoke, thanks to the fan control delivering 100 percent hardwood flavor at temperatures between 165°F and 225°F.

HOW TO USE THE BUILT-IN MEAT PROBE

Most Traeger models offer a built-in meat probe. This allows you to monitor the temperature of your meat during the cooking process. Each recipe in this book gives an estimated cook time, but monitoring the temperature is key to achieving perfect results. If you download the Traeger app and connect your grill to your Wi-Fi service, you can track the temperature of your food directly from your phone.

One end of the meat probe connects to the controller, and once it is connected, the screen will ask if you'd like to set a probe alarm. If you select "yes," you will be notified once your meat reaches the designated temperature. The other end of the probe will be inserted into the thickest part of the meat you're cooking. Once positioned in the meat, the meat probe will monitor the temperature for you. For a more accurate reading, make sure the probe is not touching the grill grate, and if you are cooking a bone-in cut of meat, avoid having the probe touch the bone.

This feature is also handy for timing your cook. For example, if you want the food to be ready at a certain time, you can adjust the temperature of the Traeger accordingly. If it's not cooking fast enough, increase the temperature. If it's cooking more rapidly than desired, decrease the grill temperature to the "keep warm" setting if that feature is offered with your Traeger model.

MANAGING YOUR COOK SPACE

Another fabulous thing about having a Traeger is the large amount of space you have to cook multiple items at once. This book includes recipes for appetizer and side dishes that can all be cooked at the same time as large cuts of meat.

I love cooking a large cut of pork for pulled pork and adding an appetizer for my guests during the beginning of an afternoon together. Then I'll add a few side dishes to my Traeger closer to when the pulled pork will be finished. That way dinner is ready all at once, and it was all cooked on the Traeger! My guests are usually pretty wowed by all that I can accomplish on my Traeger.

Some models offer more than one grill grate, which just increases the amount of food you can cook at once. Items that are cooked in a foil pan or cast-iron skillet are perfect for the higher grates.

Another tip is to cook more than one whole roast chicken at a time. Add one or two more chickens to the grill to be shredded—you can use the additional shredded chicken later for salads, wraps, and any other dish throughout the week.

These are some of my favorite combinations of recipes (appetizers, main course, and sides) from this book that are perfect to cook all together on the Traeger for a complete meal.

▶ Pulled Pork Potato Skins (page 26), Turkey Smothered with Creole Butter (page 86), Green Beans with Bacon (page 113), and BBQ Baked Beans (page 107)

▶ Sausage-and-Cheese-Stuffed Jalapeños (page 32), Apricot-Glazed Chicken Thighs (page 74), and Loaded Potato Rounds (page 106)

▶ Peach-Bourbon Chicken Wings (page 27), Harissa-Glazed Short Ribs (page 51), Smoked Mac and Cheese (page 120)

▶ Mushrooms Stuffed with Jalapeño Poppers (page 29), Pork Tenderloin Wrapped with Maple Bacon (page 56), Cinnamon Apples (page 118), and Sweet Potato Wedges (page 116)

Other combinations of recipes from this book go together beautifully as well, and can be made at the same time. For example, make the veggies for Smoked Salsa (page 112) at the same time as the onions for the Caramelized Balsamic Onions (page 110). Or cook the potatoes for Smoked Potato Salad (page 117) at the same time as the chicken and veggies for Smoked Chicken Corn Chowder (page 75). These are just a few of the delicious combinations I have grown to love over my years of Traeger-ing. The possibilities are endless!

SMOKING REMOTE: USING WIFIRE

As if they weren't already convenient enough to cook on, most Traeger Grills are WiFIRE enabled. I am not what you would call a tech-savvy person, so if I can manage to connect my grill to Wi-Fi and control it via the app on my phone, anyone can!

The first step is downloading the Traeger app to your phone. Select "add new grill" and then select the model grill you have, then hit "next." You will be prompted to agree to the app's terms and conditions and also to check that the selected Wi-Fi network is correct. (You can even assign a name to your new grill, which is especially handy if you need to connect more than one grill.)

The first option for connecting is a QR code. The QR code on a new grill is located on the inside of the hopper lid. Using your phone's camera, simply scan the QR code and you will be prompted to enter the password to your Wi-Fi network.

If you do not have a QR code, you will be prompted to follow the instructions on your grill's controller to locate the grill name and pass-word. The app walks you through the process very easily to find and enter the info. Enter your Wi-Fi password and you are all set!

Now you can monitor the temperature of your grill and adjust it from your phone. You can also monitor the temperature of your food via the meat probe and receive a notification when it reaches the desired temperature. Also, you can switch to "keep warm" or "shut down" mode.

If you have trouble connecting, don't worry. Just see the troubleshooting guide on page 20 for help.

Your Guide to Low and Slow, Hot and Fast, and Everything in Between

This table will come in handy when you want estimated cook times on specific cuts of meat. Remember that the most important and accurate indicator that something is finished cooking is the internal temperature of the food, not the estimated cook time. Factors such as the specific grill model and outside temperature also play huge parts in the timing of the cook, but this table will be a helpful reference when it comes to cook times and temperatures.

FOOD	GRILL TEMPERATURE	TIME	INTERNAL TEMPERATURE
CHICKEN			
Bone-in chicken breast	250°F	1½ to 2 hours	165°F
Boneless chicken breast	250°F OR 450°F to 500°F	45 minutes to 1 hour 5 to 6 minutes per side	165°F
Bone-in chicken thighs	250°F	1½ to 2 hours	165°F
Boneless chicken thighs	450°F to 500°F	5 to 6 minutes per side	165°F
Chicken drumsticks	250°F	2 hours	165°F
Whole chicken	250°F	4 hours	165°F
Chicken wings	250°F	2 to 2½ hours (option to increase the heat to high during the last 10 minutes for crispy skin)	165°F
Chicken leg quarters	250°F	2½ hours	165°F

FOOD	GRILL TEMPERATURE	TIME	INTERNAL TEMPERATURE
PORK			
Pork butt/ shoulder	225°F	1½ hours per pound	203°F (safe temperature is 145°F, but 203°F is best for pulled pork)
Ribs	225°F	5 to 6 hours	203°F (safe temperature is 145°F, but they will be most tender at 203°F)
Bone-in pork chop	450°F to 500°F	4 to 6 minutes per side	145°F
Pork loin	225°F	3 to 4 hours	145°F
Pork tenderloin	225°F	2 hours	145°F
TURKEY			
Whole turkey	250°F	20 to 25 minutes per pound	165°F
Bone-in turkey breast	250°F	20 to 25 minutes per pound	165°F
Turkey leg	250°F	3 to 4 hours	165°F

FOOD	GRILL TEMPERATURE	TIME	INTERNAL TEMPERATURE
BEEF			
Brisket	250°F	1 hour per pound	195°F (safe temperature is 145°F, but it will be most tender at 195°F)
Short ribs	225°F	6 to 8 hours	195°F (safe temperature is 145°F, but it will be most tender at 195°F)
Back ribs	225°F	4 to 5 hours	195°F (safe temperature is 145°F, most tender at 195°F)
Tri tip	250°F	30 minutes per pound	145°F (medium)
Burgers	250°F or 450°F to 500°F	1 hour 4 to 5 minutes per side	160°F
Prime rib	250°F	30 minutes per pound	135°F (medium rare)
Steaks	450°F to 500°F	4 to 6 minutes per side	145°F (medium)

FOOD	GRILL TEMPERATURE	TIME	INTERNAL TEMPERATURE
SEAFOOD			
Whole salmon fillet	400°F	25 to 35 minutes	145°F
Shrimp	250°F OR 450°F to 500°F	30 to 45 minutes 2 to 3 minutes per side	145°F
Lobster tails	225°F	45 minutes to 1 hour	140°F
Whole trout	225°F	1 to 2 hours	145°F
DUCK			
Whole duck	225°F	3½ to 4 hours	165°F
Duck breast	250°F OR 450°F	1 hour 10 to 12 minutes per side	165°F
Duck legs	250°F	3 hours	165°F
LAMB			
Rack of lamb	225°F	1½ to 2 hours	145°F (medium)
Leg of lamb	250°F	2 to 2½ hours	145°F (medium)
Bone-in lamb chop	450°F to 500°F	5 to 8 minutes per side	145°F (medium)

FOOD	GRILL TEMPERATURE	TIME	INTERNAL TEMPERATURE
VENISON			
Rack of venison	225°F	1½ hours per pound	130°F to 140°F
Venison steak	225°F	2½ to 3 hours	130°F to 140°F
Venison backstrap/ loin	225°F	1½ hours	130°F to 140°F

Fuel for the Fire: Wood Pellets

Hardwood pellets are the fuel source for the Traeger Grill. These food-grade pellets are different from heating pellets, so make sure you buy a product that is made from 100 percent hardwood for your grill. Trees for these pellets are grown in different parts of the country, which adds to their various flavor profiles.

The pellets are made from ground wood that is dried to 10 percent moisture. If the wood has too much moisture, it does not hold enough heat. Once dried, the wood is formed into pellets. There are multiple brands of hardwood pellets, and any brand can be used as long as they are 100 percent hardwood pellets with no additives. Traeger sells their own high-quality brand of pellets that you can find at most grocery stores, hardware stores, or online.

The hardwood pellets come in a variety of flavors, and certain pellets pair really well with certain types of food. Traeger and some other brands sell signature blends as well as individual flavors. You could also try mixing a few different flavors on your own once you are familiar with them to create your own personal blend. See the chart on page 18 for some ideas on which pellets to use with different types of food.

Types of Wood Pellets

WOOD	FLAVOR/AROMA	PAIRS WELL WITH
Alder	Mild, delicate	Seafood, poultry, vegetables
Apple	Mild, fruity	Pork, poultry, lamb, vegetables
Cherry	Bold, fruity flavor	Beef, venison, poultry, pork
Hickory	Strong, bold flavor	Barbecue, beef, venison, pork
Maple	Hint of sweetness, mild	Pork, poultry, vegetables
Mesquite	Strong, smoky flavor	Beef, pork, seafood
Oak	Medium smoke flavor	Lamb, beef, venison
Pecan	Slightly nutty flavor	Lamb, poultry

HOW MUCH YOU NEED

It's a good idea to always keep your hopper full of pellets, even though you probably won't use the whole hopper during one cook. In general, the grill will burn though 1 to 3 pounds of pellets per hour. Lower temperatures burn pellets at a slower rate compared with higher temperatures that burn pellets more quickly.

Most Traeger models have a hopper sensor that will alert you if your hopper is getting low and needs to be refilled. I check mine often, especially during long cooks.

HOW TO STORE YOUR PELLETS

I have seen many creative ideas for storing pellets. As long as you keep them in an airtight container in a dry area away from flames, you can store them however you like. A few good ideas for storing are lidded buckets sold at any hardware store,

plastic bins with lids, or containers with pour spouts that are made specifically for wood pellets.

It's best to label the pellets once they are out of the bag to avoid mixing them up. You can either label the container or cut out the label from the bag you purchased them in and tape it to the storage container.

Keeping Your Traeger in Tip-Top Condition

To keep your Traeger running in prime condition, the best thing you can do is to keep it clean. It will make your new grill last longer and keep it working safely and effectively. It is recommended to clean your grill after every three to five times you use it.

Here are some tips and tricks on the best way to clean a Traeger. You'll need a grill brush, paper towels, a small putty knife, a small vacuum with a hose, spray bottle of grill cleaner, and optional foil liner and grease bucket liners.

CLEANING THE HOPPER

Remove the pellets from the inside of the hopper, vacuum it, and wipe it down. Dust from the pellets can collect at the bottom of the hopper so it's best to remove that. Vacuum the pellets by the auger and check the auger to make sure nothing is stuck.

CLEANING THE GRILL GRATES

Brush the grates with the grill brush, starting with the top shelf. Then remove the top shelf (be careful not to hit the temperature probe in the grill), turn it upside down over the grill, and brush the back side. Repeat with the remaining shelves and set the grates aside.

CLEANING THE INSIDE AND DRIP TRAY

Use the putty knife to gently scrape the inside of the lid, sides, and racks for the grill grates. For the drip tray, I use foil liners made by Traeger to catch all the grease and keep the drip tray clean. If using those, simply discard and replace

the liner. If you don't use these liners, use the putty knife to scrape the drip tray clean. Remove the heat baffle and wipe with a paper towel. Vacuum the ashes from the bottom of the grill and the sides and racks for the grill grates.

CLEANING THE FIREPOT

Vacuum the pellets in the firepot and the pellets by the auger. Check to make sure everything looks clean and nothing is stuck. Once everything is clean, put the heat baffle, drip tray (with new foil liner, if using), and grill grates back into place, and fill the hopper with new wood pellets of your choice.

CLEANING THE GREASE BUCKET AND OUTER GRILL

If using foil grease bucket liners, simply discard the liner, wipe the grease tray with a paper towel, and replace with a new liner. If not using the liners, empty and discard the grease in the bucket and wash with dish soap and warm water.

Close the lid and spray the outer grill with grill cleaner, taking care to avoid the controller. Let the cleaner sit for a minute or two, then wipe clean with paper towels.

STORING THE GRILL

Store your grill under a covered patio or in a shed or garage. You want to make sure the controller remains dry and is not exposed to outside elements. If you are keeping the grill outside under a covered patio, I recommend using a fitted cover to help protect it even more.

Troubleshooting Your Wood Pellet Grill

You can avoid most issues by using quality, dry hardwood pellets, and keeping your grill clean and in a dry, covered environment. If you do run into problems, here's how to fix a few of the most common ones.

Q: What should I do if the pellets won't ignite?

A: It is normal for the grill to take 5 to 10 minutes to ignite, especially the first time. If after 10 minutes it still won't ignite, turn the grill off and unplug it. Check to make sure the hopper is full and the pellets are not wet or soft. Check the firepot to make sure there are pellets and vacuum out any extra ashes. Check to make sure the auger is not jammed, the fan is working correctly, and all parts are in place. Check the hot rod for any loose or cut wires. If any of these parts need to be replaced, call 1-800-TRAEGER to order them.

Q: What should I do if the auger is jammed?

A: Turn off the grill and unplug it. Use a screwdriver to remove the controller. It will be attached with wires; loosely place it back in the hole. Remove the hopper, being careful that the controller doesn't fall on the ground. Remove the burner assembly box and use some tools to help clear the jam, then put everything back together.

Q: What should I do if the temperature isn't staying steady?

A: Colder outdoor temperatures and opening the lid during the cooking process greatly affect the grill's temperature. Making sure your grill is clean and you're using high-quality, dry pellets will help keep the temperature steady. If maintaining a steady temperature is still an issue, start by cleaning the temperature probe in the grill and checking to see if the firepot looks rusty or corroded. If so, call 1-800-TRAEGER to order a new firepot.

Q: What should I do if I can't connect my grill to Wi-Fi?

A: Make sure your grill is turned on and your Wi-Fi has a strong connection. If you still cannot connect, call 1-800-TRAEGER to make sure your controller has the correct firmware version. If it doesn't, it means there's a disconnect between the firmware and the current app version, in which case they will send you a new controller at no cost.

Q: What should I do if I hear a clicking sound?

A: Check the auger first. If it is bent or won't roll smoothly call 1-800-TRAEGER to order a new one. If the auger is not bent, the issue is most likely with the auger fan. Call to order a replacement fan.

The Recipes

For this collection of recipes, my goal was to showcase the range of foods that can be cooked on the Traeger Grill. From cooking large cuts of meat low and slow for that incredible fall-off-the-bone tenderness and super smoked flavor, to cooking at higher temperatures for a perfect sear, to cooking oven dishes like lasagna and enchiladas quickly with a kiss of wood-fired flavor, your Traeger can do it all. The wide variety of recipes found in this book will give you a real feel for the versatility of your new Traeger. With every recipe I have included estimated prep times, suggested wood pellet flavors, grill temperatures, cook times, and even recipe variations and savvy tips that will make you a grill pro in no time.

Chipotle-Rubbed Chicken Wings, page 31

Appetizers

Pulled Pork Potato Skins

SUGGESTED PELLETS: ALDER, OAK

MAKES 10 POTATO SKINS

PREP TIME: 15 minutes

COOK TIME: 3 hours

TEMPERATURE: 250°F

---

5 medium-size russet
potatoes

2 tablespoons olive oil

Kosher salt

Freshly ground black pepper

3 to 4 cups pulled pork

¾ cup barbecue sauce
of choice

2 cups shredded
cheddar cheese

Sour cream, for serving
(optional)

Pickled jalapeños peppers,
for serving (optional)

You'll quickly learn as a new Traeger owner that you will end up with *lots* of leftover pulled pork—and this is not a bad problem to have! I have made pulled pork quesadillas and nachos, but these potato skins are one of my all-time-favorite ways to enjoy that delicious leftover pork.

1. Turn the Traeger on and set the temperature to 250°F.

2. Brush all sides of the potatoes with olive oil and season with salt and black pepper. Put the potatoes right on the grill grate for 2½ hours.

3. Remove the potatoes and cut them in half lengthwise. Let them cool slightly.

4. Using a spoon, scoop out most of the potato flesh from the skins. (Discard this or save it for another dish.) Divide the pulled pork evenly among each potato skin, then drizzle with barbecue sauce, and top with shredded cheese.

5. Place the potato skins back on the Traeger (still at 250°F) for 30 minutes.

6. Remove from the grill and top with sour cream and pickled jalapeños (if using).

> **VARIATION TIP: This could also be made with pulled chicken or brisket.**

Peach-Bourbon Chicken Wings

SUGGESTED PELLETS: APPLE, MAPLE

SERVES 6 TO 8 PEOPLE

PREP TIME: 10 minutes, plus marinating time

COOK TIME: 2 to 2½ hours

TEMPERATURE: 250°F

1¼ cup peach jelly or preserves

½ cup bourbon

½ cup honey

¼ cup soy sauce

¼ cup balsamic vinegar

Kosher salt

Freshly ground black pepper

Pinch red pepper flakes

5 pounds jumbo split chicken wings

Chicken wings on the smoker are insanely delicious, and they taste even better with this marinade and glaze. The smoky flavor from the Traeger combined with the peach-bourbon flavor will leave you wanting to make these over and over again.

1. In a bowl, combine the peach jelly, bourbon, honey, soy sauce, balsamic vinegar, salt, black pepper, and red pepper flakes and whisk until evenly mixed.

2. Pat the chicken wings dry with paper towels and put them in a gallon-size plastic bag. Add 1 cup of the peach-bourbon mixture to the bag and massage the bag until the wings are evenly coated. Marinate in the refrigerator for at least 1 hour or overnight. Store the remaining sauce in a sealed container in the refrigerator.

3. Once ready to cook, turn the Traeger on and set the temperature to 250°F. Place the wings on the grill grates for 2 to 2½ hours total, flipping halfway through.

4. Brush some of the reserved peach bourbon sauce on the wings during the last 15 minutes of cooking and serve the wings with the remaining sauce on the side.

VARIATION TIP: The peach-bourbon sauce can be used with salmon, shrimp, chicken thighs, and pork. You can also switch up the sauce by using the Maple-Mustard Marinade (page 130) or the Gochujang BBQ Sauce (page 129) on these chicken wings.

Crab and Artichoke Dip

SUGGESTED PELLETS: ALDER, MESQUITE

SERVES 8

PREP TIME: 10 minutes

COOK TIME: 1½ to 2 hours

TEMPERATURE: 250°F

---

8 ounces cream cheese

½ cup mayonnaise

½ cup sour cream

3½ tablespoons Cajun or seafood seasoning

2 tablespoons Worcestershire sauce

2 tablespoons freshly squeezed lemon juice

Dash hot sauce of choice (optional)

2 cups shredded Monterey Jack cheese

1 cup shredded Parmesan cheese

1 (14-ounce) jar marinated artichokes, drained and chopped

1 pound canned crabmeat

Tortilla chips or crostini, for serving

This is my tried-and-true recipe for crab and artichoke dip that I have made for my family for years. The kiss of smoke by cooking this dip on the Traeger takes the flavor to a whole new level. It's also a great way to impress your guests if you're having company. If you are going to a celebration or gathering at another location, make this dip at home, cover with foil, and bring it with you.

1. Turn the Traeger on and set the temperature to 250°F.

2. In a large bowl, combine the cream cheese, mayonnaise, sour cream, Cajun seasoning, Worcestershire sauce, lemon juice, and hot sauce (if using). Mix with a spoon or hand mixer until evenly combined.

3. Add the cheeses, artichokes, and crabmeat. Gently fold everything together with a spoon.

4. Transfer the dip to either a cast-iron skillet or 9-inch square foil pan.

5. Put the pan on the grill grate for 1½ to 2 hours.

6. Remove from the grill, let cool slightly, and serve with tortilla chips or crostini.

SMOKER SAVVY TIP: For even more smoke flavor, start the dip on the smoke or super smoke setting for the first 30 minutes, then increase the heat to 250°F for an additional 1½ hours.

Mushrooms Stuffed with Jalapeño Poppers

SUGGESTED PELLETS: ALDER, HICKORY

SERVES 6 TO 8 PEOPLE

PREP TIME: 15 minutes

COOK TIME: 20 to 30 minutes

TEMPERATURE: 350°F

---

6 slices bacon, cooked and crumbled

8 ounces cream cheese, at room temperature

2 jalapeño peppers, minced

1 cup shredded cheese of choice

Kosher salt

Freshly ground black pepper

1 pound baby portobello mushrooms, washed and dried

The creamy, cheesy bacon and minced jalapeño filling that these mushrooms are stuffed with makes for the perfect party appetizer. The Traeger cooks the mushrooms perfectly and allows them to soak up all the wood-fired flavor.

1. In a large bowl, put the bacon, cream cheese, jalapeños, shredded cheese, salt, and black pepper. Stir until evenly combined.

2. Remove the stems from the mushrooms.

3. Turn the Traeger on and set the temperature to 350°F.

4. While the Traeger preheats, divide the filling into each mushroom cap.

5. Put the stuffed mushrooms on the grill grate for 20 to 30 minutes. Remove from the grill and serve right away.

VARIATION TIP: If you make the Crab and Artichoke Dip (page 28) and have some left over, use that dip as the filling for these stuffed mushrooms. The cook time in this recipe will remain the same, 20 to 30 minutes at 350°F.

Buffalo Chicken Nachos

SUGGESTED PELLETS: HICKORY, MESQUITE

SERVES 4 TO 6 PEOPLE
PREP TIME: 10 minutes
COOK TIME: 15 minutes
TEMPERATURE: 375°F

---

8 ounces tortilla chips, divided

2 cups cooked, shredded chicken, divided

3 cups shredded cheddar cheese, divided

½ cup Buffalo sauce

½ cup ranch dressing

Yes, you read that correctly . . . you can make nachos on the Traeger! The smoky flavor turns regular nachos into something extraordinary. It's also a great way to use leftover chicken that you may have made on the Traeger the day before.

1. Turn the Traeger on and set the temperature to 375°F.

2. Put half of the chips in a single layer in a cast-iron skillet or 9-by-13-inch foil pan. Layer half of the shredded chicken and then half of the cheese over the chips.

3. Layer the rest of the chips over the chicken and cheese, then add the remaining chicken and cheese over the top.

4. Put the pan on the grill grate for 15 minutes, or until the cheese is melted.

5. Drizzle the Buffalo sauce and ranch dressing over top before serving.

> **VARIATION TIP: If you have leftover pulled pork or brisket, you can make these nachos in the same way, but try using barbecue sauce and sour cream (in the same amounts) instead of the Buffalo and ranch.**

Chipotle-Rubbed Chicken Wings

SUGGESTED PELLETS: CHERRY, HICKORY

SERVES 6 TO 8 PEOPLE
PREP TIME: 10 minutes
COOK TIME: 1 hour
TEMPERATURE: 425°F

---

5 pounds jumbo split
chicken wings

2 tablespoons chipotle
seasoning

2 tablespoons
baking powder

1 tablespoon dry mustard

1 tablespoon garlic powder

1 tablespoon chili powder

½ tablespoon cumin

Kosher salt

Freshly ground black pepper

This recipe will give you a crispier chicken wing because it's dry rubbed and grilled at a high temperature. There is also baking powder in the rub to dry the skin a bit, which is my trick for getting a crispiness that can't be beat. Enjoy these with only the rub, or toss them in your favorite sauce before serving.

1. Pat the wings dry really well with paper towels and put them in a large bowl.

2. In a smaller bowl, mix together the chipotle seasoning, baking powder, dry mustard, garlic powder, chili powder, cumin, and a pinch each of salt and pepper, then add to the chicken wings. Toss until the wings are evenly coated.

3. While the wings soak up all the flavors of the dry rub, turn the Traeger on and set the temperature to 425°F.

4. Once preheated, put the chicken wings on the grill grate for 1 hour, flipping them halfway through. Serve right away.

> **SMOKER SAVVY TIP:** For even more smoke flavor, turn on the smoke setting or super smoke for the first 10 to 15 minutes and then turn the heat up to 425°F for 45 minutes to finish cooking.

Sausage-and-Cheese-Stuffed Jalapeños

SUGGESTED PELLETS: MESQUITE, HICKORY

SERVES 6 TO 8 PEOPLE
PREP TIME: 20 minutes
COOK TIME: 20 minutes
TEMPERATURE: 350°F

---

1 pound loose ground
   Italian sausage

8 ounces cream cheese

2 cups shredded
   cheddar cheese

Kosher salt

Freshly ground black pepper

12 to 14 jalapeño peppers

The cheesy sausage filling for these jalapeños is very easy to make, making them the perfect game-day snack and a wonderful way to wow your guests. The stuffed jalapeños can be made ahead of time and packed in a sealed container if you are bringing them to a party or gathering.

1. In a medium skillet, cook the sausage over medium heat for 5 to 7 minutes, breaking it apart as it cooks. Remove the skillet from the heat and add the cream cheese, cheddar cheese, salt, and black pepper. Stir until melted together, then set aside to let this mixture cool.

2. Cut the jalapeños in half lengthwise and use a spoon to scrape out the seeds and white parts out of each.

3. Turn the Traeger on and set the temperature to 350°F.

4. While the Traeger preheats, stuff the jalapeños with the sausage-and-cheese filling.

5. Place the stuffed jalapeños on the grill grate for 20 minutes, then serve immediately.

> **VARIATION TIP: You can mix up the filling for these stuffed jalapeños by using chorizo sausage or a pound of cooked, crumbled bacon in place of the Italian sausage.**

Pig and Fig Flatbread

SERVES 8 PEOPLE
PREP TIME: 10 minutes
COOK TIME: 12 to 15 minutes
TEMPERATURE: 375°F

---

4 naan flatbreads

2 tablespoons olive oil

Kosher salt

Freshly ground black pepper

¾ to 1 cup fig jam

4 ounces crumbled
goat cheese

Pork of choice (1 pound
cooked and crumbled
bacon, 6 ounces
sliced prosciutto, or
2 cups pulled pork)

3 cups shredded
mozzarella cheese

1 cup arugula

With an adorable name like pig and fig flatbread, you can't help but want to make this quick and easy recipe. It uses store-bought, already-cooked flatbread topped with fig jam and your choice of the "pig" addition. Cut this into slices and serve as the perfect appetizer, or it could even be served as a main course for four.

1. Turn the Traeger on and set the temp to 375°F.

2. Brush the flatbreads with olive oil and season with salt and pepper. Spread the fig jam evenly over each flatbread.

3. Divide the goat cheese, pork of choice, and mozzarella cheese evenly on each flatbread.

4. Place the flatbreads on the grill grates and cook for 12 to 15 minutes.

5. Remove from the Traeger and top each with some arugula.

6. Cut into slices and serve.

> **VARIATION TIP: This flatbread is also amazing if you substitute the Gochujang BBQ Sauce (page 129) for the fig jam.**

Chicken and Bacon Ranch Flatbread

SUGGESTED PELLETS: MESQUITE, HICKORY

SERVES 8 PEOPLE

PREP TIME: 10 minutes

COOK TIME: 12 to 15 minutes

TEMPERATURE: 375°F

---

4 naan flatbreads

2 tablespoons olive oil

1 cup ranch dressing

1½ cups cooked, shredded chicken

½ pound cooked, crumbled bacon

3 cups shredded mozzarella cheese

When you have leftover smoked chicken, this is the perfect appetizer to make. This could even be a quick weeknight meal for four. When I'm smoking a whole chicken, I plan ahead and make more than I know we will eat so I can use them in other recipes throughout the week. It's a super convenient and time-saving trick!

1. Turn the Traeger on and set the temperature to 375°F.

2. Brush each flatbread with olive oil and drizzle the ranch dressing evenly on each.

3. Top each flatbread with the chicken, bacon, and mozzarella cheese.

4. Put the flatbreads on the grill grates for 12 to 15 minutes.

5. Cut each flatbread into slices and serve.

SERVE WITH: A great addition to these flatbreads is the Caramelized Balsamic Onions (page 110)! They add even more smoked flavor and a hint of sweetness that pairs amazingly with the salty bacon.

Chorizo-Queso Dip

SUGGESTED PELLETS: MESQUITE, HICKORY

SERVES 8 TO 10 PEOPLE
PREP TIME: 10 minutes
COOK TIME: 1½ hours
TEMPERATURE: 250°F

---

1 pound chorizo sausage

1 onion, diced

1 (16-ounce) block
Velveeta cheese

2 (8-ounce) blocks
cream cheese

2 cups shredded cheese
of choice

2 (4-ounce) cans
green chiles

1 cup milk

Tortilla chips, for serving

This dip is fantastic for feeding a crowd—everyone always raves about how addictive it is! Chorizo has such a great flavor, with just a hint of spice that goes well with the creamy cheese. Serve with your favorite chips for dipping.

1. Turn the Traeger on and set the temperature to 250°F.

2. In a skillet, cook the chorizo over medium heat for 5 to 7 minutes, breaking it apart as it cooks. Drain the excess grease, then put the chorizo in a cast-iron skillet or 9-by-13-inch foil pan.

3. Add the diced onion, Velveeta cheese, cream cheese, shredded cheese, green chiles, and milk. No need to mix at this point.

4. Put the pan on the grill grate for 1½ hours, stirring a few times throughout.

5. Once it's all melted and mixed together, serve with your favorite tortilla chips for dipping.

> **SMOKER SAVVY TIP:** Since the Traeger has so much cooking space, this is perfect to make at the same time as a pulled pork or brisket. They can cook together and at the same temperature—just time it so this dip is finished first so it can be served before dinner. You may even have time to add BBQ Baked Beans (page 107) to the Traeger to serve as a dinner side.

Lamb Kebabs with Lemon-Dill Sauce, page 41

CHAPTER 3

Lamb, Beef, and Venison

Burgers Stuffed with Bacon and Cheddar

SUGGESTED PELLETS: MESQUITE, HICKORY

SERVES 4 PEOPLE

PREP TIME: 10 minutes

COOK TIME: 8 to
10 minutes or 1 hour

TEMPERATURE:
250°F or 500°F

1½ pounds ground beef

6 slices cooked and
crumbled bacon

1 (8-ounce) block
cheddar cheese

1 tablespoon
Worcestershire sauce

Kosher salt

Freshly ground black pepper

4 burger buns

Toppings of choice, such
as ketchup, lettuce,
pickles, etc.

These burgers are super flavorful and juicy, packed with flavor in every single bite because they're stuffed with bacon bits and cubes of cheddar cheese. There are two cooking options for these stuffed burgers. You can smoke them low and slow at 250°F for an hour, or if you want them done quickly with gorgeous grill marks, cook them on the high temperature setting of 500°F for about 10 minutes.

1. In a large bowl, combine the ground beef and bacon.

2. Cut the block of cheese in half. Cut one half into tiny cubes and add those cubes to the bowl with the ground beef and bacon. Cut the other half of the block of cheese into four thin slices and set aside.

3. Add the Worcestershire sauce, salt, and pepper to the ground beef. Mix with your hands until evenly combined, then form into four burger patties.

4. Turn the Traeger on and set to the desired temperature (see headnote).

5. Once preheated, put the burgers on the grill grate. No matter if you're cooking them at 250° for 1 hour or at 500° for 8 to 10 minutes, flip them halfway through the cooking time. Top burgers with the sliced cheddar cheese during the last minute or two of cooking.

6. Serve on burger buns with toppings of choice.

> **SERVE WITH: Top these burgers with the Chipotle BBQ Sauce (page 133) to add some tang and spice.**

Ginger-Soy Steak Kebabs
with Yum Yum Sauce

SUGGESTED PELLETS: HICKORY, OAK

SERVES 4 PEOPLE

PREP TIME: 15 minutes, plus marinating time

COOK TIME: 15 to 18 minutes

TEMPERATURE: 450°F

⅔ cup mayonnaise

¼ cup ketchup

1 tablespoon sugar

1 teaspoon paprika

1 teaspoon garlic powder

3 tablespoons soy sauce

1 tablespoon honey

1½ tablespoons ginger paste

1½ tablespoons garlic paste

1½ pounds flat iron steak

8 to 10 kebab skewers (if using wooden skewers, soak in water for at least 30 minutes before placing on the grill to prevent burning)

8 ounces baby portobello mushrooms, roughly cut into bite-size chunks

1 onion, roughly cut into bite-size chunks

This delicious dish is cubes of marinated steak cooked on skewers with fresh veggies, served with an easy homemade yum yum sauce. This is our go-to for when we want an extra-special steak dinner.

1. In a bowl, combine the mayonnaise, ketchup, sugar, paprika, and garlic powder. Whisk until evenly combined. Store this yum yum sauce in a covered container in the refrigerator until ready to use.

2. In another bowl, whisk together the soy sauce, honey, ginger paste, and garlic paste until evenly combined.

3. Cut the steak into bite-size cubes and place the cubes in a gallon-size plastic bag. Add half of the soy sauce mixture to the steak. Massage the bag until the steak is evenly coated. Marinate in the refrigerator for several hours or overnight. Store the remaining soy sauce mixture in the refrigerator.

4. When ready to make the kebabs, turn the Traeger on and set it to 450°F. Toss the mushroom and onion chunks with the remaining soy sauce mixture.

5. Thread the steak, mushrooms, and onions on skewers. Place them on the grill grate for 15 to 18 minutes, turning halfway through.

6. Serve the kebabs immediately with the yum yum sauce on the side.

VARIATION TIP: You can easily substitute chicken, pork, or venison in place of the steak. Including more veggies such as red pepper or zucchini would also be an amazing addition to these kebabs.

Reverse-Seared Filet Mignon

SUGGESTED PELLETS: HICKORY, OAK

SERVES 4 PEOPLE

PREP TIME: 5 minutes

COOK TIME: 45 minutes
to 1 hour

TEMPERATURE:
180°F and 500°F

---

4 filet mignon steaks
(2 inches thick is ideal)

1 tablespoon olive oil

Kosher salt

Freshly ground black pepper

Reverse searing is a cooking technique that starts with smoking the steak at a very low temperature of 180°F for about an hour, then quickly searing it at an extremely high temperature of 500°F to seal in all the juices. It creates a tender and juicy steak with lots of smoked flavor.

1. Turn the Traeger on and set it to 180°F. For some (Rare: 125°F; Medium Rare: 135°F; Medium: 145°F; Medium Well: 150°F; Well: 155°F) Traeger models, this is the smoke setting. If your model has a super smoke setting, use that.

2. Brush the steaks with olive oil and season with salt and pepper.

3. Once preheated to 180°F, put the steaks on the grill grate for 45 minutes to 1 hour, or until the internal temperature reaches 120 to 130°F.

4. Remove the steaks and turn the Traeger to the highest heat setting.

5. Once preheated, put the steaks on the grill grate for 1½ to 2½ minutes per side, or until they reach the desired internal temperature.

> **VARIATION TIP:** Searing can also be done in a cast-iron skillet over high heat on the stove if you desire more of an even sear. These steaks are excellent with the Whiskey Cream Sauce (page 124) served as an accompaniment.

Lamb Kebabs with Lemon-Dill Sauce

SUGGESTED PELLETS: OAK, PECAN

SERVES 4 PEOPLE

PREP TIME: 15 minutes, plus marinating time

COOK TIME: 10 to 12 minutes

TEMPERATURE: 450°F

---

2 pounds boneless lamb (shoulder or leg)

10 ounces Greek yogurt

2 tablespoons mayonnaise

2 tablespoons freshly squeezed lemon juice

2 tablespoons chopped fresh dill

1 tablespoon garlic paste

Kosher salt

Freshly ground black pepper

4 to 6 kebab skewers (if using wooden skewers, soak in water for at least 30 minutes to prevent burning)

These luscious lamb kebabs are marinated in the lemon-dill sauce, then used as a dipping sauce. Tender, juicy lamb cooks quickly on the Traeger, which adds that beautiful kiss of smoked flavor. You could serve these kebabs with grilled pita brushed with olive oil—just set the pita on the grill grate during the last few minutes of cooking.

1. Cut the lamb into 1-inch pieces and place them in a gallon-size plastic bag.

2. To make the lemon-dill sauce, in a bowl, combine the Greek yogurt, mayonnaise, lemon juice, dill, garlic paste, salt, and pepper and stir together. Place 2 to 3 tablespoons of the lemon-dill sauce into the bag with the lamb and massage the bag until the lamb is evenly coated. Marinate in the refrigerator for 2 to 3 hours.

3. Turn the Traeger on and set it to 450°F. While the Traeger preheats, thread the lamb on the kebab skewers.

4. Once preheated, put the kebabs on the grill grate for 10 to 12 minutes, turning a few times throughout.

5. Remove from the grill and serve the lamb kebabs with the remaining lemon-dill sauce for dipping.

> **VARIATION TIP: You could add bell pepper and red onion pieces to these kebabs to include some veggies, making this more of a complete meal. Another variation is adding feta cheese crumbles to the lemon-dill dipping sauce.**

Bacon-Wrapped Venison Backstrap

SUGGESTED PELLETS: CHERRY, OAK

SERVES 4 PEOPLE

PREP TIME: 10 minutes

COOK TIME: 25 to 35 minutes

TEMPERATURE: 375°F

---

1 (2-pound) venison backstrap or tenderloin

Kosher salt

Freshly ground black pepper

6 slices regular-cut bacon (not thick sliced)

BBQ Dry Rub (page 125) (optional)

Venison backstrap is the most tender cut of deer meat. It is very lean, so it has a tendency to dry out, but wrapping it in bacon keeps the meat moist and it will come out perfect each and every time. The ideal temperature at which to enjoy this venison is medium rare to medium for maximum tenderness.

1. Turn the Traeger on and set it to 375°F.

2. Season the venison with salt and pepper. Then wrap the bacon slices around the venison, overlapping slightly. Season the bacon with the dry rub (if using).

3. Once the grill is preheated, place the backstrap on the grill grate for 25 to 35 minutes, or until the internal temperature reaches 130 to 140°F.

4. Let the meat rest for 10 minutes before slicing.

> **SERVE WITH:** The Whiskey Cream Sauce (page 124) is heavenly with this venison backstrap. I also highly recommend making the Loaded Potato Rounds (page 106) at the same time as the venison for the perfect side dish.

Beer-Brined Rack of Venison

SUGGESTED PELLETS: CHERRY, OAK

SERVES 4 TO 6 PEOPLE

PREP TIME: 10 minutes, plus brining time

COOK TIME: 25 to 30 minutes

TEMPERATURE: 375°F

---

2 cans beer of choice

1 cup water

¼ cup kosher salt

¼ cup brown sugar

4 tablespoons BBQ Dry Rub (page 125), divided

1 (2- to 2½-pound) rack of venison

Rack of venison makes for a stunning presentation. It needs to brine for 24 hours, so plan ahead when making this. It's the tenderloin cut without the bones removed. Most butchers or online meat distributors sell this cut of meat "frenched," which means the ends of the bones have been cleaned very well. This makes them stand out from the meat and look extra elegant when serving. The beer brine creates a juicier and more flavorful venison, as well as helping to remove some of the gaminess.

1. In a saucepan, combine the beer, water, salt, brown sugar, and 2 tablespoons of dry rub over medium heat, stirring until the salt and sugar are dissolved, then set aside to let cool.

2. Place the venison in a large container. Once the brine has cooled, pour it over the venison, covering it completely. Place a lid on the container or cover tightly with foil, then store in the refrigerator for at least 24 hours.

3. When ready to cook, turn the Traeger on and set the temperature to 375°F. Remove the venison from the brine and pat it dry. Season with the remaining 2 tablespoons of dry rub.

4. Place the rack of venison on the grill grate for 25 to 30 minutes, or until the internal temperature reaches 130 to 140°F.

5. Let the meat rest for 10 minutes before slicing and serving.

> **SMOKER SAVVY TIP: Letting the venison come to room temperature before placing on the Traeger will help it cook more evenly, creating a more tender, juicier meat.**

Garlic-Parmesan Meatballs

SUGGESTED PELLETS: MESQUITE, OAK

MAKES 22 MEATBALLS

PREP TIME: 15 minutes

COOK TIME: 55 minutes
to 1 hour

TEMPERATURE:
225°F and 450°F

---

1 pound ground beef

½ cup Italian bread crumbs

4 garlic cloves, minced

1 egg

¼ cup grated
Parmesan cheese

Kosher salt

Freshly ground black pepper

These meatballs are a perfect addition to spaghetti. They also make amazing meatball subs or sliders, and are delicious just dipped in your favorite marinara or barbecue sauce. You can even mix it up and use sausage, ground chicken, or ground venison in place of the beef.

1. In a large bowl, combine the ground beef, bread crumbs, garlic, egg, Parmesan cheese, salt, and pepper. Mix together with your hands and roll the mixture into 1½-inch meatballs.

2. Turn the Traeger on and set the temperature to 225°F.

3. Once preheated, place the meatballs on the grill grates for 45 minutes. Turn the temperature up to 450°F for 10 to 15 minutes, or until the meatballs reach an internal temperature of 165°F. You can flip them, if desired, during the last few minutes.

> **SMOKER SAVVY TIP:** These meatballs can be made the day before and stored in the refrigerator on a baking sheet or tray in a single layer, covered with foil or plastic wrap. You can also double or triple this recipe, then freeze some of the meatballs in gallon-size plastic bags for future use. They can be stored in the freezer for up to 4 months.

Brisket with Coffee Rub

SERVES 10 TO 14 PEOPLE
PREP TIME: 10 minutes
COOK TIME: 12 to 18 hours
TEMPERATURE: 225°F

---

1 (8- to 12-pound)
    whole brisket

2 tablespoons ground coffee

2 tablespoons kosher salt

2 tablespoons chili powder

1 tablespoon freshly
    ground black pepper

1 tablespoon garlic powder

1 tablespoon paprika

½ cup apple cider vinegar

¼ cup water

Brisket is one of the most rewarding things you can cook on the Traeger! When buying the brisket, make sure you are getting a whole brisket, and not just the "flat" of the brisket. Low and slow is the way to go for maximum smoked flavor, a gorgeous bark, and meat as tender and juicy as possible. Brisket takes hours to cook, so make sure you start early and with a clean grill with plenty of pellets. The end result is extraordinary and so worth your efforts! Note: It takes about 1½ hours per pound at 225°F to cook brisket, but monitoring the temperature is most important.

1. If your brisket has not already been trimmed by a butcher, trim most of the fat off of the brisket with a good-quality, sharp knife. Leave a thin layer of fat on the top (this is called the fat cap).

2. In a small bowl, put the coffee, salt, chili powder, pepper, garlic powder, and paprika and stir to combine. Rub this mixture over all sides of the brisket.

3. Turn the Traeger on and set it to 225°F. While the grill is preheating, mix the apple cider vinegar and water in a spray bottle. Put the brisket on the grill grate for 12 to 18 hours, or until the internal temperature reaches 200°F. Spray with the apple cider vinegar mixture every 45 minutes (start this after the brisket has been smoking for 3 hours).

4. Let the brisket rest for 1 to 2 hours before slicing. Slice the brisket against the grain.

> **SMOKER SAVVY TIP:** Some people prefer the fat cap–side up; some prefer the fat cap–side down. I have done both and have not noticed a difference in flavor.

Chili-Rubbed Porterhouse Steak

SUGGESTED PELLETS: CHERRY, OAK

SERVES 4 PEOPLE

PREP TIME: 5 minutes, plus time to let steak come to room temperature

COOK TIME: 10 to 14 minutes

TEMPERATURE: 450°F or 500°F

---

2 (1- to 1¼-inch-thick) porterhouse steaks

2 tablespoons chili powder

1 tablespoon paprika

1 tablespoon brown sugar

Kosher salt

Freshly ground black pepper

The porterhouse is the king of steaks in my opinion. It is a strip steak and a tenderloin (filet mignon) connected by a T-shaped bone. A porterhouse is a thicker cut compared to a T-bone, and also cut from the back end of the short loin, making the tenderloin portion larger. The marbling of this steak is gorgeous! The chili rub adds something extra special to an already extraordinary steak.

1. Let the steaks come to room temperature for about 45 minutes. In a small bowl, combine the chili powder, paprika, brown sugar, salt, and pepper. Rub the mixture on all sides of the steaks.

2. Turn the Traeger on and set it to the highest setting, either 450 or 500°F depending on which model you have.

3. Once preheated, put the steaks on the grill grate and cook for 5 to 7 minutes per side. The cook time will depend on thickness and how you want them done. Remove the steaks when they have reached the desired internal temperature.

4. Let the meat rest for 10 minutes before slicing.

VARIATION TIP: **You can use the reverse-sear method with these porterhouse steaks if you prefer. Just follow the reverse-sear directions for the Reverse-Seared Filet Mignon (page 40).**

Curry-Rubbed Leg of Lamb

SUGGESTED PELLETS: APPLES, PECAN

SERVES 10 TO 12 PEOPLE
PREP TIME: 10 minutes
COOK TIME: 2½ to 3 hours
TEMPERATURE: 250°F

---

1 (5- to 6-pound) bone-in
   leg of lamb

¼ cup Dijon mustard

2 tablespoons curry powder

1 teaspoon garlic powder

1 teaspoon ginger powder

1 teaspoon ground cumin

1 teaspoon ground coriander

Kosher salt

Freshly ground black pepper

Leg of lamb can seem a bit intimidating if you've never cooked one. It is seriously one of the easiest cuts of meat to make and turns out perfect and juicy every time. This curry rub complements the flavor of the lamb beautifully. It's fabulous for feeding a crowd and certainly brings that wow factor when served.

1. Brush the leg of lamb with the Dijon mustard on all sides.

2. In a small bowl, mix the curry powder, garlic powder, ginger powder, cumin, coriander, salt, and pepper until evenly combined. Rub the mixture into the Dijon mustard on all sides of the lamb.

3. While the curry rub soaks into the lamb, turn the Traeger on and set the temperature to 250°F.

4. Once preheated, put the leg of lamb on the Traeger for 2½ to 3 hours, or until the internal temperature reaches 145°F.

5. Let the lamb rest for 20 to 30 minutes before serving.

SERVE WITH: The Caribbean Jerk Dry Rub (page 127) is another great rub to use with this leg of lamb. In place of the Dijon mustard, rub the leg of lamb with 2 tablespoons of soy sauce, then rub with 3 to 4 tablespoons of Caribbean Jerk Dry Rub. Follow the same cook time and temperature, 250°F for 2½ to 3 hours.

Lamb Burgers with Basil-Feta Sauce

SERVES 4 PEOPLE

PREP TIME: 15 minutes

COOK TIME: 6 to 10 minutes

TEMPERATURE:
450°F or 500°F

1½ pounds ground lamb

1 teaspoon garlic powder

1 teaspoon paprika

1 teaspoon ground cumin

Kosher salt

Freshly ground black pepper

6 ounces plain Greek yogurt

2 ounces crumbled
feta cheese

5 or 6 basil leaves, chopped

1 tablespoon freshly
squeezed lemon juice

4 burger buns

Toppings of choice: lettuce,
tomato, onions, etc.

These yummy burgers are made with ground lamb with a mixture of spices, then grilled on high heat to seal in all the juices. They're served topped with a basil-feta sauce that brings out the flavor of the lamb perfectly. I also love serving these burgers on slices of pita or naan bread that has been slightly grilled on the Traeger in place of buns.

1. Turn on the Traeger and set it to the highest temperature, either 450 or 500°F depending on the model you have.

2. In a bowl, combine the garlic powder, paprika, cumin, salt, and pepper. Mix it with your hands, being careful not to overwork it, and form into four patties.

3. In a separate bowl, combine the Greek yogurt, feta, basil, lemon juice, and a pinch each of salt and pepper and stir until evenly mixed, then set aside.

4. Once the Traeger is preheated, put the lamb burgers on the grill grate for 3 to 5 minutes per side.

5. Toast the burger buns on the Traeger during the last minute of cooking the burgers.

6. Serve the lamb burgers on buns and top with the basil-feta sauce and any additional toppings of choice such as lettuce, tomato, or onions, if desired.

VARIATION TIP: For even more flavor in these burgers, mix some extra feta cheese crumbles and chopped basil in the lamb mixture before forming the patties. You'll have even more feta and basil in each scrumptious bite!

Smoked Prime Rib

SUGGESTED PELLETS: CHERRY, OAK

SERVES 4 TO 6 PEOPLE

PREP TIME: 10 minutes

COOK TIME: 3½ to 4 hours

TEMPERATURE: 250°F

---

4 tablespoons butter

4 garlic cloves, minced

1 (5 to 6-pound) bone-in prime rib roast

Kosher salt

Freshly ground black pepper

Prime rib is one of my favorite meals to make on the Traeger. It's perfect for a holiday or special celebration. This recipe is for a 5- to 6-pound prime rib. If you have a different size, plan on 30 minutes of cook time per pound.

1. Turn the Traeger on and set the temperature to 250°F.

2. In a bowl, mix the butter with the garlic (this is easiest if the butter is at room temperature). Rub the butter on all sides of the prime rib, then season all sides with salt and pepper.

3. Once the grill is preheated, put the prime rib on the grill grate for 3½ to 4 hours or until the internal temperature reaches 130 to 140°F for medium rare to medium doneness.

4. Let the prime rib rest for 30 minutes before slicing.

> **SERVE WITH:** The Garlic-Herb Compound Butter (page 132) pairs beautifully with this prime rib. The Twice-Smoked Potatoes (page 119) make an amazing side dish, since the potatoes are cooked at the same temperature and on very similar timing.

Harissa-Glazed Short Ribs

SERVES 4 PEOPLE
PREP TIME: 10 minutes
COOK TIME: 6 to 8 hours
TEMPERATURE: 225°F

---

4 pounds beef short ribs

2 tablespoons olive oil

Kosher salt

Freshly ground black pepper

½ cup beef stock, poured in a spray bottle

½ cup harissa paste

½ cup honey

1 tablespoon freshly squeezed lime juice

2 teaspoons garlic powder

2 teaspoons ground cumin

1 teaspoon ground cinnamon

Leave plenty of time for these beef short ribs and start them early—they cook low and slow but the end result is phenomenal. They will fall off the bone and the harissa glaze is the perfect sweet and spicy sauce to complement these ribs. Harissa is a Moroccan chile paste with a slight kick, but isn't overwhelmingly spicy. It can be found in most grocery stores or online.

1. Turn the Traeger on and set the temperature to 225°F.

2. Brush the short ribs all over with olive oil and season them with salt and pepper.

3. Once preheated, put the short ribs on the grill grates. After 3 hours, start spraying them with the beef stock every 45 minutes.

4. While the ribs cook, in a bowl, whisk together the harissa paste, honey, lime juice, garlic powder, cumin, cinnamon, and a pinch each of salt and pepper until evenly combined.

5. These ribs will take 6 to 8 hours total to cook. When the internal temperature reaches 195°F, start brushing the harissa glaze on the ribs. Remove the ribs when the internal temperature reaches 205°F and serve with the remaining sauce.

VARIATION TIP: This harissa sauce can also be brushed on chicken wings, whole chickens, and pork tenderloin, too! Simply brush the sauce on whatever meat you are cooking during the last half hour of cooking and it will caramelize and give tremendous flavor. Serve any extra sauce for dipping.

Skirt Steak Fajitas

SUGGESTED PELLETS: MESQUITE, OAK

SERVES 4 TO 6 PEOPLE
PREP TIME: 15 minutes
COOK TIME: 16 to 20 minutes
TEMPERATURE:
450°F or 500°F

---

1 (2-pound) skirt steak

2 tablespoons olive oil, divided

2 to 3 tablespoons fajita seasoning, divided

Kosher salt

Freshly ground black pepper

1 red bell pepper, seeded, stemmed, and sliced

1 yellow bell pepper, seeded, stemmed, and sliced

1 poblano pepper, seeded, stemmed, and sliced

1 onion, sliced

3 garlic cloves, minced

Tortillas, for serving

Pico de gallo and Guacamole (optional)

To keep things easy, both the steak and the fajita veggies cook on the Traeger at the same time for this recipe. These are some of the tastiest fajitas I have ever made and they are a great weeknight dinner ready in a flash, or a wonderful addition to a taco bar if feeding a crowd.

1. Place a cast-iron skillet on the grill grate, then turn the Traeger on and set the temperature to the highest heat setting, either 450 or 500°F.

2. Brush the skirt steak with 1 tablespoon of olive oil and season with 1 tablespoon of fajita seasoning, the salt, and pepper. In a bowl, put the bell peppers, poblano pepper, onion, and garlic and toss with remaining 1 tablespoon of olive oil, 1 to 2 tablespoons of fajita seasoning, and a pinch each of salt and black pepper to evenly coat the veggies.

3. Once the grill is preheated, carefully pour the veggies into the hot cast-iron skillet on the Traeger. Use tongs to spread them evenly in the skillet and cook for 10 minutes.

4. After 10 minutes, put the skirt steak directly on the grill grate for 3 to 5 minutes per side. Stir the veggies with the tongs when adding and flipping the steak.

5. Remove the steak and allow to rest before slicing. Remove the veggies when they are cooked to your liking. Serve the steak and veggies with tortillas and additional fajita toppings of choice if desired.

> **SERVE WITH: These fajitas are amazing served with the Chorizo-Queso Dip (page 35) and also with the Street Corn Salad (page 114)! You can have a whole fiesta all cooked on the Traeger.**

Herb-Crusted Rack of Lamb

SUGGESTED PELLETS: APPLE, PECAN

SERVES 4 PEOPLE
PREP TIME: 10 minutes
COOK TIME: 2 hours
TEMPERATURE: 225°F

2 tablespoons olive oil

4 garlic cloves, minced

1 tablespoon dried rosemary

1 tablespoon dried thyme

1 tablespoon dried basil

Kosher salt

Freshly ground black pepper

1 (2-pound) rack of lamb

Rack of lamb is a gorgeous cut of meat. It's tender and juicy and soaks up all the wood-fired flavor on the Traeger. This herb-crusted lamb is easy to make, but the presentation makes it look like you spent a lot more time and effort on it, and you will feel like a true chef!

1. Turn the Traeger on and set the temperature to 225°F.

2. In a small bowl, mix together the olive oil, garlic, rosemary, thyme, basil, salt, and pepper. Use your hands to rub this mixture over all sides of the lamb.

3. Put the lamb on the grill grate for 2 hours, or until the internal temperature reaches 135 to 145°F for medium rare to medium. Let it rest for 15 minutes before slicing.

SERVE WITH: This lamb does not necessarily need an accompanying sauce, but if you do want to serve it with one, I recommend the Lemon-Dill Sauce (page 41).

Sriracha-Bourbon Spare Ribs, page 67

Pork

Pork Tenderloin Wrapped with Maple Bacon

SUGGESTED PELLETS: APPLE, MAPLE

SERVES 4 PEOPLE

PREP TIME: 10 minutes

COOK TIME: 40 to 50 minutes

TEMPERATURE: 375°F

---

1 pork tenderloin (roughly 1 pound)

Kosher salt

Freshly ground black pepper

5 or 6 slices regular-cut bacon

¼ cup pure maple syrup

The only thing better than pork is wrapping it in more pork! This is a simple dish that is big on flavor. Brushing the bacon with maple syrup creates a gorgeous glaze and brings a nice hint of sweetness that pairs perfectly with the savory pork. It is important to use regular-cut bacon and not thick cut, so the bacon cooks properly.

1. Turn the Traeger on and set it to 375°F.

2. Season the pork tenderloin with salt and pepper on all sides.

3. Starting at one end, wrap the bacon slices around the pork tenderloin, overlapping them slightly.

4. Put the pork tenderloin on the grill grate for 40 to 50 minutes, or until it reaches an internal temperature of 145°F. Brush the bacon with the maple syrup during the last 10 minutes.

SERVE WITH: To add even more flavor, season this pork tenderloin with the BBQ Dry Rub (page 125). You can season the pork itself with the rub and also the outer layer of bacon. I would also suggest serving it with Cinnamon Apples (page 118) as a side dish.

Classic BBQ Baby Back Ribs

SERVES 4 PEOPLE
PREP TIME: 10 minutes
COOK TIME: 6 hours
TEMPERATURE: 225°F

---

2 full racks pork baby back ribs

½ cup store-bought barbecue seasoning, or 1 batch BBQ Dry Rub (page 125)

2 cups store-bought barbecue sauce, or either the Chipotle BBQ Sauce (page 133) or Gochujang BBQ Sauce (page 129)

This rib recipe uses the 3-2-1 cooking method: 3 hours directly on the Traeger, then another 2 hours while wrapped in foil. Water is added to the foil packet, which helps steam the ribs. The ribs spend the final hour on the grill unwrapped and glazed with barbecue sauce. They are the most tender, fall-off-the-bone ribs I have ever made.

1. Turn the Traeger on and set it to 225°F.

2. Remove the silver skin from the ribs if it hasn't been removed already. Pat the ribs dry and rub them with the barbecue seasoning. Put the ribs on the grill grate for 3 hours.

3. After 3 hours, carefully wrap each rack in foil and add a little water to each foil packet. Put the wrapped ribs back on the grill grate for 2 hours more.

4. Unwrap the ribs and put them back on the grill grate for 1 hour more, brushing with some barbecue sauce a few times as they finish.

5. Serve with any remaining barbecue sauce on the side.

> **SMOKER SAVVY TIP:** Cutting the rack of ribs in half makes wrapping them in foil a little easier. Also, transferring the ribs to a baking sheet or tray to wrap them works really well. If you prefer, you could add beer or even apple juice in place of the water in step 3 to add more flavor.

Smoked Pepperoni Calzones

SUGGESTED PELLETS: APPLE, MESQUITE

SERVES 4 PEOPLE

PREP TIME: 10 minutes

COOK TIME: 16 to 18 minutes

TEMPERATURE: 425°F

---

1 (13.8-ounce) tube prepared pizza dough

2 cups shredded mozzarella cheese

24 slices pepperoni

3 tablespoons melted butter

½ teaspoon garlic powder

½ teaspoon Italian seasoning

Your Traeger can be used just like your oven, so you can make cheesy calzones with a golden-brown crust and wood-fired flavor in a snap. These calzones are simply made with cheese and pepperoni, but the possibilities are endless when it comes to the different flavor combinations you can come up with.

1. Turn the Traeger on and set the temperature to 425°F.

2. Use a rolling pin to roll out the pizza dough on a flat surface and create a rectangle of even thickness. Use a pizza cutter to cut the dough in half both vertically and horizontally, creating four equal-size rectangles.

3. On one side of each piece of dough, add some shredded mozzarella cheese and 6 slices of pepperoni. Fold the empty side of dough over the filled side, then use a fork to press the seams closed. Repeat with the remaining dough, cheese, and pepperoni slices.

4. Gently transfer the calzones to a baking sheet. Mix the butter with the garlic powder and Italian seasoning and brush this mixture over each calzone.

5. Place the baking sheet on the Traeger for 16 to 18 minutes or until the crust is golden brown.

6. Serve the calzones with dipping sauce of choice, such as pizza sauce, garlic butter, or ranch dressing.

> **VARIATION TIP: As a Traeger owner, you might find yourself wondering what to do with leftover pulled pork or brisket. Try making these calzones with that leftover meat instead of the pepperoni, use cheddar cheese in place of the mozzarella, and dip them in barbecue sauce.**

Teriyaki Pork Burgers

SUGGESTED PELLETS: APPLE, MESQUITE

SERVES 4 PEOPLE

PREP TIME: 10 minutes

COOK TIME: 1 hour or
8 to 10 minutes

TEMPERATURE:
250°F or 500°F

---

1 pound ground pork

¼ cup teriyaki sauce

1 medium carrot, grated

¼ cup chopped scallions

3 garlic cloves, minced

½ cup mayonnaise

1 to 2 tablespoons sriracha,
plus more as needed

4 burger buns

These burgers have an incredible flavor on their own, but adding that wood-fired flavor from the Traeger makes them extraordinary. You have two cooking options with these: You can cook them low and slow for extra wood-fired goodness, or quickly for a busy weekday and to get a good sear on the burger. Add whatever toppings you like, such as more teriyaki sauce, cilantro, or kimchi!

1. Turn the Traeger on and set the temperature to either 250°F or 500°F, depending on how you want to cook them.

2. In a bowl, combine the ground pork, teriyaki sauce, carrot, scallion, and garlic. Form four patties.

3. In a separate bowl, mix together the mayonnaise and sriracha to taste and set aside.

4. Put the pork burgers on the grill grate for either 1 hour at 250°F, flipping halfway through, or 8 to 10 minutes at 500°F, flipping halfway through.

5. Place the pork burgers on the burger buns and top with the sriracha mayo and additional toppings of your choice, such as grilled pineapple rings and/or grilled onion.

> **SERVE WITH:** You can make the Gochujang BBQ Sauce (page 129) to use in place of the teriyaki sauce for an amazing twist on these burgers. Top the burgers with kimchi for an unbeatable flavor pairing.

BBQ Pulled Pork

SUGGESTED PELLETS: APPLE, HICKORY

SERVES 8 TO 10 PEOPLE
PREP TIME: 10 minutes
COOK TIME: 5 to 7 hours
TEMPERATURE: 250°F

1 (5- to 8-pound) bone-in
   pork shoulder

1 tablespoon yellow mustard

2 tablespoons brown sugar

1 tablespoon chili powder

1 tablespoon paprika

1 tablespoon garlic powder

1 tablespoon kosher salt

½ tablespoon freshly ground
   black pepper

½ cup apple cider vinegar,
   poured in a spray bottle

The ability to make tender, juicy, fall-apart pulled pork is most likely one of the top reasons to own a Traeger grill. This is my tried-and-true recipe for the best barbecue pulled pork, and it's one of my family's favorite dishes. It's perfect for sandwiches, quesadillas, nachos, and whatever else you can think of!

1. Place the pork shoulder on a tray or baking sheet and brush the mustard on all sides of the pork.

2. In a small bowl, combine the brown sugar, chili powder, paprika, garlic powder, salt, and pepper. Whisk until evenly combined and rub this mixture on all sides of the pork. Cover the pork and refrigerate overnight, or you can smoke it right away.

3. Turn the Traeger on and set the temperature to 250°F. Put the pork on the grill grate for 5 to 7 hours, or until the internal temperature reaches 195 to 200°F. Spray the apple cider vinegar on the pork several times each hour.

4. Shred the pork and enjoy!

> **SMOKER SAVVY TIP:** For extra-tender pork, remove the pork from the Traeger at 195°F, wrap it in foil, then wrap a towel around it. Place the pork in an empty cooler for an hour to let it rest and steam.

Smoked Sausage Lasagna

SUGGESTED PELLETS: HICKORY, MESQUITE

SERVES 8 PEOPLE

PREP TIME: 15 minutes

COOK TIME: 45 minutes
to 1 hour

TEMPERATURE: 375°F

---

1 pound ground Italian
sausage

2 (18-ounce) jars marinara
sauce, divided

1 package oven-ready
lasagna noodles, divided

1 (15-ounce) container
ricotta cheese, divided

4 cups shredded mozzarella
cheese, divided

Lasagna is one dish you might never have thought of to cook on a grill, but cooking your lasagna on the Traeger makes it extra delicious! This is a great recipe when feeding a crowd, and everyone will love the twist that the wood-fired flavor gives the lasagna. It's so good that this is the only way I will cook a lasagna.

1. In a large skillet, cook the Italian sausage over medium heat for 5 to 7 minutes, breaking it apart as it cooks.

2. Turn the Traeger on and set the temperature to 375°F.

3. Pour 1 cup of marinara sauce into a 9-by-13-inch casserole dish (I suggest a disposable foil pan for easy cleanup). Spread the sauce evenly and lay 4 lasagna noodles over the sauce.

4. Spread one-third of the ricotta over the noodles, then one-third of the cooked Italian sausage over the ricotta. Layer 1 cup of mozzarella cheese, followed by 1 cup of marinara sauce. Lay 4 lasagna noodles over the marinara, followed by one-third of the ricotta, then one-third of the Italian sausage, then 1 cup of mozzarella. Repeat in this order with the remaining noodles, ricotta, Italian sausage, and mozzarella.

5. Place the lasagna on the grill grates for 30 to 40 minutes. Top with the remaining mozzarella cheese and cook for 15 to 20 minutes more.

SMOKER SAVVY TIP: For even more smoked flavor, start the lasagna at 180°F, and turn on the super smoke feature if your model has it, for 30 minutes. Then turn the heat up to 375°F to finish cooking according to this recipe.

Apple-Stuffed Pork Loin

SUGGESTED PELLETS: APPLE, CHERRY

SERVES 6 TO 8 PEOPLE
PREP TIME: 15 minutes
COOK TIME: 3 hours
TEMPERATURE: 225°F

---

1 (5-pound) pork loin (not tenderloin)

2 apples, cut into half-inch slices

Kosher salt

Freshly ground black pepper

1 teaspoon ground cinnamon

1 teaspoon ground cumin

½ cup hoisin sauce

¼ cup pure maple syrup

Apples and pork complement each other beautifully, so why not make them together into one amazing meal?! This one is very simple and easy to prepare. The pork soaks up all the flavor of the apples and the apples help create a moist and delicious pork loin.

1. Turn the Traeger on and set the temperature to 225°F.

2. Using a sharp, knife cut about twelve 3-inch-deep slits in the pork. Divide the apples into each slit with the skin-side up. Season the pork on all sides with salt, pepper, cinnamon, and cumin.

3. In a small bowl, mix the hoisin sauce and maple syrup together and set aside.

4. Cook the pork for about 3 hours, or until the internal temperature reaches 145°F. Brush the pork with the hoisin and maple syrup mixture a few times during the last hour of cooking. Let it rest for 10 minutes before slicing. Serve with remaining hoisin maple syrup.

> **SERVE WITH: A great side dish that can be made at the same time and temperature as this pork is the BBQ Baked Beans (page 107). And if you want even more apples to go with the pork, try the Cinnamon Apples (page 118).**

Sausage Biscuit Sandwiches

SUGGESTED PELLETS: CHERRY, MAPLE

MAKES 5 SANDWICHES
PREP TIME: 10 minutes
COOK TIME: 15 minutes
TEMPERATURE: 425°F

---

1 package jumbo-size
  biscuits (5 count)

1 pound breakfast sausage

Optional toppings: cheese,
  egg, maple syrup

This is a quick and easy breakfast, or breakfast-for-dinner sandwich. The biscuits and the sausage patties are cooked on the Traeger for extra wood-fired goodness added to your meal, no matter when you eat these tasty sandwiches.

1. Turn the Traeger on and set the temperature to 425°F.

2. Put the jumbo biscuits on foil or a greased baking sheet.

3. Form the sausage into five patties.

4. Once the grill is preheated, place the foil or baking sheet with the biscuits on the grill grate. Put the patties directly on the grill grate for 15 minutes. Flip the sausage halfway through.

5. Cut the biscuits in half and top each one with a sausage patty. If using, top with cheese, egg, and syrup and serve.

VARIATION TIP: **You can substitute turkey sausage and make these in the same way.**

Cheese-Stuffed Chorizo Meatballs

SUGGESTED PELLETS: MAPLE, MESQUITE

MAKES 12 MEATBALLS

PREP TIME: 15 minutes

COOK TIME: 12 to 15 minutes

TEMPERATURE: 450°F

---

2 pounds ground chorizo sausage

12 (1-inch) cubes cheddar cheese

Barbecue sauce, for dipping (optional)

Chorizo is one of my favorite types of sausage. Because it packs such a punch of flavor on its own, you really don't need to add anything to it. The only thing that makes these meatballs even better is that they are stuffed with cheese! These meatballs can be eaten on their own or added to almost any dish for a quick and tasty meal.

1. Turn the Traeger on and set the temperature to 450°F.

2. Form the chorizo around each cube of cheese into 12 meatballs.

3. Place the meatballs on the grill grate for 12 to 15 minutes total. Turn them a few times as they cook.

4. Serve with barbecue sauce (if using).

VARIATION TIP: These would be a great addition and fun twist on traditional spaghetti and meatballs. They are also amazing served on a sub, sandwich, or on slider buns with barbecue sauce. You can spice this recipe up even more by using pepper Jack cheese in place of the cheddar.

Spicy Gochujang Pork Chops

SUGGESTED PELLETS: CHERRY, MESQUITE

SERVES 4

PREP TIME: 10 minutes, plus overnight marinating time

COOK TIME: 8 to 12 minutes

TEMPERATURE:
450°F or 500°F

---

4 bone-in pork chops

1 tablespoon gochujang chile paste

1 tablespoon soy sauce

1 tablespoon garlic paste

1 tablespoon ginger paste

1 tablespoon honey

The marinade and sauce for these pork chops is absolutely amazing. Gochujang is a Korean chile paste that can easily be found in most grocery stores or online. It has a slight spice, but it is not overwhelming.

1. Place the pork chops in a gallon-size plastic bag. In a bowl, whisk together the gochujang paste, soy sauce, garlic paste, ginger paste, and honey until evenly combined. Add this mixture to the bag with the pork and massage the bag until the pork is evenly coated. Marinate in the refrigerator overnight.

2. When ready to cook, turn the Traeger on and set the temperature to the highest temperature, 450 or 500°F, depending on which model you have.

3. Once preheated, place the pork chops on the grill grate for 4 to 6 minutes per side, depending on how thick they are. They will be done when the internal temperature reaches 145°F.

4. Serve the pork chops on their own, or double the gochujang sauce in step 1 and reserve half to serve alongside the pork as a dipping sauce. (Discard any sauce that was used as the marinade.)

VARIATION TIP: This marinade is perfect for chicken, flank steak, and pork tenderloin. Follow this recipe for marinating your choice of meat, and use the cooking times chart on page 13.

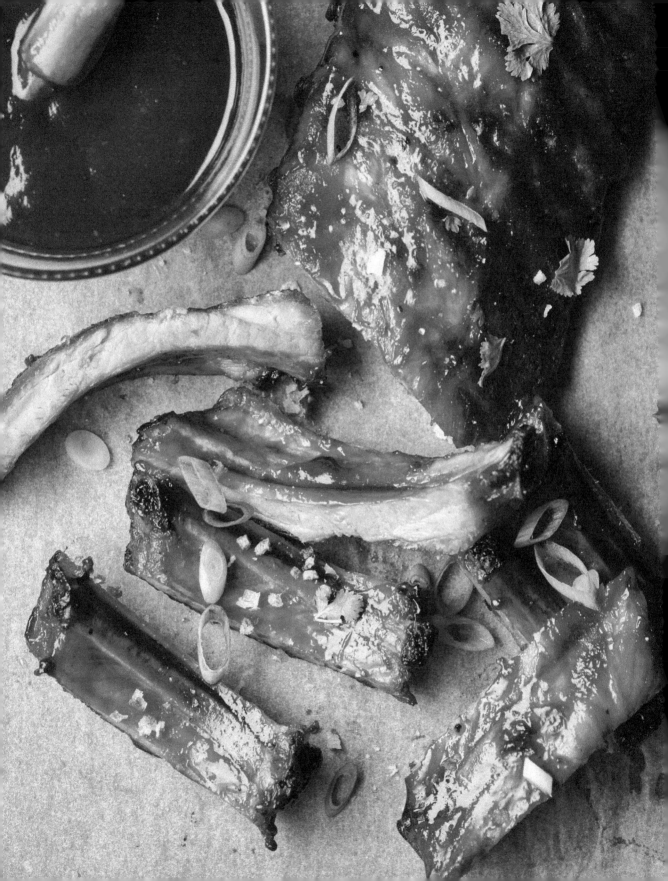

Sriracha-Bourbon Spare Ribs

SUGGESTED PELLETS: CHERRY, HICKORY

SERVES 4 PEOPLE
PREP TIME: 15 minutes
COOK TIME: 4 to 5 hours
TEMPERATURE: 250°F

1¼ cups brown sugar, divided

¾ cup bourbon

¾ cup ketchup

¼ cup apple cider vinegar

2 to 4 tablespoons sriracha

1 tablespoon soy sauce

Kosher salt

Freshly ground black pepper

1 rack pork spare ribs

1 tablespoon garlic powder

Spare ribs are larger and have more meat on them compared to baby back ribs. Baby back ribs typically are leaner and more tender, but spare ribs are more flavorful and more budget-friendly. Because it is a very different cut of pork rib compared to baby back, the cook time and temperature are different to get maximum tenderness from this cut of meat.

1. In a saucepan over medium heat, mix 1 cup of brown sugar, the bourbon, ketchup, apple cider vinegar, sriracha to taste, soy sauce, salt, and pepper. Bring to a boil and reduce the heat to a simmer for 10 to 12 minutes, stirring a few times, then remove from the heat and set aside.

2. Turn the Traeger on and set the temperature to 250°F.

3. Rub the spare ribs with the remaining ¼ cup of brown sugar, the garlic powder, and a pinch each of salt and pepper. Place them on the smoker for 4 to 5 hours, or until the internal temperature reaches 195 to 203°F. Brush the ribs with the sriracha bourbon sauce a few times after the first 2 hours of cooking.

> **SMOKER SAVVY TIP:** There's a great debate between master grillers and smokers on the perfect temperature to enjoy the most tender ribs. A safe temperature to consume pork is 145°F, but for tougher cuts of meat, cooking low and slow to a temperature between 195° and 203°F makes the meat fall off the bone. Try experimenting with different temperatures between 195° and 203°F to see what you think creates the most delicious rib.

Smoked Sausage and Veggies

SUGGESTED PELLETS: CHERRY, MESQUITE

SERVES 4 PEOPLE

PREP TIME: 10 minutes

COOK TIME: 45 to 50 minutes

TEMPERATURE: 425°F

---

1 (12-ounce) package smoked sausage, cut into 1-inch-thick pieces

1 red bell pepper, seeded, stemmed, and cut into 1-inch-thick pieces

1 yellow bell pepper, seeded, stemmed, and cut into 1-inch-thick pieces

1 red onion, cut into 1-inch-thick pieces

1 zucchini, cut into 1-inch-thick pieces

2 tablespoons olive oil

1 tablespoon balsamic vinegar

1 tablespoon garlic powder

Kosher salt

Freshly ground black pepper

Pinch red pepper flakes

Goat cheese, crumbled, for topping (optional)

Fresh basil, for topping (optional)

This easy-to-make one-pan meal has the benefit of added veggies and is overall delicious. Sliced smoked sausage and vegetables cooked on the Traeger with wood-fired flavor might become your favorite way to eat your veggies.

1. Turn the Traeger on and set the temperature to 425°F.

2. On a baking sheet, place the sausage, bell peppers, onion, and zucchini in an even layer.

3. Add the olive oil, balsamic vinegar, garlic powder, and a pinch each of salt, black pepper, and red pepper flakes to the sausage and veggies. Toss until everything is evenly coated.

4. Put the baking sheet on the grill grate for 45 to 50 minutes, tossing the sausage and veggies halfway through.

5. If using, serve topped with goat cheese and basil.

VARIATION TIP: You can substitute smoked chicken or turkey sausage for the smoked sausage. You can also add other veggies such as mushrooms or summer squash. Just make sure to cut everything a similar size so they will cook perfectly together at the same time.

Goetta Sliders with Spicy Syrup

SUGGESTED PELLETS: HICKORY, MESQUITE

SERVES 4 PEOPLE

PREP TIME: 10 minutes

COOK TIME: 24 to 28 minutes

TEMPERATURE: 350°F

---

2 pounds goetta

½ cup pure maple syrup

Few dashes hot
sauce of choice

4 slices Colby Jack
cheese, quartered

8 slider buns

Goetta is a mixture of pork, oats, and spices made into a sausage-like roll. When sliced and cooked on the Traeger, it gets crispy on the outside and tender on the inside. It's traditionally a breakfast meat, so you could have these sliders for breakfast, brunch, or everyone's favorite—breakfast for dinner. This recipe was inspired by my friend's son during a late-night camping adventure, so it's also the perfect late-night snack.

1. Turn the Traeger on and set the temperature to 350°F.

2. Slice the goetta into eight (¾-inch-thick) patties. In a small bowl, mix together the maple syrup and hot sauce.

3. Once the grill is preheated, place the slices of goetta on the grill grate for 12 to 14 minutes per side. Spoon some of the spicy syrup on top of the patties during the last minute of cooking and place a slice of cheese on each patty. Close the grill lid until the cheese melts.

4. Serve the goetta patties on the slider buns with the remaining spicy syrup.

> **SERVE WITH:** I highly recommend making these sliders at the same time as Loaded Potato Rounds (page 106) and having them as a side dish. The cook time and temperature are exactly the same and they pair perfectly together.

Reverse-Seared BBQ Pork Chops

SERVES 4 PEOPLE

PREP TIME: 10 minutes

COOK TIME: 45 minutes
to 1 hour

TEMPERATURE:
180°F and 500°F

---

1 tablespoon olive oil

4 bone-in pork chops
(1½ to 2 inches thick)

Kosher salt

Freshly ground black pepper

2 to 3 tablespoons store-
bought barbecue
seasoning, or BBQ
Dry Rub (page 125)

Barbecue sauce of
your choice, for
serving (optional)

Reverse searing is a cooking method that guarantees a moist and juicy pork chop each and every time. The pork chop is smoked low and slow, then seared at a higher temperature to lock in all the flavor and juices.

1. Turn the Traeger on and set the temperature to 180°F. For some models, this is the smoke setting. If your model has the super smoke option, turn that on.

2. Brush olive oil on both sides of the pork chops and season them with salt, pepper, and barbecue seasoning. Place the pork chops on the grill grates for 45 minutes to an hour, or until the internal temperature reaches 120°F.

3. Remove the pork chops and crank the heat dial to the highest setting, either 450 or 500°F depending on the model Traeger you have.

4. Once the grill is preheated, place the pork chops on the grill grate for 1½ to 2½ minutes per side, or until the internal temperature reaches 145°F.

SERVE WITH: If you choose to have these succulent pork chops with barbecue sauce, I suggest the Chipotle BBQ Sauce (page 133) or the Gochujang BBQ Sauce (page 129). Both are easy to make and a fun spin on traditional barbecue sauces.

Pork Belly Burnt Ends

SUGGESTED PELLETS: MAPLE, MESQUITE

SERVES 8 TO 10 PEOPLE

PREP TIME: 45 minutes

COOK TIME: 4 hours

TEMPERATURE: 225°F

---

8 to 10 pounds pork belly

½ cup olive oil

2 cups brown sugar

1 cup flavored seasoning of choice

2 cups barbecue sauce of choice

½ cup honey

4 tablespoons cold butter

My good friend Rich is the talented smoker behind this recipe. He came to my house and walked me step-by-step through his tried-and-true recipe for these amazing pork belly burnt ends. One might even call these luscious nuggets of pork belly "meat candy"—they're that good.

1. Trim some of the thicker pieces of fat from the pork belly, then cut it into 1- to 2-inch cubes with a good-quality sharp knife. Place the pork belly cubes in a large bowl and coat with the olive oil.

2. In a small bowl, whisk together the brown sugar and seasoning, then add to the bowl with the pork belly and toss to combine.

3. Turn the Traeger on and set the temperature to 225°F. Place the pork belly cubes on the grill grate for 3 hours, flipping them halfway through, until the internal temperature reaches 165°F.

4. In a bowl, whisk together the barbecue sauce, honey, and butter, until the butter breaks up into smaller pieces. Transfer the pork belly from the Traeger to a 9-by-13-inch foil pan and toss with the barbecue-honey mixture. Cover with foil and place the pan back on the Traeger for 1 hour.

VARIATION TIP: The conversation with Rich and my family when we were enjoying these pork belly bites was all about the different things you could do with leftovers. Some ideas included pork belly tacos and nachos, topping mac and cheese with pork belly, and also a pork belly egg roll dipped in barbecue sauce. Like many of the recipes in this book, the things you could do with these bites of meat candy are endless!

Duck with Orange-Cranberry Glaze, page 77

Poultry

Apricot-Glazed Chicken Thighs

SUGGESTED PELLETS: APPLE, CHERRY

SERVES 4 TO 6 PEOPLE

PREP TIME: 10 minutes, plus overnight marinating time

COOK TIME: 1½ to 2 hours

TEMPERATURE: 250°F

1¼ cups apricot jam or jelly

⅓ cup soy sauce

⅓ cup balsamic vinegar

⅓ cup honey

1 tablespoon garlic paste

1 teaspoon red pepper flakes

4 to 5 pounds chicken thighs (about 10 thighs)

Kosher salt

Freshly ground black pepper

Chicken thighs are a great cut of meat to cook on the Traeger. They're very budget-friendly and they always come out moist and yummy. This apricot glaze is the perfect complement for them.

1. To make the apricot glaze, in a bowl, whisk together the apricot jam, soy sauce, balsamic vinegar, honey, garlic paste, and red pepper flakes until evenly combined.

2. Trim the extra skin from the chicken thighs if needed, and put them in a gallon-size plastic bag. Add 1 cup of the apricot glaze mixture to the chicken thighs and massage the bag until the chicken is evenly coated. Marinate in the refrigerator overnight and store the remaining apricot glaze in a sealed container in the refrigerator.

3. Turn the Traeger on and set the temperature to 250°F. Once preheated, put the chicken thighs on the grill grate and sprinkle with salt and black pepper.

4. Cook for 1½ to 2 hours, flipping halfway through. Once the internal temperature reaches 165°F, remove from the grill and brush with the reserved apricot glaze. Serve with remaining apricot glaze.

VARIATION TIP: This glaze is excellent on pork tenderloin, pork chops, salmon, and chicken breasts. Follow the suggested cook times and temperatures in the chart on page 13. You can also use different jams and jellies such as peach, apple, and red pepper.

Smoked Chicken Corn Chowder

SUGGESTED PELLETS: HICKORY, MESQUITE

SERVES 6 TO 8 PEOPLE
PREP TIME: 15 minutes
COOK TIME: 1½ hours
TEMPERATURE: 250°F

---

2 pounds boneless, skinless chicken breast

1 pound red potatoes

1 onion, thickly sliced

1 jalapeño pepper

1 poblano pepper

1 red bell pepper

6 ears corn, shucked

2 tablespoons olive oil

Kosher salt

Freshly ground black pepper

4 garlic cloves, minced

5 cups chicken broth

1½ tablespoons Cajun seasoning

½ tablespoon Italian seasoning

8 ounces cream cheese

Optional: chives, tortilla strips

The chicken and veggies are smoked to perfection and then transformed into a unique spin on corn chowder in this recipe. This is comfort food at its finest, and perfect for when summer corn is in season. This chowder can be frozen and reheated as needed.

1. Turn the Traeger on and set the temperature to 250°F.

2. Put the chicken breast, potatoes, onion, jalapeño, poblano pepper, bell pepper, and corn on a baking sheet. Brush them with olive oil and season with salt and black pepper.

3. Once the grill is preheated, place the baking sheet on the grill grate for 1 hour.

4. After 1 hour, remove the chicken and veggies from the grate and set aside to let cool. Dice the chicken and onion slices. Remove the seeds and stems from the peppers and dice them, then slice the kernels off the corncobs.

5. In a large stockpot over medium heat, place the smoked chicken and veggies along with the garlic, chicken broth, Cajun seasoning, Italian seasoning, and cream cheese. Bring to a boil and simmer for 30 minutes, stirring a few times throughout. Taste for seasoning and add more salt and black pepper if needed.

6. If using, top with chives and tortilla strips and serve.

SMOKER SAVVY TIP: Plan ahead to make the Smoked Chicken Salad (page 78) or Poblano Chicken Enchiladas (page 80). Save some time and some pellets by cooking the chicken for the chicken salad or enchiladas at the same time as the chicken and veggies for the chowder.

Duck with Orange-Cranberry Glaze

SERVES 4 PEOPLE

PREP TIME: 15 minutes, plus overnight marinating time

COOK TIME: 3½ hours to 4 hours

TEMPERATURE: 225°F

---

1 (5-pound) duck

2 tablespoons kosher salt

2 teaspoons ground ginger, divided

1 teaspoon freshly ground black pepper

1 teaspoon garlic powder

½ cup orange juice

½ cup jellied cranberry sauce

1 tablespoon soy sauce

1 tablespoon honey

Orange is a classic flavor pairing with duck. The cranberry adds a little more zing and this glaze creates a showstopping presentation. Duck is a richer, fattier meat compared to chicken or turkey, so the amount of flavor it has is unmatched and something you have to experience. This recipe requires extra prep time because the skin needs to dry overnight, but it will be worth the wait.

1. The day before serving, pat the duck dry very well with paper towels. Use a sharp knife to make superficial cuts in the skin (being careful not to go all the way to the meat) in a crisscross pattern, or poke the skin with the tip of the knife all over. Rub the salt, 1 teaspoon of ginger, the pepper, and garlic powder all over the duck. Place the duck, uncovered, in the refrigerator overnight.

2. To make the orange-cranberry glaze, in a saucepan over medium heat, stir together the orange juice, cranberry sauce, soy sauce, honey, and remaining 1 teaspoon of ginger. Stir until the cranberry sauce is melted and the mixture has the consistency of a glaze.

3. When ready to cook the duck, turn the Traeger on and set the temperature to 225°F. Place the duck on the grill grate for 3½ to 4 hours or until the internal temperature reaches 165°F. Brush the duck with the orange-cranberry glaze during the last hour a few times.

4. For a crispy skin, you can broil the duck in the oven for a few minutes. After cooking, let the duck rest for 10 minutes before serving with the remaining orange-cranberry glaze.

Smoked Chicken Salad

SUGGESTED PELLETS: HICKORY, MESQUITE

SERVES 8 PEOPLE

PREP TIME: 10 minutes

COOK TIME: 45 minutes
to 1 hour

TEMPERATURE: 250°F

---

2 pounds boneless, skinless
chicken breasts

1 tablespoon olive oil

Kosher salt

Freshly ground black pepper

1 cup mayonnaise

3 celery stalks, minced

3 scallions, sliced

Smoking chicken on the Traeger makes the tastiest chicken salad around! If you smoke the chicken at the same time as another recipe that cooks at 250°F, it's a great time- and pellet-saving trick.

1. Turn the Traeger on and set the temperature to 250°F.

2. Coat the chicken with olive oil and season both sides with salt and pepper. Place the chicken on the grill grate and cook for 45 minutes to an hour, until the internal temperature reaches 165°F.

3. Remove the chicken from the grill, let cool, then dice it and place in a large bowl. Add the mayonnaise, celery, and scallions. Taste for seasoning and add more salt and pepper if needed.

VARIATION TIP: The smoke flavor that the Traeger gives the chicken is the star in this otherwise basic recipe. Get as creative as you'd like by adding fresh herbs, Cajun seasoning, grapes, dried cranberries, candied pecans, or even some smoked red pepper to your chicken salad.

Lemonade Chicken Drumsticks

SUGGESTED PELLETS: APPLE, CHERRY

SERVES 4 PEOPLE

PREP TIME: 10 minutes, plus overnight marinating time

COOK TIME: 2 hours

TEMPERATURE: 250°F

---

2 to 3 pounds chicken drumsticks

¾ cup brown sugar

½ cup soy sauce

¼ cup freshly squeezed lemon juice (about 2 lemons)

Fresh lemon juice mixed with some sweet brown sugar creates a lovely marinade for these chicken drumsticks that remind me of lemonade. My kids and husband request these drumsticks quite often and they devour them each and every time.

1. Put the chicken in a gallon-size plastic bag. Add the brown sugar, soy sauce, and lemon juice and massage the bag until the brown sugar is dissolved and chicken is evenly coated. Marinate in the refrigerator overnight.

2. When ready to cook the chicken, turn the Traeger on and set the temperature to 250°F.

3. Place the chicken on the grill grates for 2 hours, or until internal temperature reaches 165°F, flipping halfway through cooking.

> **VARIATION TIP: If you want a more quick-cooking meal, set the temperature of the Traeger to 400°F and grill these drumsticks for about 30 minutes, flipping them a few times throughout.**

Poblano Chicken Enchiladas

SUGGESTED PELLETS: APPLE, HICKORY

SERVES 4 TO 6 PEOPLE
PREP TIME: 15 minutes
COOK TIME: 30 minutes
TEMPERATURE: 400°F

---

2 poblano peppers, seeded, stems removed, and diced

2 tablespoons olive oil, divided

1 (14-ounce) can green enchilada sauce

1 cup sour cream

2 cups shredded cheese of choice, divided

3 cups cooked, shredded chicken

6 fajita-size tortillas (corn or flour)

I am always looking for creative ways to use leftover shredded chicken, whether it's from a smoked chicken or a store-bought rotisserie chicken. These enchiladas are easy to make on the Traeger, and even better if you are using leftover smoked chicken that was also made on the grill!

1. In a skillet, put the poblano peppers and 1 tablespoon of olive oil over medium heat. Cook for 4 to 5 minutes, then set aside and let cool.

2. Turn the Traeger on and set the temperature to 400°F.

3. In a bowl, put the enchilada sauce, sour cream, and poblanos peppers and mix. In a separate bowl, combine 1 cup of the poblano mixture and 1 cup of cheese with the shredded chicken.

4. Spread the remaining 1 tablespoon of olive oil in the bottom of a 9-by-13-inch casserole dish or foil pan. Then spread a spoonful of the enchilada sauce mixture on the bottom to prevent sticking.

5. Divide the chicken mixture into each tortilla and roll them up one by one. Place the enchiladas in the casserole dish, seam-side down. Pour the rest of the enchilada and sour cream mixture over top and sprinkle the remaining 1 cup of cheese over top.

6. Place the casserole dish on the grill grate and cook for 30 minutes, then serve hot.

SMOKER SAVVY TIP: Plan ahead when making this dish and a day or two before you make it, smoke the poblano peppers at the same time you cook another meal. They will add more smoked flavor to the dish and eliminate the need to cook them in a skillet. Just put them directly on the grill grate at 225 to 300°F for 45 minutes to an hour, then dice them and store in the refrigerator until you are ready to make these enchiladas.

Honey-Sriracha Chicken Breast

SERVES 4 PEOPLE

PREP TIME: 10 minutes

COOK TIME: 8 to 12 minutes

TEMPERATURE: 450°F

¾ cup honey

2 to 4 tablespoons sriracha

1 tablespoon soy sauce

1 tablespoon olive oil

4 chicken breasts

Kosher salt

Freshly ground black pepper

This sweet and spicy sauce turns boring chicken breasts into something extraordinary! It's a quick and easy meal to prepare, and dinner is ready in just a few minutes. Some of the sauce is brushed on the chicken during cooking, which creates a gorgeous glaze and becomes caramelized on the Traeger. The rest makes the perfect dipping sauce.

1. Turn the Traeger on and set the temperature to 450°F.

2. To make the honey-sriracha sauce, in a small bowl, whisk together the honey, sriracha to taste, and soy sauce until combined.

3. Brush the olive oil on both sides of the chicken and season the chicken with salt and pepper.

4. Place the chicken breasts on the grill grate and cook for 4 to 6 minutes per side. Brush the chicken with the honey-sriracha sauce during the last 2 minutes of cooking.

5. Serve the chicken with the remaining sauce for dipping.

> **VARIATION TIP:** This honey-sriracha sauce can be used on any cut of chicken, including boneless chicken thighs, chicken wings, or drumsticks. Just follow the cooking times on the chart on page 13 and brush the sauce on during the last few minutes of cooking.

Whole Smoked BBQ Chicken

SERVES 4 PEOPLE

PREP TIME: 10 minutes

COOK TIME: 4 to 5 hours

TEMPERATURE: 250°F

---

1 whole chicken (about 5 pounds)

4 tablespoons dry barbecue seasoning, store bought or BBQ Dry Rub (page 125)

Barbecue sauce, for serving (optional)

Cooking a whole chicken will quickly become one of your new favorite foods to make on the Traeger. It's one of the easiest things to make on it, and you can switch up the seasoning and sauces to create many different flavors. You can even experiment with flavor injections to add even more yumminess to the chicken.

1. Turn the Traeger on and set the temperature to 250°F.

2. Pat the chicken dry with paper towels. Rub the barbecue seasoning on all sides of the chicken, including under the skin.

3. Place the chicken directly on the grill grate for 4 to 5 hours, or until the internal temperature is 165°F.

4. Let the chicken rest 10 minutes before shredding or slicing. Serve with barbecue sauce (if using).

> **SMOKER SAVVY TIP: Make two or even three chickens at once to feed a crowd. Or use the leftover shredded chicken throughout the week in other meals. It's perfect on salads, wraps, tacos, or in the Poblano Chicken Enchiladas (page 80). Adding more chickens will not increase the cook time; they will all still cook in 4 to 5 hours.**

Quail Stuffed with Apple and Sage

SUGGESTED PELLETS: APPLE, MAPLE

SERVES 4 PEOPLE

PREP TIME: 15 minutes

COOK TIME: 45 minutes

TEMPERATURE: 275°F

---

2 tablespoons olive oil, divided

1 onion, diced

1 apple, diced

Kosher salt

Freshly ground black pepper

2 garlic cloves, minced

3 tablespoons butter

¼ cup fresh chopped sage

3 slices bread, cubed

8 whole quail

Quail is very tender, juicy, and extremely easy to cook on the Traeger. The stuffing brings even more flavor to this dish. Because quail are so small, they cook quickly, which is a plus for a busy weeknight. If you're making this recipe for guests, plan on serving two quail per adult.

1. To make the apple and sage stuffing, in a large skillet over medium heat, place 1 tablespoon of olive oil, the onion, apple, and a pinch each of salt and pepper. Cook for 4 to 5 minutes, then add the garlic, butter, and sage. Stir and cook for 1 minute more. Remove from the heat, then fold in the bread.

2. While the stuffing cools, turn the Traeger on and set the temperature to 275°F.

3. Place an equal amount of stuffing into the cavity of each quail. Brush the outside of the quail with the remaining 1 tablespoon of olive oil and season the quail with salt and pepper on all sides.

4. Place the stuffed quail on the grill grate for 45 minutes, or until the internal temperature is 150°F.

> **SERVE WITH: The Green Beans with Bacon (page 113) is a great side dish to serve with the quail. It will cook on the Traeger at the same time and temperature. The bacon in the green beans is a perfect complement to the apple and sage stuffing.**

Buffalo Chicken Sliders

SUGGESTED PELLETS: APPLE, PECAN

SERVES 4 PEOPLE

PREP TIME: 10 minutes, plus marinating time

COOK TIME: 8 to 12 minutes

TEMPERATURE:
450°F or 500°F

---

4 boneless, skinless chicken thighs

1 cup buffalo sauce, divided

Kosher salt

Freshly ground black pepper

8 slider buns

Optional toppings: blue cheese crumbles, ranch dressing, more Buffalo sauce, lettuce

These sliders are a fun and easy dinner, or can even be served as a game-day snack. Using boneless, skinless chicken thighs makes them extra juicy and flavorful, but you can easily substitute chicken breasts if you prefer. You can also enjoy the chicken by itself instead of serving on slider buns. This Buffalo chicken is so easy and tasty any way you have it!

1. Cut each chicken thigh in half so they are the perfect size for the slider buns. Put them in a gallon-size plastic bag with ½ cup of Buffalo sauce and a pinch each of salt and pepper. Massage the bag until the chicken is coated evenly, then marinate in the refrigerator for 1 hour or overnight.

2. When ready to grill the chicken, turn the Traeger on and set the temperature to 450°F or 500°F, whatever your grill's highest temperature is.

3. Put the chicken on the grill grate and cook for 4 to 6 minutes per side. Brush with the remaining Buffalo sauce during the last few minutes of cooking.

4. Serve the chicken on the slider buns with your choice of toppings.

> **VARIATION TIP: You can make these chicken sliders with any flavor in place of the Buffalo, including your favorite barbecue sauce or the Honey-Balsamic Marinade (page 128).**

Pickle-Brined Chicken Thighs

SUGGESTED PELLETS: APPLE, HICKORY

SERVES 4 TO 6 PEOPLE

PREP TIME: 10 minutes, plus overnight marinating time

COOK TIME: 1½ to 2 hours

TEMPERATURE: 250°F

---

4 to 5 pounds chicken thighs (about 10 thighs)

2 cups pickle juice

½ cup brown sugar

Pinch seasoned salt

I bet I caught your attention with the title of this recipe. You might not think of using pickle juice to brine meat, but it gives a truly unique flavor to the chicken with just a subtle hint of dill flavor.

1. Trim the extra skin from the chicken thighs if needed and place them in a gallon-size plastic bag. Add the pickle juice and brown sugar to the bag and massage until the brown sugar dissolves. Place in the refrigerator to marinate overnight.

2. When ready to make the chicken, turn the Traeger on and set the temperature to 250°F.

3. Remove the chicken thighs from the marinade, pat them dry with paper towels, and sprinkle with seasoned salt on all sides. Place the chicken on the grill grate for 1½ to 2 hours, flipping halfway through until the internal temperature reaches 165°F.

> **VARIATION TIP: If you want a more quick-cooking meal, use boneless, skinless chicken thighs or chicken breasts. They will cook on the Traeger set to 450°F or 500°F for 4 to 6 minutes per side.**

Turkey Smothered with Creole Butter

SERVES 8 PEOPLE

PREP TIME: 15 minutes

COOK TIME: 6 to 8 hours

TEMPERATURE: 250°F

---

1 stick butter

3 tablespoons Cajun or Creole seasoning, divided

1 (14- to 16-pound) turkey

Kosher salt

Freshly ground black pepper

1 onion, cut into wedges

1 apple, cut into wedges

Injecting this turkey with Creole butter makes it super flavorful and juicy throughout the whole bird. This is a great holiday recipe, perfect for feeding a crowd, and wonderful to enjoy as a leftover turkey sandwich. You will need a meat injector, which you can find at most hardware stores, the cooking section of larger grocery stores, or online.

1. Turn the Traeger on and set the temperature to 250°F.

2. In a bowl, melt the butter and mix in 2 tablespoons of Cajun seasoning. Fill the meat injector with three-quarters of the butter mixture and inject it into several parts of the turkey. Brush the remaining butter mixture over all sides of the turkey and season with the remaining 1 tablespoon of Cajun or Creole seasoning, the salt, and pepper.

3. Stuff the turkey cavity with the onion and apple.

4. Place the turkey on the grill grate for 6 to 8 hours (about 20 to 25 minutes per pound) or until the internal temperature reaches 165°F.

> **SMOKER SAVVY TIP:** With such a long cook time for this turkey, make sure you are starting with a clean grill and plenty of pellets. Also, I suggest using the meat probe throughout so you can monitor the temperature and adjust as needed.

Bacon-Wrapped Chicken Bombs

SERVES 4 TO 6 PEOPLE

PREP TIME: 15 minutes

COOK TIME: 40 to 45 minutes

TEMPERATURE: 375°F

---

6 boneless, skinless chicken thighs

1½ tablespoons BBQ Dry Rub (page 125), divided

Kosher salt

Freshly ground black pepper

6 (1-inch) cubes cheddar cheese

12 slices regular-cut bacon

Barbecue sauce, for serving (optional)

Boneless chicken thighs stuffed with cheese and wrapped in bacon—are you drooling yet? The explosion of flavor with these chicken bombs is unbelievable! They are especially good dipped in barbecue sauce.

1. Turn the Traeger on and set the temperature to 375°F.

2. Pound the chicken thighs if they are fairly thick. Season both sides with 1 tablespoon of dry rub and a pinch each of salt and pepper.

3. Place a cube of cheese in the center of each thigh and wrap the chicken around the cheese. Wrap each thigh with two slices of bacon and season the outside with the remaining ½ tablespoon of dry rub.

4. Place the chicken on the grill grate and cook for 40 to 45 minutes. Use tongs to turn them a few times as they cook.

5. Serve the chicken with barbecue sauce (if using).

> **VARIATION TIP:** Mix this recipe up by using a different seasoning in place of the BBQ Dry Rub such as a Cajun seasoning or the Caribbean Jerk Dry Rub (page 127). You can also use pepper Jack or Swiss cheese in place of the cheddar.

Rosemary-Balsamic Duck

SUGGESTED PELLETS: MAPLE, PECAN

SERVES 4 PEOPLE

PREP TIME: 15 minutes

COOK TIME: 8 to 12 minutes

TEMPERATURE: 450°F

½ cup balsamic vinegar

½ cup orange juice

1 chopped rosemary sprig

3 tablespoons butter

Kosher salt

Freshly ground black pepper

4 duck breasts, skin scored

Duck breast comes out perfectly grilled every time on the Traeger. To achieve the crispy skin on your duck breast, score the fat with a sharp knife, making sure to only cut slices in the fat and not the meat. The rosemary-balsamic glaze complements the duck beautifully and would also be perfect with chicken and pork.

1. To make the rosemary-balsamic glaze, in a small saucepan over high heat, combine the balsamic vinegar, orange juice, and rosemary. Once boiling, reduce the heat to low and simmer for 4 to 6 minutes until the sauce reduces and thickens, stirring a few times. Remove from the heat and stir in the butter and a pinch each of salt and pepper until the butter is melted.

2. Turn the Traeger on and set the temperature to 450°F.

3. Season the duck on both sides with salt and pepper. Once the grill is preheated, place the duck breasts, skin-side down, on the grill grate for 6 to 8 minutes. Brush each breast with the rosemary-balsamic glaze, then flip them. Cook for another 2 to 4 minutes, brushing with the glaze a few more times.

4. Serve the duck alongside the remaining rosemary-balsamic glaze.

> **SMOKER SAVVY TIP: If you prefer a smokier flavor, you can cook the duck breast at 250°F on the Traeger for 1 to 1½ hours, skin-side up. For a crispy skin, sear the breasts, skin-side down, in a cast-iron skillet until the skin is crisp.**

Teriyaki Turkey Breast Tenderloin

SUGGESTED PELLETS: CHERRY, PECAN

SERVES 4 PEOPLE

PREP TIME: 10 minutes

COOK TIME: 20 to 25 minutes

TEMPERATURE: 400°F

---

1 boneless turkey tenderloin (about 1½ to 2 pounds)

Kosher salt

Freshly ground black pepper

1 cup teriyaki sauce

Turkey tenderloin is a great cut of meat and a wonderful way to enjoy turkey as a quick and easy weeknight meal. The teriyaki sauce pairs very well with the turkey, and by using store-bought teriyaki sauce, dinner is simple and served up in no time.

1. Turn the Traeger on and set the temperature to 400°F.

2. Season the turkey tenderloin with salt and pepper. Once the grill is preheated, put the turkey on the grill grate for 20 to 25 minutes, flipping halfway through. Brush the turkey with the teriyaki sauce a few times throughout and cook until the internal temperature reaches 165°F.

3. Serve with the remaining teriyaki sauce on the side.

> **SERVE WITH: Try making the Pull-Apart Garlic Bread (page 111) as a side dish to accompany the turkey. It has a very similar cook time and temperature as the turkey, so you'll have a complete meal all done on the Traeger.**

Blackened Fish Tacos, page 101

CHAPTER 6

Seafood

Spicy BBQ Shrimp

SUGGESTED PELLETS: ALDER, HICKORY

SERVES 4 PEOPLE

PREP TIME: 10 minutes

COOK TIME: 30 to 40 minutes

TEMPERATURE: 250°F

---

1 pound jumbo shrimp, peeled and deveined

1 tablespoon olive oil

1 to 2 tablespoons BBQ Dry Rub (page 125)

Pinch cayenne pepper

This shrimp is great for a snack or light meal. You can also use it to make tacos, or to top a salad or nachos. You can control the amount of spice by adding as much or as little of the cayenne pepper as you like. You'll love the wonderful smoky, barbecue flavor!

1. Turn the Traeger on and set the temperature to 250°F.

2. In a large bowl, toss the shrimp with the olive oil, dry rub, and cayenne pepper to taste until the shrimp is coated evenly.

3. Place the shrimp on the grill grate for 30 to 40 minutes, flipping halfway through.

VARIATION TIP: You can easily switch up this shrimp recipe by using different seasonings such as Cajun, Caribbean Jerk Dry Rub (page 127), or the Cilantro-Lime Marinade (page 131).

Bourbon-Candied Salmon Bites

SUGGESTED PELLETS: ALDER, MESQUITE

SERVES 4 TO 6 PEOPLE

PREP TIME: 15 minutes, plus marinating time

COOK TIME: 3 to 4 hours

TEMPERATURE: 180°F

---

2 pounds salmon fillets

1 cup bourbon

½ cup brown sugar

½ cup water

¼ cup kosher salt

½ cup pure maple syrup

These are a treat you will just have to experience for yourself. The texture and flavor are unbelievable, and you can enjoy them warm or cold. The salmon bites will stay good in a sealed container in the refrigerator for up to a week, but I can assure you they won't last that long.

1. Remove the skin from the salmon and cut into 1- to 2-inch pieces.

2. In a large container or bowl, mix together the bourbon, brown sugar, water, and salt. Stir until the brown sugar and salt dissolve; this may take a few minutes and it's okay if they don't completely dissolve before adding the salmon. Add the salmon bites to this mixture, cover, and refrigerate for 8 to 10 hours.

3. Remove the salmon bites, pat dry, and place them on a baking sheet or foil. Let them air-dry for an hour.

4. Turn the Traeger on and set the temperature to 180°F.

5. Place the baking sheet or foil with the salmon on the grill grate for 3 to 4 hours. Brush with the maple syrup a few times during the last hour.

> **VARIATION TIP: If you don't want to add bourbon, use 1½ cups of water. You can also use whiskey or tequila in place of the bourbon for a different flavor profile. Another option is to brush the salmon bites with honey in place of the maple syrup.**

Lobster Tails with Herb Butter

SUGGESTED PELLETS: ALDER, OAK

SERVES 4 PEOPLE

PREP TIME: 10 minutes

COOK TIME: 45 minutes to 1 hour

TEMPERATURE: 225°F

---

4 lobster tails

1½ sticks butter, divided

1 rosemary sprig

1 thyme sprig

Lobster tails are so easy to make on the Traeger and are made extra succulent with the herb butter, which also picks up the wood-fired flavor. This recipe is perfect for a date night in, or an extra-special occasion.

1. Turn the Traeger on and set the temperature to 225°F.

2. Place the lobster tails, cut-side up, in a cast-iron skillet or 9-inch square foil pan. Cut up 1 stick of the butter into smaller pieces and place around the lobster tails in the pan along with the rosemary and thyme.

3. Place the pan on the grill grate for 45 minutes to an hour. Spoon the herb butter over the lobster tails a few times as they cook.

4. Once the lobster is done, melt the remaining ½ stick of butter and serve alongside the lobster for dipping.

SERVE WITH: Turn your lobster dinner into a surf-and-turf meal by making one of the steak recipes in chapter 3. Remove the lobster once it's cooked, then crank the Traeger up to 450°F or 500°F to grill the perfect steak.

Garlic-Soy Tuna Steaks

SERVES 4 PEOPLE

PREP TIME: 10 minutes, plus marinating time

COOK TIME: 8 to 12 minutes

TEMPERATURE: 450°F

---

4 yellowfin tuna steaks

½ cup soy sauce

2 tablespoons olive oil

3 or 4 garlic cloves, minced

1 tablespoon honey

Tuna is a very meaty fish, making it perfect for grilling at higher temperatures. This recipe is very easy to make and the garlic-soy marinade brings maximum flavor. Yellowfin tuna can be found fresh at the seafood counter at most grocery stores or in the frozen seafood section.

1. Poke the tuna steaks all over a few times with a fork, then place them in a gallon-size plastic bag.

2. To make the garlic-soy marinade, in a small bowl, whisk together the soy sauce, olive oil, garlic, and honey until combined. Pour half of this mixture into the bag with the tuna and massage the bag until the fish is evenly coated. Cover the remaining garlic-soy mixture and place in the refrigerator along with the bagged fish to marinate for 1 to 2 hours.

3. Turn the Traeger on and set the temperature to 450°F. Remove the tuna from the refrigerator and discard the marinade. Once the grill is preheated, place the tuna on the grill grates and cook for 4 to 6 minutes per side. Brush with the reserved garlic-soy sauce during the last few minutes of cooking.

4. Serve with any remaining garlic-soy sauce for dipping.

> **SERVE WITH:** These tuna steaks would also be amazing with the Honey-Balsamic Marinade (page 128) or the Cilantro-Lime Marinade (page 131). Use half of whatever sauce you like to marinate the tuna, and save the other half for brushing over top of the fish during cooking and to use as a dipping sauce.

Cajun and Garlic Butter Shrimp Pasta

SUGGESTED PELLETS: MESQUITE, ALDER

SERVES 6 PEOPLE

PREP TIME: 15 minutes

COOK TIME: 1 hour to
1 hour 15 minutes

TEMPERATURE: 225°F

2½ sticks butter, melted

6 garlic cloves, minced

2 tablespoons Cajun
seasoning

2 tablespoons freshly
squeezed lime juice

½ cup chopped fresh
parsley

Kosher salt

Freshly ground black pepper

2 pounds jumbo shrimp,
peeled and deveined

1 pound pasta of choice

This smoked pasta dish really brings the wow factor, especially when serving to dinner guests. It's one of my favorite comfort food meals made on the Traeger. It reheats really well, too, if you are lucky enough to have leftovers.

1. Turn the Traeger on and set the temperature to 225°F.

2. Place the butter, garlic, Cajun seasoning, lime juice, parsley, and a pinch each of salt and pepper in a cast-iron skillet or 9-by-13-inch foil pan.

3. Add the shrimp to the pan and toss until the shrimp are coated. Place the pan on the grill grate and cook for 45 minutes to an hour, tossing the shrimp a few times throughout.

4. Boil the pasta according to the package directions, drain, then add the cooked pasta to the pan with the shrimp. Toss everything to combine and continue to cook on the Traeger for 15 minutes more.

SMOKER SAVVY TIP: For even more smoke flavor, turn the super smoke feature on during the last 15 minutes, if your Traeger has that feature. It will blast even more wood-fired flavor into the pasta!

Lemon Pepper Whole Trout

SUGGESTED PELLETS: APPLE, HICKORY

SERVES 4 PEOPLE
PREP TIME: 10 minutes
COOK TIME: 14 to 16 minutes
TEMPERATURE: 400°F

---

2 whole trout (about 10 ounces each, cavity completely cleaned)

Kosher salt

Freshly ground black pepper

1 tablespoon lemon pepper seasoning

1 lemon, sliced thinly into rounds, plus lemon wedges (optional)

3 garlic cloves, minced

2 dill sprigs

2 thyme sprigs

1 tablespoon olive oil

Serving a whole trout is such a beautiful presentation. This trout is stuffed with lemon, garlic, and herbs, creating a very flavorful fish that is tender and flaky. You can plan on about half a fish to be one serving, and you can easily double or triple this recipe if feeding a crowd.

1. Turn the Traeger on and set the temperature to 400°F.

2. Season the trout with salt, black pepper, and lemon pepper seasoning on the outside and inside of the fish. Stuff each cavity with the lemon slices, garlic, dill, and thyme. Brush olive oil on the outside of each fish.

3. Place the trout on the grill grate and cook for 7 to 8 minutes per side.

4. Serve with lemon wedges on the side, (if using).

VARIATION TIP: **If you want more of a smoked fish, prepare the fish in the same way but cook it at 200°F for 2 to 3 hours, or until the internal temperature reaches 160°F. The Garlic-Herb Compound Butter (page 132) would be a great accompaniment to this trout.**

Crab Cakes with Spicy Mayo

SUGGESTED PELLETS: MESQUITE, ALDER

SERVES 4 PEOPLE

PREP TIME: 20 minutes, plus 1 hour refrigerating time

COOK TIME: 20 minutes

TEMPERATURE: 450°F or 500°F

---

3 tablespoons olive oil, divided

1 red bell pepper, seeded, stemmed, and diced

1 onion, diced

3 celery stalks, diced

Kosher salt

Freshly ground black pepper

Pinch red pepper flakes

3 garlic cloves, minced

2 tablespoons freshly squeezed lemon juice, divided

1½ tablespoons seafood seasoning, divided

1 pound cooked jumbo lump crabmeat

2 eggs, beaten

1 cup panko bread crumbs

1 cup mayonnaise

A few dashes hot sauce of choice

Lemon wedges, for serving (optional)

This is the tried-and-true recipe developed by my incredible dad, which he has perfected over the years. When we made these crab cakes together on the Traeger, even he agreed the wood-fired flavor made them extra special. The simple spicy mayo is the perfect sauce for these fabulous crab cakes—don't skip it!

1. In a large skillet, heat 1 tablespoon of olive oil over medium-high heat. Once hot, add the bell pepper, onion, celery, and a pinch each of salt, black pepper, and red pepper flakes. Cook for 8 to 10 minutes, stirring occasionally.

2. Add the garlic, 1 tablespoon of lemon juice, and ½ tablespoon of seafood seasoning and cook for 1 minute more. Remove from the heat and set the mixture aside to cool. (Cooling is important because if you add the eggs while it's still hot, the eggs will cook and not bind the crab cakes together properly.)

3. Once the mixture has cooled, add the crabmeat, eggs, and bread crumbs. Gently mix this together and form eight patties with your hands. Place them on a tray or baking sheet and refrigerate for 1 hour.

4. When ready to make the crab cakes, place a cast-iron skillet or baking sheet on the grill grate, then turn the Traeger on and set the temperature to the highest setting, either 450 or 500°F depending on the model Traeger you have.

5. Once it reaches the highest temperature, wait another 10 minutes to let the skillet preheat.

6. Drizzle the remaining 2 tablespoons of olive oil into the skillet or and place the crab cakes in it, being careful not to crowd them.

7. Flip the crab cakes after 10 minutes and cook for 10 minutes more. While the crab cakes cook, mix together the mayonnaise, hot sauce, remaining 1 tablespoon of lemon juice, and remaining 1 tablespoon of seafood seasoning.

8. Serve the crab cakes with the spicy mayo on the side and lemon wedges (if using).

SMOKER SAVVY TIP: When we tested this recipe, we found that we achieved a better sear on the crab cakes with the cast-iron skillet compared to the baking sheet. You may need to use two cast-iron skillets depending on the size you have. If you only have one cast-iron skillet, you can place both a cast-iron skillet and baking sheet on the grill to make sure there's enough room for all of the crab cakes.

Blackened Fish Tacos

SUGGESTED PELLETS: MESQUITE, HICKORY

SERVES 4 PEOPLE

PREP TIME: 10 minutes

COOK TIME: 8 to 10 minutes

TEMPERATURE:
450°F or 500°F

---

4 tilapia fillets

2 tablespoons blackened seasoning

1 tablespoon olive oil

8-12 Tortillas of choice (flour or corn)

Optional toppings: lettuce, salsa, pickled jalapeño peppers, guacamole, etc.

These fish tacos are easy to cook and make for such a fun dinner. Set out all the fixings and everyone can build their own tacos just the way they like. I mix tartar sauce with my favorite hot sauce to bring a spicy kick to these already delicious tacos.

1. Place a cast-iron skillet or baking sheet on the grill grate, then turn the Traeger on and set the temperature to the highest setting, either 450 or 500°F depending on the model of your grill.

2. Sprinkle the blackened seasoning on both sides of the tilapia.

3. When the grill reaches temperature, wait another 10 minutes so the skillet or baking sheet is nice and hot.

4. Drizzle the olive oil into the skillet or baking sheet and place the tilapia fillets on top of the oil. Cook the tilapia for 4 to 5 minutes per side. Place the tortillas on the grill grates for a minute or two to warm them.

5. Remove the fish from the grill, flake it into smaller pieces, and assemble the tacos with your choice of toppings.

SERVE WITH: Plan ahead to make the Smoked Salsa (page 112) to put on these tacos. The salsa would also make a great side dish for the tacos served with some chips.

Ginger-Soy Mahimahi with Bang Bang Sauce

SUGGESTED PELLETS: APPLE, MESQUITE

SERVES 4 PEOPLE

PREP TIME: 10 minutes, plus marinating time

COOK TIME: 12 to 16 minutes

TEMPERATURE: 400°F

---

4 mahimahi fillets

¼ cup soy sauce

1 tablespoon olive oil

1 tablespoon ginger paste

½ tablespoon garlic paste

½ cup mayonnaise

½ cup sweet Thai chile sauce

2 tablespoons sriracha

Mahimahi is a great fish for the grill because it's firm enough to not fall apart on the grill grate like some other flakier fishes might. The ginger-soy marinade is nearly universal and can easily be used on any cut of meat. But what really makes this dish extraordinary is the homemade bang bang sauce. You'll want to put it on everything!

1. Place the mahimahi fillets in a gallon-size plastic bag. In a small bowl, whisk together the soy sauce, olive oil, ginger paste, and garlic paste until combined, then add the sauce to the bag with the mahimahi. Massage the bag until the fish is coated. Marinate for 1 hour in the refrigerator.

2. Turn the Traeger on and set the temperature to 400°F. Once preheated, put the fish on the grill grate for 6 to 8 minutes per side.

3. While the fish cooks, make the bang bang sauce. In a small bowl, mix together the mayonnaise, chile sauce, and sriracha until combined.

4. Serve the mahimahi with the bang bang sauce on the side.

> **SERVE WITH:** For a complete meal all cooked on the Traeger, try the Cajun Garlic Butter Corn on the Cob (page 108). The corn and the mahimahi cook at the same time and temperature.

Hot Smoked Salmon

SERVES 6 TO 8 PEOPLE

PREP TIME: 10 minutes, plus curing time

COOK TIME: 3 to 4 hours

TEMPERATURE: 180°F

1 cup brown sugar

½ cup kosher salt

1 (3-pound) salmon fillet

Hot smoked salmon is a must-try! It's perfect to use in appetizers such as crostini, bagels topped with cream cheese and smoked salmon, or in smoked salmon dip. It's also great to add to pasta with an Alfredo cream sauce, and it's addicting just to snack on by itself, too.

1. In a small bowl, mix together the brown sugar and salt. Spread a thin layer of this mixture in the bottom of a 9-by-13-inch casserole dish. Place the salmon fillet over the top and then cover the salmon with the rest of the brown sugar mixture. Cover and refrigerate for 10 to 12 hours.

2. Remove the salmon from the refrigerator and pat dry very well. Let it sit out and air-dry for 2 hours.

3. Turn the Traeger on and set the temperature to 180°F. Place the salmon on the grill grate for 3 to 4 hours.

> **SMOKER SAVVY TIP:** Air-drying the salmon allows a film called a pellicle to form on the outer layer of the salmon. This will increase the wood-fired flavor your fish will get from the grill and also prevents it from tasting too salty from curing with the dry brine, so make sure to allow time for this important step.

Jalapeño-Cheddar Corn Bread, page 109

Sides

Loaded Potato Rounds

SUGGESTED PELLETS: ALDER, APPLE

SERVES 4 TO 6 PEOPLE
PREP TIME: 5 minutes
COOK TIME: 30 to
40 minutes
TEMPERATURE: 350°F

2 russet potatoes

2 tablespoons olive oil

Kosher salt

Freshly ground black pepper

1½ cups shredded cheese
of choice

6 slices cooked,
crumbled bacon

Optional toppings: sour
cream, chives

This is the perfect potato side dish for burgers and steaks. Thin-sliced potatoes are grilled and then topped with cheese and bacon. They're super easy to make at the same time as your main dish on the Traeger and always a huge hit.

1. Turn the Traeger on and set the temperature to 350°F.

2. Slice the potatoes into quarter-inch rounds. Brush both sides with olive oil and season with salt and pepper.

3. Once the grill is preheated, lay the potatoes in a single layer on the grill grate.

4. Close the lid and grill for 15 to 20 minutes, then flip them, close the lid, and grill for an additional 15 to 20 minutes.

5. Top the potatoes with the shredded cheese and bacon. Close the lid and allow the cheese to melt.

6. If using, top with sour cream and chives and serve.

VARIATION TIP: The possibilities for topping these potato rounds are endless. You can top them with leftover pulled pork and cheddar cheese, garlic and Parmesan cheese, or even serve them plain with your favorite dipping sauce.

BBQ Baked Beans

SUGGESTED PELLETS: HICKORY, MESQUITE

SERVES 8 PEOPLE

PREP TIME: 10 minutes

COOK TIME: 1½ to 2 hours

TEMPERATURE: 250°F

---

3 (28-ounce) cans
   baked beans

¾ cup barbecue sauce
   of choice

½ cup yellow mustard

½ cup brown sugar

2 tablespoons
   Worcestershire sauce

These beans make an excellent side dish served with any large cut of meat such as pulled pork, pork tenderloin, or brisket. They cook in a cast-iron skillet or foil pan at the same time as your main dish right on the Traeger.

1. Turn the Traeger on and set the temperature to 250°F.

2. Pour the beans into a 10-inch cast-iron skillet or 9-by-13-inch foil pan. Add the barbecue sauce, mustard, brown sugar, and Worcestershire sauce. Stir until combined.

3. Place the pan on the grill for 1½ to 2 hours, stirring a few times throughout.

> **VARIATION TIP:** Add cooked, crumbled bacon or leftover pulled pork or brisket to these beans to bring even more flavor.

Cajun Garlic Butter Corn on the Cob

SUGGESTED PELLETS: ALDER, HICKORY

SERVES 6 PEOPLE

PREP TIME: 5 minutes

COOK TIME: 10 to 12 minutes
or 45 to 50 minutes

TEMPERATURE:
225°F or 400°F

---

2 tablespoons melted butter

½ tablespoon garlic paste

1 tablespoon Cajun
 seasoning, divided

Kosher salt

Freshly ground black pepper

6 ears corn on the cob,
 shucked

Fresh corn on the cob brushed with a Cajun garlic butter is one of the easiest side dishes to prepare on the Traeger. The wood-fired flavor the grill gives this corn on the cob is outstanding. Choose the temperature based on what else you are cooking so everything is ready at the same time.

1. Turn the Traeger on and set the temperature to either 225°F or 400°F (depending on what else you're cooking, or if you want low and slow or a quick grilled corn).

2. In a bowl, mix the butter, garlic paste, and 1½ teaspoons of Cajun seasoning.

3. Brush the Cajun garlic butter on all sides of the corn and sprinkle with the remaining 1½ teaspoons of Cajun seasoning and a pinch each of salt and pepper.

4. If smoking the corn at 225°F, cook for 45 to 50 minutes, turning a few times throughout. If grilling at 450°F, cook for 10 to 12 minutes, turning a few times throughout.

> **SERVE WITH: This corn is the perfect side dish to make alongside whole chicken or ribs that also cook at 225°F, or for pork chops and chicken breasts that grill at 450°F. The Garlic-Herb Compound Butter (page 132) also tastes amazing on this corn.**

Jalapeño-Cheddar Corn Bread

SUGGESTED PELLETS: APPLE, HICKORY

SERVES 8 PEOPLE

PREP TIME: 10 minutes

COOK TIME: 25 to
30 minutes

TEMPERATURE: 400°F

---

1 cup cornmeal

1 cup all-purpose flour

¼ cup sugar

2 teaspoons baking powder

½ teaspoon baking soda

Pinch Kosher salt

1½ cups buttermilk

2 eggs

5 tablespoons melted
   butter, divided

2 jalapeño peppers (minced)

1 cup shredded
   cheddar cheese

Make corn bread on your Traeger once, and you may never go back to making it in your oven again. This version spices things up a bit with the addition of jalapeño, but if you prefer something with less heat, simply omit the peppers (see tip).

1. Turn the Traeger on and set it to 400°F.

2. In a large bowl, whisk together the cornmeal, flour, sugar, baking powder, baking soda, and salt to combine.

3. Add the buttermilk, eggs, and 3 tablespoons of butter to the dry ingredients. Stir until evenly combined.

4. Gently fold in the jalapeños and shredded cheese.

5. Pour the remaining 2 tablespoons of butter in a 10-inch cast-iron skillet or 9-by-13-inch foil pan and spread evenly. Pour the corn bread batter into the pan.

6. Place the pan on the grill grate and cook for 25 to 30 minutes.

VARIATION TIP: You can play around with different additions to this corn bread. Instead of jalapeño and cheddar, you can add ¼ cup of honey to make a sweet corn bread. Add some corn kernels to add texture. I like to top leftover corn bread with pulled pork and barbecue sauce. It's super good!

Caramelized Balsamic Onions

SERVES 4 TO 6 PEOPLE

PREP TIME: 15 minutes

COOK TIME: 3 hours

TEMPERATURE: 275°F

---

4 yellow onions

4 tablespoons butter

3 tablespoons brown sugar

3 tablespoons balsamic vinegar

Kosher salt

Freshly ground black pepper

These caramelized onions get soft and develop a sweet flavor after a few hours on the Traeger. They are perfect as a side for steak and brisket, but also for topping burgers, flatbreads, or making them into a caramelized onion dip. They will stay fresh in the refrigerator for a week, so you can plan to use them in a few recipes throughout the week.

1. Turn the Traeger on and set the temperature to 275°F.

2. Thinly slice the onions and place them in a 10-inch cast-iron skillet or foil pan. Cut the butter into smaller pieces and add to the onions along with the brown sugar, balsamic vinegar, and a pinch each of salt and pepper.

3. Place the pan on the grill grate for about 3 hours, stirring the onions every half hour.

SMOKER SAVVY TIP: The total cook time will depend largely on the thickness of the onions. Just keep an eye on them toward the end, and add a bit of water and stir if they look like they are drying out.

Pull-Apart Garlic Bread

SUGGESTED PELLETS: ALDER, HICKORY

SERVES 6 TO 8 PEOPLE
PREP TIME: 15 minutes
COOK TIME: 30 minutes
TEMPERATURE: 350°F

2 (11-ounce) tubes
French bread dough

1 stick butter, melted

2 tablespoons garlic paste

Kosher salt

Freshly ground black pepper

This recipe is perfect for a crowd—just set it on the table and everyone can pull off pieces of garlic bread at dinner. It's very easy to make because store-bought French bread dough in a tube is transformed into this amazing side dish!

1. Turn the Traeger on and set the temperature to 350°F.

2. Cut the bread dough into 1-inch pieces. In a small bowl, mix the butter, garlic paste, and a pinch each of salt and pepper.

3. Dip each bread piece into the garlic butter and place in a 9-by-13-inch casserole dish or foil pan. Pour any remaining garlic butter over top.

4. Place the pan on the grill grate and cook for 30 minutes.

VARIATION TIP: Adding fresh herbs or Italian seasoning will bring even more flavor. You could also add shredded Parmesan or mozzarella cheese. These delicious nuggets of garlic bread also taste delicious dipped in pizza sauce!

Smoked Salsa

SUGGESTED PELLETS: HICKORY, MESQUITE

SERVES 8 PEOPLE

PREP TIME: 20 minutes

COOK TIME: 1½ hours

TEMPERATURE: 225°F

---

6 to 8 Roma tomatoes, halved

1 large onion, quartered

1 red bell pepper, halved lengthwise with seeds removed

2 jalapeño peppers, halved lengthwise with seeds removed

3 or 4 garlic cloves

1 tablespoon olive oil

Kosher salt

Freshly ground black pepper

1 cup chopped fresh cilantro

2 to 3 tablespoons freshly squeezed lime juice

1 teaspoon sugar

I developed this recipe years ago with my kids. We make a large batch of it every year and can it in mason jars to enjoy for months. It's the perfect addition to any taco night as a side dish with chips for dipping.

1. Turn the Traeger on and set the temperature to 225°F.

2. Place the tomatoes, onion, bell pepper, jalapeños, and garlic in a 9-by-13-inch foil pan. Add the olive oil and a pinch each of salt and pepper and toss until everything is coated.

3. Put the pan of veggies on the grill grate and cook for 1½ hours, tossing halfway through. Remove the pan from the grill and let cool.

4. Once cooled, add the smoked veggies to a food processor or blender along with the cilantro, lime juice, and sugar. This may need to be done in smaller batches. Taste to adjust seasoning and add more salt and pepper if needed.

VARIATION TIP: For a spicy salsa, feel free to leave a few jalapeño seeds in for a nice kick. You could also add corn on the cob to the veggie pan to smoke, cut the kernels off the cob, and stir in the corn after the salsa has been blended. Adding a poblano pepper would also be a nice flavor variation.

Green Beans with Bacon

SUGGESTED PELLETS: MAPLE, PECAN

SERVES 4 TO 6 PEOPLE
PREP TIME: 10 minutes
COOK TIME: 30 minutes
TEMPERATURE: 225°F

6 slices bacon

1 onion, diced

4 garlic cloves, minced

4 (15-ounce) cans cut
green beans, drained

2 tablespoons butter

Kosher salt

Freshly ground black pepper

Pinch seasoned salt

Everything is better with bacon in my opinion! This bacon and green bean side dish goes great with any meal and is very simple to prepare. Everything is already cooked before you place it on the grill, but the Traeger gives it an extra-special flavor. Cook time and temperature is versatile since it only needs to be warmed, so adjust if needed if your main course is also being cooked on the Traeger at a different time or temperature.

1. Turn the Traeger on and set the temperature to 225°F.

2. Set a large skillet over medium heat on your stove. Use kitchen scissors to cut the bacon into bite-size pieces right into the skillet. Cook the bacon for 4 to 5 minutes, then drain off some of the bacon grease.

3. Add the onion to the skillet with the bacon and cook for 4 to 5 minutes more.

4. Add the garlic, green beans, butter, and a pinch each of kosher salt, pepper, and seasoned salt. Cook for 1 to 2 minutes more.

5. Place the skillet on the Traeger grill grate for 30 minutes.

VARIATION TIP: Fresh green beans can be used in place of the canned beans. Trim 1 pound of fresh green beans, boil them in salted water for 5 minutes, then add them to the skillet.

Street Corn Salad

SERVES 4 TO 6 PEOPLE
PREP TIME: 15 minutes
COOK TIME: 10 to 12 minutes
TEMPERATURE: 450°F

---

2 tablespoons olive oil

8 ears corn on the cob, shucked

2 jalapeño peppers

1 red bell pepper

1 red onion, thickly sliced

Kosher salt

Freshly ground black pepper

½ cup mayonnaise

½ cup sour cream

1 tablespoon chili powder

1 teaspoon garlic powder

Pinch cayenne pepper

1 cup Cotija cheese

½ cup chopped fresh cilantro

This salad is so unique and delicious. It's perfect to serve on the side at dinner, or to bring to a party or gathering. You can serve this warm, at room temperature, or cold. This dish combines everything yummy about street corn while served as a salad.

1. Turn the Traeger on and set the temperature to 450°F.

2. Brush olive oil on all sides of the corn, jalapeños, bell pepper, and onion. Season everything with salt and black pepper.

3. Place the corn, jalapeños, bell pepper, and onion on the grill grate and cook for 10 to 12 minutes, turning a few times.

4. Let the veggies cool after removing them from the grill. Cut the corn kernels off the cob and place in a large bowl. Remove the stems and seeds from the peppers and dice them. Dice the onion and place everything into the bowl with the corn.

5. Add the mayonnaise, sour cream, chili powder, garlic powder, cayenne pepper to taste, Cotija cheese, and cilantro. Stir to combine. Taste to adjust seasoning and add more salt and black pepper if needed.

SERVE WITH: This salad is great to make with any grilled chicken, steak, or pork chop recipe in the book. They grill at the same time and temperature, and while the meat rests, just prepare the salad for it all to be ready at the same time.

Smoked Deviled Eggs

MAKES 24 DEVILED EGGS
PREP TIME: 20 minutes
COOK TIME: 45 minutes
TEMPERATURE: 180°F

---

12 eggs

½ cup mayonnaise

½ cup yellow mustard

Kosher salt

Freshly ground black pepper

1 teaspoon paprika

One of my favorite summer side dishes is deviled eggs. This is my tried-and-true recipe with a smoked twist that brings extra yumminess. I've even included my trick for making the eggs easier to peel.

1. Gently place the eggs in a large pot and cover with water. Bring to a boil, then reduce the heat to low and simmer for 10 minutes. Turn the stove off and let the eggs sit in the hot water for 45 minutes.

2. Turn the Traeger on and set the temperature to 180°F.

3. Place a few ice cubes in the water with the eggs to cool them slightly, but they should still be warm and easy to peel. Peel the eggs and place them on the grill grate for 45 minutes. If your grill has the super smoke feature, turn it on.

4. Cut the eggs in half lengthwise, remove the yolks, and put the yolks in a large bowl. Place the whites, cut-side up, on a tray.

5. In the bowl with the yolks, add the mayonnaise, mustard, and a pinch each of salt and pepper. Beat with a hand mixer for 1 minute, and taste to adjust seasoning. Divide this mixture evenly among each egg white.

6. Sprinkle with the paprika and store in the refrigerator until ready to serve.

> **VARIATION TIP: There are so many things you can add to the deviled egg filling to mix it up. Bacon, chopped jalapeño, hot sauce, barbecue sauce, or even Buffalo sauce would add a nice twist.**

Sweet Potato Wedges

SERVES 4 PEOPLE

PREP TIME: 10 minutes

COOK TIME: 30 minutes

TEMPERATURE: 350°F

---

2 sweet potatoes

2 tablespoons olive oil

1 teaspoon chili powder

1 teaspoon ground cumin

1 teaspoon ground cinnamon

Kosher salt

Freshly ground black pepper

This is one of the simplest side dishes, yet one of my all-time favorites. Sweet potatoes are so healthy and really soak in all the smokiness from the wood pellets. I love dipping them in honey mustard, ketchup, or spicy mayo.

1. Turn the Traeger on and set the temperature to 350°F.

2. Cut each sweet potato in half lengthwise, then cut each half into 6 wedges (for a total of 24 wedges). Brush olive oil on all sides of the wedges and sprinkle with chili powder, cumin, cinnamon, and a pinch each of salt and pepper.

3. Place the sweet potato wedges on the grill grate for 15 minutes, then flip them and cook for another 15 minutes.

4. Serve as is or with a dipping sauce of your choice.

> **SERVE WITH: The Pork Tenderloin Wrapped with Maple Bacon (page 56) and the Goetta Sliders with Spicy Syrup (page 69) have just about the same cook time and temperature as these Sweet Potato Wedges. Make them all together at once for a complete meal.**

Smoked Potato Salad

SERVES 8 PEOPLE

PREP TIME: 15 minutes, plus time for cooling

COOK TIME: 1 hour

TEMPERATURE: 250°F

---

3 pounds red potatoes

2 tablespoons olive oil

Kosher salt

Freshly ground black pepper

1 cup mayonnaise

¼ cup yellow mustard

3 celery stalks, minced

3 scallions, sliced

This is the perfect summer side dish to bring to a party or gathering. Your friends and family will be left wondering what is so extra special about your potato salad. It's up to you if you want to let them in on your Traeger secret weapon!

1. Turn the Traeger on and set the temperature to 250°F.

2. Dice the red potatoes (I like to leave the skin on, but it's up to you whether or not to remove it) and put them in a 9-by-13-inch casserole dish or foil pan. Add the olive oil and a pinch each of salt and pepper and toss until the potatoes are coated. Place the pan on the grill grate and cook for 1 hour. (The cook time will vary depending on the size of the potatoes, so check to make sure they are fully cooked before taking them off the grill.)

3. Refrigerate the potatoes until they are completely cool—this is very important to keep them from turning to mashed potatoes when making the salad.

4. Add the cooled potatoes to a large bowl along with the mayonnaise, mustard, celery, and scallions. Gently toss to combine. Taste to adjust for seasoning and add more salt and pepper if needed.

> **VARIATION TIP:** You can add so much to this potato salad recipe to make it your own. Some suggested additions are bacon, fresh dill, a few chopped hard-boiled eggs, hot sauce, or seasoned salt.

Cinnamon Apples

SUGGESTED PELLETS: APPLE, MAPLE

SERVES 4 PEOPLE

PREP TIME: 10 minutes

COOK TIME: 1 hour

TEMPERATURE: 250°F

---

4 large Honeycrisp or
Granny Smith apples

4 tablespoons butter

2 teaspoons ground
cinnamon

1 teaspoon kosher salt

3 to 5 tablespoons brown
sugar (more or less
depending on how sweet
you want the apples to be)

Apples are the *best* side dish to go with pork, a classic duo like peanut butter and jelly! These apples are not super sweet and they complement the flavor of the pork perfectly. The temperature is the same as BBQ Pulled Pork (page 60), so just add the apples an hour before the pork is finished cooking and it's all done at the same time.

1. Turn the Traeger on and set the temperature to 250°F.

2. Cut the apples into thick slices (I leave the skin on but it's up to you whether or not to remove it) and put them in a 9-by-13-inch casserole dish or foil pan. Cut the butter into smaller pieces and scatter it around the apples along with the cinnamon, salt, and brown sugar.

3. Place the pan on the grill grate and cook for 1 hour, tossing a few times throughout. (The cook time will vary depending on the thickness of the apples and how you like them cooked.)

VARIATION TIP: This may sound weird, but I suggest adding ¼ cup of cinnamon-flavored whiskey to the apples. The alcohol will evaporate during the cooking process but it gives this side dish a unique flavor.

Twice-Smoked Potatoes

SUGGESTED PELLETS: ALDER, MESQUITE

MAKES 10 POTATOES
PREP TIME: 15 minutes
COOK TIME: 3 hours
TEMPERATURE: 250°F

---

5 russet potatoes

2 tablespoons olive oil

Kosher salt

Freshly ground black pepper

1½ cups whole milk, warmed

1 stick butter, softened

2 cups shredded
   cheddar cheese

These are a showstopping potato side dish, great for feeding a lot of people. You can make the twice-smoked potatoes the day before and warm them back up on the Traeger if you like.

1. Turn the Traeger on and set the temperature to 250°F.

2. Brush the russet potatoes with olive oil and season all sides with salt and pepper. Place the potatoes on the grill grate and cook for 2½ hours.

3. Remove the potatoes and cut them in half lengthwise. Let them cool slightly.

4. Scoop most of the potato out of the skin with a spoon and put the potato in a large bowl. Add the milk, butter, and a pinch each of salt and pepper. Beat with a hand mixer for 1 minute. Taste to adjust the seasoning and add more salt and pepper if needed.

5. Stir in the shredded cheese, then divide this mixture evenly among the potato skins. Place them back on the Traeger for 30 minutes.

VARIATION TIP: I have made this recipe multiple times and love coming up with new twists. Adding some barbecue seasoning to the potato mixture is amazing, and of course adding bacon is always a great idea. You can mix up the cheese by using pepper Jack, sharp white cheddar, or mozzarella in place of the cheddar.

Smoked Mac and Cheese

SUGGESTED PELLETS: MESQUITE, OAK

SERVES 8 PEOPLE

PREP TIME: 20 minutes

COOK TIME: 30 to
45 minutes

TEMPERATURE: 400°F

---

1 pound short-cut pasta
(macaroni, shells, penne)

2½ cups whole milk

1 (12-ounce) can
evaporated milk

1 stick butter

8 ounces cream cheese

8 ounces shredded
Gouda cheese

16 ounces shredded Colby
Jack cheese

1 tablespoon kosher salt

1 teaspoon ground mustard

½ teaspoon freshly ground
black pepper

Mac and cheese is the ultimate comfort food. If your kids are picky eaters, a sure way to make them happy is serving creamy, decadent mac and cheese as a side dish. This recipe is super simple because it does not require making a roux. It starts very thin, but thickens as it cooks on the Traeger.

1. Boil the pasta according to package directions in salted water. Drain and rinse with cold water so the pasta does not get mushy.

2. Turn the Traeger on and set the temperature to 400°F.

3. Put the same pot that you boiled the pasta in on the stove over medium heat. Combine the whole milk, evaporated milk, butter, cream cheese, Gouda and Colby Jack cheeses, salt, ground mustard, and pepper and stir until the cheese melts, about 10 minutes. Add the cooked pasta to the pot and stir to combine. Put the mac and cheese in a 9-by-13-inch casserole dish. Note: The sauce will look very thin, but it will thicken as it cooks.

4. Put the casserole dish on the grill grate and cook for 30 to 45 minutes (no need to stir).

SERVE WITH: If you make the BBQ Pulled Pork (page 60), or the Whole Smoked BBQ Chicken (page 82), top this mac and cheese with the leftovers and a little barbecue sauce drizzled over the top to make this side dish a complete meal.

Rubs, Marinades, and Sauces

Whiskey Cream Sauce

YIELDS ABOUT 2 CUPS

PREP TIME: 10 minutes

COOK TIME: 15 minutes

1 (14-ounce) can beef broth

1 cup whiskey, divided

2 tablespoons Dijon mustard

1 cup heavy
  (whipping) cream

1 teaspoon garlic powder

1½ tablespoons cornstarch

This one is a family favorite! I started by just making it for special occasions and holidays, but now we have it at least once a month because it's so addicting.

1. In a small saucepan over high heat, bring the beef broth, ¾ cup of whiskey, and the Dijon mustard to a boil, then reduce the heat to low and simmer for 10 minutes.

2. Add the heavy cream and garlic powder to the saucepan. In a small bowl, mix the remaining ¼ cup of whiskey with the cornstarch, then add that to the saucepan. Simmer for 5 minutes more. Store in airtight container and refrigerate for up to 3-to-4 days.

SERVE WITH: This sauce is excellent with any steak and also so good with pork chops. I recommend serving it with mashed potatoes as this sauce is like a gravy. The perfect bite is steak, mashed potatoes, and this sauce . . . *yum*!

BBQ Dry Rub

YIELDS 1/2 CUP

PREP TIME: 5 minutes

1/4 cup brown sugar

2 tablespoons chili powder

2 tablespoons paprika

1 tablespoon garlic powder

1 tablespoon onion powder

1 tablespoon kosher salt

1/2 tablespoon freshly ground black pepper

1/2 tablespoon dry mustard

This dry rub is so easy to make and better than any store-bought variety I have tried. Feel free to double or triple the recipe to use multiple times.

In a small bowl, whisk together the sugar, chili powder, paprika, garlic powder, onion powder, salt, black pepper, and mustard until evenly combined. Store this dry rub in a sealed container until ready to use.

SERVE WITH: This dry rub can be used with chicken, steak, pork, and even seafood. If you want to add some heat to this rub, add some cayenne pepper for a spicy kick.

Maple and Brown Sugar Rub

YIELDS 1¹/₂ CUPS

PREP TIME: 5 minutes

¾ cup brown sugar

½ cup pure maple syrup

2 tablespoons soy sauce

2 tablespoons sriracha

Maple and brown sugar pair so well together. This sweet and spicy rub brings a unique flavor with just a few simple ingredients.

In a small bowl, whisk together the sugar, maple syrup, soy sauce, and sriracha until combined.

SERVE WITH: This rub is amazing on pork tenderloin, pork chops, steak, and chicken. Just rub on your meat of choice and cook according to the times and temperatures in the chart on page 13.

Caribbean Jerk Dry Rub

YIELDS 1¹/₂ CUPS

PREP TIME: 10 minutes

1 cup brown sugar

4 tablespoons ground allspice

2 tablespoons kosher salt

¹/₂ tablespoon ground cloves

¹/₂ tablespoon freshly ground black pepper

¹/₂ tablespoon turmeric

¹/₂ tablespoon cinnamon

¹/₂ tablespoon cumin

¹/₂ tablespoon paprika

¹/₂ tablespoon thyme

¹/₂ tablespoon red pepper flakes

This rub has lots of ingredients, but it's well worth making. It's way better than any store-bought rub I have found and you can make extra to keep in a container to use over and over.

In a bowl, mix together the sugar, allspice, salt, cloves, black pepper, turmeric, cinnamon, cumin, paprika, thyme, and red pepper flakes until combined. Store in a sealed container until ready to use.

SERVE WITH: This can be used as a dry rub, or you can combine it with soy sauce for a wet rub on any cut of chicken or pork. I love using this on ribs—just follow the recipe for Classic BBQ Baby Back Ribs (page 57) and substitute this seasoning.

Honey-Balsamic Marinade

YIELDS ¹/₂ CUP

PREP TIME: 10 minutes

¼ cup balsamic vinegar

2 tablespoons honey

1 tablespoon Dijon mustard

1 tablespoon garlic paste

1 tablespoon Italian
  seasoning

This marinade is super flavorful and so easy to make. The honey brings just a hint of sweetness that caramelizes as it cooks.

In a small bowl, whisk together the balsamic vinegar, honey, mustard, garlic paste, and Italian seasoning until combined.

SERVE WITH: This marinade can be used for any cut of meat. Simply place the meat in a gallon-size plastic bag, add the marinade, and massage the bag until the meat is coated. Marinate in the refrigerator for an hour or even overnight. Marinating seafood in it takes only about 10 minutes.

Gochujang BBQ Sauce

YIELDS ABOUT 2 CUPS
PREP TIME: 5 minutes
COOK TIME: 5 minutes

1 cup ketchup

¼ cup white vinegar

¼ cup gochujang chile paste

¼ cup honey

1 tablespoon soy sauce

1 tablespoon ginger paste

1 tablespoon garlic paste

Gochujang can be easily found in the Asian section of most grocery stores. It's a Korean chile paste that has a slight spice and brings a definite wow factor to this barbecue sauce.

In a small saucepan, bring the ketchup, vinegar, chile paste, honey, soy sauce, ginger paste, and garlic paste to a boil, then reduce the heat to low and simmer for 5 minutes, stirring a few times. Store in airtight container and refrigerate for up to 3-to-4 days.

SERVE WITH: You can double or even triple this recipe and keep it in the refrigerator to use on everything. It's a great twist on traditional barbecue sauce to use on ribs, pulled pork, and chicken.

Maple-Mustard Marinade

YIELDS 1 CUP

PREP TIME: 5 minutes

½ **cup pure maple syrup**

½ **cup Dijon mustard**

1 tablespoon soy sauce

Kosher salt

Freshly ground black pepper

Pinch red pepper flakes

I love this marinade, which doubles as a dipping sauce if you save some. Maple syrup paired with mustard is a magical combo!

In a small bowl, whisk together the maple syrup, mustard, soy sauce, salt, black pepper, and red pepper flakes until combined.

SERVE WITH: Pork chops, salmon, or chicken wings— really this marinade can be used on any cut of meat. Use half to marinate the meat and save the rest for dipping.

Cilantro-Lime Marinade

YIELDS ¾ CUP

PREP TIME: 10 minutes

Juice of 1 lime

2 tablespoons olive oil

½ cup chopped fresh cilantro

2 garlic cloves, minced

1 teaspoon chili powder

1 teaspoon cumin

Kosher salt

Freshly ground black pepper

This is such a light and refreshing marinade. Lime brings a burst of bright flavor when paired with the fresh cilantro and garlic.

In a small bowl, mix together the lime juice, olive oil, cilantro, garlic, chili powder, cumin, salt, and black pepper until combined.

SERVE WITH: This is a great marinade for seafood. It's incredible with shrimp, salmon, tilapia, and lobster, but could also be used for chicken. If marinating any seafood, it only takes about 10 minutes, but for chicken you should marinate for several hours.

Garlic-Herb Compound Butter

YIELDS 1 CUP

PREP TIME: 10 minutes

---

2 sticks butter, at room
temperature

2 to 3 tablespoons
garlic paste

2 tablespoons chopped
fresh basil

1 tablespoon chopped
fresh thyme leaves

1 tablespoon chopped
fresh rosemary

Butter just makes everything better, and butter mixed with garlic and herbs brings even more flavor!

1. Using a handheld mixer in a small bowl, combine the butter, garlic paste, and herbs for 1 minute.

2. Store the butter rolled in plastic wrap, or in an ice cube tray in the freezer for individual portions.

SERVE WITH: Cut off a slice of this compound butter to top a hot-off-the-grill steak. It melts into the steak, bringing even more flavor and juiciness. It's also great melted over grilled corn on the cob.

Chipotle BBQ Sauce

1 cup ketchup

¼ cup white vinegar

¼ cup brown sugar

1 (4-ounce) can chipotle peppers in adobo sauce

This is an incredible barbecue sauce with the spicy flavor of chipotle peppers, the perfect way to heat up traditional barbecue sauce.

1. In a blender or food processor, blend the ketchup, vinegar, sugar, and chipotle peppers until combined.

2. Pour the mixture into a small saucepan, bring to a boil, then reduce the heat to simmer for 5 minutes, stirring a few times. Store in airtight container and refrigerate for up to 3-to-4 days.

SERVE WITH: This spicy barbecue sauce has so much flavor thanks to the chipotle peppers in adobo sauce—it's perfect for pulled pork, brisket, and ribs. If you don't want quite as much spice, just reduce the amount of chipotle peppers.

Sriracha-Bourbon Spare Ribs, page 67

MEASUREMENT CONVERSIONS

VOLUME EQUIVALENTS	US STANDARD	US STANDARD (OUNCES)	METRIC (APPROXIMATE)
LIQUID	2 tablespoons	1 fl. oz.	30 mL
	¼ cup	2 fl. oz.	60 mL
	½ cup	4 fl. oz.	120 mL
	1 cup	8 fl. oz.	240 mL
	1½ cups	12 fl. oz.	355 mL
	2 cups or 1 pint	16 fl. oz.	475 mL
	4 cups or 1 quart	32 fl. oz.	1 L
	1 gallon	128 fl. oz.	4 L
DRY	⅛ teaspoon		0.5 mL
	¼ teaspoon		1 mL
	½ teaspoon		2 mL
	¾ teaspoon		4 mL
	1 teaspoon		5 mL
	1 tablespoon		15 mL
	¼ cup		59 mL
	⅓ cup		79 mL
	½ cup		118 mL
	⅔ cup		156 mL
	¾ cup		177 mL
	1 cup		235 mL
	2 cups or 1 pint		475 mL
	3 cups		700 mL
	4 cups or 1 quart		1 L
	½ gallon		2 L
	1 gallon		4 L

OVEN TEMPERATURES

FAHRENHEIT	CELSIUS (APPROXIMATE)
250°F	120°C
300°F	150°C
325°F	165°C
350°F	180°C
375°F	190°C
400°F	200°C
425°F	220°C
450°F	230°C

WEIGHT EQUIVALENTS

US STANDARD	METRIC (APPROXIMATE)
½ ounce	15 g
1 ounce	30 g
2 ounces	60 g
4 ounces	115 g
8 ounces	225 g
12 ounces	340 g
16 ounces or 1 pound	455 g

INDEX

ACKNOWLEDGMENTS

I would love to acknowledge my family for supporting me during the crazy hours that come with writing a cookbook. Their love and many words of encouragement kept me going. To my husband, Shannon; my kids, Kelsey, Kaitlyn, Rachel, and Tyson; and my amazing parents, Rita and Jim—thank you and I love you all! I would also like to acknowledge the wonderful editors and publishers at Callisto Media for believing in me and helping me through the process of writing my first cookbook.

ABOUT THE AUTHOR

 **CHERI RENEÉ** lives in a small town in Indiana with her husband and four kids. She is a second-grade teacher in addition to running the successful food blog CooksWellWithOthers.com, where she posts lots of Traeger recipes in addition to many other recipes. Her love and passion for cooking started when she was a young mom and wanted to enjoy good food at home without having to take all the kids to a restaurant. She is a self-taught home cook who is dedicated to developing amazing recipes for others to enjoy at home.

CPSIA information can be obtained
at www.ICGtesting.com
Printed in the USA
JSHW011514190921
18780JS00005B/7

Made in the USA
Columbia, SC
24 August 2017